MARIAN L. SALZMAN is a successful editor/writer and management/marketing consultant. After graduating with honors from Brown University and studying at Harvard University's Graduate School of Arts and Sciences, she co-founded *Career Insights* magazine. She authors a bi-monthly newsletter, *The Campus Report* (Gordon Associates), for human resources executives. Her first book, *Inside Management Training*, was published by NAL/Plume in 1985 and was closely followed by *MBA Jobs!* (Amacom, 1986), which she co-authored with Nancy Marx Better. Marian Salzman is director of media relations for Kehoe, White, Savage & Company, a shareholder relations firm in New York City. She has been editor of *Management Review*, consultant to several corporate college relations offices, published in *Bottomline/Personal*, *Business Week*'s "Guide to Careers," *Forbes*, *Ms.*, and *Self*, and featured in articles in *Glamour*, *Savvy*, and *Women's Wear Daily*.

NANCY MARX BETTER is a free-lance writer in the San Francisco area. She graduated cum laude from Yale University in 1984 and went on to become a staff reporter at *Fortune*. Soon afterward, she became a staff reporter and feature writer for *Manhattan, inc.* magazine. She has contributed to *Self*, *Management Review*, and, most extensively, the San Jose *Mercury News* and *The Wall Street Journal*. Her first book, *MBA Jobs!*, co-authored by Marian Salzman, was published by Amacom in 1986.

WANTED:
LIBERAL ARTS GRADUATES

Wanted: Liberal Arts Graduates

*The Career Guide to Companies
That Hire Smart People*

*Marian L. Salzman and
Nancy Marx Better*

Doubleday

NEW YORK   LONDON   TORONTO   SYDNEY   AUCKLAND

Published by Doubleday, a division of
Bantam Doubleday Dell Publishing Group, Inc.,
666 Fifth Avenue, New York, New York 10103.

Doubleday and the portrayal of an anchor with a
dolphin are trademarks of Doubleday, a division of
Bantam Doubleday Dell Publishing Group, Inc.

Library of Congress Cataloging in Publication Data

Salzman, Marian L.
  Wanted, liberal arts graduates.

  1. Job hunting—United States. 2. Vocational guidance
—United States. 3. College graduates—Employment—
United States. 4. Bachelor of arts degree. 5. Master
of arts degree. I. Title.
HF5382.75.U6S27   1987   650.1'4   87–8846
ISBN 0-385-24008-2

2 4 6 8 9 7 5 3

BG

For our parents, who taught us to think smart.

CONTENTS

FOREWORD: Heather Evans, Chief Financial
   Officer, Program Development, Inc.   *xi*

Introduction: A Brave New World for
   Liberal Arts Grads   *1*

1 Liberal Arts Grads Can Make Good   *5*

2 Who Said They're Not Looking for
   Thinking People?   *14*

3 In Search of the Right First Job   *20*

4 Pathways Into and Up the Organization   *28*

5 What Liberal Arts Grads Need to Know   *46*

6 How to Make the Smart Choice   *68*

7 Internships   *74*

8 Getting Inside Organizations That
   Hire Smart People   *78*

9 The Profiles: The Best Employers
   of Liberal Arts Grads   *82*

NOTES   *289*

APPENDICES   *291*
   Sources for Smart People   *291*
   Glamour Jobs in the Big Apple   *302*
   Companies That Hire Smart People
   (Organized by Industry)   *311*

FOREWORD

You will have to be a well-armed hunter in order to satisfy your appetite for job satisfaction. That's because your appetite for current job satisfaction is likely to be much stronger than your parents', yet most companies haven't redesigned their job structure to satisfy it. The first employer that stumbles into your trap may not offer the challenges you crave. You had better target the jobs that will keep you fat and happy.

To understand how your needs and expectations differ from what most American companies have grown to expect, compare yourself to a typical college graduate of your parents' generation. Your father probably landed his first job in the early 1960s. Pretty soon you or your older sibling were "on the way," taking your mother out of the work force. Two more children followed fast. In the beginning, your parents struggled just to make ends meet and then to enjoy the rewards of success, moving from that tiny first apartment to a comfortable suburban home. At that stage, around forty and an executive in a major corporation, your father may have finally found time to wonder whether the struggle was worth it.

Now that you're graduating, you will start at a higher salary in real terms than those paid a generation ago. In addition, without military service and in a competitive job environment, you are getting onto a career track earlier than the average professional in your parents' generation. You will probably marry later and have children much later. The result is that your income in real dollars will soon be several times what your parents had for an entire family when they were your age.

Without severe financial pressure and sole responsibility for a family, you will be able early on to afford to factor fulfillment into your career decisions. Family, friends, and community will seem necessities, not luxuries. You will be less likely to be caught up in the vicious circle of work absorption.

Competition, hope, and financial necessity previously kept the best young executives on the path toward top positions. Today the best talent demands satisfaction in the here and now.

Unfortunately, not only will you have enough leisure time to gain perspective, you also face a cost-benefit equation in which the prospects of hard work being rewarded are *truly* worse; each of you has a smaller chance at a top management position. The baby boom produced an enormous crop of well-educated young professionals. In the old pyramid-shaped corporate organization, there's only so much room at the top.

Sacrifices of time and relationships appear more onerous when the expected value of future rewards is smaller. Or, in other words, you are not going to wait around twenty-five years for a chance at a gold watch. Public opinion analyst Daniel Yankelovich calls you fulfillment seekers: bright, educated, and introspective men and women who choose work on the basis of an organization's ability to provide significant, creative, and satisfying work.

Psychologists find that the amount of fulfillment derived from any job depends mostly on *challenge*, which one study defined as the variety of tasks, opportunity for learning, job/skill fit, and decision-making responsibility. Achievement contributes to the enjoyment of work because the higher the prestige, the greater the challenge. Salary and promotions per se are relatively unimportant.

The best news yet for both you and your prospective employers is that the decentralized, flexible organizations that will attract and motivate today's young talent are also the ones that are best able to compete in today's business environment. Corporations have plenty of challenging work to offer; however, in the traditional hierarchical corporate structure, inherent challenge is often limited to a few top positions.

In order to become more flexible and innovative in their marketplaces, some corporations have already implemented policies that disperse responsibility and broaden the variety of tasks in lower-level positions.

Marian Salzman and Nancy Marx Better have identified the flexible and innovative corporations that are looking for flexible, innovative young people—i.e., liberal arts graduates like you. The descriptions they provide in this book will help you identify which ones offer work that you personally will find challenging. As the authors point out here and in their past writings, there is no "ideal" job, only ideal matches between particular individuals and particular situations.

So, first, before you get excited about all the great jobs that are out there, read about how to gauge your own requirements and likes and dislikes within the range of job pathways. Follow the authors' advice about how to maximize your success rate among your targeted employers. Most of all: plan ahead.

You and your peers are likely to be demanding employees. This book will teach you how to job-hunt and show you the flock of possibilities. Hunt selectively—and feast on *choice* rewards.

> Heather Evans
> Chief Financial Officer
> Program Development, Inc.

New York City
March 1987

ACKNOWLEDGMENTS

ACKNOWLEDGMENTS

Writing this book in a matter of months would have been impossible without the help of many liberal arts grads who assisted us in every way possible. They shared their job-hunting experiences and told us what they did right and wrong. They told us about their workplaces and what made them good or bad. They led us to countless friends, classmates, and colleagues, who opened up and made candid observations on their careers. Without this ever-growing network of people, we couldn't have finished our job. Their enthusiasm for the project kept us going when we were exhausted. Over and over, we were told, "I wish such a book had been available when I graduated!" Well, so did we, and here it is.

In addition to thanking the hundreds of liberal arts grads who participated in our work, we'd like to express our gratitude to several individuals who made key contributions. Joel Kaufman and Kimberly Witherspoon offered their expert research skills, as well as an enormous measure of support and encouragement. Alison Schechter was a first-rate bibliographical sleuth and tracked down many of the sources in our appendices. The career counseling and placement offices at Yale, Brown, Stanford, Columbia, and New York universities, among others, offered invaluable research facilities. And, of course, we are grateful to the recruiters at organizations across the country who provided us with information and observations on the hiring process.

Finally, we want to thank our editor, Marshall DeBruhl, and his associate, Ceci Scott, who made the writing process a pleasure. Their confidence in two young authors who majored in sociology and history proves that there is a place in this world for liberal arts grads!

WANTED:
LIBERAL ARTS GRADUATES

Introduction:
A Brave New World for
Liberal Arts Grads

There are worse labels to bear than that of liberal arts major. Murderers, thieves, and hijackers are examples. The plight of liberal arts majors, rebuffed repeatedly after experiencing a late awakening to the drama and excitement of business, is real.
—Allan Cox, *Inside Corporate America*[1]

The liberal arts degree is far from valueless in the business world—at least as far as the good students are concerned. Some of today's top graduates with sheepskins in English, economics and history are getting offers that rival the stuff of M.B.A.s' dreams. . . . Some top B.A.s are snaring multi-phase financial packages as sophisticated as those that headhunters use to woo gold-collared senior executives.
—John Byrne, *Forbes*[2]

Once again, liberal arts graduates are getting mixed press. On one hand, the media regularly sports headlines singing the praises of students who major in business, engineering, or computer science; on the other, it touts the benefits of a well-rounded education in the arts, the sciences, and the humanities. What's the *real* scoop on the outlook for liberal arts grads?

According to one recent study of corporate executives, 33 percent expressed a strong preference for hiring liberal arts grads; 60

percent favored candidates with technical degrees.[3] Another survey reveals that in both 1985 and 1986, job opportunities for liberal arts grads surged in all parts of the country.[4] Said John Stodden, an economist and employment analyst, "Corporate America is turning to the broadly educated, as the specialists paint themselves into the corner. At the same time, liberal arts students are smart enough nowadays to pick up computer skills and business principles to facilitate their career development."[5] Likewise, *Harvard Business Review* reported, "Business is becoming disenchanted with MBAs, many of whom, after a few years, are not particularly efficient as managers and remain therefore in functional positions. In fact, many colleges record the level of good undergraduates in terms of curiosity, dedication, ability to withstand criticism, conceptualization of problems, and willingness to take risks as higher than that found within their MBA programs."[6]

Clearly there's a market for liberal arts grads—but it's not easy to crack. As a generalist, your education doesn't limit you to a narrow field of options; however, your background may not be particularly easy to sell to prospective employers. Today's liberal arts grad is a crazy hybrid, part Renaissance scholar and part fast-track manipulator.

Ready or not, you're poised to plunge into the most difficult juggling act ever undertaken by a generation. "Having it all" is the pay dirt, yet the game's rules are being modified even as play begins. Employers realize that you and your peers are life-style pioneers; however, they complain that you want too much too soon. "The problem is that patience is an old-fashioned virtue," gripes one recruiter. "Few are willing to tough it out for the relatively modest starting salaries we have to offer."

So the dilemma exists: how can you have it all when you aren't sure what's available? Thanks to the proliferation of colored parachutes, we all know that smart career planning is really life/work planning. Liberal arts grads enter the professional world, adorned in gray flannel suits and status running shoes, worried as much about succeeding on the job as off. Racing up the career ladder requires sacrifices, and you're not sure which ones you're willing to make. And with a million people graduating from America's colleges and universities each year, the competition is tough as always.

The News Isn't All That Bad

All headlines, statistics, and warnings aside, you and your liberal arts peers are rarely bad people or bad hires; what you are is confused by the endless array of choices before you. At the ripe old age of twenty-one or twenty-two, burdened by ambition and drive —not to mention by soaring rents, biological clocks, student loans, and the assorted implications of life in the eighties—you're preparing to move into organizations. Besides the pressure of trying to make it on the job, you'll agonize over what—including love—you need to stay on the fastest track. Getting into the job hunting game isn't easy, and trying to pass "Go" each time you come around the board can be impossible. You'll face rejection, you'll hit roadblocks, *and* you'll have to keep moving. The bottom line on breaking in to the work world, especially for liberal arts graduates, is that it's one game in which, strategize as hard as you might, there's no one right roll of the dice. But, according to a recent article in *Fortune*, the gloom-and-doom talk is all wrong. "The baby boomers are supposed to be feeling demoralized, their hope of doing even as well as their parents inevitably disappointed. In fact, they are filled with steely optimism: in envisioning their careers, they barely admit the possibility of being stalemated."[7]

Finding the right first job may be the toughest strategic planning, marketing, and sales problem you'll ever face. As a liberal arts student, chances are you're among the best and brightest, as well as the most confused and pressured. With so little exposure to the practical world, it's hard to decide where to begin your search. How can you know whether you'll be happiest in accounting, advertising, banking, or retailing? Would you like to work in a department store, a consumer products company, or a brokerage firm? And once you've narrowed your career possibilities, other questions remain unanswered: Do you want to work for a small, medium, or large organization? In a profit or nonprofit setting? Do you want to live in a city, a suburb, or a rural area?

There's another side of the job search question that liberal arts grads must consider: what's in it for the employers? After incurring the expense of recruiting, hiring, and training you, how can they be sure you won't skip off because another opportunity catches your fancy? Employers are wary of new hires who demand daily to know how much they're getting out of their jobs in terms of cash, comforts, and contacts. It's fine to check on your situation periodically, but remember that even on the job, there's a means (what you learn) as well as an end (what you earn).

Unreasonable Is Okay

Many years ago, George Bernard Shaw noted that "the reasonable man adapts himself to the world; the unreasonable one persists in trying to adapt the world to himself. Therefore all progress depends on the unreasonable man." So maybe it's not all that bad to be unreasonable in your expectations. But the breed of unreasonableness that prevails on campus is often a justification for refusing to begin at the bottom of the heap. Many liberal arts graduates don't understand the trade-offs that go with fast-track careers. Instant or early success is rare indeed. Today's industry giants started out in the trenches and spent thousands of hours forging their careers. If you're prepared to do the same, and you have the right stuff (ambition and smarts), you're likely to succeed.

Back when we got our liberal arts degrees, there wasn't any book available to help sociology and history majors play the corporate job hunting game. *Wanted: Liberal Arts Graduates* is filled with advice we wish we'd gotten from recruiters, career counselors, current students, and recent graduates. The following chapters should leave you convinced that if you package one part substance with one part sizzle, you'll be able to land a blue-chip offer from a company at which you'll feel genuinely comfortable and where you'll want to stick around for long enough to make a real contribution. Keep in mind that if you pick smart the first time around the board, your future searches—and your career plans—will be a whole lot easier.

Chapter **1**

Liberal Arts Grads Can Make Good

One of the all-time great philosophers, Linus in "Peanuts," lamented, "There's no heavier burden than a great potential." Among smart people with no professional experience, this complaint is common. When you have great potential, it's little wonder that you expect challenging work and genuine responsibilities. And while management training programs, which let you earn while you learn, sound appealing, you know that competition for the most selective spots is stiff. So you go on with your job hunt, worried to death that you might not land an offer and afraid that even if you do, it might not really be what's right for you.

There's no point in telling you that because you're smart, your dream job is out there waiting. Rather, the fact remains that some of the smartest job hunters have the toughest time finding the right opportunities. Unlike accounting majors who know that they've been prepared to assume entry-level jobs as staff accountants in public accounting firms, all you know is that you can communicate, problem solve, and think. But how many classified advertisements have you seen that read like this:

Wanted: Liberal arts graduates. Able to speak, write, and think clearly. Willing to do research, to compare and to

> *contrast information. Experienced in reading vast quantities of material, in performing analysis and in synthesizing ideas. No practical background required.*

Unless you're willing to settle for the most basic job of all, administrative assistant (translation: "go-fer" and observer), the hardest part of your job hunt is going to be figuring out what it is you're looking for. What that step requires, first and foremost, is looking inside yourself.

In the midst of determining if you're analytical, people-oriented, and persuasive, there's the added pressure of knowing that sooner or later, the explanation that you're busy "finding yourself" isn't going to satisfy your family and friends. Fathers (mothers, or whoever) always think they know best when it comes to the work world. If you're not ready to get married, you won't accept a proposal. Likewise, if you're not ready to accept a job offer, don't jump at your first prospect. Just because your college clock is running out and you're tired of fumbling around, don't start hunting for a job simply because career anxiety has gotten the best of you.

Professor Jeanne M. Lynch, of Rensselaer Polytechnic Institute, cautions against what she has termed the lottery of life approach to employment. She suggests that you develop some perspective; put some effort into the job search; and anticipate and combat the pressure you're feeling. If you allow yourself enough time, you won't be forced into leaping without having looked.

There are two ways to arrange for the requisite time to conduct an appropriate job search. (We define "appropriate" as at least two months for sizing yourself up and another two for exploring the employment market.) The first plan calls for beginning the process during the fall of your senior year; the second allows for starting after commencement, when you'll have plenty of time to research career possibilities as well as specific opportunities. One caveat: some of the most exclusive employers, especially those who start college graduates in management training programs, have fixed hiring quotas at different times of the year. While several of the best-managed retailing companies start executive trainees six or more times per year, most of the bluest-chip investment banks start their college hires in early summer *only*. The word is out on which organizations have the most structured hiring programs, so think ahead and ask around. If Merrill Lynch hasn't hired anyone in the summer for the past three years, don't hold your breath in anticipation that you're the rare exception, the one worthy of the company creating a new position—and just because you've granted a personnel officer the honor of reviewing your cover letter and résumé.

It's important to choose your job search time frame before the pressure heats up. Inform all interested parties before they become worried and end up adding to your pressure. No one wants to hear about the trials and tribulations of his father's postgraduation job hunt when he's embarking on his own. Further, the experience of looking for a career twenty or thirty years ago was completely different than it is today. When your parents got out of school, college grads had different expectations of what kinds of work were acceptable for a bright, eager young person. Today's job hunter is approaching a brave new world in which starting salaries are often astronomical and fast-track jockeying is the name of the strategy game.

Let's look at Edward Meyer, chairman of Grey Advertising. When Meyer left Cornell University in 1949 with a liberal arts degree, he wanted to enter the advertising field desperately. However, back then, all college graduates began their careers in the mail room—which just didn't appeal to Meyer. So he accepted a position at Bloomingdale's and spent three years in the retail rat race before moving over to the Biow Agency, which at the time was one of the top ten agencies in America. In an interview three decades later, Meyer explained that he was offered the position at Biow because he and his interviewer shared a common major—English—and a common work experience—retailing.

Like Meyer, Young & Rubicam's long-time chairman and chief executive officer, Edward Ney, is a liberal arts man. He earned his B.A. in history from Amherst College in 1947 and then, after being refused a job in Benton & Bowles's mail room, he landed an offer from Batten, Barton, Durstine & Osborn as a management trainee. When asked about the value of a liberal arts education for those bound for Madison Avenue, he replied, "The wide-open humanistic experience—interest in the arts, in music, in history, and in writing—is marvelous preparation for a career in advertising."[1]

Edward Finkelstein, who has just led Macy's through a highly publicized leveraged buyout, began his career at Macy's. But unlike today's trainees, who beg and moan if they haven't been promoted from job one—sales manager—to job two—assistant buyer—within two years, Finkelstein spent his first eight years as manager of the curtains and drapes department in the Herald Square store. "Your aspirations and goals grow as you move step by step up the ladder," said Finkelstein. "It's counterproductive to think too far ahead, but it's realistic to imagine how you would do in the next job. When presented with the opportunity, you won't be surprised or overwhelmed." He added, "I think that an individual's most productive effort in getting to the next management level is performing well in his present assignment. That's how I viewed each step."[2]

As proof that Finkelstein's career philosophy prevails at Macy's —if not throughout the retailing industry—one need only look at the career paths of the two dozen executives who joined him in the management buyout. Nearly all the major players are homegrown, graduates of a training squad *The Wall Street Journal* has labeled the "Harvard of retailing." These executives toughed it out in branch stores, through store-line and buying-line assignments, putting in long, long hours and years of six-day work weeks. The result is the kind of rapid career progression that is possible for the best and brightest liberal arts grads—provided you're willing to work mighty hard and don't mind sacrificing your ego for the sake of the bottom line.

Times have changed, however. Take a recent graduate from Brown University who majored in political science. She spent more than a year training at Macy's before moving over to the corporate buying offices of May Department Stores. "It's hard to motivate yourself to go through the semiannual job rotations when you know that there's good experience and more immediate payoffs in following a different career path," she said. "When you accept a career track that involves store assignments, you choose to put the rest of your life on hold during the months, even years, when you're managing the selling floor. Stores are open long hours and, as management, you're expected to be on the front line, motivating your people to keep up the merchandising and the selling." She continued, "After you go through one Christmas and inventory season, you begin to feel that your education and talent are being wasted as a sales manager. That's when I began to seriously consider other career opportunities within the retail business. After I was promoted to assistant buyer, I started looking for situations that wouldn't force me to move back into stores for future promotions."

Still, while that particular liberal arts grad is happier in a staff function, May's chairman of the board, David Farrell, suggests that the future leaders of his company are generalists who share his fifties orientation toward hard work and then more hard work. "Retailing is like a competitive game," he said. "To remain at the forefront of merchandising developments, retail executives must outposition and outthink the competition. Shifts and changes in the industry require us to maintain constant vigilance in order to keep up with customers' tastes; in any given retail season, the element of risk adds to the general excitement. And although buyers do have some authority to choose the merchandise they market and although their decisions determine the range of good from which customers can make selections, consumer response is the bottom line."[3] Farrell, who has been with the May Company since his 1956 graduation from Antioch College, gives strong testimony to the benefits of a liberal arts education. "Since our industry mirrors what's happening in the world, we look for people who are good students of social trends. Fashion doesn't happen in a vacuum; it's a creative response to what's going on in people's lives. Therefore, since a liberal arts background prepares individuals to understand social movements, it's ideal preparation for a successful career in retailing."[4]

Liberal Arts Grads Make Good Across the Board

Liberal arts graduates make good in all industries, not just advertising and retailing, which are typically considered to be the most creative. In his keynote address at the 1984 Conference on the Humanities and Careers in Business, Roger B. Smith, chairman of General Motors, insisted, "There is almost no phase of

business life that can be successfully conducted without the benefit of humanistic values and insights." He noted that "studying the
humanities gives you a sense of perspective. In discussions of corporate management nowadays, we often find the word 'steward-
ship'—and with good reason. Certainly, a corporation must serve
the interest of its customers, employees, and shareholders. But
that alone is not enough. In the cities and towns where its facilities
are located, it must also act with a sense of responsibility for the
natural environment, for the economic health of the country, and
ultimately, for the welfare of future generations. People who have
studied history and philosophy find it easy to maintain such a
broad perspective. They know that what a corporation does can
have moral implications that may reach far beyond the making of
goods and the earning of profits." Smith added that in business, "to
thrive—even to survive—you have to be able to envision new
things, as well as new ways of doing old things. You have to extrap-
olate on the basis of what worked in the past. You have to be able to
organize and reorganize your operations to achieve economy and
eliminate redundancy. And you need the power to imagine how
the course of events might be changed, and by what kinds of
intervention."

For these reasons, megamanufacturers like General Motors recruit, hire, and retain large numbers of liberal arts graduates.
According to Smith, "They're successful not because they did or
did not major in philosophy or French, but because they've had
the wit and the resources to absorb what they've been taught and
to employ it in an imaginative and creative way." In other words,
it's the learning how to learn that you have mastered as a liberal
arts student—and it's this ability to "quick study" that must be
illustrated to convince potential employers that you're worth the
investment.

Cynthia Burr, senior vice president of Connecticut General Life
Insurance Company, earned a B.A. in French from Connecticut
College and joined CIGNA's group insurance department immediately following graduation. She advised that "each company has
its own personality, and when you begin your job search, it's important to keep in mind that you can't draw a common profile of
what it is all companies look for in new employees."[5] Burr explained, "We look for generalists, people with good analytical and

conceptual skills, common sense and 'smarts.' It's important that you convince us that you're mature, have a desire to work hard, and have the self-confidence to learn from others. This last trait includes the desire to learn from those who may be a couple of rungs below you on the ladder. We don't hire people for one-way careers, which means that even though we may steer you to the most obvious opening initially, there's a good deal of movement among people with great potential."[6]

Once you prove that you've got the skills an employer needs, what matters most is "fit"—whether you're the kind of colleague the executive who's doing the hiring seeks. According to Terrence R. Connelly, a managing director of Salomon Brothers who earned a B.A. in politics from Catholic University, when working professionals are selecting new hires, they focus as much on the candidate's personal characteristics as on the specifics of his academic package. Indeed, there are many hidden networks job hunters can join, through extracurricular activities and interests. One example is what's known around Wall Street as the lacrosse connection. Said Barbara-Jan Wilson, director of career development at Wesleyan University, "When someone [an employer] played or plays lacrosse, he is able to appreciate the qualities and skill that predict success. He looks at the player and the player's position and has insight into how the player fits into the business environment."[7] Bill Meckel, a liberal arts graduate of Brown University who is president of a brokerage firm, agreed. "At the risk of sounding corny, I think that lacrosse is a microcosm of life . . . players do business in the same manner as they play the game."[8]

The bond, the connection, the contact—call it what you will—is what makes it even easier for you young old boys and you young new girls to break into the job market. The tough stuff is knowing what breaks you're looking to make in today's unconventional working world—and knowing how to appear patient enough to get them. Heather Evans, a quintessential yuppie superstar (she became a vice president at Bear, Stearns just five years after graduating from Harvard with a B.A. in philosophy), explains the catch-22 that liberal arts graduates can find themselves trapped in. "In our short hair and crisp suits, we look just like the young managers of the 1960s. We are driven, ambitious and politically conservative, like our predecessors. One difference, however, is that managers now in their late twenties to early thirties are better off in their careers, yet statistically are less likely to reach the top. These differences make them less responsive to the psychological pressures that kept our predecessors hanging on to the corporate ladder. In general, we've become too smart too soon to fall for the old stick-and-carrot trick; we are focusing on the here-and-now. We want success sooner rather than later."[9]

Like it or not, what Evans points out is true. Fulfillment does—or at least should—factor into career decisions for today's liberal arts graduates. It's a luxury that Macy's Finkelstein and Grey's Meyer, to name just two industry leaders, didn't have. If you're seeking total fulfillment, keep in mind the importance of getting inside yourself to figure out what really satisfies you and how you can sustain a sense of well-being.

If you pay attention to the media, it's clear that those who study social trends have noted how today's graduates demand satisfaction here and now. Companies are aware that they must do what they can to change the traditional structure that put challenging, creative work years out of the grasp of new hires. The flip side of this awareness is that corporate recruiters, as well as line managers, are often on the lookout for those who have unreal expectations of first and subsequent jobs. A recruiter for a leading management consulting firm jokes, "He wants to be a CEO . . . so what else is new? I'm tired of hearing about how a student would initiate changes in our long-term strategy. I'm more interested in hearing about how excited he is about rolling up his sleeves and joining the team. When I recruit rookies, I'm looking for naive enthusiasm, maybe just a touch of competitive spirit. A rookie isn't a senior vice president, isn't eligible for a corner office, and shouldn't have any delusions of grandeur. It's a tough balance, for what I see most times are students who are undecided but talk big, or students who are overdecided and who are looking for very specific situations which just can't be found at the entry level."

One more bit of getting-started advice: when you're ready to throw yourself into the job hunting game, the more you know about the rules and your competitors, the better. Even though it may be difficult to convince yourself and your important others about the value of careful planning before jumping in, we promise you that preparation will pay off once you're on the job, once your career has begun. Knowing *what* you want and *why* is the key to a successful job hunt; it's easy to sell yourself into an opportunity once you thoroughly understand the product and the marketplace. So take your great potential in hand, and get started!

Chapter **2**

Who Said They're Not Looking for Thinking People?

Although your roommate may have known from the time she was seven that she wanted to be a doctor, and the guy next door may have decided to major in computer science after interning for a high-tech company, few of us are fortunate enough to choose our careers so easily. Said one college career counselor, "By the start of senior year, less than a quarter of our liberal arts students have a definite idea of what they want to do after graduation—let alone for the rest of their lives." So the other three-quarters must get prepared to embark upon an arduous search to discover what they have to offer employers, and vice versa.

Choosing a career is a two-way street. You must know yourself— your skills, knowledge, and strengths—and you must know the market for these abilities. The successful job hunter uses many of the same tactics that are used in selling a product. As a liberal arts major, you are offering your general capabilities, in particular your capacity to learn quickly. You're usually an employer's best bargain, since you'll do top-flight work for an entry-level salary. "We find that liberal arts students come with less baggage than those who've specialized early," said one recruiting coordinator from a commercial bank. "They don't have any bad habits to break, and they can be trained from the ground up. They're often our best hires."

Although there are (in theory, at least) hundreds of careers open to liberal arts majors, the endless possibilities may be paralyzing. And since there's no clear relationship between your undergraduate major and various occupational labels, it may be difficult to get started. "I'm really jealous of my friends who majored in engineering," said one political science major. "They know exactly what to do with their degrees, and all the big companies are courting them. Nobody's begging me to take a job as a political scientist!" Many students put off making a choice for fear of rejecting the "right" profession and forever mourning the road not taken. That's why developing a strategic marketing plan is essential. Once you've assessed yourself, you'll be able to take stock of your future. You'll be able to set goals and make plans *without* worrying about whether you've overlooked the most appropriate avenues.

Most sales campaigns follow a three-pronged approach:

1. analysis of the product and its uses;
2. research of the marketplace to figure out where the product is needed and where it may be used effectively; and
3. examination of methods to get the product into the marketplace and ways to make it appealing to buyers.

In this chapter we cover the first step, product analysis, commonly known as self-assessment. Webster's defines a skill as "a developed aptitude or ability." Each of us has hundreds of skills, some that we were born with and some that we learned. Obviously there are certain abilities that employers expect the liberal arts major to have mastered by the time of graduation. You should be able to conduct and comprehend research; to compare and contrast information; to read and write with a critical eye; and to convey your ideas to others clearly, both orally and in writing. At a time when the world is becoming more and more technically oriented, the well-rounded generalist is expected to offer a breath of fresh air. As William Lawrence, professor of economics at Pace University, explained, "Students who have no sense of history or literature are missing so much. Those who do can be more creative and objective."[1] Likewise James Gibbons, dean of engineering at Stanford University, recently stated his belief that most significant issues had qualitative and subjective dimensions "best approached through studies of literature, history, art and social sciences."[2]

For the purpose of product analysis, divide your abilities into three groups: basic skills (what you can do), knowledge (what you know about), and strengths (what your personal characteristics are). To fully understand the product—your abilities and long-term potential—you must take the self-assessment process seriously. Although it may seem tedious, you'll be paving the way for creating a top-flight résumé and for answering the most challenging interview questions. In effect, you'll be developing your sales pitch. Sitting down for ten minutes and thinking about the subject won't help; you need to know *what* you are qualified for and *why*. "I find so few students have a realistic perception of their qualifications," said an investment bank recruiter. "They throw around a lot of vague superlatives about their achievements, but they often can't back them up with any hard facts."

P.S. Negatives Count as Positives

Don't forget to include negatives as well as positives. Discovering and defining your weaknesses is just as important as elaborating on your strengths. Employers may perceive your soft points through omission, or they may ask you directly what they are. Be prepared. Like an expert salesperson, you should be familiar with your product's weaknesses and be able to turn them into selling points.

Keep in mind that the results of your self-assessment must be as thorough as a product analysis. Coke is it for a reason. If Procter & Gamble wouldn't try to sell a new brand of detergent without fully researching its applications, why should you sell yourself without fully researching your abilities? Your self-analysis must be realistic and provide the basis for approaching the job market with all the background information you need to sell yourself to the right employer. Like a good scout, be honest with yourself. Pretending you're someone you're not will only hurt you. On the other hand, don't be afraid to show off your abilities; a good salesman never sells his product short. Unlike a seller of used cars, you're lucky enough to be peddling a prestige product—one that will make the right buyer mighty happy.

Following is a suggested outline for organizing your self-assessment. While comprehensive, it's by no means complete. As you work through it, add to or alter the categories as you see fit. We suggest using a point system to further define your abilities. Give yourself a 1 if you have an elementary level of proficiency with the subject; a 2 if you have an intermediate level of proficiency; and a 3 if you have an advanced or expert level of proficiency.

Be aware that this list is meant to guide you in selling yourself to employers. After completing the exercises, go over each listing and ask yourself, "Why did I say this?" and "Why do I feel this way?" Dig deep into your background, since the successful marketer understands his product in depth as well as breadth. Give yourself several hours to write down your attributes and to illustrate them with concrete examples. For example, if you volunteer part-time at a day care center, you probably use supervising, planning, monitoring, and coordinating skills; you have gained knowledge of teaching children; and you have demonstrated strengths in tolerance, patience, and, of course, your high energy level! If you sold T-shirts for the big homecoming game, you probably used organizing, administering, delegating, and strategizing skills; you have gained knowledge of retail merchandising; and you have demonstrated strengths in resourcefulness, initiative, and ambition. If you were the entrepreneur behind such a drive, be sure to recognize the independence that such an effort illustrates.

You might try asking a friend to join you in the self-assessment process and to trade work sheets when you're done. (Be sure, however, not to take your friend's assessment too seriously if an underlying tension exists because you're both pursuing spots in a highly exclusive training program.) Chances are you'll be able to add substantial items to each other's lists. When you've finished, put your work sheet away for a few days and then come back to it for revisions or additions. Refer to it throughout your job hunt to remember at a glance who you are and what you can do. Be prepared to grow and change as you become more savvy about the job market. Keep in mind that it's difficult to choose your goals when you're not certain about your abilities. Once you've chosen to commit yourself to a continuing process of self-evaluation, your job search will be made much simpler.

SKILLS:

Communication Skills

Reading	Drawing/	Defining
Writing	Illustrating	Interpreting
Speaking	Reporting	Explaining
Listening	Negotiating	Persuading
Editing	Describing	

Research Skills

Collecting	Investigating	Classifying
Analyzing	Evaluating	Compiling
Synthesizing	Examining	Hypothesizing
Clarifying	Critiquing	Coordinating
Surveying	Interpreting	

Management Skills

Planning	Counseling	Coaching
Organizing	Teaching	Interviewing
Supervising	Monitoring	Deciding
Developing	Relating	Motivating
Delegating	Guiding	Strategizing
Leading		

KNOWLEDGE:

(These are examples; each individual has a unique body of knowledge to sell to an employer. This is where you're really figuring out why you are *it!*)

Foreign language
Computer operation
Graphic design

STRENGTHS:

High energy level	Direction	Determination
Initiative	Leadership	Resourcefulness
Flexibility	Diplomacy	Objectivity
Intelligence	Tolerance	Enthusiasm
Perspective	Competitiveness	Patience
Judgment	Dependability	Ability to work
Cooperation	Creativity	under pressure
Common sense	Ambition	

Once you've taken stock of your skills, knowledge, and strengths, you'll have a clearer, more organized view of your present and future capabilities. The next step is to ask yourself the following questions:

How well do I make use of my abilities?

Which of my abilities do people most often praise? Which do they criticize?

What interests and challenges me?

What do I do best and what do I like to do most?

How have I distinguished myself from my peers at school? Outside school?

What have been my most satisfying and most disappointing experiences in school? Outside school?

What kinds of experiences do I hope to encounter in the next few years?

If, after completing the self-assessment exercises and answering the foregoing questions, you feel a need to explore yourself further, you may want to take a professionally administered personality inventory or vocational aptitude test. The most common tests used to determine career direction are the Strong-Campbell Interest Inventory, the Myers-Briggs Personality Type Indicator, and the Minnesota Multiphasic Test. Consult your school's career placement center to find out where you can take these tests. Although they can't predict with certainty your success in any given field, they may help to reveal what careers other people with a similar personality makeup have found satisfying. Armed with a thorough self-analysis, you should feel confident about approaching the next step in your marketing plan: determining what you want to do and where you want to do it.

Chapter 3

In Search of the Right First Job

Once you've analyzed the product, you're ready to research the marketplace. From day one of your job hunt, consider yourself a professional and act accordingly. Treat your investigation of the marketplace as a serious campaign, and you'll produce substantive results. Rome wasn't built in a day; dream jobs are created by selling the right you into the right organization for you. And knowing what's right takes plenty of research.

You should start by asking, "What looks like an interesting career?" rather than "Who's hiring?" Often, beginning job hunters get hung up on media projections and statistics that proclaim the dearth of jobs in one profession or another. Be wary of what you read, because occupational forecasts are frequently inaccurate. As Richard Bolles, author of *What Color Is Your Parachute?*, has said, "There are openings for every job in the world. All that forecasts do . . . is to define 'the degree of competition.' "[1]

As a rule, the earlier you begin career planning, the better chance you'll have of getting what you want. Waiting too long to start looking can slow the progress of your search and undermine your ability to focus on your goals. Being able to space the job hunting process over several months—or even a year—is an advantage you shouldn't pass up. Learn to weave your job hunting activities into your daily schedule. "If I could give one piece of advice to the entire senior class," said a career counselor at a large state university, "it's start early! All too often I find students panicked because they've left only a few weeks to decide what industry, what company, and what city they want to work in. If you don't take an interest in career planning several months before graduation, it's highly unlikely that you'll be happy in your first job."

Searching for meaningful work can be a stressful, tension-filled experience. It's a vicious cycle—the more anxious you are, the more likely you are to be filled with self-doubt and indecisiveness. Many liberal arts graduates suffer from anxieties created by the high—and often unrealistic—expectations that have been imposed upon them by their family, their school, their peers, and themselves. Lots of students who breezed through high school and were admitted to their first-choice college panic when faced with the recruiting process; after all, in the past, they were able to prove themselves on the basis of previous experience. This time around, they have to sell themselves on potential alone. It's the SATs times one hundred, in terms of cold, sweaty-palm pressure.

In addition, students frequently make the mistake of deciding on a career without understanding their values and motivations. They pass over the work settings that best utilize their abilities in favor of jobs they see as glamorous—jobs that the president of the fraternity/sorority may have accepted last year and returned to campus to brag about. Liberal arts majors are especially susceptible to what they see as the "in" careers. It may be fine for you to choose your clothes or your car because they're status symbols, but to pick a job that way is dangerous. "I thought investment banking was incredibly exciting from what my friends told me and from what I read in magazines," said one recent graduate. "I had no idea how long the hours are, or how uninteresting I find most of the work." Likewise, admitted another liberal arts major, "I'd heard that retailing was filled with chic people and international buying trips, but I didn't know that I'd have to spend most of my first year selling hosiery." Obviously, if your major sources of information are your friends and the media, you're likely to have a distorted view of what options are available to someone with your skills and interests. (How often is it reported that assistant editors at magazines are simply well-dressed typists/fact checkers?) Go ahead and examine the hottest jobs while researching the marketplace, but remember your goal: to find the niche where you, the product, can be most effectively utilized.

As a student, the place to begin your market research is in the campus planning or placement center. (If you're no longer in school, the local public library should contain a number of these resources.) Drop in, introduce yourself to a counselor, and ask to be shown around. You may be overwhelmed by the wealth of information; if that's the case, don't be afraid to call for help. Following is a sampling of the resources you'll probably find:

Counseling services. The most important service provided by any placement office is one-to-one counseling. Experienced career counselors are usually available by appointment to assist you in clarifying your goals, finding the right resources, and answering general planning questions. Make sure to use this service. Never again will you have the opportunity to attach yourself, at no extra cost, to experts in the job hunting game.

Industry notebooks or files. These offer general information on a number of topics, from accounting and advertising to insurance and retailing. Included may be broad histories, analyses, surveys, and forecasts, as well as lists of prominent companies or individuals to contact for further information.

Company files. These contain brochures, annual reports, newspaper and magazine clippings, and other materials, including whom to contact for information on employment opportunities.

Company videotapes. Usually ten to thirty minutes long, these tapes are an excellent way to see what the company's offices and employees look like. (Keep in mind that everything's spiffed up a bit for the video presentation—not many companies will invest money and time in filming the dark side of entry-level life.)

Reference books. See the appendices for starters. These detail books, registers, directories, catalogs, guides, and journals about general and specific job hunting topics. Most sources we've cited are available at your placement office.

Alumni counseling network. This service provides you with information on graduates of your alma mater who are willing to talk with you about their field, with insights into how you might conduct an appropriate job search in that area.

Group workshops. Many schools offer weekly workshops on interviewing, résumé writing, organizing a job search, and making career decisions. There may also be lectures or discussions on specific careers.

Career fairs. On campus or off, career fairs and open houses offer employers and students an informal way to meet and exchange information. Don't attend career fairs with the goal of getting a job offer; think of these events as an excellent way to collect stacks and stacks of material about job possibilities. In fact, career fairs are like career flea markets, fun to browse in but not the best place to shop.

On-campus recruiting. According to Jesse M. Smith, Jr., executive director of the College Placement Council, "The on-campus recruiting process is, without a doubt, the most effective and efficient system for filling entry-level positions."[2] Recruiters come to campuses not to extend on-the-spot job offers but to uncover a group of qualified students who will then be invited to interview more formally at the company's headquarters. Usually an employer contacts the campus to announce the number and type of positions available and to arrange interview dates. The career placement office then takes care of setting up the interview schedules. While many job offers do result from on-campus recruiting, keep in mind that the organizations that come to your school represent only a very small portion of the employment universe. As a rule, most campuses are primarily visited by large corporations rather than small companies or representatives from the arts, social services, and government. If you choose to sign up for on-campus recruiting, you should also be actively using other methods to obtain a job. Generally, employers visit campuses between January and March, although some large universities have both fall and spring recruiting schedules.

If your school doesn't have one of these services, see if you can get it started. Form a student interest group and invite executives from local companies to speak to you—chances are they'll be flattered and delighted to oblige.

As you conduct your investigation of the marketplace, develop a system to organize your research. Jotting down a contact's name on the back of your history exam isn't going to do you much good unless you then transfer it to a safe place. Over the course of your search, you'll pick up loads of information. Some of it will be immediately useful, and some of it will be completely extraneous. Save it all, because a company that bores you to tears today may become a hot prospect tomorrow. It's better to have a few extra files cluttering up your room than it is to rack your brain trying to remember the name of an interviewer who suggested you call back six months later. If you can't keep straight basic information on a company, why should they hire you?

Each individual has his own method for storing information. Our favorite is the file/folder system. For the first part, you'll need a 4-by-6-inch file box and several dozen 4-by-6-inch lined index cards. On a one-card-per-company basis, record the company's full name, address, and phone number; the name of the director of college recruiting; the name and phone number of who referred you to the company; and the name(s) and title(s) of your interviewers. Include the dates of all correspondence and interviews, and jot down any brief personal impressions. What you'll create is a quick and handy reference system. Next, you'll need several dozen letter- or legal-size files. We suggest organizing your material into company files and industry files, similar to what's found in a career placement office. You might also want to create a general file, in which you put sample résumés, cover letters, thank-you letters, and correspondence.

Once you've examined what's available on campus, you've by no means exhausted your resources—in fact, you've only just begun. Although the placement office may be the first stop on your marketing campaign, don't make it the last. After you've obtained as much knowledge as possible from published sources, go to live ones. Talk to friends, relatives, neighbors, faculty members, and former employers—anyone who will give you further advice. Often you'll find recent graduates of your school the best source of help, since they know what you're up against.

After you've done your initial round of market research, it's time to begin evaluating your opportunities. Just as you analyzed your skills, knowledge, and strengths, you must examine your values and motivations. Each employer places a different emphasis on these qualities. In the language of marketing, you must design your product's sale according to the buyer's needs. Following is a list of personal values that may affect your career strategy. Take a close look at them to see which are most important in your life.

VALUES ANALYSIS:

Achievement: Need to feel that you are doing a job well
Affection: Need to form close relationships with colleagues
Altruism: Need to feel that you are contributing to the welfare of others
Challenge: Need to be intellectually stimulated
Change: Need to engage in different activities periodically
Creativity: Need to develop new ideas or invent new works
Expertise: Need to reach an authoritative level in a specialty
Independence: Need to work at your own pace, to be responsible for yourself
Leadership: Need to have power or control over others
Prestige: Need to have your work praised or rewarded in public
Security: Need to have certainty in your life
Way of Life: Need to enjoy your life, at work and outside
Wealth: Need to earn lots of money

Once you've clarified your values, you should determine your motivations. Since you'll undoubtedly be spending a significant amount of time at work, the environment should be comfortable and satisfying. Remember that your happiness and success depend on finding the right seller/buyer fit. Different careers have different demands; you should be aware of what job factors are most critical to you. The following questions are designed to help you determine your own criteria for choosing where you, the product, will be most effectively utilized in the marketplace.

MOTIVATION ANALYSIS:

Which qualities do I want in an office: Large/small? New/old? Quiet/noisy? Competitive/noncompetitive? Structured/unstructured? My own space/bullpen?

What rewards are most important to me: Money? Benefits? Incentives? Travel? Power? Recognition? Promotion?

What kind of people do I enjoy working with: Formal/informal? Men/women? Groups/individuals? Younger/older? Traditional/creative?

What sort of feedback do I need: Frequent/occasional? Written/verbal? Scheduled/random?

Which hours do I prefer: Fixed/flexible? Weekdays/weekends? Under 50 per week/over 50?

What location do I like: Close to home/long commute? In office full-time/traveling often? Staying in one place/relocating frequently?

After you've analyzed your priorities, you'll be able to rate a company's ability to fulfill your expectations. A word of warning, however: clarifying your values and motivations can only help you determine the direction in which you should be heading. Don't get caught up in endlessly reexamining these characteristics, because you may convince yourself that no job can meet your out-of-reach criteria. Assessing yourself should open your options rather than close potential pathways. It should give you a heightened sense of your distinct abilities and interests and how they may be applied successfully to the job market.

Now that you've figured out who you are and what you want from a job, it's time to draw up a list of companies and begin outlining what they have to offer you in the near and long-term future. Keep in mind that in your parents' generation, a job and a career were one and the same, and a large corporation was usually responsible for planning both. In today's rapidly changing work environment, the individual sets his own goals and uses a variety of routes to reach them. As James Robinson III, chairman of American Express, recently said about the corporate world, "Change is the only constant we all face."[3] Thus career planning has become an art. Like an artist, you should be colorful and creative, and be willing to make frequent revisions. As you consider different employers, ask yourself the following questions:

What will it be like to work for this company?

How will my abilities be utilized and how will they be strengthened?

What sorts of challenges/problems should I expect to deal with?

How much training will I need before I make a real contribution?

How long will it take to be promoted?

What is it like to live in this company's various locations?

Does this industry/company have good growth potential?

How is this company regarded in the field?

What is this company's reputation in the community?

What is the company stereotype?

How will I feel about myself working for this company?

When you've determined the handful of companies you really want to work for, it's time for the next step in your marketing plan: packaging the product and presenting it to the buyers.

Chapter 4

Pathways Into and Up
the Organization

Understanding the differences among various pathways into organizations is a key component of your job-search strategy. Know how a line position differs from a staff function, and how a formal training program differs from informal or on-the-job learning. Once you've chosen the field that interests you, it's time to explore the various opportunities along that career track and to see which routes are most appealing. Many liberal arts graduates feel cheated or confused in their first job. The problem is usually that they didn't determine which pathway was the right one, even if they took the time to choose their employer carefully. "I went into retailing because I liked the idea of becoming a buyer," says one recent graduate. "Instead, I got stuck in store-line merchandising." Says another student in a bank training program, "I thought M & A [mergers and acquisitions] was where all the action is. But after a few months, I realized that with my personality and work style, I'm better suited for sales and trading."

Line Versus Staff

In most companies, "line" employees manage the business and "staff" employees manage the organization. According to management expert Betty Lehan Harrigan, "Line jobs are where the action is, where the money is, where the power is."[1] Line managers are directly accountable for the company's products/services. Staff managers provide support and advice behind the scenes. Although line jobs are often hailed as the fastest track to the top, staff jobs can be an excellent place to start. It's a two-way street, since line managers can't do their jobs without staff help, and vice versa. For instance, a consumer products salesman (line) can't increase the company's profits without the assistance of a financial analyst (staff) who invests his revenues. When you review the climbs made by leading corporate executives, you see that a combination of both experiences makes for the best leaders.

Both line and staff functions exist in every organization; their nature depends on the nature of the business. While an accountant in a public accounting firm is a line worker, an accountant in a manufacturing company is considered staff. Likewise, a personnel director in a human resources agency is a line manager, while a personnel director in an investment bank is known as a staffer. Ideally, you should mix staff and line positions on your way up the organization.

Take the career of John Akers, IBM's chief executive officer, for example. After graduating from Yale in 1960, he moved to California and entered IBM's sales training program. In his first year, he earned $6,500. After a year and a half as a trainee, Akers became a marketing representative and spent five years traveling around New England selling computers. By 1967, he was promoted to marketing manager, and the following year he became an assistant district manager. At this point, he was pulling in about $45,000. In 1969, he was transferred to New York, where he became a branch manager. Soon after, he was named administrative assistant to IBM's president, Frank Cary. In 1972, Akers got his first national job, as director of distribution/media industries in the company's data processing division, for a $65,000 salary—ten times what he'd earned just one decade earlier. Nine months later, he moved to Los Angeles and became vice president and regional manager of the western region's data processing division. The following year he returned to New York and became president of the data processing division, earning about $150,000. By 1976, Akers was named one of twenty-five IBM vice presidents, and in

1978, he added group executive to his title. In 1981, he became vice president and group executive for the information systems and communications group, for $335,000—or fifty times his original salary. Six months later, he became senior vice president in that area, which merited a $40,000 raise. By 1983, Akers was named president and director, earning about $600,000. The following year, he was named chief executive officer, at a salary of $750,000. Asked how he managed his amazing climb (beating out thousands of other trainees along the way), Akers answered, "I got it by being nice to everybody."[2]

Training Programs Versus On-the-Job Apprenticeships

In recent years, corporate training programs have grown and prospered—and consequently become the rage for liberal arts graduates. After all, you're used to disciplined learning, to having your professors call the shots. Wouldn't a formal training program be an ideal vehicle for entering the work world? Wouldn't it offer the structure you need, not to mention a group of co-workers who are your peers?

Yes and no. Training programs are only as good as the management behind them. They vary in length from one month to two years, and in size from six trainees to six hundred. As a trainee, you undertake classroom work and practical assignments that give you an overall grasp of the company's operations and a chance to demonstrate your abilities. In some programs, you get rotated through various departments and are then offered your choice of positions upon completion. In others, you're trained for a specific job and are placed in an appropriate position once you've picked up the necessary skills. In the best programs, trainees become junior executives or a reasonable facsimile in three to five years.

The typical training program begins with a brief orientation session, in which you read literature describing the company's philosophy and goals, and you study charts displaying its organizational structure. Next you enter the classroom for instruction in a variety of specialized skills. In a commercial bank training program, you might study accounting and finance, while in a computer sales program, you might study marketing and basic electronics. Classes are usually taught by a combination of in-house experts and outside professors from local schools. Most programs use grades on weekly exams to evaluate the rate at which you're absorbing and utilizing new information. Along the way, and after the program is complete, you're likely to be asked to attend seminars or workshops addressing select topics related to new skills, problems, or developments in the industry.

Following your classroom stint, you may begin a series of rotations through different departments and functions. These are designed to give you exposure to various areas of the company. At the same time, you're given a chance to search out the best niche for your abilities and interests. In some programs, you won't be rotated at all; instead, you'll be placed in a permanent position. From then on, you're expected to assume responsibility and start making a real contribution to the organization. Although you may only be a few months out of college, you'll have to hit the fast track running—if not sprinting. "You're thrown from the frying pan into the fire," says a retailing executive about his trainees. "Only the fittest survive."

For some liberal arts graduates, training programs offer the ideal combination of in-depth education and experience as well as hefty starting salaries (usually in the $20,000–$35,000 range). However, the competition is extremely stiff. Since nearly half of all on-campus recruiting offers go to engineering or technical graduates, liberal arts students have to be plenty aggressive—and even then, only one in fifteen generally make it into the top training programs. Across the country, college seniors have been seen camping out on career placement office steps to sign up first for interviews with companies like Procter & Gamble, Morgan Stanley, Macy's, Manufacturers Hanover, Ogilvy & Mather, and McKinsey & Company, just to name a few of today's trendiest employers. And once you get into the program, competition seems to escalate. "Whoever pulls the most all-nighters is like a god around here," says one recent graduate working for an investment bank. "You've got to be constantly on your toes or somebody else will get the best assignments and be promoted before you." We know one tale of a trainee whose appendix ruptured while she was working on a big deal at an investment bank—and she had to be forced by her peers to leave the office. "It's sickness, in more ways than one," said the recent graduate who reported this incident.

For some trainees, this sort of competition is invigorating. "There's nothing as exciting as working with an incredibly talented bunch of people who treat you like their equal," says an English major working for an advertising agency. For other trainees, it's debilitating. "I thought there'd be some comradeship and support, but it's every man out for himself," says a history major working for a management consulting firm. "I've never been so worn down in my life. I'm starting to be really negative about the job, because I just don't think I'll make it through the rest of training." Clearly, a high level of resilience is necessary for the most competitive, if not for all, training programs. If you won't feel comfortable or perform your best in such intense surroundings, you may be better off in an informal, on-the-job learning situation.

To get the most out of formal management training, carefully evaluate the program's quality, history, philosophy, and reputation before accepting an offer. Some programs were begun decades ago and are constantly being refined to meet the needs of new recruits. Others have gone several generations virtually untouched and are outmoded. Also beware of brand-new training programs, which may be defect ridden or ill defined. Trainees in recently developed programs may be victims of the "guinea pig" syndrome. In addition, examine closely the programs offered by small companies or start-ups, since they may lack the time, disposition, or wherewithal for proper training. They might also not promote as rapidly as promised, since it's tough to have growth opportunities without growth. Similarly, in places that are growing at a very rapid pace, management may be too busy coping with change and confusion to train new hires.

If the intensely collegiate feel of studying and interacting with the same group of people for several months to a year doesn't appeal to you, an informal training situation may be your best bet. This sort of hands-on learning offers greater independence and responsibility through one-on-one instruction and supervision in specific work assignments. Companies offering informal training usually have an orientation period and a seminar/workshop series similar to those in formal programs, but there aren't hours and hours of classroom study. Instead, the focus is on completing proj-

ects administered by a senior manager and then discussing what
went right and what didn't.

Just as there are pitfalls in formal programs, informal training
has its down side. You may find that a loosely managed conglomer-
ation of assignments doesn't teach you much; when you're used to
information being presented in a logical, sequential manner, a
random collection of experiences may be confusing. You also
might not have a clear relationship with your superiors. "When I
was hired, I was told that one person was to be my boss," says a
recent graduate working in a public relations firm. "Instead, everyone threw work at me, and I had no idea what my priorities
were supposed to be."

In general, the best informal training situations involve a good
mentor relationship. Finding a superior who's supportive of your
career goals and who wants to help you reach them can be tantamount to your happiness. For you students of the humanities, note
that the word "mentor" derives from Greek mythology. (Mentor
was the name of a friend of Odysseus who was entrusted with the
education of Telemachus, his son.) Thus the word implies a trusted
individual who can coach or teach you in his specialty. The ideal
mentor protects and promotes you and your interests, giving you
enough rope to take chances but not enough to hang yourself. The
worst mentor is one who begins to compete with you as soon as
your greenness acquires a luster.

Understanding Career Pathways

Once you've established the type of training that best suits you,
the next step is to investigate career pathways. Recognizing and
analyzing the differences among job functions will help you
choose the right track. While the following options don't represent
the entire spectrum of paths available to liberal arts graduates,
they are the most common. You'll find accounting, advertising,
consulting, finance, human resources, manufacturing, marketing
and sales, and public relations functions in just about every organization you examine. (Since this book's focus is on the best *companies* to work for, we haven't included categories for acting, teaching, firefighting, painting, flying, or any other function that isn't
frequently done in a corporate setting.) Bear in mind that while

the nature of jobs in different companies and industries may vary, the basic aspects of these career paths are consistent.

Accounting

Forget the green eyeshade and the mechanical pencil tucked behind your ear. Accounting has come into its own in the eighties. The old stereotype of the boring number-cruncher no longer holds true; as the accuracy of the bottom line has come under fire, accountants have emerged as the darlings of corporate América. Wherever you find money, you'll find accountants keeping track of it. The buzzword of today's accounting business is "value added," which refers to the innovative new services accountants are developing.

Essentially, accountants analyze, verify, and report the results of business transactions. With ever-increasing sophistication, they provide the financial information that is needed by all types of organizations, both profit and nonprofit, to evaluate their present condition and to make decisions about their future activities. There are almost one million accountants working in the United States today, and as the nation's tax legislation and financial reporting standards grow more complex, the field continues to expand.

A career in accounting requires strong mathematical skills as well as the ability to analyze data, communicate effectively, and work well with others. While it's not necessary to have an undergraduate accounting degree, knowledge of quantitative methods, economics, computer science, and statistics helps. There are two fields of accounting open to liberal arts graduates: management accounting and public accounting. (There are also jobs in government and education accounting, but these are mainly reserved for undergraduate accounting majors or M.B.A.s.)

The majority of accountants are found in management (or industrial) accounting. These individuals work in companies that provide a product or service to the public, from microchip manufacturers to money managers to motels. They do a variety of tasks, some simple and some highly complex. The most frequent responsibilities include internal auditing, bookkeeping, cost accounting, data processing, budget directing, and financial analysis. In general, liberal arts students enter management accounting with one of several titles: internal auditor, cost accountant, plant accountant, and data processor are common. A few years down the line, you may be promoted to chief or senior accountant, budget director, financial analyst, or data manager. Further down the road, you can make controller, treasurer, vice president, and, ultimately, president or CEO. One recent survey of executives found that more had come up through an accounting background than any other specialty.

About a quarter of the nation's accountants work for public accounting firms. You may have heard of the "Big Eight": Arthur Andersen; Arthur Young; Coopers & Lybrand; Deloitte, Haskins & Sells; Ernst & Whinney; Peat, Marwick & Mitchell; Price Waterhouse; and Touche Ross. These prestigious firms do accounting for more than three-quarters of all the companies listed on the New York Stock Exchange. They employ hundreds of accountants, many of whom are liberal arts graduates, and they recruit extensively at schools across the country. In general, while you don't need to take the Certified Public Accountant (CPA) exam to work for a management accounting firm, you do need this credential to work for a public firm. (Once you're on the job, you'll more than likely be trained to take the CPA exam.) Since CPAs generally command a slightly higher salary than noncertified accountants, public accounting is seen as a more lucrative field than management accounting.

Public accountants perform audits, give tax advice, and provide management consulting services. They often travel to the client's headquarters or branches during an audit and spend many hours investigating the company's records. It's a painstaking process; non-detail-oriented individuals need not apply. Most liberal arts graduates enter public accounting firms as accounting trainees, becoming junior or staff accountants after completing training. After several years, you may be promoted to the senior accountant position, and then to manager or partner. The top accountants in a public accounting firm are usually called senior partners. Although senior partners earn high salaries, few trainees (less than one in seven, according to our sources) make it to this point. Most people leave and get jobs in management accounting or become consultants or financial analysts.

Advertising

Advertising is the happy home of many liberal arts graduates. It's seen as a sexy, exciting, and creative business, with many opportunities for broadly educated individuals. Basically, advertising involves calling something to the attention of the public, through information found everywhere from newspapers and magazines to radio and television—and including billboards, bumper stickers, T-shirts, and matchbooks. Some six thousand advertising agencies currently operate in the United States, ranging from tiny "Mom 'n' Pop" shops to multinational giants. While more than 125,000 people work in the advertising industry, the recent spate of mergers has narrowed the field. The consolidation of several large firms into "megaagencies" has eliminated hundreds of jobs, making entry more difficult than ever.

Each year the nation's businesses spend some $60 billion advertising their products and services. Currently the top ten agencies generate nearly half of the industry's total dollar volume. These agencies design campaigns and buy space from print and broadcast organizations, then charge their clients a percentage of the total fee billed by the media. Although some agencies do accept flat service fees from advertisers, most follow the 15 percent commission structure. So if an agency has annual billings of $500 million, it's actually earning $75 million in revenues.

Here's how an ad campaign works. A company takes its product or service to agencies, looking for bidders. When an agency is assigned a campaign, it enlists an account executive, a market researcher, a media planner, a copywriter, and an art director to develop a plan. The account executive is directly responsible for dealing with the client. He acts as a liaison, handling new accounts and maintaining old ones. The media planner is responsible for analyzing various media options (television, radio, print, and billboards are examples) and developing a strategy for the advertising placement. He negotiates contracts for advertising space or air time, which involves choosing ways to reach the largest group of consumers most efficiently. The copywriter creates the words for print advertising or the scripts for commercials, using information compiled by the market researcher. The art director, supervising a staff of commercial artists, designers, and producers, generates art for the ad campaign. The whole operation is regulated by the office management and finance department, which handles agency workings and oversees budgets.

Besides working at an ad agency, there are two other major career paths available to liberal arts graduates in advertising. You can work in-house for a profit or nonprofit organization, handling any of the foregoing functions; or you can work for a magazine, newspaper, radio station, or television network, selling space to advertising agencies. Chances are that wherever you begin your career, you'll end up moving around and sampling other options within your specialty. Advertising is known as a field in which the top talent shifts around periodically.

Most liberal arts graduates enter the advertising industry as junior account executives or copywriters, market researchers, media assistants, production assistants, or sales representatives. Since advertising is a high-turnover field, entry-level jobs open frequently. However, competition is extremely stiff, and salaries can be quite low. The best qualifications for advertising include excellent communications skills, a high level of creativity, and a good background in research. If you can type and answer the telephone, that helps; since only a few large agencies have formal training programs, most recent graduates begin as glorified "gofers."

Consulting

In recent years, consulting has become one of the hottest careers for liberal arts graduates. High salaries, frequent travel, and opportunities to interact with senior management have made consultants the envy of the business world. However, with increased popularity comes competition, and consulting is perhaps the most competitive field for freshly minted B.A.s to enter. Outside the handful of top firms that offer highly selective training programs, there's little available at the entry level. Generally speaking, consulting firms seek the very best and brightest graduates. They look for new hires who are highly articulate, objective, self-confident, and resilient. "We don't have any product to sell but our people," says a recruiter from a top consulting firm. "They've got to be the absolute cream of the crop or they just won't cut it with our clients."

Exactly what do consultants do? Back in 1974, newsman Eric Sevareid joked that a consultant was "any ordinary guy more than fifty miles from home."[3] Besides traveling, consultants handle organizational, operational, and strategic issues that a company lacks the time or resources to tackle. Because they work outside of industry with no accountability to the bottom line, they offer an objective point of view. Consultants are essentially professional problem solvers. They assess the needs of an organization and develop an appropriate plan of action. Of course, anyone with a bit of experience can call himself a consultant—and many do. The United States currently has thousands of one- or two-person consulting firms that offer expertise in countless areas. Industry analysts estimate the total market to be in excess of $3 billion, about a third of which is commanded by the top twenty-five multinational firms.

Liberal arts graduates generally enter the consulting business as research associates or assistants. In this capacity, they work on a case team with several senior consultants. The size of the team varies from firm to firm and from problem to problem, just as the nature of the research associate's responsibilities vary. In the best assignment, you may analyze an industry segment or a consumer market; in the worst, you may do a considerable amount of number crunching, proofreading, and the ever-present photocopying. "I like the fact that the assignments vary so often," says one trainee at a top consulting firm. "One month I worked for a computer client and the next for a consumer products company. It's a great way to get a window on a number of different businesses."

If you enjoy moving from assignment to assignment without settling in, consulting may be for you. However, some people find the work too transient, and they complain of being seen as perpetual outsiders. "I wasn't really happy just going in, giving advice, and taking off," says one economics major who spent two years at a large firm. In addition, consulting is one of the most stressful careers; many consultants work seventy- and eighty-hour weeks, and it's not unheard of to spend a hundred hours on the job. But those who stick it out are usually well rewarded. "We always joke that you're paid by the hour," says one consultant. "If you work a fifty-hour week, you earn $50,000. If you work a seventy-five-hour week, you make $75,000. . . ."

Since the vertical structure of most consulting firms is quite lean, research associates can move up rapidly. After two to three years, you can become a senior associate or a consultant. If you perform well for several more years, you might become a manager and lead a consulting team. Following that, you can move up to senior manager and then to junior partner. The top individuals at a consulting firm are usually called partners, principals, or directors.

Finance

We probably don't need to tell you that finance has become more filled with scenes of glory and greed than "Dallas" or "Dynasty." The nation's superbrokers and arbitragers are pictured daily in the media, along with tantalizing tales of their billion-dollar deals. Carl Icahn, Saul Steinberg, Felix Rohatyn, T. Boone Pickens, and their peers have captured the imagination—and, in some cases, the wrath—of America.

There are two broad kinds of jobs in the finance industry. The first type, which are considered line positions, are in commercial banks, investment banks, and insurance companies. The second category is within industrial and service organizations, where finance jobs are usually staff functions.

Today over one and a half million people work in the country's fifteen thousand commercial banks. The vast majority of these individuals hold clerical jobs, as tellers, clerks, and secretaries, while some 300,000 people work as bank officers. Traditionally, commercial banking was a nine-to-five job, offering stability and security but not much challenge. That's all changed, however, as regulatory restrictions have loosened, allowing commercial banks to encroach on investment-bank territory (and vice versa). Instead of simply lending money and managing accounts, bank officers now handle everything from Eurobond trading to leveraged-buyout financing.

Commercial banks are among the best employers of liberal arts graduates. Each year dozens of recruiters scour the nation's campuses in search of talented students eager to enter the field. While a quantitative background is helpful, anyone with a good grade point average and an analytical mind might apply. Most banks start recent graduates as trainees, after which they become loan officers. In this position, you evaluate the credit worthiness of businesses and individuals to determine whether and how much of the bank's money should be loaned to them. You also familiarize clients with the bank's range of services. Most often, new hires are found in retail banking, which deals with private individuals and small companies, or in wholesale banking, which deals with large corporations. Some trainees are placed in other areas, such as capital markets, trust management, or operations. After several years, you can be promoted to assistant vice president or assistant secretary. From there, you may become a vice president, credit manager, or treasurer.

The investment bank has many different specialty areas. The corporate (or public) finance department issues stocks and bonds; the brokerage department buys and sells these instruments; and the trading department matches buyers and sellers to earn money on fluctuations in the marketplace. Behind these functions exists the research department—which analyzes industries, companies, and securities—and the operations department, which processes transactions. The hottest department today is mergers and acquisitions (the famous M & A), which buys and sells companies, often at a dizzying pace. Competition for entry-level jobs or training spots within the top investment banks is tough; some only offer positions to one in twenty applicants. It's a dynamic, high-energy industry in which new hires must sink or swim. While trainees have frequent contact with senior management, much of their work is of a semiclerical nature. Hundred-hour work weeks are generally the rule, not the exception. After two years as an analyst, many liberal arts graduates go on to business school and then return as associates. Next on the ladder is assistant vice president, followed by vice president. At the top of public firms are the managing directors; in private firms, these big cigars are called managing partners.

The insurance business is today a multibillion-dollar industry, employing more than one and a half million people. In recent years, the field has lost its dull, conservative image; now most major insurance companies oversee everything from money management to real estate development. There are three kinds of insurance companies: property and casualty (which insure individuals and businesses against property loss and on-the-job casualties); generic life (which provides annuities, health insurance, life insurance, and employee-benefits plans); and multiple line (which performs all these functions). The assets of the country's five thousand insurance firms totals about $600 billion and pays annual benefits approaching $60 billion. The insurance business is intimately related to the investment business, since some 25 percent of its earnings come from stocks, bonds, mortgages, and other financial instruments. Indeed, some insurance companies have investment portfolios worth as much as $60 billion. Thus the value of securities across the country is affected by the decisions of insurance company executives.

Liberal arts graduates usually enter insurance companies as actuaries, claims representatives, underwriters, agents, or brokers. Actuaries are responsible for studying and assimilating statistics, such as probabilities of injury, sickness, death, and unemployment. Their calculations determine what premium rates should be for insurance policies. Claims representatives, known as adjusters and examiners, settle claims by using various reports, evidence, and testimony of witnesses. Underwriters analyze whether prospective purchasers of insurance are good or bad risks. Agents and brokers are the people who go out and sell insurance policies to individuals and organizations. While no specific degree is best for a career in insurance, you should have good quantitative, analytical, and rational abilities. Course work in statistics and mathematics is a help. Most of the nation's top insurance companies do recruit aggressively for entry-level candidates. Liberal arts graduates are usually trained for several weeks or months before going out into the field or handling policies independently.

If you don't choose to work in a commercial bank, an investment bank, or an insurance firm, you may find a finance position in an industrial or a service organization. Most large companies have quite extensive finance departments, in which specialists perform every function from sales and trading to research and M & A. Entry-level jobs are usually found in the controller's office, which examines the company's performance and develops financial plans; and in the treasury area, which invests surplus funds and generates access to outside capital. Liberal arts graduates looking for staff finance jobs should have a quantitative background, since nonfinancial organizations generally won't devote months to teaching these skills.

Human Resources

As corporations increasingly recognize the importance of organizational efficiency and effectiveness, human resources plays a vital role in American business. After all, in a service-oriented economy, the most important national resource is people. Once known as personnel, the human resources function exists in all areas of private and public industry as well as in government and education. Basically it involves recruiting and placing people at all levels of an organization, as well as performing union negotiations and developing and administering compensation plans. In addition, human resources specialists deal with innovative areas, such as training and development, affirmative action, employee counseling, organizational strategy, and career planning.

Entry-level jobs for liberal arts graduates interested in human resources are generally found in three departments: training and development, labor relations, and recruiting and placement. The best background for human resources includes course work in sociology and psychology sciences, as well as having excellent interpersonal skills.

Manufacturing

Lately manufacturing has been making a bit of a comeback as a popular field. As Harvard Business School professor Robert Hayes advised, "Get experience early on in making it, designing it, selling it—not counting it."[4] Manufacturing careers include many areas of specialization. Liberal arts graduates interested in a career in industrial management generally take one of the following paths: production, inventory control, purchasing, or merchandising. Production involves coordinating plant organization and manufacturing capacity, and making sales forecasts and cost estimates. Inventory control is concerned with checking expenditures and filing reports, as well as coordinating the ordering, receiving, storing, and shipping of materials, supplies, and equipment. Purchasing relates to the buying of goods or services necessary for the operation of an organization. Merchandising involves warehousing and distributing products, as well as serving customers and maintaining stores. Whether an enterprise produces chemicals, clothing, or computers, all these functions are usually present. Some occur at the production facilities, while others take place at the wholesale or retail level.

While manufacturing jobs don't currently have a place in the limelight, they shouldn't be discounted. Often they're the best pathway up an organization, since on a day-to-day basis, they involve the "real thing"—producing products. An entry-level manufacturing job offers the opportunity to develop a broad base of skills and experiences. It also allows a recent graduate to make a very real impact on a company's bottom line. "Even though I've only been working in merchandising for a few months, I'm already handling millions of dollars worth of inventory," says one history major who works for a sportswear manufacturer. "Most of my friends are still standing around at the copy machine, shuffling papers for senior execs." This sentiment is echoed by other liberal arts graduates in manufacturing jobs, who agree that while they don't get the biggest payoff, they do get greater responsibility in a shorter time than their peers do in most other functional areas.

Marketing and Sales

While "marketing" and "sales" are used interchangeably by many people, there is an important difference between these functions. Marketing involves finding new products and services and improving existing ones, while sales involves finding customers who will buy these goods. Both areas are excellent employers of liberal arts graduates; each year representatives of most of the nation's biggest corporations hire dozens of freshly minted B.A.s to market and sell their products and services. No prior experience is needed; in fact, many companies actually prefer to hire people with no experience, so they can be trained in their particular methods. Marketing and sales professionals can be found everywhere, trying to interest the public in anything from Reeboks and Redskins tickets to radios and real estate.

Imagination, intuition, and initiative play a big role in marketing, which deals with consumer research and product/service evaluation. Liberal arts graduates usually enter this area as marketing assistants, working with brand managers to learn how consumer needs can be met better, faster, and cheaper. If you've studied psychology or sociology, you've probably dealt with several marketing terms; did you know, for example, that the term "baby boomer" was coined by marketing experts to describe a group of consumers? Some of the best training programs in this area are found within consumer product firms, such as Procter & Gamble, General Mills, and Clorox. After a few months of training, new hires work on a team that handles a specific product, such as Tide, Ruffles, Crest, or Jell-O. This team makes decisions on everything from advertising to packaging—and keeps an eye on what the competition is doing. After two or three years, a marketing assistant may be promoted to assistant brand manager, and then to brand manager.

It's often said that sales requires the Three Ps: personality, persuasiveness, and perseverance. If you're thinking of a career in sales, you should be articulate and optimistic. While sales is usually seen as a less complex area than marketing, it requires an in-depth knowledge of the product/service, the retailers, and the consumers. Sales representatives must be self-starters, and they must be able to face rejection. Most large companies train liberal arts graduates for several months and then put them out in the field to sell. In addition to calling on clients, sales representatives are expected to provide their organization with volume forecasts, market trends, and other data. Sales managers are responsible for recruiting, hiring, training, supervising, planning, budgeting, and promoting. It's usually easy to measure a salesman's success, since most are paid on a salary/bonus or salary/commission scale.

Public Relations

Webster's dictionary defines public relations as "the art or science of developing reciprocal understanding and goodwill between a person, firm, or institution and the public." Public relations deals with creating and molding a company's image, through the collection, analysis, and dissemination of information. Unlike advertising, in which a company pays for its messages to appear, public relations relies on the print and broadcast media for free editorial coverage. As the media become increasingly sophisticated, companies have to work harder and harder at building and maintaining favorable public opinion. More and more, an organization's image, profitability, and even its continued existence are linked to how it presents its goals and policies to the public.

Public relations is an excellent career for liberal arts graduates. Currently more than 150,000 people are employed in the industry, working as writers, editors, researchers, speakers, producers, and managers. The majority of individuals in public relations work for corporations, ranging from accounting firms and banks to consumer products companies and department stores. The next largest group works for nonprofit organizations, such as foundations, cultural agencies, research institutes, schools, hospitals, labor unions, political parties, and government agencies. The smallest number of public relations employees work for the country's four thousand independent public relations agencies. Often the best place to train, these agencies handle from one to one hundred different accounts. Some agencies focus exclusively on one industry, while others handle a broad range of clients.

Although no particular background is needed to enter public relations, course work in journalism, communications, and English is useful. If you've worked for a school publication or a television or radio station, you'll be a good candidate for an entry-level spot. You'll be expected to have excellent writing and speaking skills, and to be creative with ideas and language. You should also be quite poised, since you'll be dealing with high-level executives and contacts. Since few organizations offer formal training programs in public relations, most new hires learn by working on press releases, speech writing, employee publications, company newsletters, shareholder reports, and other internal/external communications. Liberal arts graduates generally enter as assistant account executives and are promoted after two or three years to account executives. Next on the ladder is account supervisor or vice president, leading to the title of manager, president, or principal.

Chapter 5

What Liberal Arts Grads Need to Know

After you've analyzed the product and the marketplace, you're ready to package your goods and sell them. Be prepared to razzle and dazzle, to sing your praises loud and clear. "No matter how terrific a student may be, he's never going to get a great job if his appearance is sloppy—on paper or in person," says a career counselor. This chapter helps you to develop marketing aids, from résumés and cover letters to interviewing techniques and follow-up plans. Keep in mind that Alka-Seltzer wasn't launched overnight, and Doritos spent months being tested in the snack market. Like these products, you must be prepared for some test marketing. It could be two weeks or two months—whatever it takes to feel at ease with your sales pitch.

The Résumé: Your Best Advertisement

A résumé is a one-page advertisement for your abilities and achievements. It enables employers to learn the basic facts about you in a single glance. Thirty seconds are typically allotted to skimming a candidate's résumé, so make it concise, well organized, and easy to read. Since it's the first example of your work that an employer will see, your résumé has to be exemplary. Good ad copy sells; good résumé copy does, too.

Creating a résumé gives you the forum to review your education and experience. As you compile and organize your background information, you'll learn more about your talents and potential. A good way to begin designing your résumé is with the following work sheet. Just as a marketing manager lists all the pertinent data on his product before dreaming up a sales campaign, so you should compile your personal data. Laying out your universe of skills and accomplishments will help you decide what to include, stress, and omit on your résumé. Once you've created a comprehensive personal catalog, you'll find a thousand and one applications for it, particularly as you begin filling out job applications and going for interviews.

Creating the Perfect Résumé

Many liberal arts graduates wonder why they don't get invited to interview for the jobs they want most. One reason is their failure to spend the necessary time refining their résumés. Remember, you aren't offering recruiters a life history; you're presenting them with a business document that sells your assets as an employee. Don't take a "kitchen sink" approach and drown the reader in a sea of useless information. "A well-thought-out résumé indicates that you can organize your thoughts," says a recruiter for a large aerospace company. The facts you choose to include—and the manner in which you organize them—usually determine whether and when you'll get an interview.

There is no "best" format for a résumé. However, there are a few widely agreed upon conventions. A one-page résumé, offset or copied on good-quality paper, is considered appropriate for recent college grads. Remember that if you're having your résumé typeset (or printed by laser, which closely resembles typesetting), you can get more on a page. You may want to experiment with several different spatial arrangements before choosing the one you like most. Whatever design you select, don't pack the page with print; use empty space to invite reading. Where possible, use underlining, boldface, italics, and capital letters to set off names and categories from the body of the résumé. Aim for a fresh, creative

RÉSUMÉ WORKSHEET

VITAL STATISTICS

Name _____

Address _____

Telephone _____

EDUCATIONAL BACKGROUND

College _____

Location _____

Date completed _____

Degree received _____

Major _____

Names of courses relevant to career interest _____

_____

Senior thesis, research papers, or special projects _____

_____

Honors, scholarships, and other academic awards _____

_____

Extracurricular activities _____

WORK EXPERIENCE (repeat this category for every major job held)

Organization _____

Department _____

Location _____

Dates of employment _____

Boss's name _____

Job description _____

Accomplishments on the job _____

_____

Abilities gained from job _____

_____

PERSONAL INFORMATION

Hobbies _____

Sports _____

Languages _____

Other interests _____

look, but avoid being trendy or gimmicky. Your packaging strategy matters a great deal. If you're headed for Madison Avenue, you'll want a different look than if you're headed for Wall Street.

Above all, the key to an effective résumé is straightforward language. As a student of the liberal arts, you're expected to present yourself clearly and efficiently. You can aid and impress employers by condensing your writing—by shortening their reading time. Don't bury your abilities and accomplishments in vague or verbose descriptions. Keep sentences short, and leave out articles such as "the," "a," and "an." Avoid using personal pronouns, since the repeated use of "I" or "me" tends to make you appear self-centered. It's also downright boring. Stay away from abbreviations (except for state names), and watch out for colloquial language. Whenever possible, start sentences with action words (see list on p. 52) that explain what you did rather than what you were. This will help convince the reader that you are a "doer," someone who makes things happen. If you say your "responsibilities included" raising funds for underprivileged children, it's not clear whether you actually got any money. Say "raised $2,500 for underprivileged children," and it's apparent that you did just that. Give concrete examples of what you've done; numbers talk, so quantify whenever possible.

When you've finished a first draft of your résumé, give it to a friend, teacher, career counselor, or parent to read. After you've had it reviewed by an objective source or two, go over it again carefully. Is there anything you can't speak knowledgeably about? Are you certain all the information is accurate? Says one recruiter from an investment bank, "I find it hard to believe a candidate is detail-oriented when he's misspelled words and used poor grammar on his résumé. If he didn't care enough to make it perfect, how do we know he'll care about any work we give him?" One caveat: if you're a novice hiker, don't list technical climbing as a hobby. You may just get Mountain Mike for an interviewer, and he'll grill you on the sport's finer points. Likewise, if you don't speak Russian fluently, save yourself the embarrassment of getting flustered when your interviewer decides to conduct the interview in Russian.

Résumé Guidelines

1. *Identification*

Your full name, address, and phone number should be at the top of your résumé. If you'll be moving home or somewhere else after graduation, give that information too.

2. *Job Objective*

The job objective is a one-sentence statement of your specific career interests. It should be a logical extension of your abilities and accomplishments, and you should be able to explain it easily to employers. Stating a job objective is useful if you are certain of what you want to do. It's a double-edged sword, however, since it may increase your possibilities with some employers and decrease them with others. Some students attempt to solve this dilemma by creating several résumés, each with a different job objective. This can work, but we don't generally recommend such a strategy. Résumés tend to get passed around within large companies, and if your "marketing" résumé and your "finance" résumé happen to collide, chances are that an employer won't take either one—or you—seriously. In addition, an executive in one fully staffed department may read your résumé and consider passing it along to a colleague. But a job objective may prevent him from doing so. In general, liberal arts grads who are unsure of their objective are best off stating their specific interests in personalized cover letters.

3. *Education*

Recent college graduates should place educational background ahead of work experience, since this category contains their primary qualifications. (An exception is the student who's taken significant time off to work for the chairman of a large corporation or start up a successful enterprise.) Give the names and locations of schools attended, as well as the dates of attendance and degrees received. Indicate your concentration or major, and any honors and awards. Include extracurricular activities that you participated in, but avoid stretching a minor involvement into a major commitment. No one cares if you spent one afternoon each semester volunteering at an old folks' home.

4. *Experience*

If you've had little or no significant work experience, don't worry—and don't fake it. Employers can smell B.S. miles away. Once you've lied on your résumé, you never know when it's going to catch up with you. In the worst scenario, you might become involved in a classified project that requires security clearance, or you might be the target of an investigative journalist. Wiping a bogus credential off your résumé isn't easy when it's locked up in a personnel file. If you've been a full-time student for most of your life, you're not expected to have had an impressive array of high-level jobs. However, you should have some work experience on your résumé that illustrates your initiative, dedication, and responsibility, as well as your capacity for working with others. Include all significant jobs, part-time or summer, paid or volunteer. For every item you list, give the organization's name and location, your job title, the dates of your employment, and a description of what you did. Don't forget to use active language. While you shouldn't falsify any facts, try to present your experience in the most attractive light possible.

5. *Additional Information*

Use this section to mention any abilities or achievements that don't fit in the education or experience sections. You might note fluency in a language; musical expertise; or computer programming, for example. Although material in this section of your résumé isn't usually a critical hiring factor, it helps to define you as a unique and interesting person. Many interviewers use this information as an ice-breaker, to get a feel for what you're really like outside school or work. "I put the fact that I'd traveled through Australia on my résumé," says one recent graduate who works in public relations. "It was pure luck that my interviewer had just been there, and we spent most of the hour comparing experiences. By the time I left his office, I felt like we were old friends."

6. *References*

The phrase "References available upon request" means that when an employer asks for references, you can provide them instantly. To prepare for this, develop a list of people (teachers and former employers are usually the best sources) who know you well and can speak with authority about your potential to succeed.

Keep the names, titles, organizations, addresses, and phone numbers of your references handy, so you can offer an employer two or three on the spot. Remember to ask permission from these individuals before passing their names along. And, for your sake as well as theirs, don't forget to give them a copy of your résumé so they'll be updated on your goals and progress.

SAMPLE ACTION WORDS

accomplished	delegated	interpreted	purchased
achieved	demonstrated	interviewed	recommended
addressed	designed	introduced	recruited
administered	determined	invented	redesigned
advised	developed	invested	reduced
affected	devised	investigated	reported
analyzed	doubled	launched	researched
anticipated	drafted	led	resolved
appraised	edited	maintained	revised
approached	established	managed	revitalized
approved	evaluated	marketed	saved
arranged	examined	mediated	scheduled
assembled	executed	merchandised	served
assessed	expanded	minimized	shaped
assigned	expedited	modified	simplified
assisted	facilitated	monitored	sold
budgeted	familiarized	motivated	solved
built	formulated	negotiated	stimulated
calculated	fund-raised	obtained	studied
clarified	generated	operated	supervised
collaborated	guided	organized	supported
communicated	handled	originated	surveyed
conceived	hired	participated	synthesized
conceptualized	identified	performed	taught
conducted	implemented	planned	tested
coordinated	improved	presented	traded
counseled	increased	processed	trained
created	initiated	produced	translated
decided	inspected	proposed	utilized
decreased	instructed	provided	wrote
defined	integrated	published	

SAMPLE RESUME #1 (With Job Objective)

Julie Ann Benson

Present Address:
2000 University Avenue
Philadelphia, PA 19019
(215) 555-6148

Permanent Address:
35 Delamine Road
Miami, FL 10572
(213) 555-7234

JOB OBJECTIVE   To obtain a position as a sales representative with a consumer products company.

EDUCATION
1983–1987

Miller College, Philadelphia, PA
B.A. in Art History, June 1987. Minor in French. Completing senior thesis entitled, "Art and Business: Will the Twain Ever Meet?" Course work includes sociology, political science, economics, and psychology. Member, Senior Class Council; Alumni Fund Agent.

Fall 1985

Ecole Parisienne, Paris, France
Studied art history and literature during semester abroad. Volunteered at the Louvre as an English-speaking tour guide.

EXPERIENCE
2/86–present

Senior Class T-Shirt Agency
Developed and managed agency that sells T-shirts at football games and other sporting events to finance senior class activities. Supervise planning and inventory control. Train and oversee staff of six students. Sold $4,500 of T-shirts over three months in 1986.

Summers
1985, 1986

Arawa Sailing Camp, Cape Cod, MA
Counselor at eight-week sailing camp. Taught campers aged seven to fifteen sailing, wind surfing, and swimming. Promoted after first summer to assistant waterfront director.

ADDITIONAL
INFORMATION

Fluent in French. Have traveled through Europe and the United States. Enjoy sailing, tennis, and art.

REFERENCES AVAILABLE UPON REQUEST

SAMPLE RESUME #2 (Without Job Objective)

Michael Stone

Present Address:
603 College Way
Los Angeles, CA 91425
(213) 555-8294

Permanent Address:
127 Willow Lane
Dallas, TX 12345
(713) 555-3017

EDUCATION

Spring State University, Los Angeles, CA
B.A. degree in political science, June 1987. Minor in economics. Dean's list, four semesters. Course work includes accounting, computer science, and philosophy. Running back, varsity football team.

EXPERIENCE
9/86–present

Vice President, Alpha Tau Omega fraternity.
Organize and coordinate all house activities and meetings. Supervised freshman rush and fall orientation. Arranged housing lottery for 126 fraternity members. Coordinated budget of $5000 for 1986–1987 school year.

Summer 1986

Handyman, Two Guys Repair Company, Dallas, TX
Performed residential home repairs and maintenance work. Painted interiors/exteriors, fixed plumbing and wiring problems, and reinstalled roofing.

9/85–6/86

Office Assistant, Spring State Dean's Office
Provided administrative support to undergraduate dean's secretary. Processed registration and grades, and distributed handouts from dean. Gained familiarity with IBM PC-AT, and software including Lotus 1-2-3 and Microsoft Word.

ADDITIONAL
INFORMATION

Born in Massachusetts. Raised in Texas. Enjoy skiing and photography.

REFERENCES AVAILABLE UPON REQUEST

The Information Interview: You Call the Shots

Many liberal arts graduates find informational interviewing a useful way to discover what it's like to work in a particular field. An information interview allows you to learn more about a prospective career by talking with a professional. For beginning job hunters who lack a broad network, this can be an excellent way of developing contacts.

To locate interview subjects, ask career counselors or faculty members for suggestions. You can also check the industry and/or company files in your career library for alumni sources. Once you've got a list of possibilities, send a brief letter (see example on p. 58) explaining why you'd like an information interview. Make sure it's absolutely clear that you're not requesting a formal job interview. Offer to meet with anyone in the individual's organization who might give you advice. In general, top executives have crowded schedules and are unwilling to spend their precious time with students who are researching careers. Your best bet is to approach employees who are relative newcomers to the work force. Often they'll be flattered by a request for job hunting assistance, and since they have little or no hiring responsibility, they'll give you the real lowdown on what it's like to work for their firm. In addition, someone closer to your age and experience may advise you on how to handle difficult interviewers at his company, or even offer to help you get a job interview.

Keep in mind that the purpose of an information interview is research, not job search. You should never pressure your subject or seem as if you have another motive than that expressed. Anyone granting you an information interview is doing you a big favor. Show your appreciation by researching the company thoroughly before your visit. Since your objective is to learn as much as you can about the career field, you should arrive with a list of intelligent, specific questions. Begin by stressing the positive, to get your subject talking about what he enjoys doing. Once you've established an easy rapport, you can ask about negative job aspects.

Although information interviews are often quite casual, act as you would at a full-fledged job interview. If you're meeting your subject at his office, wear a suit or jacket and slacks/skirt. Showing up in jeans and a sweater, with your portable stereo hanging out of your knapsack, doesn't suggest that you're on the verge of entering the professional world. Even if you're just meeting for a cup of coffee at the local diner, dress neatly and appropriately. Arrive early, and keep an eye on your watch. If you've asked for half an hour, get ready to leave after twenty-five minutes. It's fine to bring a résumé along, in case your subject asks to see it. Even if he doesn't, you can invite him to have a look and make suggestions. You should also bring a pad for taking notes, so that you can write down any useful tips, contacts, or ideas. After the interview, send your subject a short thank-you letter, reiterating your appreciation for his time. What follows is a list of questions you may want to ask. Adapt them to the situation, and improvise when necessary.

Suggested Questions for Information Interviews

How do you spend a typical day/week?

What do you enjoy most about your work? What do you enjoy least?

How closely do you work with others? What kinds of people do you interact with?

What has been your career progression?

Do you travel often? Where to? Would you like to travel more/less?

How many hours do you work per week? Are your work hours flexible? If not, does this create pressure in your life?

What parts of your job are the most challenging? Which are the most tedious?

What would you like to get done that you haven't, due to either personal choice or lack of time?

What is the criterion for success in your job? How is success rewarded?

How many years do most people stay in your job? What is the job below yours like? What is the one above like?

How does the feedback system work at your company? Are you satisfied with it?

Are the skills gained in your job easily transferable?

What sort of training have you had? Is it ongoing?

What do you wish you had known about your career field before you entered it? What do you wish you had known about your employer?

How is your organization structured?

To whom do you report, and whom do you supervise?

What is the most common form of communication in your company? How do you know what is going on around the office?

What are your long-term career goals?

Are there opportunities for self-employment in your field? For part-time employment?

What are the trends/projections for your company? For your industry?

Do you believe there's a demand for people in this field?

What do you see as the best way for me to get into this field?

What journals or magazines do you recommend I read?

With who else do you recommend I speak for more information?

The Cover Letter: Your Best Introduction

No matter how fabulous your résumé may be, it can't arrive naked at an employer's office when you're trying to get a job interview. You must clothe it in a cover letter. The cover letter is a critical sales tool, since it serves to introduce you to a potential employer. Without one, your package is incomplete. And unless the cover letter is well written and informative, your résumé may never get read. "Too many times I've seen a brilliant résumé ruined by a mediocre letter," says one recruiter for an advertising agency. "It's always a disappointment, particularly if the student is applying for a job that involves writing."

The ideal cover letter is short and to the point, designed to be read by an individual with limited time. Just as your résumé shows off your capacity for conciseness and organization, so your cover letter should demonstrate your ability to think and write clearly. Although it's business correspondence, it should have a friendly, down-to-earth tone. Don't be afraid to seem enthusiastic. An overly cool letter can indicate a lack of personal warmth. And don't get caught up in trying to write a Pulitzer prizewinner; the cover letter doesn't lend itself to lofty literary aspirations.

While every cover letter should be individually written and original, there are several generally accepted features. Your letter

SAMPLE COVER LETTER FOR
INFORMATION INTERVIEW

Date

Ms. Barbara Wilson
Assistant Vice President
Copco Consumer Products
300 Pine Street
Philadelphia, PA 19010

Dear Ms. Wilson,

Sam Arnold, director of career placement at Miller College, suggested that I write to you for some career advice.

I will be receiving my B.A. degree from Miller in June, and I'm extremely interested in a sales career. In order to improve my knowledge of the field in general, and about Copco in particular, I'd like to arrange a brief information interview with you or one of your colleagues.

I'll give you a call early next week to see if we can arrange an appointment at your convenience. Thank you very much for considering my request. I look forward to learning more about careers in sales.

Sincerely,

Julie Ann Benson

should be composed of three to four paragraphs, and fit on one page. It should be typed on good-quality paper, with no errors in spelling or grammar. Watch out for run-on sentences, redundant phrases, and clichés. Avoid excessive use of personal pronouns, because they give your writing a monotonous tone. As you compose your letter, ask yourself: Does it capture the reader's attention? Does it make him want to read the accompanying résumé to learn more about me?

Cover Letter Guidelines

Opening

Make sure your letter is addressed to the correct person—the one who has responsibility for hiring you. Always double check the individual's name, title, and address. There may be two vice presidents named William Richards at a large corporation, so use a middle initial if it's available.

First Paragraph

Open your letter by briefly introducing yourself and explaining your interest in the company. If you have a specific position in mind, mention it here. If you are writing at the suggestion of a contact, refer to that individual.

Second Paragraph

In this paragraph, you should elaborate on why you are interested in and qualified for a position in the company. Without repeating your life story as chronicled in your résumé (do mention that it's enclosed), highlight a few relevant achievements. Let the reader know that you've done your homework by alluding to your research on the organization. Try to show why you would be right for the company and vice versa.

Third Paragraph

In your conclusion, you should discuss your plan of action. If you request an interview with the person to whom you have written, state a particular time frame in which you will call to make arrangements. (If you promise to follow up your letter with a call, don't forget to do it.) Finally, thank the employer for his time and consideration.

SAMPLE COVER LETTER

Date

Mr. John Smith
Recruiting Coordinator
Best Consumer Products
1000 Michigan Avenue
Chicago, IL 60605

Dear Mr. Smith,

In June, I will receive my B.A. degree in history from Miller College. For some time, I have been interested in a career in sales, and your organization has been recommended to me as one with an excellent management training program.

As the enclosed résumé indicates, I've had my first hands-on experience this past year in sales and found it very exciting. I developed and managed a campus T-shirt company that sold $4,500 worth of shirts during the fall football season alone.

Your recruiting brochure suggests that candidates for jobs at Best Consumer Products be highly motivated and dedicated individuals. I believe that I'm just the type of person who could, with training, make a real contribution as a Best sales representative.

If possible, I'd appreciate the opportunity to meet with you to discuss how my education and experience fit your hiring needs. I'll call your office next week to see if we can arrange a mutually convenient appointment. Thanks for your consideration. I look forward to meeting you.

Sincerely,

Julie Ann Benson

The Job Interview: How Smart People Get Hired

Okay, okay, we know this is the hardest part for every job hunter, old or new. But if you've thoroughly analyzed yourself and the marketplace, and packaged yourself accordingly, you might actually *enjoy* your interviews.

There are two ways to get rid of (or at least calm down) those preinterview jitters: preparation and practice. As a minimum, read everything available in the campus library or placement center about the companies you plan to interview with. This way you won't waste the interviewer's time asking questions you could easily have answered yourself. You also should do several mock interviews (if possible, try one on videotape), in order to gain experience thinking swiftly on your feet. Learn to talk about yourself and your career goals with ease, so that you are confident and persuasive. "It's crucial that students take the interviewing process seriously," says one recruiter for a commercial bank. "If they haven't done their homework, we can tell in a minute." In general, you must be ready to explain, justify, and expand on everything in your résumé. Over and over, you will be asked the bottom-line questions: Why this industry? Why this company? Why this job?

Accept the fact that interviewing is a difficult process for both parties, and your job search will be easier. Think about a time when you had to pass judgment on another person. You may have had to vote on someone's admission to a club, team, publication, or campus government. What did you seek in that person? Chances are you looked for sincerity, intelligence, enthusiasm, humor, articulateness, trustworthiness, maturity, poise, and common sense. You probably also favored the neatly attired, attractively groomed candidate over the sloppy one. You may have also had the dilemma of finding more good candidates than available spaces. Realize that employers feel the same way. They're turned off by superficial, cocky, inconsiderate people and turned on by natural, modest, gracious people. And they often can't offer jobs to everyone they'd like to hire.

No doubt you've heard that hiring decisions are sometimes made very early in the interview. Like it or not, first impressions are often critical. Always confirm your appointment the day before, and make sure to arrive a few minutes early. Dress simply and conservatively. There are no hard-and-fast fashion rules for interviews. Wear whatever makes you look and feel your most comfortable and professional. Keep in mind that clothes speak louder than words. "They can communicate confidence, attention to detail, and creativity—or self-doubt and carelessness," says one expert. Make sure your business manners are as attractive as your appearance. Maintain eye contact when speaking, show off your best posture when seated, and offer a firm handshake and a smile when you enter and leave the room. Heed the advice of a businessman who says, "When you have to make a choice between two people for a promotion—assuming all else is equal—you're going to lean toward the one with the sharp image. It's good advertising for your firm to send out someone with the right appearance, someone who can generate enthusiasm before he even opens his mouth."

If you're interviewing on campus, keep in mind that many recruiters are on the kind of whirlwind tour that would make Bruce Springsteen or Michael Jackson wince. They often see as many as a hundred students a week, and they become awfully tired of repeating the same old stuff. Be courteous and respectful around your interviewer, but don't be afraid to relax. "I'm really impressed by a candidate who puts himself at ease in a strange new situation," says one recruiter for an accounting firm. "It's always a pleasure to kick back a bit and get to know someone on a more informal level." Realize that interviewers come in many forms. Some want to lead the discussion, and some want to let you lead. Some have a sense of humor and some don't. Some are hard-hitting and some are soft-spoken. Some seem eager and some seem bored. Some will ask highly structured questions and others will ask open-ended ones. In general, the more experienced the interviewer, the more comfortable he'll try to make you. Look for keys to his style early on in the interview, and try to react accordingly.

The best interview involves an active exchange of ideas and information between two people. The process has four elements, all equally important. First, the interviewer is gathering information about you, in order to decide whether you're right for the company. Next, he's trying to present the company in an attractive light, so that you'll want to work there. Meanwhile, you're seeking to impress the interviewer with your qualifications. Finally, you're evaluating the company as a potential place to work.

Sample Job Interview Questions

Can you tell me about yourself and your background?

What was your major? What courses are most applicable to this field?

Why did you choose your major? What have you learned most from it? What did you like and dislike about it?

Why did you choose to go to this school? Did it fulfill your expectations?

What have been your biggest accomplishments in college? What have been your biggest disappointments?

How would your friends describe you? What would your teachers and former employers have to say about you?

Have you ever failed at anything significant? What did you learn from the experience?

What are your greatest strengths? What are your major weaknesses?

What do you consider the best decision you've ever made? What was the worst?

Are you a leader? Can you give an example of your leadership?

Do you prefer to work by yourself or on a team?

What was the most challenging activity or assignment you've ever handled? How did you deal with it?

What makes you stand out from your peers?

What are the attributes of your ideal job?

What makes you think you could succeed in this field?

How are you judging the companies you're interviewing with?

What have you read about our company lately, aside from the recruiting materials?

Are you competitive? How do you plan to get ahead on the job?

Have you ever worked under extreme pressure? How did you do?

How do you feel about traveling? Are you willing to relocate?

What's the last book you read? The last movie you saw? The last lecture you attended?

What do you expect to get out of your career?

Where do you want to be in five years? On what do you base this?

What are your goals in life?

At some point during most interviews, you'll be asked if you have any questions. Be prepared to inquire about several points not covered in the company's literature, so that you can show your interest in the organization and the research you've done. Don't be redundant or rhetorical; it's just as important to ask intelligent questions as it is to give intelligent answers. Never tell an interviewer that you don't have any questions for him, since this will be interpreted as a lack of interest on your part. Later on, you may wish you'd asked about the evaluation process, the overtime hours, or the rate of turnover. Many students are so eager to find employment that they pass up this opportunity to get past the company's PR and find out if the job is really right for them.

Sample Questions to Ask at a Job Interview

What do you consider the company's strengths and weaknesses?

Where do you think the best opportunities are in this firm for liberal arts graduates?

How is the company dealing with changes in the industry?

How do you expect a trainee to distinguish himself? What are his principal responsibilities and obligations during the first year?

How important do you think it is to have previous experience in this field?

Do trainees work independently or in groups? How are they supervised?

Does the company provide opportunities for continuing education?

How are assignments made? Are there frequent deadlines?

Is there much contact among different departments?

What is a typical career path within the company?

Do trainees travel? How often and for how long?

How often are trainees evaluated? Formally or informally?
Is there a high rate of turnover in this company/field?
How would you describe the company's philosophy?

What Turns Interviewers Off

lateness	apologizing for your lack of
sloppiness	experience
evasiveness	making inappropriate jokes
arrogance	trying too hard to please
flippancy	lack of self-control
abrasiveness	discussing irrelevant topics
indecisiveness	focusing too much on salary
not being yourself	and vacation time
lack of preparation	uncertainty about future goals
negative attitude	chewing gum or smoking
interrupting frequently	overstaying your welcome
begging for a job	

The Follow-up: Your Best Conclusion

As soon as possible after each interview, take a few minutes to evaluate your impressions. Jot down the questions and answers you remember, and make a note of what you might have left out. Describe your interviewer briefly and how you think he assessed you as a candidate. This way you'll be able to refer to your experience and improve your performance in the future. You'll also use this information when thanking the interviewer and when weighing the pros and cons of the job offer.

Once you've recorded your thoughts, send your interviewer a brief letter of thanks, neatly typed on business stationery. This is the final step in your marketing package; after all the hard work you put into producing a first-rate résumé and cover letter, don't blow it now. The best thank-you letter is written in a friendly, warm tone. After all, you now *know* the person you're writing to. Express your appreciation for the interviewer's time and consideration, mention a few salient points made by each of you during the discussion, and reiterate your interest in the company. You may also want to introduce any significant facts you omitted during the interview.

SAMPLE FOLLOW-UP LETTER

Date

Mr. John Smith
Recruiting Coordinator
Best Consumer Products
1000 Michigan Avenue
Chicago, IL 60605

Dear Mr. Smith,

It was a pleasure to meet with you last Wednesday afternoon to discuss career opportunities in Best's sales department.

Our talk was highly informative, and you left me feeling very enthusiastic about Best's sales representative training program. With my broad education and travel experience, as well as my job running the Senior Class T-Shirt Agency, I believe I'd be an excellent trainee. From what I've read about Best, in addition to the information you gave me, it seems like an ideal place for someone with my qualifications. I'll be graduating in June and I'd like to start working after a short vacation.

As you suggested, I've enclosed my latest sales plan for the T-shirt agency. I'd greatly appreciate your comments on it.

Again, many thanks for meeting with me. I look forward to learning more about Best, and I hope to hear from you soon.

Sincerely,

Julie Ann Benson

In the case of on-campus interviewing, a thank-you letter may not be necessary or timely. If you know that the hiring decision will be made before a note can arrive at the interviewer's office, it doesn't make much sense to send one. However, if the company's recruiters are sticking around town for a day or two before making offers, you might try dropping off a brief letter at their hotel, or leaving one at the career placement center.

Chapter 6

How to Make the Smart Choice

If you've packaged yourself properly, you should have at least one or two employers biting. Some liberal arts graduates who've mastered the art of selling themselves become hot items and are pursued by five or six organizations. Either way, it's the right job offer that counts. When it comes, celebrate your success. Then, after you're done partying, take the time to be sure that you're making the smart career choice.

Think of job interviews as the first segment of "The Dating Game." Rarely are offers made after the first round of questions. Often candidates are called back for second and third interviews before receiving offers by letter or phone call. In the euphoria of getting the much-awaited good news, pay close attention to four factors: what position you're being offered, where you'll be located, what the starting salary is, and, most important, when you must respond. Make sure you understand these details—the *real* offer—clearly, or you may run into trouble later. If possible, get written confirmation. Otherwise take good notes from your phone calls and type them up for reference.

If the employer doesn't give you a deadline to respond to his offer, try to make a decision within two or three days—even if you just decide to ask for an extension. While a quick answer is always appreciated, most companies realize that you may be negotiating with other companies. As soon as your first offer comes in—one you're considering seriously—notify the rest of your prospects and explain the situation, saying that you'll need to hear from them by "X date" to make your decision. At this point, you should have one thing on your mind: getting all the facts on the table as fast as possible. If you've kept good files on your prospective employers, you're all set. If not, get started scrambling around to gather information. Refer to your placement office, alumni, professional associations, surveys. When time permits, you may want to make another visit to the company, to get a further idea of what it's like to work there. (In order to help you compare job offers, we've included a form at the end of this chapter.) Now is the time to play private eye and dig deep for information that will help you determine whether the company has what you seek—and whether that's what the offer is about.

As you evaluate job offers, consider the *real* value of each compensation package. Keep in mind that a $25,000 salary goes a lot further in Cleveland than it does in New York. Research the cost of living in each company's town before comparing offers. Also examine nonsalary items or "perks," such as moving expenses, vacation time, expense account, medical/dental coverage, life insurance, pension plan, commissions, stock options, and profit sharing. Some of these extras might come in the form of status symbols, such as a more advanced title, a secretary, or a corner office. You'll also want to check into the company's education policy, to see whether you'll be reimbursed for study at local institutions. In addition, find out what the procedures are for salary reviews and increases. Think about it. After one good salary review, the low-offer employer might pay you more than the organization that starts you off with a big bang and follows up with 2 percent increments. And don't forget that money isn't everything. As H. L. Mencken once said, "The chief value of money lies in the fact that one lives in a world in which it is overestimated."

By completing the self-assessment and values analysis exercises in chapters two and three, you should have developed a set of criteria for selecting an employer. Refer back to your personal profile, and keep asking yourself the following questions:

Does this company's philosophy fit with my personality? Am I comfortable with what it stands for?

What are the opportunities for professional and personal growth?

Is the industry generally healthy?

Does the company have a solid record and good growth potential?

Will the job challenge and excite me?

Is the feedback system adequate?

Does senior management care about the quality of my training?

Is the mood within the organization friendly and supportive?

Am I likely to be happy and successful in this position? Do I find the total life/work package acceptable?

Salary negotiations can be one of the toughest parts of your job search. You're at the end of a long road, and you're probably tired of marketing yourself. In addition, you're so happy to simply *have* a job offer that you don't want to rock the boat. "I thought entry-level salaries were fixed," says one liberal arts graduate who works for a department store. "But then I found out that some people in my training program were making $3000 more than me, and I was furious. I hadn't even bothered to discuss my salary, because I thought I was so lucky just to get an offer." When it comes to negotiating your salary, always start with a range rather than an exact figure. Do your homework and find out what individuals with your background and experience are earning in other companies in the same industry. While you don't want to price yourself out of a great job, don't sell yourself short. Inform the employer that pay is just one of many factors you're considering, implying that you're willing to discuss several alternatives, such as accelerated review dates and a postponed starting date. "I admire students who aren't afraid to drive a hard bargain," says a recruiter for an investment bank. "If they're really good, the best in their class, they're probably in great demand. There's no reason they shouldn't ask for the competitive salary."

Before you enter negotiations, develop your position. Convince yourself that you're worth it by reviewing the strengths and abilities that you feel qualify you for a high price tag. Also make sure you thoroughly understand the company's compensation plan, so that you won't get backed into a corner, in the short or long run. If you've been able to discover how the pay scale works, ask for a salary near, but not at, the top. If you've heard the highest amount paid to liberal arts graduates is $25,000 and you ask for that amount, you're unlikely to get a penny more. But if you describe your asking price as a range "from $25,000 to $35,000, depending on the rest of the package," you're likely to get at least your bottom bid. Whatever you do, don't drag in unrelated issues, for example, your student loans, your car payments, or your new working wardrobe. Realize that you and the employer have already expressed mutual admiration; now's the time to show off your diplomatic ability. After all, if you can haggle with finesse for your salary, you're likely to do the same for the company.

To bring your salary negotiations to a successful culmination, act the true professional. When you're bargaining for a used car, you can afford to lose your cool; when you're bargaining for your salary, you can't afford to be anything but your buttoned-up best. Above all, don't start your new career on the wrong foot. Show your gratitude for concessions won, and be gracious about those lost. Prove that you're the most desirable of team players—a good sport.

Once you've accepted a job offer, consider it a binding contract. Request the final terms in writing, so that both parties are absolutely clear on what's what. When you've received written verification, send a brief confirmation note stating your delight at being hired and indicating the date you'll begin. Immediately notify other potential employers that you're no longer available. Thank them for their consideration, and suggest that perhaps you remain in touch. If you've gotten your job through an on-campus placement office, let the director know, especially since your dropping out of the job hunt may open opportunities for others. Good job hunting etiquette never stops. Then take a deep breath and congratulate yourself—you've closed the sale!

Checklist for Evaluating a Job Offer

The Company:

Company Name:
Parent Company:

Products/Services:
Years in Business:
Number of Employees:
Publicly or Privately Held:
Annual Sales/Income:
Five-Year Growth in Sales/Income:
Current Financial Condition:
Future Financial Outlook:
Position Within Industry:
Outlook for Industry:
Recent Expansions:
Products/Services Being Developed:
Major Competitors:
Principal Customers:
Principal Suppliers:

The Job:

Formal or On-the-Job Training:
Advancement Opportunities:
Performance Review:
Abilities Utilized:
Quality of Co-workers and Supervisors:
Major Challenges:
Travel Opportunities:

The Compensation Package:

Salary:
Bonus:
Medical and Health Insurance:
Life Insurance:
Dental Insurance:
Family Coverage:
Retirement/Pension Plan:
Stock Options:
Profit Sharing:
Vacation Time:
Holidays:
Sick Days:
Tuition Assistance:
Expense Account:
Company Car:

Club Memberships:
Moving Expenses:
Other Benefits:

The Life-style:

Location:
Cost of Living:
Why Should I Accept this Offer? (The Pros)
Why Should I Turn Down this Offer? (The Cons)

Chapter 7

Internships

An internship is like taste testing in your favorite ice cream parlor. Why settle for heavenly hash without sampling it—and several other flavors? Internships are often the best way for liberal arts students to be exposed to work roles and to make career choices. As an intern, you'll gain practical experience by meeting new challenges and acquiring new skills. Since internships offer a unique perspective on people, events, and issues in a real-life situation, they provide unlimited learning opportunities, or taste tests. Said *The Wall Street Journal,* "Most [interns] come bearing little or no practical experience, an abundance of preconceptions and, frequently, a wish to learn all there is to be taught. They leave, if not much richer, invariably wiser."[1] Adds a college placement officer, "Students who've completed one or more internships usually find they have an edge in the job market over their less experienced peers. If you've forgone a summer vacation to work long hours for minimal pay, it proves you're serious."

Internships vary from forest ranger jobs in state parks to investment banking positions on Wall Street. They can be part-time, full-time, paid, or for credit. Most often, they span a summer or a semester. An internship may be an informal apprenticeship, in which you work as an aide or assistant to an executive, or it may be a formal training program, in which you rotate through different departments and are given a series of specific assignments. The best internships involve advanced decision-making opportunities and plenty of independence. The worst require tedious "go-fer" work and constant supervision. No matter what you end up with, grin and bear it: the experience is bound to be worthwhile in the long run. There are also résumé credits to be collected. You'll meet and exceed your expectations in any job if you gain insights into the field and expand your career horizons.

To find an internship, consult the career placement office at your school for information. It's possible to find an internship in almost any profession that appeals to you. Many government, publishing, financial, medical, legal, cultural, and public-service internships are run on an annual basis. You'll find dozens of national internships, available to students across the country, as well as a number of opportunities open only to members of your school or community. More exotic jobs tend to operate on a somewhat erratic schedule. Frequently students devise internships by persuading employers to let them join their staff for the summer, promising to help out with clerical work in return for learning opportunities. Following are several good sources for information on internships: *Directory of Internships, Work Experience, and On-the-Job Training Opportunities; Directory of Undergraduate Internships; A Guide to Federal Internships for Students;* and *National Directory of Summer Internships.*

Although an internship is *not* the same thing as a job, it's important to act in a professional manner. Don't act as if you're just passing through to soak up the atmosphere—make a deep commitment to both work responsibilities and personal relationships. Your accomplishments and attitudes toward others will be evaluated carefully by your employer when the summer or semester is over. "At first, I dressed very casually, and I raced out the door at five o'clock sharp every evening," says one international relations major who interned for a law firm. "But pretty soon I started picking up signals, and I realized that if I was going to act like a college student, I'd be treated like one. On the other hand, when I began dressing more appropriately and working longer hours, people treated me much more as their equal."

Successful interns demonstrate a high level of interest and motivation, and they take the initiative in discovering and taking advantage of learning opportunities. You should use an internship to improve your ability to set, refine, and fulfill goals, while making certain that you consistently contribute to the organization and community in every possible way. If you're unhappy with the internship, talk to your superiors and see what alternatives are available. If there's no way out, keep in mind that it's only a brief stint. "In some ways, my internship was a big letdown," says a student who interned for a software company. "It seemed like the receptionists were always getting sick, and I spent most of the summer filling in for them. To keep myself busy, I reorganized the phone system a bit, trying to cut down on the number of calls that got lost or unanswered. By the end of the summer, my boss had received a lot of good feedback on my reorganization project, and he wrote me a really nice recommendation."

Before beginning an internship, research it as thoroughly as possible. Find out who'll be in charge of you and what he'll expect. Knowing what you're responsible for and who you're responsible to can eliminate a lot of confusion and frustration on both ends. Over the course of your internship, don't hesitate to talk with other employees, to find out why they like or dislike their jobs, what their backgrounds and training are, and what advice they have to offer you in your career search. You'll be surprised how much people enjoy talking about themselves once they feel relaxed around you. It's to your great advantage to begin forming a network of contacts who can help you later on when you're looking for postgraduate employment.

At the end of an internship, don't leave loose ends. Say good-bye and thanks to everyone you worked with, and if you're interested in returning to work for the organization, let your supervisors know. Over lunch, or in a letter, tell your immediate boss (and relevant others) how you felt about the job you did and how your academic and career goals were affected by the experience. Discuss how the experience confirmed your interest in the field, and mention any relevant courses you plan to pursue. Promise to keep them up to date on your future achievements, and arrange to visit when you're back in town or have some free time.

Finally, when you return to school, let the placement office know what you thought of your internship. Your input can help other students approach—or avoid—similar opportunities. You may also want to write a few pages about your experience, so that you'll have specific examples of your work to refer to when you apply for a full-time job. Do this when the memories are fresh and you'll have plenty of colorful interview material later on.

Whether your internship is a dream or a nightmare, try to learn all you can from it. Remember that you're just testing the waters; if you don't care to swim in them, you won't have to. When your two, twelve, or twenty weeks with an employer come to an end, you can walk away and never return. At worst, a bad internship costs you a few sunny afternoons at the beach; at best, it provides you with a clearer idea of your career plans. Either way, it adds to your experience and makes you a better job candidate. In fact, it sometimes seems as if interning has become to college students of the eighties what protesting was to students of the sixties. "We estimate that in any given academic year, one in every five undergraduates is involved in an internship," said Jane Kendall, executive director of the National Society for Internships and Experiential Education. Why shouldn't you be one of them?

Chapter **8**

Getting Inside Organizations That Hire Smart People

In choosing which companies to include in *Wanted: Liberal Arts Graduates*, we utilized journalistic, rather than scientific, methods for targeting the best places for liberal arts graduates to work. We began by putting our ears to the ground and borrowing the ears of friends and colleagues, in an attempt to learn as much as possible about the mood within possible "best" organizations. Over and over, we asked: Are there appropriate entry level jobs for liberal arts grads? Do liberal arts grads have a good shot at being trained to assume leadership roles? Will they suffer any for not having technical degrees? Is senior management committed to involving liberal arts grads in meaningful work, through some combination of formal and on-the-job training? Do liberal arts grads have access to liberal arts mentors who can guide their progress? Does the organization's philosophy have a humanistic bent?

We collected insights from college placement officials, academicians, corporate recruiters, students, recent alumni, and executives working in countless organizations. We asked them where the best jobs were for liberal arts grads and why. Although we investigated hundreds of excellent opportunities in profit and nonprofit organizations, we focused on those companies that have demonstrated a strong commitment to hiring and training liberal arts graduates. After refining our list, we turned to employees inside the recommended organizations to learn more about what they do, how satisfied they are, and what attitudes prevail toward liberal arts grads. Finally we interviewed the college relations officers of the best organizations to get specifics about whom they hire and why; starting salaries and benefits; and training and career paths.

Many of the people who talked to us did so based upon our promise to allow them anonymity. (Once you're on the job, you'll realize quickly that in big organizations, new hires feel more pressure to blend into the corporate culture than to self-promote. During years one through five of your career, unless you're an extraordinary superstar in a media-crazed company, you'll probably choose to work hard and to work smart—which means that you won't be holding press briefings to discuss your career progress!) And although most organizations were cooperative, several failed to make certain information available to us. In these cases, we've based our remarks on extensive research.

While we've attempted to offer the most up-to-date information possible, bear in mind that corporate America is undergoing dramatic changes at a breathless pace. Every day we read about companies that are growing, shrinking, merging, and divesting. Thus, Burroughs and Sperry became Unisys, and U.S. Steel (which found itself largely in the energy and not the metal business) became USX. In every industry, from advertising and retailing to finance and manufacturing, corporations are altering their names and makeup with regularity.

How to Use the Company Profiles

The company profiles, in alphabetical order, are organized in a standard format. Most contain all the information described in the following paragraphs, although companies in different industries require modifications on occasion. For example, we offer total billings for advertising agencies; total sales for manufacturing companies; and assets, deposits, and loans for commercial banks. We've omitted information when it was unavailable from company sources, and when current employees couldn't verify what we were told. Keep in mind that in some cases, we are profiling a division of a large diversified corporation. Thus what we tell you about Jordan Marsh may or may not apply to the twenty-plus other divisions of Allied Department Stores.

Company Name: The full name of the company appears. When you address correspondence to a company, always be certain you have its name correct. This means that Goldman Sachs is Goldman, Sachs & Co. and Salomon Brothers is Salomon Brothers Inc (without the period!). Beware phonetic spellings; if it sounds like Marian it could be Marianne, Maryann, or Mary Ann. And there's always the possibility that John Smith is actually Jon Smythe. Get the point? The best way to find out the incontrovertibly correct way to spell a person's or an organization's name is simply to call and ask. If you're afraid that whoever answers the phone is going to report you as an idiot, don't give your real name. Simply dial the company's number, and say, "My name is Mary Jones and I'd like to double-check the spelling of Bob Smith's name." No one will be the wiser but you—and you'll rest assured that your letter is going to the right place. This applies for contact information, too.

Contact Information: We give you the full name and title of the organization's leader and the full name, title, address, and telephone number of its key college relations representative. In a few cases—such as the Macy's—we provide you with the addresses of several operating divisions, since the company recruits on a decentralized basis. Similarly, for organizations such as IBM and Procter & Gamble—the national giants—we offer regional contacts so that you can get in touch with someone in your preferred part of the country.

The Numbers: Whenever this information is available, we provide some basic numbers that should help you understand the magnitude of the employer's business. Although sales and profits are the financials in most cases, you'll find billings or professional revenues for management consulting firms, advertising agencies, and accounting firms. Keep in mind that while there may be a point in comparing the professional revenues of Bain & Company to the Boston Consulting Group, it doesn't make much sense to compare Bain to Arthur Andersen, or Arthur Andersen to Leo Burnett.

The Organization: We describe the company's chief products/

services, and offer information on its background. Included is an explanation of how the organization is structured and where its subsidiaries and divisions are located.

The Jobs: What kinds of entry-level jobs does the organization offer to liberal arts graduates? How can you get yourself hired for these jobs? We provide specific advice about what the people who are hiring look for in liberal arts applicants, and what sort of orientation and training are available. We also discuss possible career paths you might travel and the types of professional development you can expect in the future.

The Payoff: What's in it for you in terms of pay and benefits? When specific salary information, or at least a numerical range, is unavailable, we speculate on where the company fits into the industry and across the board when it comes to paying off its entry-level liberal arts grads.

The Word: This is where we give you the word as we've heard it about what it's really like to join the organization. What's the difference among the Big Eight accounting firms? Will Macy's or Bloomingdale's give you a better head start on your retailing career? Is it true that at The Morgan Bank, there is such a thing as a free lunch, served daily to all executives to promote comradeship across the ranks? Do you really get a complimentary white Brooks Brothers shirt for pulling an all-nighter at Shearson Lehman? In this category, we try to debunk myths, dispel rumors, and reveal truths. We offer the inside scoop from those who know best—the employees who not so long ago were standing in your shoes.

Chapter 9

The Profiles:
The Best Employers
of Liberal Arts Grads

ABRAHAM & STRAUS

(a division of Federated Department Stores, Inc.)

Contact Info:

Chaim Edelstein, Chairman

Walter J. Davis, Director, Executive Recruitment
420 Fulton Street
Brooklyn, New York 11201
(718) 802-7500

Financials (1985):

Sales: $767.5 million

The Organization

Abraham & Straus, which is about 120 years old, is currently New York State's second largest department store and one of the top ten in the United States. New store openings and increased business in its existing stores added almost $300 million in volume in the past decade. A&S is the leading retailer on Long Island and is firmly established in New Jersey. Pennsylvania is a new market for A&S, and the department store has opened its second store in the Philadelphia area.

What's unique about A&S is that its departments are operated as independent profit centers, which means that the managers function more like entrepreneurs and are accountable for both operations and most aspects of profitability.

The parent company, Federated Department Stores, Inc., is a diversified retail firm serving customers across the nation through its department stores, mass merchandising stores, supermarkets, and other retail divisions. By the end of 1985, Federated had sixteen operating divisions and 604 stores in the major retail markets of thirty-six states. Each of the franchises operates on a decentralized basis and, for example, A&S operates in some of the same markets as Bloomingdale's, The Children's Place, and Filene's Basement, although only Bloomingdale's, which is also a department store company, is a similar type of operation.

The Jobs

Like most department store companies, A&S offers an executive development program, which primarily consists of on-the-job training and continues throughout an individual's career. Each job assignment is designed to enhance the merchandising and managerial skills of the individual and, at the same time, to provide immediate challenge and responsibility. Experience is supplemented by formal training at the beginning of an A&S career and later with advanced seminars.

At A&S, you begin your career in merchandising by participating in one of two executive training programs. The company offers an assistant buyer training program, which initially focuses on a buying career path, and a sales manager training program, concentrating at the outset on a store merchandising direction. However, you're not locked in to either career path.

As an assistant buyer trainee, you gain on-the-job experience in a buying office during your ten-week orientation. You work closely with a buyer to acquire skills in inventory management, analysis of a business, sales promotion, and vendor relations.

If you decide to enter as a sales manager trainee, you participate in a thirteen-week program in one of A&S's stores. You work with a department manager, learning to present merchandise, manage a selling floor for profit, supervise and motivate a sales staff, and control inventories.

In both programs, your training involves two different merchandising assignments in two different types of departments. Your on-the-job experience is supplemented by weekly seminars and scheduled workshops that introduce you to A&S's merchandising philosophy, techniques, and systems. Each week of the program covers a separate retail management topic, and the seminars are led by A&S executives—experts in their fields.

You are assigned a personal sponsor, usually a senior executive, who can help you answer any questions you have about A&S and your progress. You receive feedback through two performance reviews, one each by the buyers or department managers with whom you have trained. You're also guided by an executive development specialist.

With the first job assignment comes early responsibility. When you finish the assistant buyer training program, you are made an assistant buyer. Within six months, you have responsibility for an entire merchandise classification. When you complete the sales manager training program, you're placed as a sales manager in the main store or in a branch store and, within the same time frame, have responsibility for managing merchandise and people in a specific merchandise area. Beyond the actual job responsibilities, your goal as a new merchant is to learn merchandising through actual experience, for this is the best preparation for the larger responsibilities that await you.

How you progress, the timing of promotions, and how far you go depend on your interest, performance, and skills, as well as on available opportunities. For those who choose the central merchandising line, the career path is executive trainee, assistant buyer, department manager, associate buyer, buyer, divisional merchandise manager, merchandise vice president, and general merchandise manager. For those who choose the store merchandising line, the career path is executive trainee, sales manager, department manager, group department manager, group manager, divisional group manager, store manager, and group vice president.

The Payoff

Benefits are comprehensive and include discounts on most purchases as well as paid holidays and a liberal vacation policy. A&S offers starting salaries that are competitive with the other New York City–based department store companies. Expect an offer of an annual salary of twenty thousand dollars, plus or minus one or two thousand, depending on where you attended college and the record you compiled.

The Word

A & S: All week and Sundays, or at least that's what recent grads have to say about the retailing life. The hours are no worse than what comes with an entry-level position anywhere in the industry and this company's management is known for its commitment to training and developing the recent graduates they hire. Chairman Edelstein earned his B.A. from Bar Illan University in Israel.

The store has surely come a long way since 1865 when twenty-two year old Abraham Abraham and his friend Joseph Wechsler opened the store on Valentine's Day. What they had was $5000 each; three clerks; and a family tradition as merchants. Today, A&S is a Brooklyn institution (Did you know that Brooklyn is the fourth largest city in the United States?) that has grown to serve all of Long Island and most of the New York metropolitan area, while still maintaining its vital role in the commercial, cultural, and philanthropic development of Brooklyn first fostered by its founder.

Best of all, Brooklyn has finally taken off and is now chic. The Heights, Cobble Hill, Carroll Gardens, and Park Slope—all neighborhoods near the flagship store—are great places to live.

ADDISON-WESLEY PUBLISHING COMPANY

Contact Info:

Donald R. Hammonds, President and Chief Executive Officer

Roger L. Drumm, Corporate Recruiter
Reading, Massachusetts 01867
(617) 944-3700

Financials (1985):

Sales: $139,402,000
Profits: $6,666,000

The Organization

Addison-Wesley Publishing Company, Inc., is one of the fastest growing, most respected publishers in the college publishing industry. From modest beginnings more than thirty-five years ago, the company has earned a reputation as a leading publisher of high-quality texts, reference books, and educational products.

Addison-Wesley's roots go back to 1942, when Melbourne W. Cummings was the Boston-area sales manager for Lew A. Cummings Company, a New Hampshire printing firm. The company printed, among other publications, a textbook on optics written by Francis Sears, an MIT professor. In early 1942, Sears brought Melbourne Cummings his newest manuscript and proposed that he perform the function of publisher as well as printer. Accordingly, Addison-Wesley Press was born and named for its two unrelated founders, Lew Addison Cummings and Melbourne Wesley Cummings.

Today the company publishes a wide range of books and educational materials for colleges, elementary and high schools, nursing and medical schools, training programs, professionals, and the general population. Its products and offices are located worldwide.

The Higher Education Division is the largest and oldest part of the company, publishing outstanding undergraduate- and graduate-level products in a wide range of disciplines. Addison-Wesley is an industry leader in computer science, mathematics, and science, and is quickly growing book publishing units in business and decision science and engineering.

The Jobs

The best pathway into Addison-Wesley is as higher education marketing representative. Nearly everyone in high levels of responsibility received an introduction to publishing as a marketing rep. This is the best position from which to gain the knowledge of educational needs, trends, and markets—knowledge essential in every aspect of publishing, including marketing, editorial acquisition or development, production, promotion, and sales. Then, once you have established a sales, marketing, and editorial track record in the field, there are several directions in which you can advance: sales; sales/marketing management; marketing; and editorial.

There is a published profile of who achieves success at Addison-Wesley. "A college graduate . . . intelligent, articulate and outgoing, with an inquisitive mind . . . ambitious, eager to participate, contribute, and succeed . . . committed to excellence . . . possessing proven leadership qualities and the ability to manage your own time and responsibilities."

Determining the textbook and supplemental teaching needs for professors and demonstrating how Addison-Wesley products meet these needs are major functions of the marketing representative. As a rep, you will meet with college and university educators on a regular basis to stay current on their specific requirements and to keep them apprised of new educational packages, new trends in the field, and future publications. You will further be responsible for serving your accounts, handling individual, departmental, institutional, and bookstore needs.

Another aspect of the marketing representatives' job is searching for new, quality products—manuscripts, software packages, course ware, testing materials, and the like—and for exceptional scholars and teachers. The company relies on marketing representatives to report manuscript leads, new product ideas, and information about the marketplace, and to encourage gifted teachers and writers to publish with Addison-Wesley.

In addition to your meetings, and encompassing both your sales and editorial responsibilities, is the marketing role. Marketing is the ongoing process of gathering, synthesizing, and analyzing information about the company's educational materials and competitors' products; students' and professors' needs; trends and changes in curriculum and methods of teaching and learning; and similarities and differences in a variety of learning environments and disciplines. This is an integral part of the publishing process and, as field rep, you're the marketing specialist within your territory.

Traditionally the role of marketing rep has been carried out one on one, by reps in the field meeting with potential buyers. Today Addison-Wesley also employs telemarketing representatives who complete the same tasks by telephone.

As an Addison-Wesley rep, you will also deal with managers of college bookstores, retail bookstores, libraries, teacher-supply stores, and wholesalers. You may call upon the sales potential of government agencies, professional organizations, and industry itself, which all offer in-house workshops that require print materials.

Addison-Wesley has a comprehensive ongoing program for training reps in basic sales, marketing, editorial, and financial techniques and skills. The training program develops interviewing, listening, probing, synthesizing, and reporting skills within the publishing context. Throughout the training process, market and product knowledge is emphasized, and important closing skills are reinforced. Basic organizational procedures are also taught, and all appropriate company policies and procedures are introduced.

Both formal and informal training continue once you're on the job and are usually organized around seasonal goals, priorities, and emphases.

While formal training takes place at the corporate headquarters and during national sales/marketing meetings, regional training focuses on programs, experiences, and more specific needs. Much of the training is highly individualized, taking place on campuses that you'll visit under a supervisor assigned to work with you throughout the year.

Still, almost from the beginning, you are in charge of your days and your results. There is a team of experts to back you up: your supervisor and regional manager, regional and national acquisition editors, plus a regional and national staff of editorial, marketing, sales, and support personnel.

The Payoff

Besides a base salary that is competitive within the publishing industry, Addison-Wesley offers an incentive plan for making and surpassing sales goals and targets; an editorial bonus plan for each manuscript you sign; a company car or car allowance and expenses; insurance; vacation and holidays; and tuition assistance. One plus is that Addison-Wesley offers geographic flexibility and has regional headquarters in Wakefield, Massachusetts; Atlanta, Georgia; Rolling Hills, Illinois; and Redwood City, California.

The Word

Even though the thought of traveling by car from college town to college town within a region may sound dreary, the reality is that Addison-Wesley offers an outstanding opportunity for those who want to combine marketing with product development and for those who want to stay in touch with the world of education while working in the world of commerce.

"I wasn't sure how I would feel about my New England territory at first," says an Ivy League grad who hails from a Connecticut suburb. "What I have discovered is that I love staying in touch with the college campuses that I visit, and that the professors I call upon are a bright, eager group of professionals. Many afternoons I think that there's no other job where my background in science would matter so much. I am tossing ideas around with the best of them. And at the same time, what I'm doing is devising new ways to market information. That's the key—translating educational trends into marketable products and programs. . . ."

AETNA LIFE & CASUALTY COMPANY

Contact Info:

William O. Bailey, President

Kathy P. McKendree, College Program and Staffing
151 Farmington Avenue
Hartford, Connecticut 06156
(203) 273-3315

The Organization

Aetna, headquartered in the insurance capital of America, Hartford, Connecticut, is one of the largest diversified financial organizations in the country. Its main products include virtually every form of insurance, bond, and pension program. The company is also involved in real estate, land development, business financing, investment management, and technology enterprises.

The company is organized into six major areas, each of which is run by its own management team.

Personal Financial Security Division—sells and services all forms of life and health insurance, pension products to individuals, and auto and homeowners policies.

Employee Benefits Division—sells and services life and health insurance and pension products to groups, usually businesses.

Commercial Insurance Division—sells and services all forms of casualty and property insurance, and fidelity and surety bonds.

Financial Division—develops and implements plans to invest productively Aetna's financial resources, and coordinates long-range corporate planning.

Corporate Administration—has responsibility for staff services that support Aetna's business and runs the home office.

Diversified Business Division—manages Aetna's various operations and recommends and implements acquisition of businesses outside the insurance field.

Aetna is among the top twenty *Fortune* "500" companies and is the largest shareholder-owned insurer in terms of revenue, assets, and insurance in force. It is the largest fidelity and surety bond writer in terms of income; the largest writer of dental insurance; first in number of individually written corporate pension plans sold; and a major partner in Satellite Business Systems, a company that provides speed data, voice, and facsimile communications services to large businesses.

The Jobs

More often than not, liberal arts graduates begin their careers with Aetna in the Commercial Insurance Division, for the commercial insurance field offices are "where the action is." The field offices are Aetna's front line and are responsible for the entire operation in a specific territory. About one-third of the company's forty thousand employees are Hartford-based; the rest work throughout the country, and it's these folks who deal mostly with the company's independent agents and policyholders.

There are seven typical entry level jobs to consider: administration department supervisor, bond representative, claims representative, commercial insurance underwriter, commercial insurance engineer, commercial account representative, and premium auditor.

Take, for example, the bond representative's job. Bonds are versatile instruments that help protect people and get jobs done. Surety bonds provide a third-party guarantee, an essential link between people who pay for a service and the person or company hired to do the job. If a contractor goes bankrupt or fails to finish a job, Aetna, as the surety, either sees that the job is completed or pays its bondholder.

Surety bonds are an extension of credit, an assurance of financial responsibility and a guarantee that when a job is promised, it will be done.

Fidelity bonds protect companies and financial institutions against dishonesty by employees and against theft and loss. They are, in effect, honesty insurance.

As the leading contract surety bond writer, Aetna covers construction of manufacturing plants, airports, commercial buildings, hospitals, schools, and power plants. Its projects include the

United Nations headquarters, the Hoover Dam, and the Niagara Falls power project.

As a bond representative, you'll counsel agents and their clients on financial and technical matters relating to bonding qualifications. You'll become an expert in bond guidelines by dealing with contractors, engineers, lawyers, bankers, brokers, political leaders, public officials, and top managers in all kinds of businesses.

Therefore, feeling they will be most successful in this position, Aetna seeks liberal arts grads who are "comfortable meeting people; able to evaluate people, companies, and situations; and who, based on those analyses, are confident making decisions involving substantial amounts of money."

The size and scope of the bond business requires you to be highly trained, including one year of formal training that includes classroom instruction and on-the-job experience in a field office. The opportunities for advancement are great.

Similarly, as a commercial insurance underwriter, you will be extensively trained, including on-the-job experience in a field office and classroom training at the home office. Fairly quickly, you'll be making and influencing important decisions about insuring different kinds of businesses. Manufacturers, contractors, retail stores, apartment buildings, restaurants, and other businesses need insurance to reduce the risk of financial loss from the unforeseen and uncontrollable. Since there is always risk, the critical question is: how much risk is involved in the particular business seeking insurance, and how much of a premium should they pay?

That's where the analytical skills that are nurtured in liberal arts course work come in. It'll be your job to make that decision, by examining all relevant information about that company. As an underwriter, your liberal arts talents will count, since communication skills matter most. You'll be dealing directly with the independent agents who sell Aetna's insurance and will be helping customers solve complex insurance problems. All in all, insurance, particularly underwriting, is "a people business!"

William O. Bailey told *Career Insights*, "Fifteen years ago insurance companies were considered dull and conservative—the standard impression was that insurance companies were run by a few salesmen who pressed you to buy their products. Today, in contrast, insurance is part of the whole financial services industry.

. . . Ours is a moderately conservative business in the best sense since insurance is a present promise of future performance. Those who like Russian roulette or riverboat gambling probably won't be attracted to the insurance industry, which, as a consequence of its fiduciary responsibility to people, needs prudent managers." He advised, "Although not many of us know where we want to be twenty years from now, insurance companies offer young people the opportunity to learn and to be productive."

The Payoff

The company pays starting salaries in the low twenties for B.A. hires and offers an extensive benefits package. (It makes sense, considering that the company sells just that to thousands of other employers, too.) Performance evaluations are annual, and raises reflect achievement, initiative, and increasing responsibility. One unique aspect of the Aetna compensation package is an incentive savings plan that kicks in once you've been on the job for a year. Participants can contribute up to 15 percent of their salary in a variety of investment options. The company matches your contribution dollar for dollar, up to 5 percent of your salary. Tuition reimbursement for up to two courses a semester is another Aetna extra.

The Word

The only bad thing about the company is the corny tag line, which runs on many of its recruitment advertisements: "Aetna, we're glad we met ya!" It's unfortunate that the company's great success story as an employer can get lost in low-grade advertising copy that screams "boring" with slogans like: "Here's stand-up proof that liberal arts majors can succeed hands-down in business." The truth is that Aetna offers a very attractive financial services alternative to credit-analysis management training programs in money center banks. President Bailey is an econ major from Dartmouth, and a large number of the people who run the company come from the arts and sciences, even from the humanities!

BBDO INTERNATIONAL

Contact Info:

Allen Rosenshine, President and Chief Executive Officer

Christopher Carey, Manager of Training and Development
383 Madison Avenue
New York, New York 10017-2565
(212) 415-5000

Financials (1985):

Billings: $2.5 billion
Net Revenue: $377 million

The Organization

BBDO International, New York, is part of a new holding company, Omnicom Group, with Needham Harper Worldwide and Doyle Dane Bernbach. Even as BBDO International, Inc., it is one of the largest advertising agency groups worldwide, with over 156 offices in forty-two countries. BBDO does business in markets that account for over 95 percent of world advertising expenditures.

BBDO is best known for its agency personality. The fundamental personality is reflected in the quality of the clients served. These clients include American Cyanamid, Black & Decker, Campbell Soup, Chrysler, General Electric, Gillette, Lorillard, PepsiCo, Scott Paper, and Visa U.S.A.

It's an agency with a fresh outlook and with a management team that is accomplished and progressive. BBDO is also an agency where marketing ability is highly regarded. The marketing and research capabilities are deep, including the most excellent management science techniques in the agency field. Clients depend on these techniques when they formulate their own marketing plans.

BBDO is a highly creative agency, and its campaigns on behalf of clients are among the most appealing and innovative. In all cases, campaigns result from concise strategic thinking.

BBDO's management stresses the importance of training. Account managers are advertising generalists and are seasoned in every discipline: marketing, media, creative, and business skills. BBDO's Account Management Training Program was developed to train future agency leaders with these skills.

The Jobs

College hires enter the program with the title of assistant account executive and are assigned to accounts that can immediately use their skills and can help them develop new ones. These accounts typically require involvement with all marketing disciplines and offer the opportunity for exposure to client companies with sophisticated professional managers and marketing departments. Assistant account executives start throughout the year, and training normally lasts for about eighteen months, depending on an individual's progress.

At BBDO, professional development is from four sources: on-the-job training, a seminar series, marketing problem-solving workshops, and quarterly performance evaluation, with extensive career counseling.

During your first months as an assistant account executive, you meet representatives from every department to understand how BBDO operates. You also begin workshops to sharpen your communication skills. Working with account executives, you have ongoing involvement in the evaluation of research needs, interpretation of research data, and presentation of findings to clients; liaison with clients, conference reports, production estimates, and store checks; copy strategy development and follow-up, legal clearance, presentation to clients, production, scheduling, and competitive evaluation; development of media strategies, planning, buying, postbuy analysis, and competitive media evaluation; and billing process and manpower/profit planning.

After about nine months, the assistant moves to another account, for the belief here is that rotation diversifies the training experience.

The second source of professional development is a series of management seminars conducted by senior agency executives. Independent projects are assigned periodically. Some of the seminars may include agency finance, marketing fundamentals, commercial testing techniques, and advertising and the law.

In addition, you will be expected to attend marketing problem-solving workshops, which are held three times a year, with four or five trainees in each group. Account supervisors are group leaders, and they bring a current marketing issue to the group. The goals are to build strategic thinking beyond what you will have mastered from your account experience; to provide exposure to market categories; to enhance presentation and selling skills; and to foster a sense of teamwork among assistants. Sample problems are to develop a marketing plan for Chrysler's Northeast zone, or to resolve the positioning of Lever Brothers Wisk's new detergent powder. Groups meet every week or so for two months and eventually produce a final presentation, which is made to the account with which the issue originated, as well as to the agency's senior management.

Assistants are evaluated quarterly on their oral and written communication skills, analytical ability, and sensitivity to the copy, marketing, and research processes. They're evaluated against a uniform set of objectives by supervisors and are invited to confer with the personnel department's career counselors. Management supervisors have final responsibility for training and for evaluation.

On the basis of evaluation, the Account Management Development Committee determines the length of an individual's training, and you will be promoted to account executive and will receive an account assignment as soon as you're prepared to handle the responsibility.

The Payoff

Salary is consistent with the Madison Avenue norm of mid-twenties for assistant account executives. Comprehensive benefits are part of the compensation package.

The Word

BBDO was the advertising agency of the year in 1985, and even with the proliferation of mergers and all the assorted implications for the old-line firm of Batten, Barton, Durstine & Osborn, all is still healthy within the ranks of its personnel. Omnicom may be its

parent, but BBDO is still a strong agency in its own right, and
account executives report great faith that they're moving right
along, right up, and that the merger spells opportunity more than
anything else. There is a BBDO tradition that is honored each
spring at the agency breakfast. Each year at that time, the BBDO
Founders Award is presented to "honor members of the crew." If
what you're looking for is to row with the crew, this is one agency
at which those who work hard to keep it moving full steam ahead
will be well rewarded today and in the future.

BAIN & COMPANY

Contact Info:

William Bain, Jr., President

Joan Courtney, Director of Recruiting
Two Copley Place
Boston, Massachusetts 02116
(617) 572-2000

The Organization

Bain & Company has become so hot it sizzles. Although the firm
does little in the way of public promotion, word of mouth has
made it the top choice of liberal arts graduates seeking consulting
jobs. The company was founded in 1973 by Bill Bain, along with
four fellow refugees from the Boston Consulting Group. In less
than fifteen years, it has achieved an astonishing growth record,
mushrooming from a handful of consultants to a staff of more than
seven hundred. It's currently the largest strategic consulting firm
in the world, with major offices located in Boston, San Francisco,
London, Munich, Tokyo, and Paris. In 1985, total revenue ex-
ceeded $100 million for the first time, and that figure is expected
to multiply rapidly.

What is it that makes Bain so appealing? For one thing, it's the
only major consulting firm that never works for directly competing companies—even when the competitors are in different coun-

tries. This way there's never a conflict-of-interest problem, and each client's position can be advanced unhampered. According to Bill Bain, "A winning competitive strategy requires a highly partisan attitude on the part of the consulting firm. It's obviously harder to feel that way if you're sitting on both sides of the table." Another unique element of Bain's philosophy is its innovative view of client relationships. The firm presents itself as a long-term investment rather than a short-term cost. Periodically Bain evaluates the amount of value it's added to a client's business and divides that figure by its fee. If the rate of return is significant—as it almost always is—the client is likely to continue the collaboration. Overall, Bain has a higher number of long-term clients than any of its peers.

But most important is Bain's distinctive approach to the consulting business. According to the firm, "The principal thrust of [our] practice is to assist our clients in the design and implementation of strategies that will enhance each client's competitive position and that will help the client create significant economic value." To accomplish these objectives, Bain's activities are divided into three broad areas: corporate strategy, business unit strategy, and implementation assistance. Corporate strategy involves allocating scarce resources among a client's businesses so as to maximize financial performance. Business unit strategy involves analyzing competitive advantage by comparing a client's product or service to alternative products and services, conducting market research, and evaluating competitors' financial resources and intentions. Implementation assistance involves putting recommendations into effect and ensuring that businesses perform according to Bain's strategy analysis. Generally the firm's projects include developing and establishing strategy; creating marketing programs; assisting clients with acquisitions, divestitures, and other major asset deployments; and helping clients improve their total management process.

The Jobs

From what we've heard, getting hired by Bain ranks up there with being admitted to Harvard, winning a Rhodes scholarship, and so on. The firm's training program, which is widely acknowledged as one of the best in the industry, is constantly being improved and refined. In reality, anyone with a good academic background, excellent interpersonal skills, and a high level of motivation can get in the door. There seems to be a definite Bain type, and there's only one word for it: well rounded. While the firm does employ a fair share of rocket scientists, brains clearly aren't everything. Athletes are popular, as are campus leaders. Keep in mind that all Bain has to offer clients is its staff—so the selection process can be arduous. While your interviewer may be an incredibly nice person, he'll be testing you in a number of ways. You must be able to demonstrate a great deal of physical and mental energy as well as an ability to think on your feet and make a persuasive presentation. Since you may have to be in a room for hours on end with clients and fellow team members, you should also indicate that you have a sense of humor. Most important, perhaps, is a strong drive to find solutions to difficult problems. As the firm points out, "If problems were easy, clients would not be seeking outside help." And a word to the wise: Bain is known for stringing recruits along, so don't worry if you're called back for third and fourth interviews—and if, after that, you don't hear anything for a week.

If you're Bain material, you'll be hired as an associate consultant, which is the entry-level position available to non-M.B.A.s. In this job, you'll gain extensive training in fundamental business concepts and analytical techniques, and have extensive client contact. You'll participate on case teams that handle a number of different objectives: corporate portfolio development, relative cost analysis, value management, marketing/pricing strategy, competitor analysis, or acquisitions/divestitures. Typical assignments include interviewing clients' customers and personnel, designing and executing quantitative analyses, and serving on task forces in the client organization. You'll be exposed to a broad range of industries, and the roles you'll play will vary according to the case objective and to your progress. The associate consultant position is generally a two-year job, after which you head back to business or law school. However, outstanding associate consultants may be promoted to consultant without acquiring a graduate degree. Unlike many of its competitors, Bain presents the position as open ended and tends to encourage qualified people to stay on. In addition, the firm provides tuition reimbursement to some associate consultants who plan to return after graduate school. And recently Bain has begun new programs to support associate consultants who make the transition to consultant without leaving. In the past couple of years, the firm claims it has "devoted more staff time and expense investment to formal training to build skills of current staff members than to recruiting and new client development combined."

The Payoff

Bain offers some of the highest starting salaries in the field. With raises and bonuses, some top liberal arts grads earn upward of $40,000 after only a short time at the firm. Bain's comprehensive benefits package includes full-service medical and life insurance plans. In addition, the firm offers a vast array of perks. When you travel, it's all expenses paid, and that can include trips overseas. After the completion of a big project, you'll often be treated to a lavish dinner or perhaps a cocktail party aboard a ship. Fun is important to Bain, so many perks come in the form of postproject play.

The Word

From what we've heard, Bain is it. The combination of rapid learning, early responsibility, and constant teamwork seems to give the firm an edge over its competitors in attracting top talent. Bain boasts of offering "nearly unequaled opportunity for motivated people to make a difference," and this appears to be true. Unlike trainees at leading investment banks, who often complain of doing useless number crunching for weeks on end, associate consultants referred to their work as "tremendously challenging" and "extremely stimulating." Says the firm, "Not only is there enormous potential for making a positive impact on client firms, but our people can readily identify their personal contributions and observe the tangible results in a relatively short period of time." Whether your goal is to remain at Bain, return to school, or change professions, two years spent as an associate consultant is an invaluable experience.

Keep in mind that a key word at Bain is "competition": you'll hear it used over and over, both in reference to clients and to employees. In a recent speech made to the Harvard Business School Club of Chicago, Bill Bain explained his competitive theory. He defined the goal of developing a competitive strategy as giving the client a sustainable advantage, and said, "In other words, you are trying to devise ways to put his competitors at a permanent *dis*advantage." Bain then quoted Oscar Wilde as saying, "It isn't enough that I succeed, my enemies must also fail." The point is, you've got to be ultracompetitive to make it as a Bain consultant—and you've got to be willing to see everyone else in your client's industry get hurt. It's a bit of a compromise for some people, who find it hard to be simultaneously sweet and tough as nails.

BANK OF AMERICA

Contact Info:

A. W. Clausen, Chairman

Cynthia Yee, Manager of College Recruiting
400 California Street
San Francisco, California 94104
(415) 765-2630

Financials (1985):
   Assets: $117.7 billion
   Deposits: $94 billion
   Loans: $84 billion

The Organization

Bank of America is the principal subsidary of BankAmerica Corporation, the second largest bank holding company in the nation. Founded by retired produce merchant A. P. Giannini in 1904 as the Bank of Italy, B of A's first home was in a remodeled tavern. Giannini was fond of calling it The Little Fellow's Bank, and he was said to make loans as small as $25. Through consolidation and mergers with several other banks in California, Bank of Italy became the third largest bank in the nation by 1927, and three years later, it officially changed its name to Bank of America. In 1931, the bank opened its first international office, in London, and by 1945, it was the world's largest bank in terms of deposits. After A. P. Giannini's death four years later, his son Mario took over the reins and guided the bank into the future.

During the past few years, B of A has taken over several regional banks, as well as Seafirst Bank in Washington State and Charles Schwab, a national discount brokerage house. (Earlier this year, in a much-publicized battle, Schwab bought his firm back.) Besides regular commercial banking activities, B of A has a computer leasing and financial data processing unit, an investment research unit, an insurance arm, and a real estate investment unit. Today Bank of America operates in over 1,700 branches and offices worldwide. In California alone, the bank has 903 branches and 1,330 automated teller machines. In addition to its San Francisco headquarters, B of A has divisional headquarters in Los Angeles, New York, London, Caracas, and Tokyo.

The Jobs

B of A employs about eighty thousand people. Each year several dozen B.A.s are hired into its various training programs, including branch management, consumer credit, and business and corporate banking. The cream of the crop join the Commercial Banker Development Program, which trains officers to handle the highly competitive "middle market." This program encompasses a year of classroom training and field experience. Generally it involves 30 percent classroom study and 70 percent on-the-job learning. The idea is to develop financial and product knowledge while developing technical, negotiating, sales, and marketing skills. In addition, trainees are expected to study B of A's branch system, its approach to banking, and the bank's culture and personality, in retail, business, and corporate banking. Trainees are recruited from top colleges and universities around the country, with an emphasis on California institutions. Generally the training stint involves rotating through different branches of the bank and then being assigned to a particular branch or department.

The Payoff

Most freshly minted B.A.s are offered starting salaries in the low-to mid-twenties range. Benefits include medical, dental, and life insurance coverage, as well as reduced loan rates, free checking, a savings plan, reduced Visa card rates, and reduced mortgage rates. In addition, since staffers tend to be moved around at semifrequent intervals, the bank offers an excellent relocation package.

The Word

B of A has had its share of troubles. By the middle of 1986, the bank had suffered operating losses over seven quarters approaching $1.5 billion. At this point, First Interstate Bank made an aggressive takeover bid. In a widely publicized battle, the board of directors voted to oust its chairman, Sam Armacost, and replace him with former chairman A. W. Clausen. Then B of A began restructuring to divest itself of nonessential businesses in order to raise its book value. B of A sold off a number of ailing operations and ultimately stalled First Interstate's bid. However, the bank was left seriously shaken and is taking time to regroup.

Much maligned in the press for mismanagement, B of A has fought hard to maintain its respectable, responsible image. Staffers say the large size and decentralization encourage cliques to form, and they complain about lack of communication among local, regional, and corporate offices. However, many recent hires extol the opportunities for rapid advancement. "The bank's undergoing a real transition, and there's lots of latitude for aggressive people," says one liberal arts major. "If you're willing to work long hours, you're likely to move up very quickly. The bank is really looking for a new breed of managers."

BANK OF BOSTON

Contact Info:

William L. Brown, Chairman and CEO

Gail Kelley, Director of College Relations
100 Federal Street
P.O. Box 1976
Boston, Massachusetts 02110
(617) 434-2200

Financials (1985):

Assets: $22 billion
Deposits: $15 billion
Loans: $14 billion

The Organization

Bank of Boston is the oldest and largest bank in New England. It was founded during the Federalist period, and some of its earliest customers were among the nation's architects. In 1984, employees at the Federal Street headquarters celebrated the bank's bicentennial—and its growth from a tiny lending operation to one of the top twenty banks in the nation. Today BOB provides financing to a wide variety of industries, ranging from transportation to entertainment. The bank has a foothold throughout New England, except the states of Vermont and New Hampshire, which haven't approved interstate banking yet. Due to the growth of high technology, the region is expected to have excellent potential as a lending market in the future. Outside the Northeast, it has more than a hundred international offices, primarily in Argentina and Brazil.

Recently BOB reorganized into five operating groups: corporate, international, New England, real estate, and treasury/investment. Each group is responsible for serving carefully defined segments of the bank's market and for managing its own resources and profitability. In addition, a new core group of senior staffers called the Corporate Center helps establish and support the bank's strategic direction, overall management, and policy implementation.

The Jobs

BOB, which employs sixteen thousand people worldwide, hires B.A.s who "communicate effectively, both orally and in writing, and demonstrate leadership, maturity, and enthusiasm." In addition, the bank seeks candidates who demonstrate "talent, imagination, determination, and entrepreneurial spirit." The potential for strong analytical, negotiating, and decision-making skills is also required. If you're interested in an international banking job, you should have appropriate language skills and be willing to travel.

Most B.A.s enter BOB's Loan Officer Development Program (LODP) to train for international and domestic lending positions. The stated purpose of the LODP is "to prepare men and women to initiate and maintain mutually beneficial relationships between the Bank and its commercial customers." The program combines course work, case studies, and project assignments with internships in various divisions. The length of the program is tailored to the needs of the individual; according to the bank, "We want to leverage each candidate's unique background and fill in the gaps, not teach you what you already know." The two-phase program involves basic training in credit analysis and commercial banking (four to twelve months), followed by a series of rotational internships (six to nine months). These "tours" provide line experience in several different divisions, including most of the geographic and specialty lending divisions and many of the bank's overseas offices.

Individuals who haven't had any full-time work experience or relevant course work begin the program with a four-month internship in a division such as audit, cash management, or letter of credit. This internship doesn't lengthen your total training experience, since it displaces one of your later internships. Throughout the program, you work closely with one LODP adviser who has primary responsibility for your development. This adviser monitors your work assignments, performance reviews, and salary reviews. Upon satisfactory completion of the program's second phase, a division assignment is made. Depending on your skills—

and initiative—you'll be promoted to loan officer after six to nine months.

The Payoff

BOB's salary and benefits programs are described by the company as "nationally competitive." From what we hear, B.A.s are offered packages similar to those their peers in other cities (e.g., New York) get. Which means, of course, BOB trainees have an extra edge in terms of disposable income. Benefits include up to ten days of vacation for trainees; full health coverage; a staff health center; and life and disability insurance. Staffers also receive free checking account services and reduced rates on selected loans. In addition, BOB offers a Thrift Incentive Plan, which allows you to share in the bank's growth and profits. Education benefits include a multitude of annual in-house programs as well as tuition assistance for bank-related courses at local institutions.

The Word

BOB is apparently the place to be if you want to bank in Boston. Many recent graduates find it an ideal place to spread their career wings, especially those who enjoy a familial atmosphere. Long attractive to students, Boston has emerged as one of the country's most exciting and livable cities. "The quality of life is really superior," says one BOB trainee. "I have my own apartment, and it's nearly twice as big as those of my friends working in New York. And I can actually afford to eat in the restaurants and go to an occasional concert or show!" Beyond the major money center banks in Manhattan, BOB enjoys a reputation as the premier commercial banking institution in the Northeast. And as New England's well-diversified economy picks up, opportunities are bound to increase. Says one recent BOB hire, "There's still a lot of relatively new territory to cover in this area. If you're willing to explore new options, this is a great place to be." By most accounts, BOB is a safe bet if you want a rigorous introduction to commercial banking and you prefer a slightly slower-paced life-style. There seems to be just as much challenge and stimulation as at the New

York banks, but you're not as likely to be a little fish lost in a gigantic pond.

BANKERS TRUST

Contact Info:

Alfred Brittain, III, Chairman

Nina Jahn, Director of College Relations
299 Park Avenue
New York, New York 10017
(212) 250-2500

Financials (1985):

Assets: $45 billion
Deposits: $25.6 billion
Loans: $23 billion

The Organization

Bankers Trust, one of the ten largest commercial banks in the country, has one major difference from its brethren: it doesn't take individual consumer deposits. You won't find any automated teller machines at BT, because there's no such thing as a BT cash card. Between 1980 and 1984, the bank sold off its retail business in order to concentrate on merchant banking. Today BT's clients are mainly large organizations and high-income individuals. The bank ranks as one of the nation's most prestigious financial institutions and as one of the most diverse financial organizations in the world. BT provides sophisticated quality services to multinational, domestic, and foreign corporations, as well as to financial institutions and governments. It has offices in cities including Atlanta, Miami, Chicago, Dallas, Houston, Los Angeles, and San Francisco, as well as in three dozen countries worldwide.

BT's business is broken down into four sectors: wholesale banking, corporate financial services, money and securities markets, and fiduciary activities. Along with Morgan Guaranty, BT is considered to have pushed the furthest against the Glass-Steagall Act of 1933 (which separated the activities of commercial banks from those of investment banks) by getting involved in private placements, mergers and acquisitions, and Eurobond trading. The bank's corporate financial services staff is comparable in size to that of many major investment banks, and some of the key executives are veterans of successful Wall Street careers. In just one week during 1986, the bank's corporate finance department played a leading role in $8 billion worth of deals by pledging to arrange financing for about $4 billion.

The Jobs

BT employs approximately 10,500 people and hires several dozen liberal arts grads each spring. The bank's recruiting team scours colleges and universities across the nation for candidates who have "high levels of energy and tenacity, a commitment to excellence in all endeavors, and a large capacity for innovation." Even though the bank's recruiting rhetoric is similar to that of its competitors, at BT, it's true that only the very best and brightest are hired. Recently BT's recruiters stated, "We prize independence of thought. We seek problem solvers, people with initiative and inventiveness. In the intensely competitive banking environment of today, we cannot afford individuals who are afraid to voice unconventional ideas or propose novel solutions."

If you're looking for a nine-to-five commercial banking job, don't look at BT. The bank is renowned for running one of the most rigorous account officer training programs in the industry; it involves on-the-job exposure as well as class work in credit, accounting, and finance. B.A.s are often mixed with M.B.A.s in this program, but you must first take introductory courses before joining the M.B.A.s. About a year after graduating from the officer training program, successful trainees become assistant treasurers. You're likely to do your first stint at BT in the wholesale banking, corporate finance, money market, or fiduciary department. In wholesale banking, you coordinate products and services throughout the bank that may be of use to customers; you cultivate relationships with clients; and you enhance the profitability of accounts. In corporate finance, you're involved in the bank's nonlending financial services: private placements, mergers and acquisitions, lease financing, project financing, and a variety of advisory services. In the money market center, you must be able to "think quickly, exercise judgment, and make rapid decisions involving large sums of money," since you'll buy, sell, and trade financial instruments for the bank and its customers. In the fiduciary area, you'll concentrate upon trust administration, investment management, investment research, or technical investment consulting. Some positions are also available in the strategic planning division, the operations department, the auditing area, and the marketing group. Whichever function or group you enter, BT offers early responsibility and opportunities for rapid advancement. Individuals are encouraged to design their own careers, as generalists or specialists.

The Payoff

BT offers some of the best starting salaries in the field. (The only place you're likely to do better is at J. P. Morgan.) The bank sets its pay scale with an eye toward what its biggest competitors, on and off Wall Street, are offering. In general, liberal arts grads begin in the high-twenties range. BT's benefits package is likewise considered quite choice. It includes medical, dental, and life insurance coverage as well as free checking, a savings plan, and a tuition reimbursement program. BT also provides relocation and apartment-finding assistance upon hiring or transferring employees.

The Word

Although investment banking may seem sexier than commercial banking, BT isn't lacking in sex appeal. The bank's popularity has increased as its reputation for quality training and innovative techniques has grown. In an industry in which many of the biggest players have been undergoing rapid change and consolidation, BT has delivered one of the consistently best performances. Analysts predict a bright future for BT; as the walls between investment and commercial banking tumble further, BT's position will be extremely attractive. By the 1990s, the bank is expected to move full force into many of the areas currently dominated by its Wall Street competitors. By most money center standards, BT's asset quality is very good; it has one of the largest loan loss reserves in the world.

The only complaint we found about BT was the "fence-straddling" dilemma. While liberal arts grads say the bank provides tremendously exciting opportunities, some find the environment a bit confusing. On the one hand, BT carries much of the heavy bureaucracy of a commercial bank, but employees are required to turn deals around as fast as an investment bank—and usually without the hefty bonuses. "If I'd wanted to work for an investment bank, I would have gone to Wall Street," says one trainee. "It's not that I thought it would be easy—I just never thought it would be like this!" However, BT has recently begun to emphasize that bonuses will play a greater role, and many top-level financiers have been lured away from competing firms. Clearly, if you come prepared for BT's maverick business philosophy, you'll find the work stimulating. "Instead of worrying about maintaining accounts for small customers, I have a chance to get involved with major deals," explains one trainee in corporate finance.

BAXTER TRAVENOL LABORATORIES, INC.

Contact Info:

Vernon R. Loucks, Jr., President and Chief Executive Officer

Linden V. T. Smith, Corporate Manager of College Relations
One Baxter Parkway
Deerfield, Illinois 60015
(312) 940-5000

Financials (1985):

Sales: $2,355 million
Profits: $137 million

The Organization

Baxter Travenol Laboratories, Inc., is an international manufacturer and distributor of health care products, systems, and services. The new Baxter Travenol—a company created by the merger of Baxter Travenol and American Hospital Supply Company in 1985—is a company with the breadth of resources to help health care providers deliver quality care more efficiently.

The new Baxter Travenol is capable of providing important health care products, systems, and services to virtually every area inside and outside the hospital, from central supply to the operating room, from the nursing stations to the pharmacy, and from data processing to outpatient services and beyond. Moreover, Baxter Travenol is committed to helping hospitals and other health care providers contain costs without sacrificing quality.

The new company has been organized into ten operating groups. Each group, and the chief executive who leads it, is charged with the responsibility of finding innovative solutions that meet consumers' needs in today's cost-conscious marketplace. The ten groups are: corporate marketing, healthcare services, parenterals, medical products, alternate site, distribution, surgical/critical care, diagnostics, blood products, and world trade.

With the merger, Baxter Travenol now has 61,000 employees and 120,000 products serving health care providers through these ten operating groups. It manufactures products in twenty-three countries and markets its products and services in more than one hundred countries. The company has combined annual sales in excess of five billion dollars.

Today the health care industry represents 11 percent of the U.S. gross national product, and it is a growing industry. New products, technologies, and methods of distribution are increasing both the capabilities and the efficiencies of health care providers. At the same time, economic pressures are forcing every health care provider and supplier to deliver more cost-effectively than ever before.

The Jobs

Career opportunities open to liberal arts graduates include information systems (any major provided you've had nine to twelve hours of programming, including three hours of COBOL) for positions as programmer/analyst and materials management systems associate; manufacturing for positions as buyer trainee and production planner trainee; research for positions as research assistant and chemist; sales for positions as sales representative and territory manager; operations for positions as management understudy, distribution analyst, traffic analyst, and materials planning analyst; accounting and finance for positions as staff accountant, financial associate, and credit trainee; and consulting for positions as research associate.

The Payoff

Baxter Travenol places a high premium on its employees' quality of life. Benefits are excellent and opportunities for growth abound. When you join the company, your career development will hinge upon your performance record. The company pays a competitive package of direct and indirect compensation. In addition to annual starting salaries in the $20,000- to $30,000-range, you'll receive a benefits package that includes family medical and dental coverage, disability benefits, life insurance, a pension plan, and a discounted stock purchase plan.

As a health care company, Baxter Travenol is committed to maintaining a healthy work environment. The company offers programs for fitness, nutrition, smoking cessation, stress reduction, and other activities related to wellness.

Baxter Travenol plays an active role in meeting other employee needs through a credit union, tuition reimbursement programs, and day care assistance. There is also an employee purchase program that provides substantial discounts on merchandise.

Corporate headquarters are in a suburban location about twenty miles north of Chicago. Major facilities are located in Southern California and in other major U.S. cities and around the world.

The Word

Bill Gantz, Baxter Travenol's chief operating officer, graduated from Princeton with a degree in economics. His first postgraduation job was selling group health insurance for three years. He's been with Baxter Laboratories in one capacity or another since 1966. He told *Pharmaceutical Executive,* "I think the most gratifying thing for me is doing things that really make a difference in the world. We're in a business that is very much a caring business. We're dealing with very sick people with most of the products we have. For instance, with kidney dialysis, I see people today able to lead relatively normal lives who could never have done so ten or fifteen years ago." He continued, "When I look back, I want people to say, 'Here is a person who has made a difference in the world. Because he's been here, we've been able to accomplish things that could not have otherwise been done.'"

The merger of American and Baxter screams big opportunities for those who can contribute. With a "smart" role model like Gantz, and there are many men and women like him in the organization, it's no wonder that you're concluding that this is still one of the "100 best companies to work for," if not even more attractive than that.

THE BIG NINE

Thomas J. Nessinger, Firm Director of Recruiting
Arthur Andersen & Co.
69 West Washington Street
Chicago, Illinois 60602
(312) 580-0069

John P. Prendergast, National Director of Personnel
   Development
Arthur Young & Co.
277 Park Avenue
New York, New York 10172
(212) 407-2309

Jeffrey D. Pronty, Manager of College Relations
Coopers & Lybrand
1251 Avenue of the Americas
New York, New York 10020
(212) 536-2729

James C. Older, National Coordinator of Recruitment
Deloitte Haskins & Sells
1114 Avenue of the Americas
New York, New York 10036
(212) 790-0591

Nicholas F. Rago, Senior Manager, National Recruiting
Ernst & Whinney
2000 National City Center
Cleveland, Ohio 44114
(216) 861-5000, ex. 5465

Samuel A. Vitkoski, Director, Professional Recruitment
KMG/Main Hurdman
Park Avenue Plaza, 55 East 52nd Street
New York, New York 10055
(212) 909-5605

Bernard J. Milano, Partner-in-Charge of Recruiting
Peat, Marwick, Mitchell & Co.
345 Park Avenue
New York, New York 10154
(212) 758-9700, ex. 4056

Larry P. Scott, Director, National Recruitment
Price Waterhouse
1251 Avenue of the Americas
New York, New York 10020
(212) 819-5028

Roger C. Eickhoff, Director of Human Resources
Touche Ross
225 Peachtree Street, N.E., Suite 1400
Atlanta, Georgia 30303
(404) 586-6740

No book about jobs for smart people would be complete without noting that the Big Eight (plus Main Hurdman) hire a small number of the best and brightest arts and sciences grads each year. Accounting firms recruit liberal arts majors for tax and consulting career tracks as well as for auditing careers. In fact, the aforementioned accounting firms have joined forces for the past few years to provide certified public accounting training for liberal arts grads. In conjunction with New York University, Northeastern University, Rutgers University, and the University of Hartford, these public accounting firms offer top students the opportunity to earn a Master of Science degree in accounting while working at full pay within their firms. This *intense* fifteen-month work-study program offers you the technical expertise that is essential for on-the-job challenges that come with job one—junior auditor—in all these firms.

While each of these firms offer similar career tracks and long-range opportunities, and the climb from junior to partner almost always takes about a decade, what you have to ask yourself is whether you will feel comfortable with this group of colleagues. There are some differences among firms, and the best advice is to get inside and figure out where you'll thrive. If you do the M.S.-in-accounting pathway, you'll be getting top-notch training; just choose the right top-notch clients and colleagues.

BLOOMINGDALE'S

(a division of Federated Department Stores, Inc.)

Contact Info:

Marvin S. Traub, Chairman

William Regan, Executive Recruiter
1000 Third Avenue
New York, New York 10022
(212) 705-2383

Financials (1985):

Sales: $955.2 million

The Organization

Bloomingdale's was founded in 1872 by Lyman and Joseph Bloomingdale. Opening day saw a gross of $3.68, but within six years the "El" roared uptown and 1878 sales went over the $850,000 mark.

It was the right place at the right time. New York's "Silk Stocking" district grew up around it. The building, originally on 56th Street, moved to its permanent location on 59th and by 1931 covered the entire square block (59th to 60th Street, Lexington Avenue to Third Avenue).

Bloomingdale's has been described more as a lifestyle than simply a store, creating a pattern of shopping habits not only for New Yorkers but for visitors from everywhere in the world. It is a "neighborhood" store that all kinds of customers, young to old, have labeled "my favorite store."

Bloomingdale's stores currently include seven department stores in New York City and its tri-state suburbs; two in the Philadelphia area; a home furnishings specialty store in the Boston suburbs; a clearance center on Long Island; two department stores in the suburbs of Washington, and a fashion apparel store across the street from the home furnishings store in Chestnut Hill, Massachusetts. Bloomingdale's now operates in Texas and Florida, too, with a total of sixteen stores.

The parent company, Federated Department Stores, Inc., is a diversified retail firm serving customers across the nation through its department stores, mass merchandising stores, supermarkets, and other retail divisions. By the end of 1985, Federated had sixteen operating divisions and 604 stores in the major retail markets of thirty-six states. Each of the franchises operates on a decentralized basis and Bloomingdale's does operate in some of the same markets as Abraham & Straus, Burdine's, The Children's Place, Filene's, and Filene's Basement, although none of these stores is quite like Bloomingdale's. In fact, Bloomie's has a slogan: "Like no other store in the world. . . ."

The Jobs

Andrea Jung, a graduate of Princeton, is divisional merchandise manager for intimate apparel. Only a year after she joined the executive training program, she became department manager of sweaters in the Massachusetts store. Two years later, she returned to New York City as associate buyer of swimwear. Three months later she was promoted to buyer. As Andrea built the volume of her departments, she was given increasing responsibilities, first as group buyer, then as a divisional merchandise manager. That kind of career success is possible at Bloomie's, where an ambitious future is the name of the game for bright liberal arts grads.

To meet its aggressive expansion plans while continuing its practice of promoting from within, Bloomingdale's hires and develops dozens of top-quality junior executives each year. They're trained in the classroom and on the job and are provided with career opportunities in operations and merchandising.

Operations executives may oversee the movement of merchandise in the warehouse and in and out of the stores. They may be responsible for directing the receiving and ticketing of merchandise, for managing Bloomie's phone order operation, or for overseeing the flow of items being sent to customers. On the selling floor, operations executives schedule and supervise a full staff of sales and stock people. All the jobs are managed within expense and productivity objectives.

From the first job assignment, operation executives have accountability for the budgeting, staffing, training, and supplying of an area or a department, including up to dozens of people. If you choose this career path, you're not quite thrown to the wolves—a training counselor guides you and supports you during the early phases of your career. Once you demonstrate mastery of your first assignment, you're eligible for promotion to the next level in one of the support departments: credit, distribution, internal audit, shortage control, training, or selling services. Later you may be assigned to other departments, gathering the rounded experience you'll need so that you'll be prepared to manage a department of your own.

When you join Bloomie's as a merchandising trainee, you'll be assigned to work with a seasoned department manager on the selling floor of the famous flagship store. You'll assist with displaying merchandise and monitoring stock levels and will be able to put to use what you're learning in the classroom. The department manager will give you feedback.

While you are a trainee, you'll report to the executive training squad manager, who will be reviewing your progress and determining your placement in various departments. As a trainee, you'll rotate through several departments in various merchandising divisions to gain a broad understanding of the company's procedures and systems.

Usually the first permanent assignment—assistant department manager—comes after three months. Your daily responsibilities will include merchandise presentation, record keeping, stock maintenance, and inventory control. From assistant department manager, the career path is central assistant buyer, then department manager, then associate buyer or buyer. From there, you'll move into senior management positions, beginning with store divisional merchandise manager, central divisional merchandise manager, and vice president.

The training process at Bloomingdale's begins on your first day on the job. Topics include merchandise math, purchase order management, consumer buying habits, forecasting, buying concepts, merchandise presentation, and business writing. Even after you begin to move through the ranks, you'll return to the classroom on occasion to sharpen your skills and to participate in management training of greater depth.

The Payoff

Salaries at Bloomie's are just like all other stores in New York City—low- to mid-twenties, give or take a bit. In addition to salary, there is a generous discount on all purchases, which "increases your spending power significantly." Bloomie's is quite generous with vacation time and offers you most major holidays plus up to three weeks in the first year. Benefits are on the generous side of standard and include partial tuition reimbursement for work-related courses.

The Word

Bloomingdale's is the all-time department store innovator. It was the first to sell the sizzle along with the steak. As far back as the Bloomingdale brothers, there was great innovation happening in the "East Side Bazaar," and they knew that publicity counted, that shopping had to be made fun. When other stores were using elevators only to move merchandise, Bloomingdale's decorated an elevator in mahogany and velvet, and called it a sky carriage to carry customers.

In recent years, Bloomie's has confronted real competition in the New York market, and observers have commented that she's over the hill, that soon people will say "we knew her when." But, for now, Bloomingdale's, led by Harvard B.A. Traub, continues to grow and prosper, in its creative tradition of plenty of sizzle.

THE BOSTON CONSULTING GROUP, INC.

Contact Info:
Alan J. Zakon, Chairman

Lisa Lyons, Recruiting Director
Exchange Place
Boston, Massachusetts 02109
(617) 973-1200

The Organization

The Boston Consulting Group (BCG) is an international leader in corporate strategy. Founded in 1963 with two consultants working out of a single room, the firm has grown at a furious pace. By 1966, BCG moved into a twenty-room suite, and four years later, it expanded to an entire floor. Growth for the first eleven years was a whopping 35 percent compounded annually. By 1977, there were over 200 professionals working for BCG, with nearly half that number overseas. Today the firm has more than 350 consultants working out of New York, Chicago, Los Angeles, San Francisco, London, Paris, Milan, Munich, Düsseldorf, and Tokyo, as well as the Boston headquarters.

BCG's founders had a vision: "that a small, eclectic group of well-trained but unconventional business thinkers could change the world; that by helping companies to think more deeply and creatively about their businesses and to act on those insights, we could create greater wealth in the world, and disproportionately greater wealth for our clients." The firm's clients are typically the chief executive officers and senior line managers of major corporations worldwide, many of whom have been clients for a number of years. Known as a haven for brainy types, BCG's focus is on solving highly complex business problems. Increasingly the firm is focusing on the management of innovation, by working with traditional clients to develop new businesses and redirect existing businesses. BCG is also working with entrepreneurial companies and smaller ventures within established companies to commercialize new technologies and ideas.

The Jobs

BCG's recruiting efforts are directed at campus superstars across the country. Since the firm goes in for heavy analytical and conceptual thinking, high grades are important. In fact, BCG prides itself on being "uniquely a place to sustain the pace of learning experienced in a top academic program." You'll find more Phi Beta Kappas at BCG than you will at most firms its size—perhaps because the primary recruiting targets are Harvard, Yale, Stanford, Princeton, Brown, Dartmouth, and the University of Pennsylvania. According to the firm, the best candidates have "superior academic training, an intense curiosity about the world, and abundant personal energy." Interviews are notoriously tough for entry-level consulting jobs; most students report being drilled and grilled nearly to the point of distraction. If you've taken—and done well on—the GMAT or LSAT, make sure to submit your scores with your résumé. They'll help substantiate any claims you make about your quantitative abilities.

Each year BCG hires a couple of dozen research associates for a two-year training stint. Following a brief orientation, you'll be put on a team, which usually consists of an officer, a manager, two or three consultants, and an associate consultant. Each member of your team will assume initial responsibility for a portion of the project, and together you'll work through the conclusions and implications with the client. While you'll be encouraged to learn from the senior members of your team, you'll also be expected to maximize your individual autonomy. As a new associate, you'll perform financial analyses, conduct field interviews, acquire data, and prepare and deliver presentations. Some of this work may be of a highly theoretical nature; BCG is frequently involved in considering a company's future position rather than how to make existing operations more efficient.

BCG's offices are purposely kept small, and staffing is lean. This way you'll be able to maintain close working relationships and a free flow of ideas. You may work on broad issues, such as resource deployment, financial policy, and international competition, or on specific questions of pricing, product and market focus, manufacturing structure, and sales policy. You'll learn how to look through your clients' eyes at themselves, their competition, and their markets. To a large extent, you'll be expected to determine your own role in the firm, as a function of your aptitudes and interests. You'll be responsible for maintaining your own schedule and managing your own time. While you won't be expected to develop client assignments yourself, you will be encouraged to develop close relationships with senior staffers. Travel will be an essential part of your job, and you may be on the road for several days each month. After two years, most associates return to graduate school for a business or law degree, although a few stellar candidates may continue on and be promoted to consultant. After two or three years as a consultant, the next step is manager. Following six or seven more years, successful managers will become vice presidents and have a partnership stake in the firm.

The Payoff

BCG offers an extremely competitive salary and benefits package, including major medical, disability, and group life insurance. According to the firm, "Salary levels at hiring must necessarily reflect education, experience, and maturity. There will not be exact fits to potential performance. Initial rates may or may not reflect the initial value to the organization. However, salary levels after the first year will rapidly reflect the actual contribution to the organization's performance." The normal rate of salary progress is around 15 percent annually in real terms—which means that your salary should quadruple between the age of twenty-five and thirty-five. If you're making substantially less, the firm considers it "a good indication that consulting should not be considered a lifetime career and election as an officer is unlikely." BCG's system of performance measurement and recognition is simple. Your project managers report on your progress, and you get an appropriate raise.

The Word

Liberal arts grads give BCG top marks for training. "At first, I was a bit overwhelmed by the caliber of work I was expected to do," says one former associate. "But I got up to speed quickly and began to really enjoy the challenge." The firm's corporate culture is highly supportive, and people seem to matter a great deal. Indeed, BCG describes itself as "a group of professionals who share an extraordinary level of talent and a common set of values. We respect one another's abilities and independence, and enjoy one another's company." Modest it's not, but this statement does ring true. The firm has a low attrition rate, and when professionals leave, they generally go off to become heads of major companies or to start their own firms. One of BCG's most famous émigrés is Bill Bain, who started the company that bears his name and has become twice as big as his former home.

From what we've heard, self-motivation is the key to success at BCG. Since you won't be supervised in the usual sense, you'll have to be driven from within. Sometimes you may have to balance contradictory aims, such as appearing outwardly passive while remaining inwardly aggressive. The complexity of client-consultant relationships demands an unusual combination of skills, and to make it at BCG, you'll have to reconcile conflicting characteristics. While the firm is low key, it is high performance. As it says, "For the right person, BCG is the best job in the business."

BOOZ, ALLEN & HAMILTON INC.

Contact Info:

Michael McCullough, Chairman and CEO

Nancee Martin, Manager of University Relations

101 Park Avenue

New York, New York 10178
(212) 697-1900

The Organization

Booz, Allen & Hamilton is the granddaddy of management consulting in America. As the nation's oldest and largest consulting firm, it's been around for two and three times as long as many of its toughest competitors. Since 1914, Booz, Allen has advised businesses, governments, and institutions across the world. Known as a general consulting firm, it handles issues relating to organization, planning, manufacturing, marketing, information systems, personnel, administration, finance, and strategy. Many of Booz, Allen's clients are *Fortune* "500" top management, although it also deals with the managers of smaller, up-and-coming businesses. As consulting has boomed in recent years, the firm has scrambled a bit to keep up with rapid change. However, since the industry has an annual growth rate of 20 percent, there appears to be room for both the young mavericks and the more traditional firms. And one advantage Booz, Allen clearly has is a vast network of offices spanning the globe. The firm is represented everywhere from Cleveland and Caracas to San Francisco and São Paulo.

The Jobs

Booz, Allen employs more than sixteen hundred professionals and hires several dozen new consultants each year. Liberal arts grads are hired for the research analyst position, which offers some of the best training in the industry. While the firm has expressed a particular interest in students who major in economics, engineering, computer science, or business, anyone with good grades (usually in the top 10 percent of the class) and a high motivation level is welcome to apply. Booz, Allen is known for hiring a lion's share of Ivy Leaguers, although many other colleges and universities are also represented. Well-rounded types are favored, particularly those who've demonstrated leadership in a sport or a student organization. Since the firm maintains a clubby atmosphere, it's important that you fit in with the corporate culture. Typically, research analysts are on the road one or two days a week, although some projects may take you away for weeks at a time. So stay-at-home types need not apply.

When you arrive at Booz, Allen, you'll be trained in basic consulting techniques. You'll learn analytical and research procedures, and how to make oral and written presentations. Once you've mastered the essential skills, you'll be assigned to a case team, which is at the heart of your experience. As a new team member, you're likely to act as a fact finder, defining problems and researching in-depth solutions to them. You'll be responsible for developing recommendations, writing reports, and making presentations. Booz, Allen believes in giving new recruits plenty of exposure to clients, so you'll probably do a fair amount of traveling. While senior staffers will be available to offer guidance, you'll be expected to manage yourself to a great extent. As you progress, you should develop an ability to generalize and conceptualize from your exposure. In other words, you should be able to apply what your first experience teaches you to your second, and so on. Although most analysts return to graduate school after two years, on occasion, an exceptionally talented individual will be invited to remain and move up the career ladder.

The Payoff

Apparently seven decades have shown Booz, Allen that the best salaries command the best staffers. Liberal arts grads generally start in the low-thirties range and are given generous bonuses—and often raises—within the first year. The firm's comprehensive benefits package includes medical, health, and life insurance. Perks are abundant in the consulting business, and Booz, Allen is no exception. When you travel, you travel in high style—and that's anywhere from Abu Dhabi to Algiers.

The Word

Management consulting is still a relatively young field. The rules are changing all the time, and new firms seem to enter the business daily. While Booz, Allen has a stronghold on most of its long-term clients, some of its sexier competitors are stealing away the hottest raw talent. To be sure, the firm still interviews more than ten candidates for every one it hires, and thousands of résumés still flood the recruiting office. However, to remain competitive, Booz, Allen has to become increasingly creative and innovative. "A few of the Boston-based start-ups have really stolen the firm's thunder," says one former analyst. "It's time the people at the top realized that they've got to make it more attractive to an entrepreneurial generation."

From what we've heard, Booz, Allen offers an environment that is simultaneously stimulating and friendly. The words "cutthroat" and "individualistic" were never mentioned. Instead, present and former staffers talked about the "open," "warm," and "familial" atmosphere. "There's no need for a dog-eat-dog mentality," says one analyst. "Since we've been around so long, we've proved our excellence over and over." If you want a top training experience without working in ultracompetitive surroundings, Booz, Allen may be the perfect spot.

LEO BURNETT COMPANY, INC.

Contact Info:

John J. Kinsella, President and Chief Executive Officer

Debbie Kamykowski, Recruitment Coordinator
Prudential Plaza
Chicago, Illinois 60601
(312) 565-5959

Financials (1985):

Billings: $1.868 billion
Net Income: $269.4 million

The Organization

Leo Burnett Company, Inc. is a worldwide organization consisting of forty offices in thirty-four countries. Its headquarters are in Chicago and it is one of two United States advertising agencies in the "top ten" that are headquartered outside New York. In the United States, its current client list numbers twenty-seven accounts; ten of these accounts have been with Leo Burnett for twenty-five years or longer. Clients include Allstate Insurance, General Motors, H. J. Heinz, Hewlett-Packard, Maytag, Pillsbury, Procter & Gamble, 7-Up, and United Airlines.

Leo Burnett is best known for its apples, despite the fact that its trademark is a hand reaching for a cluster of stars. (This symbol sums up the company's philosophy in the words of Leo Burnett himself: "When you reach for the stars, you may not quite get one, but you won't come up with a handful of mud either.") The first day Leo Burnett opened for business, August 5, 1935, the receptionist set out a bowl of fresh apples to welcome visitors to the agency. Since then, apples have said welcome to very visitor and client coming through Leo Burnett doors each business day, everywhere in the world. In 1985, the agency gave away 440,713 apples.

The Jobs

Smart people are best advised to do what they can to get into one of the two dozen or so spots that go to trainees who are hired directly off college campuses. Starting dates are staggered throughout the year. Deb Kamykowski looks for people who are creative, intelligent problem-solvers with excellent communication and interpersonal skills for the Burnett Client Service Development Program. "We seek people who have a superior track record of accomplishments and leadership. While prior experience is not necessary, since we provide extensive on-the-job training, we seek strong interest in advertising and marketing."

The Client Service Program combines on-the-job training with supplemental programs that are intended to groom outstanding account executives. The first job is client service trainee, and initial training takes about a year, sometimes longer. The trainee learns the ropes and develops, produces, and airs superior advertising, all the while reporting to an account executive.

Every four months trainees are evaluated and, once superior performance is demonstrated, the client service trainee is promoted to assistant account executive. In that capacity, you learn to lead and manage your accounts by building upon the skills you have already begun to develop. Assistant account executives are assigned to a single client brand, for this assignment is intended to expose you to a broad range of both marketing analysis and advertising developments. Concurrently the assistant account executive is expected to successfully manage two major projects, from initial plans through client presentations.

The agency's top management, as well as outside executives, supplement on-the-job training with two series of after-hours seminars. All trainees attend the "Wednesday Seminar Program," and the "Advanced Seminar Program" is attended by those trainees who are assigned to the Client Service Division. Each trainee participates in another series of ten media training classes sponsored by the Media Research Department.

And while you're getting started, you're encouraged to turn to a mentor. The adviser program extends to the assistant account executive stage, and your adviser/mentor is there to show you the ropes, to be a sympathetic ear, and to help you formulate realistic career goals—all in strict confidence.

The goal of the entire training program is to prepare you to assume full responsibility as an account executive with your own brand.

The Payoff

Leo Burnett is a nine-star employer in terms of pay and benefits, according to the authors of *The 100 Best Companies to Work for in America*. From profit sharing to tuition reimbursement, the company offers all the perks you could be hoping for, plus some. With entry-level salaries in the twenty-thousand-dollar range, it's no wonder that the decision to accept an offer to head for the Windy City is often no decision at all. "For me, it was simply a question of when I would start," says an assistant account executive hired off the Dartmouth campus two years ago.

The Word

"Friendly" and "homey" are two ways that Leo Burnett's ambience is often described. A 1985 story in *Business Week* about Leo Burnett was titled, "A Folksy Ad Agency Goes on the Offensive." It concluded in a very upbeat tone, "Suddenly, after years of dismissing Burnett as an old pair of loafers—worn out and comfortable—everyone is taking note."

Just like its legendary character Charlie the Tuna, Leo Burnett has a classic style that makes many people feel right at home from their first day at work. Ask yourself if you feel comfortable with tradition and then ask yourself if you want to be part of making some tradition. While its advertising can sometimes be homespun, Leo Burnett certainly is well lauded for just that by companies like Kellogg and United Airlines, who recognize that heartwarming advertising will always be fashionable.

Anyone for an apple?

CENTRAL INTELLIGENCE AGENCY

Contact Info:

Robert M. Gates, Director of Central Intelligence

Herbert Simmons, Chief, Washington Area Recruitment
P.O. Box 12406
Arlington, Virginia 22209
(703) 351-2028

Robert D. Peterson, Personnel Representative
P.O. Box 4688
Atlanta, Georgia 30302
(404) 221-6669

Kent Cargile, Personnel Representative
P.O. Box 50611
Dallas, Texas 75250
(214) 767-8550

Stephen Conn, Personnel Representative
P.O. Box 9111
John F. Kennedy Post Office
Boston, Massachusetts 02114
(617) 223-0443

Gerald Crawford, Personnel Representative
P.O. Box 1412
Chicago, Illinois 60690
(312) 353-0311

R. Stephen Gunn, Personnel Representative
P.O. Box 3009
Cincinnati, Ohio 45201
(513) 684-3860

Thomas White, Personnel Representative
P.O. Box 38428
Denver, Colorado 80238
(303) 388-2226

A. Maughan Lee, Personnel Representative
P.O. Box 3127
South El Monte, California 91733
(818) 442-0267

James T. Fitzgerald, Personnel Representative
P.O. Box 2303
South Hackensack, New Jersey
(201) 342-8835

Russell Miller, Personnel Representative
P.O. Box 1255
Pittsburgh, Pennsylvania 15230
(412) 644-2813

The Organization

The Central Intelligence credo is the following: "We are the
Central Intelligence Agency. We produce timely and high quality
intelligence for the President and the Government of the United
States. We provide objective and unbiased evaluations and are
always open to new perceptions and ready to challenge conventional wisdom. We perform special intelligence tasks at the request of the President. We conduct our activities and ourselves
according to the highest standards of integrity, morality, and
honor and according to the spirit and letter of our law and Consti-

tution. We measure our success by contribution to the protection and enhancement of American values, security, and national interest. We believe our people are the Agency's most important resource. We seek the best and work to make them better. We subordinate our desire for public recognition to the need for confidentiality. We strive for continuing professional improvement. We give unfailing loyalty to each other and to our common purpose. We seek through our leaders to stimulate initiative, a commitment to excellence and a propensity for action; to protect and reward Agency personnel for their special responsibilities, contributions, and sacrifices, to promote a sense of mutual trust and shared responsibility. We get our inspiration and commitment to excellence from the inscription in our foyer: 'And Ye shall know the truth and the truth shall make you free.' "

The Agency has no law enforcement or security functions, either at home or abroad. It is governed by presidential executive order and law, and the nation's elected officials oversee all U.S. intelligence activities through the congressional oversight process.

Neither the number of employees nor the size of the Agency's budget can be publicly disclosed. Only the President can direct the Agency to undertake a covert action. Such actions are recommended by the National Security Council. Once asked, the director of Central Intelligence must notify the intelligence oversight committees of the Congress. Covert actions are considered when the National Security Council judges that U.S. foreign policy objectives may not be fully realized by normal diplomatic means and when military action is deemed too extreme an option. Therefore, the Agency may be directed to conduct a special activity abroad in support of foreign policy such that the role of the U.S. government is neither apparent nor publicly acknowledged.

The Jobs

The Agency carefully selects well-qualified people in nearly all fields of study. Scientists, economists, linguists, and mathematicians are but a few of the disciplines continually in demand. Many people are generalists, people who have demonstrated their qualifications to hold the many varied positions that make up the bulk of the domestic and overseas staffs.

Agency professionals whose job it is to deal with subjects like politics, economics, military strategy, and geography are highly trained and educated. In its constant pursuit of information, the CIA is very much like a university. And like a university, it has a place for people with a wide range of specialties. For example, historians, political scientists, area specialists, and linguists find producing current intelligence and working with people overseas challenging assignments. Others produce biographic studies or translate foreign language documents. Geographers can prepare specialized reports and maps concerned primarily with the environmental characteristics of foreign areas. And there is also the demanding work of managing the Agency itself; managers come from liberal arts backgrounds, too.

The Payoff

Government salaries are generous at the entry level, in the high teens to mid-twenties easily, depending upon your qualifications. The benefits package is extensive, too.

The Word

What can we tell you about the pros and cons of joining the elite ranks of intelligence? Just remember that entry-level life is still entry-level life, even if you're working for the world's most mysterious employer.

CHASE MANHATTAN BANK

Contact Info:

Willard C. Butcher, Chairman

Robert Mollusky, Manager of College Relations
One Chase Manhattan Plaza
New York, New York 10081
(212) 676-2771

Financials (1985):

Assets: $86.9 billion
Deposits: $59.7 billion
Loans: $61.2 billion

The Organization

Chase Manhattan's roots lie in a 1955 merger between the Chase National Bank and the Bank of Manhattan, two venerable New York financial institutions. The merger was engineered by John J. McCloy, the brilliant international lawyer who was lionized by the post–World War II generation. Chase Manhattan has close ties with David Rockefeller, who controls about 5 percent of Chase stock. Rockefeller served as president, chief executive, and chairman of the bank in the 1960s and 1970s. In 1981, he turned the reins over to Willard Butcher, who has worked for Chase since his graduation from Brown University in 1947.

Currently Chase ranks after Citibank as the largest bank in New York and after Bank of America as the third largest bank in the United States. It's got more than three hundred domestic branches, fifty major subsidiaries, and operations in more than a hundred countries. In addition, Chase is moving rapidly into interstate banking, with banks in Delaware, Florida, Maryland, and Ohio. An aggressive marketer, Chase provides a full range of financial services to corporations, banks, governments, and individuals around the world. Chase is known in the industry as a banker's bank, since it utilizes an extensive correspondent network. Over the past few years, Chase has closed several branches in lower-income areas to focus on its most profitable sectors; today the bank specializes in moving money around for large-scale customers. Always a big player in foreign exchange trading, Chase has lately benefited from active international markets. In addition, Chase's fee-based services, such as credit cards, investment banking, and trusts, have performed well over the past couple of years.

Recently senior management made a fundamental reassessment of the future for Chase and developed an "integrated set of specific strategic thrusts" to accomplish. These goals include continuing the bank's long-standing commitment to the corporate marketplace and adopting a global approach to selected corporate industries; marketing consumer services beyond the current New York base and focusing on the development of financial products tailored to specific market segments; aggressively pursuing the worldwide private banking market for individuals; emphasizing selected profitable products to middle-market businesses; expanding in the real estate market; and structuring government business to complement other business initiatives.

The Jobs

Chase employs about 45,000 people and hires about 200 new graduates annually. Considered one of the top places to begin a banking career, Chase mainly hires Ivy Leaguers and graduates of other prestigious schools. Less than 10 percent of undergraduates interviewed generally receive job offers. According to the bank, candidates should have three broad categories of credentials: traditional professional business skills; a solid grounding in management theory and capability of understanding and applying management skills; and "a philosophy and vision that encompasses social forces well beyond the immediate concerns of business at hand." Most liberal arts grads enter Chase's Credit Development Program as preparation for the relationship manager position. This program proceeds through two phases: first, a period of formal credit development and analysis work, for six to eight months; and second, a line assignment offering exposure to Chase's business units and an opportunity to refine credit analysis skills. At the conclusion of the program, you may be placed in one of the following banking areas: International, Corporate Industries, Institutional Banking, Real Estate, Asset-based Finance, or Credit Audit. Limited opportunities also exist in the Treasury, Operations, and Capital Markets divisions. While many positions exist in the New York area, relationship managers may also be placed around the country or abroad.

The Payoff

Chase offers a competitive salary and benefits package, including Blue Cross/Blue Shield coverage, tuition reimbursement, free checking, and profit sharing.

The Word

If you're thinking about going to graduate business school, training at Chase is good practice—and a mighty good credential. The bank's training program is known as one of the toughest and most demanding in the industry, and it's sink or swim all the way. Twelve-hour days aren't unusual for trainees, and weekend work is a given. "I've never gotten to know a group of people as well in such a short time," says one trainee. "It's really the ultimate bonding experience."

Chase is known as a place where the individual counts. Despite the organization's size, bureaucracy is kept to a minimum. If you're not a self-starter, don't bother applying to Chase. There's little hand-holding, even at beginning levels. Survivors of the training program remain go-getters as they proceed through the bank's ranks. Many trainees never leave the bank; for example, chairman Willard Butcher began at Chase National Bank in 1947 and spent thirty years climbing to the top. The bank's philosophy: "We believe you should take ownership of your job, your responsibilities, your decisions. You are responsible for the bank's performance. The emphasis is on delivering results. *Your* delivery. *Your* results." Chase alumni can be found at most major commercial and investment banks throughout the country, forging lucrative deals and brainstorming innovative financial tools.

CHEMICAL BANK

Contact Info:

Walter V. Shipley, Chairman

Mary DeLoache, College Relations Manager
277 Park Avenue
New York, New York 10172
(212) 310-6752

Financials (1985):
   Assets: $52.3 billion
   Deposits: $33.7 billion
   Loans: $36.9 billion

The Organization

As the sixth largest bank in the nation, Chemical Bank is a dominant force in a major money center market. One of the nation's oldest financial institutions, Chemical was originally chartered in 1824 as a subsidiary of a chemical manufacturing company. Twenty years later, it became a purely financial institution. Today the bank has a strong niche in retail, commercial, and investment banking. Currently Chemical has more than 270 domestic offices and 60 foreign branches, and about one-third of its net income comes from international business. Worldwide, the bank provides a comprehensive range of financial services to individuals, corporations, financial institutions, and governments.

Chemical's operations are broken down into six business groups: world banking group, personal and banking services, Chemical Bank investment banking, financial management, operations, and staff functions. As deregulation has begun eroding profit margins on the bank's traditional business mix, Chemical has started investigating new sources of revenue. According to the bank, "the distinctions among financial institutions are becoming hazy, and we must compete not only with other banks but also with other financial institutions such as brokerage and investment firms." Indeed, Chemical's entry into investment banking signifies its new willingness to take risks. Over several years, Chemical has developed staff for mergers and acquisitions, venture capital, private placement, merchant banking, and public financial services. With an average daily trading volume of more than $40 billion, the bank is recognized as a major market maker. Unlike other leading New York banks, Chemical has steered clear of heavy lending to the agricultural, energy, and real estate sectors, thereby protecting itself from overexposure in these volatile areas.

The Jobs

Chemical, employing twenty thousand people, is a big fan of liberal arts grads. Dozens are hired annually for the bank's many different training programs. Chemical says individuals should possess "common sense, intelligence, an aptitude for logical analysis, communicative skills, quantitative ability, and high achievement motivation." The bank offers entry-level jobs in credit training, auditing, financial accounting, data processing, capital markets operations, financial management, and general management. The credit training program prepares officers for domestic lending, international lending, middle-market lending, and real estate lending. Although the programs vary, most involve about six months of credit training courses and case analysis. Following completion of the classroom stint, you rotate among several departments, working with experienced lending officers. Upon completion of this phase, you leave for your designated functional area. The stated goal of the program is "to develop strong credit analysts who can analyze and assess risk, and present and support their conclusions concisely." And, according to the bank, you should take "as much responsibility as you can handle—and as soon as you can accept it."

The Payoff

Chemical offers outstanding starting salaries and a comprehensive benefits program. Included are medical, dental, life, and disability coverage, as well as free checking, reduced loan and credit card rates, and a savings incentive plan. After three years of service, you're eligible for Chemical's profit sharing plan, and after one year, you're automatically enrolled in the bank's retirement plan.

The Word

Chemical is making its move into the upper reaches of commercial banking. Although the bank doesn't enjoy the lofty reputation associated with some of its peers, such as Morgan Guaranty or Bankers Trust, it's increasingly known as an up-and-coming player. Trainees say the program is difficult, and some don't make it all the way through. Failure in several parts of the course work can mean you get the boot. But Chemical plays by the rules and tries to give every trainee a fair shake. "The only guy I know who didn't make it out of the training program really didn't care. Over and over, people tried to help him, but he just wasn't into doing the quantity or quality of work," says one former trainee.

For those who do advance, Chemical offers good feedback. There are frequent performance appraisals and career planning sessions, as well as in-house management and technical programs. The bank also encourages you to pursue job-related academic study and will provide full tuition reimbursement. Unlike some of its superconservative competitors, Chemical doesn't revolve around an old-boy network or a country-club chumminess. Results seem to matter more than connections. Most of the bank's top officers worked their way up from the ground floor; Walter Shipley, the chairman, started at the bank after graduating from New York University, and Robert Lipp entered the training program immediately after finishing Harvard Business School. Likewise, executive vice presidents Edward O'Neal, Jr., and Kenneth LaVine, Jr., began their careers at Chemical as trainees.

CHUBB GROUP OF INSURANCE COMPANIES

Contact Info:

Henry L. Harder, Chairman and President

Frank M. Paolucci, National Recruiting Coordinator
15 Mountain View Road
P.O. Box 1615
Warren, New Jersey 07061
(201) 580-2219

Financials (1985):

Total Revenues: $2,394,023,000
Net Income: $70,540,000

The Organization

"While an insurance policy is a legal contract that expresses our minimum responsibility, there are many occasions when equity demands that we recognize a moral obligation beyond the strictly legal terms—and this is always a consideration in our settlements."

Hendon Chubb (1874–1960)

In 1967, Chubb & Son Inc., along with the property and liability insurance companies it manages, became a wholly owned subsidiary of a holding company called The Chubb Corporation.

Today the corporation, which includes its real estate subsidiary, Bellemead Development Corporation, and its life insurance subsidiary, Chubb LifeAmerica, has over 38 million publicly traded shares of stock. *Fortune* ranks it as the forty-second largest diversified financial organization in the United States. The largest contributor is the Chubb Group of Insurance Companies, accounting for $5.8 billion dollars in assets.

The Chubb Group demonstrates the following characteristics:

$2.3 billion in property and liability premiums for business and individual clients in 1985.

Representation by 3,000 independent agents and brokers served by 6,800 people in 50 branch offices in the United States and Canada.

An international network including offices in Latin America, South America, the Caribbean, Europe, Australia, Hong Kong, Japan, and Singapore. In addition, Chubb is represented by affiliates and liaison companies in 92 countries worldwide.

Chubb offers the conventional coverages that are the bread and butter of the insurance industry and, by emphasizing service to customers with special needs, has carved a niche for itself where experience and service are the compelling reasons for recommending and purchasing its insurance products. In personal insurance, Chubb has excelled at designing products for people who can best be described as affluent. In commercial insurance, Chubb offers products to a broad base of businesses and industries. Chubb has also developed special insurance programs to fit the individual needs of such target industries as electronics manufacturing, plastic working, metalworking, printing, and publishing. And the list of successful innovations runs on and on. For example, Chubb's unique Department of Financial Institutions is known as a leader in offering property and liability protection to banks, stock brokerages, insurance companies, and investment firms. Its Executive Protection insurance program acknowledges the growing need for coverage in the event of kidnap, for alleged mishandling of pension funds, or for damages arising out of serving on a corporation's board of directors.

The Jobs

Chubb's recruitment brochure asks, "What would it be like to work in an industry . . . where your decisions place millions of your company's dollars on the line? where market pressures are determined by daily changes in the rate of U.S. Treasury bills or the anticipated course of a hurricane? where your judgment and negotiating skills directly affect the profitability of the firm?" It suggests, "If you are searching for a career that offers this kind of challenge, the property/casualty insurance industry may be for you." There should be one other suggestion inserted as early in this company's profile as possible: that is, only the best and the brightest need apply, for Chubb is to insurance what The Morgan Bank is to commercial banking—elite and elitist.

The entry-level jobs at Chubb are in underwriting, operations, claims, loss control, and actuarial. Throughout the recruitment materials, liberal arts graduates from schools like Hobart, Princeton, and Smith are featured, along with insight into each of the career paths. The company hires less than two hundred trainees each year, many of who begin as underwriters.

The skills of successful underwriters are developed through a combination of textbook knowledge and experience. The ability to grasp theoretical underwriting concepts and effectively apply them in practical business situations is a skill you'll need.

Trainees are hired for specific underwriting departments: commercial lines, marine, personal lines, surety, executive protection, financial institutions, international, or other specialty departments, to work in one of the company's fifty offices throughout the United States and Canada. Each department has a training program that provides extensive technical knowledge and on-the-job experience during your initial nine to twelve months with Chubb. Many departments present their technical underwriting concepts during structured training seminars in Chubb's Warren, New Jersey, corporate headquarters. These seminars range from two to eleven weeks in length and involve lectures, case studies, role enactments, and discussion groups.

As a trainee, the majority of your experience will be in a branch office, working closely with an underwriter who is responsible for your development. You will analyze new and existing accounts and recommend courses of action to your supervisor. As you are exposed to an increasing number of different underwriting situations and as you exchange ideas with other members of the department, you will develop your own approach to problem solving. When you demonstrate your command of underwriting concepts, you'll begin to deliver proposals directly to agents and brokers. In order to help prepare you for these face-to-face negotiations, you'll participate in marketing/negotiating strategy workshops intended to help you refine your listening, selling, and writing skills.

Bill Specht, a Princeton grad who works in the Commercial Lines Division, said, "Chubb offered an underwriting job that called for salesmanship, judgment, and the ability to work closely with customers." He lauded his experience: "I have been challenged every step of the way. From a personal point of view, I feel I have grown with each and every challenge." The reports from people who are on the other career tracks are similar. Leslie Conti, Excess/Umbrella and International Manager, Seattle office, graduated from Dickinson College and chose the actuarial route. She said, "Chubb has advanced my career along a path both challenging and fun (yes, insurance is fun!) and Chubb accomplished this with only one geographic move on my part. This was a more difficult task than it sounds, as I work in a medium-size branch with only fifteen underwriters in six departments. As a trainee, I moved to the Northwest and decided to stay. In many companies, that decision could have doomed my career. Chubb, being an incredibly people-oriented company, has worked hard to progress my career in a rewarding and innovative manner."

The Payoff

Starting salaries are competitive with the financial services business; and, if your job performance is outstanding, greater compensation comes quickly. Formal evaluations of your performance are conducted at least once each year. The benefits package is extensive, and the quality of colleagues is a real plus.

The Word

If you're looking to work in the upper end of the financial services marketplace, the Chubb family is the right one to get adopted by. This is a family that has insured such movie stars as the ten sea gulls who were trained for the lead in *Jonathan Livingston Seagull.*

The light side of the business aside, this is a family that stresses excellence: excellent breeding, excellent education, excellent performance, excellent training. Chairman/president Harder is a Yalie, and his kind of background seems to predominate. So if you're up for moving to the horse country of Warren County, New Jersey, where Chubb's home office is located, or are interested in settling in one of the branch locations, including Atlanta, Chicago, Dallas, Los Angeles, Minneapolis, New York City, Philadelphia, Pittsburgh, San Francisco, and Toronto, get your best "dressed for success" look on, and persuade Chubb's recruiters and line executives that you're made of the right stuff. "My advice," suggested a Williams graduate, "is that you study the company and its strategy and take the approach of convincing your interviewers why you should be part of the team. When I go on campus to recruit prospective employees, everyone I take seriously is smart and presentable. What I look for is men and women who will bring added value to the office. That added value might be an interest in sailing or in wine tasting. What I mean is that we want complete people, not number crunchers or yes-men."

CITIBANK

Contact Info:

John S. Reed, Chairman

Debra Quinn, Director of Recruiting Services
1 CitiCorp Center
153 East 53 Street
New York, New York 10043
(212) 559-4875

Financials (1985):

Assets: $150.6 billion
Deposits: $90 billion
Loans: $102.7 billion

The Organization

There's no doubt about it: Citibank has remained number one in the U.S. banking industry for nearly a decade. With some twelve hundred offices in forty-two states and eighteen hundred branches in ninety-two foreign countries, the Citi's sheer magnitude is daunting. Founded in 1812 as The City Bank of New York to replace the local branch of the defunct First Bank of the United States, Citibank's growth has been nothing short of astounding. In 1914, the bank became the first in the United States to open an international office, in Buenos Aires. Two years later, Citibank purchased the International Banking Corporation, a firm with offices around the globe, and was on its way to becoming a gigantic conglomerate.

Today Citibank's total capital is the largest amount held by any privately owned financial institution in the world. Wherever you go, the Citi truly never seems to sleep. Although half of Citibank's income comes from large international transactions, the bank competes aggressively for even the smallest consumer account on home turf. Citibank pioneered many aspects of modern banking: in the late 1920s, it was the first bank to offer consumers personal loans; in the early 1960s, it invented the certificate of deposit; and in the mid-1970s, it came up with the concept of the automated teller.

Currently Citibank serves individuals, corporations, financial institutions, and governments practically across the planet. The bank refers to its core businesses as the five I's: Individual Bank Sector, Institutional Bank Sector, Investment Bank Sector, Insurance Business, and Information Business. Each of these units is run separately and directed by its own management team. Individual Banking handles transactional services, savings services, and loan services. Institutional Banking is responsible for worldwide business with corporations, governments, nonprofit organizations, and financial institutions. Investment Banking deals with securities trading and brokerage, foreign exchange and money market activities, investment management, venture capital, private placements, municipal underwriting, and other related products and services. The insurance group is engaged in "efforts . . . to eliminate regulations that prohibit chartered banks in the United States from engaging in the insurance business." The information group handles technology research and development, overseeing Citicorp's 160 data centers and 6,000 technical staffers.

The Jobs

With some 85,000 employees, Citibank just edges out Bank of America for having the largest number of bank staffers. Since the bank's hiring process is fairly decentralized, it's hard to estimate how many liberal arts grads are hired each year. In the past, you had to be mightily impressive—or aggressive—to get noticed, because applications flood into Citicorp's New York headquarters by the thousand. Says Citibank, "We want people who present their ideas in a clear, concise, informative way and who can organize their work, develop business plans and strategies, and establish priorities. We need people with analytical ability who have demonstrated that they learn rapidly and well—because our business is complex and growing and we aim for an aggressive leadership position in all our efforts." Entry-level jobs are available in several areas: marketing, corporate banking/account management, consumer sales management, services/production management, systems/data processing, financial advisory/corporate finance, financial control, security analysis/portfolio management, and global money markets. The institutional banking, individual banking, and capital markets groups hire M.B.A.s for most of these jobs, while the financial control unit hires primarily candidates interested in systems/data processing or financial control. Most new hires receive some formal classroom training along with on-the-job learning. Citibank's training program for corporate lenders is less structured than are similar programs run by other leading commercial banks; trainees are placed directly in the area to which they have been assigned rather than waiting a year or two. Promotions from within are the rule at Citibank, and most top managers have been with the bank for at least a decade.

Recently Citibank developed a new program, called Citifrontrunners. This program was "designed to identify a small group of highly talented recent college graduates and provide them with a challenging, significant, and rewarding career path at Citicorp." Initially you report to a senior manager in the U.S. Consumer Banking Group, and you're given the opportunity to develop yourself in a variety of important assignments. The consumer banking group is one of the newest organizations within the bank, and it's "dedicated to outperforming the competition in developing new and innovative financial services characterized by service excellence." Trainees in this area start by immediately being responsible for a piece of business and then participating in a number of training courses and special seminars designed to enhance management skills. In addition, the Citifrontrunner program involves a mentor system, in which officers are assigned to trainees to help them grow professionally.

The Payoff

Citibank offers competitive salary and benefits packages. Included are medical, dental, and life insurance coverage, as well as free checking, reduced loan rates, credit card discounts, and tuition reimbursement.

The Word

Right off the bat, Citibank tells you, "Because we are decentralized, there are tremendous opportunities for individuals to run their own shows." According to trainees, this translates into a popular expression: "Those who need hand-holding need not apply." Citibank celebrates individuality and boasts that "you won't find a corporate cookie cutter [here]." That's fine, but, says one recent hire, "It's hard to tell what the corporate personality is at all. You may meet people during training whom you never see again, since everything is so spread out and everyone does his own thing."

With offices from Argentina and Australia to Zaire and Zambia, it's easy to see why decentralization works best for Citicorp. However, even though management may not be on your back, it's there. Citibank has a reputation for playing hardball and putting plenty of pressure on employees to perform. Presumably that's how it stays at the top of an enormously competitive industry. If you've gone to a big university and haven't minded being a little fish in a big pond, Citibank might be the perfect place for you. "It's a very buy-sell kind of atmosphere," says one trainee. "I wanted a commercial banking environment as exciting as an investment bank, and I got it." Citicorp was one of four commercial banks to make it into *The 100 Best Companies to Work for in America*. Said the authors, "Citicorp is hell-bent on changing the nature of banking, and it wants people who prefer living in the eye of a hurricane." That about sums it up. You've got to make yourself seen and heard, and you've got to like living in a maelstrom.

DMB&B

Contact Info:

John S. Bowen, Chairman and Chief Executive Officer

Bill Haney, Associate Personnel Manager, Account
    Management
909 Third Avenue
New York, New York 10022
(212) 758-6200

Financials (1985):

Billings: $2.2 billion

Net Income: $319.5 million

The Organization

DMB&B is a worldwide communications agency serving leading national and multinational companies. Its client roster includes Anheuser Busch, a client since 1915; General Foods, since 1929; General Motors, since 1934; and Procter & Gamble, since 1941. The agency is organized into three parts: USA Division, International Division, and Diversified Communications Companies. DMB&B has nine offices in the United States and ninety worldwide. It is one of the ten largest ad agencies and one of the most diversified; its partner companies specialize in public relations, direct mail, promotion, corporate and marketing communications, health and medical advertising, industrial advertising, and television production.

DMB&B was created in 1985 through the merger of two major agencies; its full legal name is D'Arcy Masius Benton & Bowles, Inc. During its first fifty-five years, Benton & Bowles was a leading agency for packaged goods, a pioneering agency in the use of broadcast media, and an outstanding agency for consumer marketing. D'Arcy MacManus Masius was founded in 1973 through a succession of mergers. The D'Arcy Agency had its roots in St. Louis in 1906; its original successes were with Coca-Cola, Anheuser Busch, and General Tire. MacManus, John & Adams, headquartered in Detroit, with strong representation in the automotive market, merged with D'Arcy in 1971. Masius, Wynne-Williams, a London-based international agency with a strong New York office, merged with D'Arcy MacManus in 1973.

The several strengths of DMB&B today reflect its heritage: an extensive worldwide network with offices in twenty-five countries; a great creative tradition; outstanding marketing and media capabilities; new-product-launch expertise; and an unmatched client list.

The Jobs

At DMB&B, account management is at the center of the action. It's where the resources of the agency and the needs of the client connect. The effective account manager understands both sides of the equation and serves as translator between clients and creatives. At all levels—assistant account executive, account executive, account supervisor, and management supervisor—smart people will make abundant use of their liberal arts education, their experience, and their common sense.

Your mission adds up to this: make your client's business grow through marketing planning and implementation and through strategic use of advertising and promotion. It's all a matter of learning and leading—of learning the client's business, goals, and personalities and of analyzing data, designing new research, and identifying emerging needs.

What training does, in essence, is prepare you to keep studying the newest developments in marketing and media; to get you involved in the client's marketing function; and to help you hone your judgment so that you can advise candidly, develop marketing approaches, and sell your ideas with clear and thorough logic. Concurrently you're learning about the agency support groups that will turn your concepts into reality, and you will be practicing motivating and directing the development of creative work that will move your clients' products off the shelves.

The account manager, according to the DMB&B formula, requires careful preparation, which is why the agency has developed and constantly updates its Account Management Program. From day one, you will assume management responsibilities. You'll get two account assignments; each one will last for from eight months to a year. You'll be an integral part of each group, a functioning member who is guided by an account executive. During this phase, you will be totally immersed in the business of your clients. This will mean developing marketing plans, media plans, and creative plans. It might mean covering television shoots. It will mean analyzing research, reviewing competitive advertising, checking media plan implementation, maintaining daily contact with the client, taking part in strategy sessions, and working with every agency department. Soon you'll have budgeting responsibilities. And at the same time, you'll attend seminars and workshops to get an overview of the agency operations, insights into the principles of advertising, and acquainted with DMB&B's partner companies.

Some of the agency's operations seminars are "Partner and Diversified Companies: An Overview," "Media Basics," "Music Rights," and "Consumer Promotions." Advanced seminars include "Writing Workshop," "Effective Presentations Workshop," and "Communications: A Look at the 21st Century."

As part of your training, you will develop an independent research project and present your conclusions to key agency people. You'll be promoted in a matter of months—eighteen to twenty-four, to be exact. Three or four years later, you can expect to be an account supervisor.

The Payoff

DMB&B pays you off fairly, certainly competitively, and as you move up the ranks, the dollars get to be more generous. Expect the standard array of benefits and know that more await you—as soon as you're beyond job one and two.

The Word

There has been merger mania on Madison Avenue, and DMB&B grew out of just this craze. Some observers argue that these agencies are too large and that it's easy to get overlooked in the shuffle that follows the consolidation of two pretty big players in the advertising business, not to mention all their worldwide affiliates, partners, and subsidiaries. Still, if you have the right stuff for the brave new world of Madison Avenue, DMB&B is a good choice. "I weathered the merger," says one account executive, "and am beginning to see the good that's come from the reorganization. I think that the business press hypes what's happening. In terms of my day-to-day life, very little has changed. The only difference was that when times were tense, office politics intensified. But the worst seems to be over and people are getting to be more relaxed about management shifts and what they mean."

Think about the career possibility in advertising jingles for just a second and it will be easy to be bright about the agency's future and your role in it. Like client 3M, DMB&B seems to have "something on the ball." And with "grief relief" (Pepto-Bismol, The Procter & Gamble Co.) in sight, there's "excitement ahead" (Pontiac Division).

DEAN WITTER REYNOLDS INCORPORATED

Contact Info:
Robert M. Gardiner, Chairman

Sharon Klein, M.B.A. Recruiting
#2 World Trade Center
New York, New York 10048
(212) 524-5269

The Organization

In 1924, the brothers Dean and Guy Witter, along with their cousin Jean Witter, began a brokerage firm with eight employees in San Francisco. Dean Witter was a great sportsman who published three books about the outdoors. For over four decades, he ran the firm, which eventually spread across the nation and then the world. In 1967, at the time of his retirement, Dean Witter wrote, "We have a sacred trust to protect our customers, to put their interests first." A decade later, Dean Witter merged with Reynolds Securities, in what was then the largest deal ever ($165 million) between two securities-based companies. Just three years later, Dean Witter Reynolds was bought by Sears, Roebuck and Company. Along with Allstate Insurance and Caldwell Banker, the firm is now part of one of the largest and most extensive financial services companies in the world.

Since the takeover, Dean Witter has expanded its activities to encompass a broad array of financial operations. The firm's sales force and capital base have mushroomed as it moves toward its ultimate goal: "becoming the nation's preeminent provider of securities-related and consumer financial services." Headquartered in New York, Dean Witter is divided into three operating units: Capital Markets (Investment Banking, Equity, Fixed-Income, and Realty groups); Individual Financial Services (National Sales, Marketing, and Products groups); and Consumer Banking (Sears Savings Bank, Sears Mortgage Securities Corp., Allstate Enterprises Inc., Allstate Enterprises Mortgage Corp., Greenwood Trust Co., and Discover Card Services Inc.). Since the early 1980s, the firm has nearly doubled its sales force, from six thousand to eleven thousand. Today Dean Witter has more than 650 offices located around the country, with corporate and public finance offices in Atlanta, Boston, Chicago, Dallas, Houston, Los Angeles, Miami, Philadelphia, San Francisco, and London.

The Jobs

Dean Witter employs some twenty thousand people and hires several dozen B.A.s each year. The firm recruits at Harvard, Wharton, Stanford, University of Chicago, Dartmouth, Cornell, Northwestern, Colgate, and MIT, among others. Liberal arts grads can be hired into most of the firm's departments, but the best formal training program is in investment banking. The two-year analyst program is open to candidates who have a "distinguished academic record." It's also good to have had exposure to accounting, finance, economics, and computer science, since Dean Witter doesn't offer much class work. Unlike many of its peers, the firm believes in immersing analysts immediately. From day one, you'll be a member of a project team, working alongside senior officers and assuming an active role with clients. You'll participate directly in transactions and be responsible for preparing proposals, statistical exhibits, and company and industry financial analyses. Dean Witter's banking teams are generally small, and this gives you a chance to handle extremely challenging work. The firm takes a traditional service-driven, rather than a transaction-driven, approach to investment banking. This means you'll focus on establishing long-term relationships with clients instead of simply turning around deals. Some clients, like Delta Air Lines, for example, have been with Dean Witter for four decades, from a public offering in the 1950s through a merger in the 1970s to a major bond issue in the mid-1980s. You may be placed in one of the firm's

regional investment banking offices, or in a specialty group dealing with private and project finance, leveraged buyouts, master
limited partnerships, and mergers and acquisitions. In addition,
you may be put in an industry group, such as health care, regulated industries, financial institutions, technology, and energy.

The Payoff

Dean Witter doesn't offer the highest salaries in the industry,
but it does stay competitive. Most liberal arts grads start in the
high-twenties range and earn substantially more after the first
couple of reviews. In addition, analysts receive a semiannual bonus tied to performance. Dean Witter offers a comprehensive
benefits package, including medical, dental, and life insurance
coverage, as well as discounts on several financial services.

The Word

According to one analyst, "The worst part about working for
Dean Witter is having people make the same old jokes. 'Oh, you
work for Sears, don't you? Can you get me a discount on a new
lawn mower?'" Dean Witter may be part of an enormous conglomerate, but its core businesses remain unbureaucratized. The
firm's regional structure offers the best of both worlds: the capital
and distribution capabilities of a large, national brokerage house
together with the personal attention, recognition, and availability
of an intimate operation. The firm's widely recognized investment
research team consistently ranks high in the industry, and the
corporate finance department is considered an up-and-coming
power on Wall Street. Under the new leadership of Sears, Dean
Witter has become increasingly consumer-oriented, and the firm
intends to continue providing new products and services to the
retail market. From what we've heard, liberal arts grads enjoy a
good measure of autonomy while getting plenty of guidance. In
addition, Dean Witter doesn't have a "star system" that rewards
the rugged individualist; there's room at the firm for many kinds of
people.

DONALDSON, LUFKIN & JENRETTE, INCORPORATED

Contact Info:

Richard Jenrette, Chairman

Jeanne M. Ruscio, College Recruitment
140 Broadway
New York, New York 10005
(212) 504-3903

The Organization

When people on Wall Street talk about maverick firms, Donaldson, Lufkin & Jenrette comes to mind. Back in 1959, three young Harvard Business School graduates—William Donaldson, Dan Lufkin, and Richard Jenrette—pooled $100,000 to start the first major brokerage house in more than twenty-five years. Over and over, the team used a contrarian strategy to flout convention and to alter many of the industry's traditional business habits. Rather than competing for the white-shoe customers who purchase blue-chip stocks, the firm focused on institutional investors, writing research reports on smaller companies for them. Part of DLJ's astonishing growth has to do with opening this market—which today accounts for the vast majority of brokerage fees. Over the years, the "three musketeers" continued to pioneer new areas. In 1970, for example, DLJ became the first brokerage house to make a public offering of its own stock. By going public, the firm fundamentally changed Wall Street, giving it access to the huge chunks of capital that are essential for today's financial institutions—as demonstrated by the mergers sweeping the industry. In addition, DLJ made the New York Stock Exchange a more democratic organization. It opened the floodgates for institutions to indirectly join the exchange simply by purchasing a publicly owned member firm. Soon afterward, Merrill Lynch and several other industry leaders jumped on the bandwagon.

In 1984, the Equitable Life Assurance Society bought DLJ and agreed to let the firm operate as an independent subsidiary. Today

DLJ is a full-service international investment banking firm involved in institutional trading and research, investment management, and financial and correspondent services. Unlike some investment firms that cater to the mass or retail markets, DLJ mainly concentrates on large institutions and public entities. In these areas, the firm has achieved rapid growth; although DLJ is the only major investment bank to have been founded after World War II, it has gained dominant or leading positions in most sectors of its business.

DLJ is organized into several operating divisions. The Capital Markets Group includes Agency Banking, Public Finance, Fixed Income, Sprout (venture capital), Real Estate, Institutional Equities, and Research. The Financial Services Group includes the Pershing Division and DLJ's regional brokerage network. The other major businesses are Investment Management (Alliance Capital Management) and DLJ Futures. Each division within the groups is managed as a separate entity, tailoring transactions to professional investors or to corporate clients who require a high degree of strategic financial servicing (as opposed to simple transaction servicing). The firm has offices in New York, Boston, Chicago, Dallas, Houston, Miami, San Francisco, London, Paris, Geneva, and Hong Kong.

The Jobs

DLJ isn't the biggest name in the business, but it's among the most prestigious. The firm is extremely selective and generally hires fewer than 10 percent of the students it interviews. DLJ employs some four thousand people and hires a handful of undergraduates. The firm regularly recruits at the Ivy League schools as well as at several major state universities and smaller liberal arts colleges. According to DLJ, the best candidates are "highly motivated, intelligent, creative, and are stimulated by the results-oriented, entrepreneurial work environment." Which means that only self-starters need apply.

Top recruits are hired for the investment banking/corporate finance analyst position. At DLJ, analysts assume on-the-job training immediately. You'll work on a broad range of client transactions and statistical studies, generally as a member of a project team. Most of these teams include a senior vice president, a vice president, an associate, and an analyst. DLJ's philosophy is to expose analysts to a wide array of opportunities. It's likely that you'll be involved in several deals simultaneously, ranging from mergers and divestitures to private placements or public offerings. This way you'll gain an understanding of different situations and learn from your project team members. When you start as an analyst, you'll probably spend a fair amount of time doing number crunching and providing general support to your assigned department. However, you'll be expected to learn rapidly and assume greater responsibility. According to DLJ, new hires can expect continual exposure to both senior management of the firm and senior management of corporate clients. This way you can acquire the "perspective and judgment necessary for success in an investment banking environment."

The Payoff

DLJ's salary and bonus packages are highly competitive within the industry. Most liberal arts grads start in the high-twenties to mid-thirties range, and year-end bonuses are reputed to be generous. DLJ's comprehensive benefits package includes full medical and life insurance coverage as well as a pension plan, tuition reimbursement, and other options.

The Word

According to DLJ, "This work environment is refreshingly open and informal, ensuring intellectual challenge, interaction, and opportunity." While the firm has come a long way from its maverick youth, it remains one of the least stuffy major players in the financial markets. That's not to intimate that DLJ's employees don't have an extremely professional image; as a matter of fact, the firm's chairman, Richard Jenrette, is often called the last gentleman on Wall Street. In 1984, *The Wall Street Journal* wrote, "Personable and statesmanlike, he stands out in what is becoming an increasingly competitive, and occasionally cutthroat, business." Thanks to Jenrette's hands-on style, DLJ is today known as a place where initiative and independent action are valued and an aggressive, innovative spirit can thrive. "You get the feeling that people are very loyal to the firm," says one analyst. "My boss has been here for nearly a decade, and I don't think he could be wooed away for anything. Management really seems to care about keeping good people."

FILENE'S
(a division of Federated Department Stores, Inc.)

Contact Info:
Michael J. Babcock, Chairman

William L. Blaze, Divisional Vice President, Recruiting
426 Washington Street
Boston, Massachusetts 02101
(617) 357-2438

Financials (1985):
Sales: $353.5 million

The Organization

Filene's was founded by William A. Filene, a German immigrant tailor who opened his first retail store in Boston in 1852. He was a democratic and simple man, possessing qualities of honesty and fairness. These are the qualities—combined with financial judgment and careful supervision of resources and investments in merchandise—that built Filene's into a New England institution.

William Filene's main contribution to retailing history was unique: his two sons, Edward and Lincoln. The two inherited the business in 1901 when their father died. They owned equal shares and became the best-known brother team in American retailing. Edward was a merchandising wizard and Lincoln an administrative genius who managed the store and its staff. The company grew rapidly under their leadership. A series of moves and acquisitions begun in 1901 culminated in the more than 650,000-square-foot Filene's store that now occupies an entire Boston city block.

The brothers pioneered many retailing firsts during their careers. The year 1909 saw the founding of one of the greatest marketing innovations of all time—the automatic markdown basement. World famous today, Filene's Basement now operates as a separate company within the Federated family.

Edward Filene established the first retail store credit union to keep employees from borrowing money from loan sharks; he also encouraged employees to organize a Cooperative Association to arbitrate all grievances, including discharges. Lincoln brought the store accolades for its early innovations in the field of employee relations.

Committed to the traditions, taste, and life-style of New England, the store, which grew from modest beginnings, is a Boston landmark, as well as one of the best-managed businesses in the region.

The parent company, Federated Department Stores, Inc., is a diversified retail firm serving customers across the nation through its department stores, mass merchandising stores, supermarkets, and other retail divisions. By the end of 1985, Federated had sixteen operating divisions and 604 stores in the major retail markets of 36 states. Each of the franchises operates on a decentralized basis. Filene's operates sixteen stores in New England, from Maine to Connecticut, and west to Albany, New York.

The Jobs

Filene's recruits liberal arts grads for merchandising career paths, beginning with the job of assistant buyer. Following a brief orientation period, your first position gives you the immediate opportunity to analyze, create, and run a business. This position offers you the unique opportunity to learn the intricacies of buying from experienced teachers. Twelve to eighteen months later, you will be promoted to the sales manager position.

As executive trainee/sales manager, you will maintain Filene's standard of customer service while developing floor merchandising skills, supervisory skills, and organizational skills essential to your development. After establishing yourself in this position, you'll be promoted to the senior assistant buyer level.

The senior assistant buyer position is when you're expected to pull together the skills you have learned thus far and drive your own business. In this job, you're under the close supervision of a buyer and in charge of planning, analyzing, and operating your own department.

Then, as a Filene's buyer, you'll face the challenge of sole responsibility for a several-million-dollar business.

Filene's also offers numerous positions in various divisions that support its merchandising efforts. Executive trainees begin careers in management information systems, finance and expense control, and operations management. Other sales-support career paths are human resources, general accounting, and sales promotion.

The Payoff

Rumor has it on Eastern college campuses that if Filene's wants you, its recruiters will match your best retailing offer. Salaries are excellent—mid-twenties, more or less—and benefits are comprehensive, including health care, life and travel insurance, savings plan, short-term disability insurance, credit union, paid holidays and vacations, and, of course, excellent merchandise discounts.

The Word

Lincoln Filene believed that "the store could grow if it had the right people." Today's recruiters have the same belief and practice it daily, in an attempt to win campus superstars to their camp. Filene's wines and dines recruits when they visit Beantown and, as one assistant buyer remembers, "makes you feel pretty special for having gotten that far in the process."

Boston and New England offer a unique blend of old and new, of diversity and excitement. It's a toss-up between Filene's and Jordan Marsh if you want retailing and you want Boston, so be sure that you take the time to know where you'll fit best. One rule is that Jordan's is the place for the entrepreneurs and Filene's works best for organizational men and women.

THE FIRST BOSTON CORPORATION

Contact Info:

Peter T. Buchanan, President and Chief Executive Officer

Anne Leggett, College Recruiting
Park Avenue Plaza
New York, New York 10055
(212) 909-2385

The Organization

Following the Glass-Steagall Act of 1933, which caused banks to separate their investment and commercial banking activities, several firms were forced to split their operations. First Boston was the stepchild of Chase National Bank and the First National Bank of Boston. Following World War II, First Boston expanded into a broad range of financial services. The firm became a leading underwriter for many of America's largest corporations, particularly those controlled by the Mellon family, such as Gulf Oil and Alcoa. Over the next few decades, the firm entered the international arena with great success. Soon after acquiring an ownership interest in Credit Suisse, a London-based merchant banking organization, First Boston was recognized as the market leader in global underwritings.

During the past couple of decades, the firm has gained a reputation for creativity and innovation. First Boston is credited with developing new products that become industry standards; for example, the firm pioneered the nation's first interest rate swaps, public zero coupon bonds, and health equipment loan programs. Recently the company launched an asset-backed securities group and issued the largest U.S. corporate debt offering in history.

Currently First Boston is divided into three major areas: corporate finance; public finance; and sales, trading, and research. The corporate finance department has two principal groups: investment banking (securities origination, project finance, leasing, corporate reorganizations, and corporate advisory work) and mergers and acquisitions (divestitures, takeover defense, and leveraged buyouts). First Boston's public finance department deals with public sector entities, including state and local governments, special purpose authorities, and not-for-profit corporations. In sales, trading, and research, the firm analyzes, makes markets in, and sells a wide variety of taxable fixed income, tax-exempt, and equity instruments. The department also includes First Boston's mortgage products group, which originates, sells, and trades mortgage-related securities.

First Boston deals with mainly blue-chip clients from a broad range of industries. The firm's lineup includes both public and private companies, with revenues from under $100 million to over $10 billion. Besides First Boston's Manhattan headquarters, the firm maintains domestic offices in Atlanta, Boston, Chicago, Cleveland, Dallas, Denver, Houston, Los Angeles, Philadelphia, and San Francisco. Internationally, First Boston has approximately fifty investment banking specialists located in Geneva, London, Melbourne, San Juan, Sydney, Tokyo, and Toronto.

The Jobs

First Boston recruits only the best and brightest—and even then the firm interviews more than a dozen candidates for every one it hires. About 3,500 people work for the organization, and each year several dozen B.A.s are hired. Although it helps to have a background that includes some course work in accounting, economics, and finance, all majors are welcome at First Boston. It's not uncommon to find art history, English, and psychology majors working in the M&A department, especially if they went to a top school and graduated high in their class. Everything's important to First Boston's recruiters: grades, previous experience, extracurriculars, personality, and appearance. You've got to have it all to get in the door, and then you've got to keep performing at top capacity to remain on the fast track. The firm characterizes the perfect hire as possessing "keen intelligence and self-motivation combined with a sense of teamwork, a proven record of leadership, a dedication to excellence and an innovative mind."

Liberal arts grads are hired into most of First Boston's departments, and training varies with your location. If you make it into the prestigious analyst training program, you'll spend two years before either going to graduate school or (and this is rare) being offered a permanent spot. The training program involves classroom work and on-the-job learning assignments, as well as seminars on specific topics. You'll learn all about accounting and securities, as well as how to analyze complex financial transactions. Teamwork is an important part of training at First Boston; once you've mastered the fundamentals of investment banking, you'll be assigned to a client team, typically composed of one managing director or vice president, one associate, and one analyst. Be prepared for hour after hour of number crunching; much of your job is support work for associates. Most analysts conduct cash flow and financial analyses of proposals, and assist in the preparation of equity and debt offerings. The firm believes in acquiring a broad background, so you'll be exposed to a wide array of assignments during your first year or so.

The Payoff

First Boston offers some of the top starting salaries in the industry. It's not unheard of for a liberal arts grad to earn a $30,000 salary with a year-end merit bonus of 40 percent. In addition, you may be given a couple of thousand dollars as a sign-up bonus and granted six-month reviews. While the reviews determine your salary increases, the bonus size depends on both your contribution to the firm's overall earnings and the firm's revenues. First Boston's comprehensive benefits package includes medical, dental, and life insurance, as well as discounts on several financial products.

The Word

Although investment banking has taken a beating in the media, it's still a favorite of liberal arts grads. The challenge, the responsibility, and the money can't be beat. And First Boston is among the most popular firms. It's known as a classy place, where people are aggressive, but not brash. The atmosphere is conservative and corporate, but not stodgy or stuffy. Unlike the big financial supermarkets, where new recruits tend to sink or swim, First Boston pays plenty of attention to its trainees. Athletes and campus leaders are in abundance, as well as others who demonstrated lots of initiative during their undergraduate years. "The people in the program are smart, but not at all bookish," said one analyst. "There's a sense that common sense and creativity are what really count." Another thing that counts is being able to maintain a high standard of work over a long period; most trainees pull several all-nighters during their experience at First Boston. "It's important to keep smiling, even when it's 3 A.M. and you've been crunching numbers since dawn. If you complain once, you might not see a good assignment for a while." Likewise, not cooperating with members of your team is a no-no, since First Boston expects a high level of interaction and communication. Overall, the firm earns high marks from liberal arts grads on almost every count.

FIRST CHICAGO CORPORATION

Contact Info:

Barry F. Sullivan, Chairman

Agnes Alexander, Recruitment and Development Services
One First National Plaza
31st Floor
Chicago, Illinois 60670
(312) 407-4820

Financials (1985):

Assets: $39.8 billion
Deposits: $28.6 billion
Loans: $25.3 billion

The Organization

First Chicago Corporation is the holding company that owns the First National Bank of Chicago, the largest bank in the Midwest and the tenth-largest bank in the United States. The bulk of First Chicago's business falls into four categories: commercial banking (35 percent), international banking (27 percent), real estate (15 percent), and consumer banking (15 percent). Recently the bank has made several acquisitions in the suburban Chicago area, primarily regional banks geared toward middle-market business lending. With this added capital base, First Chicago is expected to perform well in upcoming years. Currently the bank has more than seventy offices in cities such as New York; Boston; Baltimore; Washington, D.C.; Atlanta; Dallas; Houston; Miami; Cleveland; Los Angeles; and San Fancisco. It also has affiliates in over thirty-five countries.

Founded under the National Banking Act of 1863, First Chicago has been run by several well-known midwestern banking figures. One of them, Melvin Traylor, was a Kentucky farm boy who worked his way through law school and ran the bank during the Depression. Traylor was so well liked by his peers that at the 1932 Democratic Convention, the Illinois delegates nominated him for vice president. Today First Chicago's stated mission is "to be the premier bank holding company in the Midwest with a reputation for excellence in serving customers nationwide and through the world. We intend to be the preferred supplier of financial products and services in the Midwest, yet we do not intend to be limited by regional boundaries."

In 1986, the bank implemented a comprehensive planning process that divided the organization into 120 "strategic business units" (SBUs). Each SBU is responsible for providing specific services and products, scanning the marketplace in search of new initiatives to support continued growth, and participating actively in strategic planning. First Chicago also reorganized its activities into three major departments: global corporate banking, consumer banking, and middle-market banking.

The Jobs

First Chicago seeks candidates with "evidence of a strong motivation to perform well; to anticipate and perceive problems; to develop workable solutions and implement them through teamwork." Mental agility, sound judgment, and personal integrity are also qualities cited by the bank's recruiters as "essential." First Chicago employs fourteen thousand people and hires several dozen liberal arts grads each year. The bank offers entry-level positions in commercial and personal banking, service and financial products, trust, asset/liability management, systems, corporate planning, control, auditing, and law. Most B.A.s enter the Relationship Manager Development program (RMD), a multiphase training program that prepares new hires to be members of the "First Team." The relationship manager is responsible for identifying and serving both credit and noncredit needs of the bank's customers; your duties as an RM include maintaining existing customer relationships and bringing in new business, as well as analyzing the credit worthiness of clients and marketing the full array of First Chicago's services and products. The program's first phase involves credit and banking courses. Following successful completion of class work, you apply and refine your newly acquired skills by performing credit analyses for actual loans/credit projects. Depending upon previous experience and current performance, this phase can last from eight to twenty-four weeks. The final phase of the RMD program involves one or two two-month rotations. Then, you take a first-level line position in the U.S. Banking Department, the Worldwide Banking Department, the Credit Policy Committee, or the Trade Finance Division. Permanent assignments reflect a blend of the individual's preferences and the bank's requirements.

In addition, First Chicago offers a program for "exceptional undergraduates" called the First Scholar Program. This program allows top students to pursue a career with the bank while simultaneously earning a master's degree in business or management. The thirty-month program combines employment with First Chicago and year-round attendance at the evening division of The University of Chicago Graduate School of Business or the J. L. Kellogg Graduate School of Management at Northwestern University. As a First Scholar, you hold a series of responsible positions in a wide variety of financial disciplines through the use of six-month rotational assignments. These assignments provide you with broad exposure to the areas of investment, commercial, and consumer banking and enable you to explore a diverse range of career options. You're required to complete two courses each quarter toward your master's degree, and all tuition fees are prepaid by the bank. If you're interested in this high-powered program, you have to apply to one or both of the graduate schools and simultaneously apply for a job at First Chicago. If you're accepted all around, and complete the First Scholar program in thirty months, you're guaranteed to hop on the fastest track possible.

The Payoff

First Chicago pays highly competitive salaries—and they go further in Chicago than they do in New York. The bank describes its compensation as "internally equitable, externally competitive, and tied directly to individual performance." Employees participate in a comprehensive benefits program that provides medical, dental, and life insurance coverage as well as liberal holiday and vacation schedules and a tuition reimbursement plan.

The Word

If you want to live in Chicago and work for a fast-paced, dynamic bank, First Chicago's your best bet. As the bank says, "Chicago's chief asset is a quality of life that remains affordable and attractive to today's professional." Increasingly, the best and brightest are taking Horace Greeley's advice and heading West, or at least Midwest.

Over the past few years, First Chicago has forged a national identity and succeeded in luring top executives away from other prestigious financial institutions. One of these recruits, Barry Sullivan, was a twenty-three-year veteran at Chase Manhattan when he left New York in 1980 to take the helm at First Chicago. With the goal of reviving the bank's management, Sullivan embarked on an ambitious program, hiring more than three hundred new officers and expanding the corporate planning staff. Clearly his efforts have paid off; the bank's profits and reputation have both risen tremendously. In general, staffers appear pleased with Sullivan's hands-on management style. "Even though the bank's growing quickly, you never feel like it's some kind of big amorphous corporation. The lines of power are clear, and there's a real emphasis on teamwork," says one trainee.

FIRST INTERSTATE BANCORP

Contact Info:

J. J. Pinola, Chairman

Gretchen Thompson, Manager of College Relations
707 Wilshire Boulevard
Los Angeles, California 90017
(213) 614-3001

Financials:

Assets: $45.5 billion
Deposits: $33.6 billion
Loans: $28.6 billion

The Organization

"Aggressive" is the word most often used lately to describe First Interstate. That has a lot to do with sixty-two-year-old Joseph J. Pinola, the bank's tremendously aggressive leader. Pinola made headlines nearly every day in late 1986 with his mighty bid to take over Bank of America, his former home. Although the deal never went through, it made Joe Pinola—and First Interstate—household words throughout the nation.

Although the name First Interstate enjoys good recognition, not many people realize that it's the largest multistate bank holding company in the United States. First Interstate banks cover nearly half the geographical area of the country; the bank has offices in California, Oregon, Arizona, Nevada, Colorado, Washington, Utah, Idaho, New Mexico, Wyoming, Montana, Wisconsin, Alaska, and Hawaii. Recently it added Indiana, Oklahoma, and North Dakota to the roster. Over the past few years, First Interstate has been transformed from Western Bancorporation, a loose confederation of regional banks, into a giant, coordinated banking company. Today it has branches in eighteen states, with over a thousand offices and forty franchisees. Its three main divisions are First Interstate Bancorp (the parent company), First Interstate, Ltd. (the merchant bank), and First Interstate Bank of California (the retail bank).

The Jobs

First Interstate employs 34,000 people, making it the fourth-largest work force of any commercial bank in the country. Recruiters look for candidates with a broad range of academic and professional credentials. Teamwork is important at First Interstate, so interpersonal skills are a must. Each year recruiters visit dozens of campuses, mainly in California. According to the bank, "The essential ingredient of our strategy is superior people. This strategy implies a heightened investment in building skills, knowledge, and expertise." First Interstate offers several highly regarded training programs, which include formal orientation, classroom instruction, and on-the-job experience. Opportunities are available in sales/credit, branch service/operations, commercial credit, real estate lending, and financial analysis.

In addition to its variety of training programs, First Interstate offers a summer internship program in which about sixty students gain firsthand exposure to the bank. Internships are available in most areas, including cash management, market planning, financial analysis, data base design, and special industries analysis. Placement is based upon your skills and interests and the bank's needs. During the internship program, interns meet once a week for seminars, workshops, and other activities. Outside working hours, interns attend sports outings, picnics, and concerts. Successful interns are often invited back to the bank upon graduation.

The Payoff

Starting salaries for B.A.s at First Interstate are generally in the $19,000 to $26,000 range, depending on the position and the candidate's background. The bank offers a competitive salary and benefits package. Included are medical, dental, and life insurance coverage, as well as free checking, credit card discounts, reduced loan rates, and tuition reimbursement.

The Word

First Interstate has acquired a reputation for playing tough. Joe Pinola is as brash and ballsy as they come; under his rule, the bank has mushroomed. As interstate banking competition heats up, First Interstate is likely to continue expanding at a breathless pace. And Pinola is prepared for battle. He has amassed a highly talented cadre of executives and built a board of directors that reads like a Who's Who of California heavyweights. Among the directors: George Keller, CEO of Chevron; Roy Anderson, chairman of Lockheed's executive committee; Dr. Jewel Plummer Cobb, president of California State University at Fullerton; and Bruce Nordstrom, chairman of Nordstrom, the department store chain.

Besides having an aggressive leader, First Interstate is known for training its employees well. For would-be bankers who fear getting lost in the shuffle at a large urban institution, First Interstate offers a somewhat more laid back alternative. However, don't arrive dressed in "jams" and toting a surfboard; trainees at First Interstate are expected to put in long hours and make themselves visible to senior management. But if you're interested in going all the way west, First Interstate's a great starting point. The finance industry is booming in the Los Angeles area, and we don't need to tell you about the beautiful beaches.

FLEET FINANCIAL GROUP

Contact Info:

J. Terrence Murray, Chairman and President

Virginia McQueen, Personnel Officer
55 Kennedy Plaza
Providence, Rhode Island 02903
(401) 278-6000

Financials:

Assets: $7 billion
Deposits: $3.9 billion
Loans: $4.8 billion

The Organization

Fleet Financial Group owns Fleet National Bank of Rhode Island, the largest bank in Rhode Island and the third largest in New England. The bank has been part of New England since the days when the first summer resort in America was established on Narragansett Bay. Founded in 1791 as the Providence Bank, it earned a profit in its first year and in 1792 paid a dividend to its stockholders —as it has continued to do every year since. In 1954, the bank's name was changed to the Industrial National Bank of Providence, and twenty-eight years later, it acquired the name Fleet, which "conveyed an image—as in a fleet of ships—of many separate entities operating under central direction and with a shared destination."

Over the decades, Fleet has gradually expanded throughout the Northeast. In 1985, the bank acquired two high-performance regional banks, First Connecticut Bancorp and Merrill Bankshares of Maine, increasing its presence to the north and south. Today Fleet is a diversified financial services company with more than three hundred offices in thirty-four states and four foreign countries. In addition to Fleet's traditional commercial and trust banking activities, the bank has major divisions that handle mortgage banking, real estate lending, asset-based lending, consumer banking, venture capital, and data processing.

In recent years, Fleet has begun to actively seek out attractive bank and nonbank acquisition candidates. To round out its New England coverage, Fleet bid for the Massachusetts-based Conifer Group in 1986. However, when the bidding turned hostile, Fleet obeyed its conservative nature and walked away. Later the Bank of New England made a deal with Conifer at a higher price. This example shows Fleet's nature: eager to grow but unwilling to take major risks. In the future, it's likely that Fleet will rely on its highly diversified portfolio of businesses. More than a third of the bank's earnings are currently generated by nonbank subsidiaries.

The Jobs

Fleet employs some five thousand employees, and one thing's for sure: the bank's not overstaffed. During the past five years, as the bank has doubled in earnings and assets, it's retained approximately the same number of workers. Fleet offers a variety of training programs, most of which involve a small percentage of classroom work and a number of internships or rotations. On-the-job learning is stressed, and trainees are expected to be self-starters. Opportunities exist in asset-based lending, auditing, branch management, cash management, commercial credit/administration, commercial credit/lending, money management, product management, and operations management. A number of other areas, such as corporate trust services, financial management, and information systems, have no formal training programs but offer extensive on-the-job learning.

Fleet's Commercial Loan Officer Development Program is popular with liberal arts graduates. This eighteen to twenty-four-month program involves participation in an intensive accounting course, followed by a seminar in analytical techniques. Upon successful completion of the classroom phase, you write analytical reports and learn to make lending decisions. You're then eligible to participate in a set of internships, including assignments in the Loan Review Department, the International Division, and the Consumer Banking Division. Additional internships are available in the lending division, operational areas, and workout groups. At the end of the program, you'll be placed as a commercial lending representative in an appropriate department.

The Payoff

Fleet offers one of the most comprehensive and competitive programs in the industry. And we don't need to tell you how much further the dollar goes in Providence than in New York. Fleet offers health, life, disability, and accident insurance, as well as a pension plan. Employees are also eligible for free checking accounts, free safe deposit boxes, and reduced rates on mortgage and personal loans. In addition, the bank has profit sharing, thrift, and stock purchase plans that are available after a certain amount of time. Fleet employees receive between two and four weeks of paid vacation each year, based on length of service and/or job level. The bank also honors eleven paid holidays annually. Tuition reimbursement for successful completion of approved courses is available. Finally, one of the biggest perks around: Rhode Island–based employees may use the Brown University athletic and recreational facilities, which are actively supported by the bank. In addition, Fleet has fully equipped fitness centers at the main office and operations center.

The Word

Rhode Island's always been known as a quirky place. The first state in the Union to declare its independence, it has retained a unique variety of life-styles. While Providence may not have a reputation as a "hot" place to live, residents cite the many recreational, entertainment, cultural, and educational activities available. Several of the nation's best universities and museums are in Rhode Island, as well as a few of the most popular vacation spots. "I wasn't so sure about being in Providence when many of my friends were going to New York," says one Fleet trainee. "But we've got the beaches in Newport and Narragansett, and we're much closer to skiing in Vermont and New Hampshire. And, of course, Boston's a short ride away."

Terrence Murray, who took over the bank at the age of forty, is known for being one of the shrewdest regional banking executives in the country. He's a real roll-up-the-sleeves type, and his team of managers is smart, young, and dynamic. Few banks are more involved in the community than Fleet. Recently the bank made a commitment to allocate up to $8.6 million of mortgage and rehabilitation loans to help meet the housing needs of low-income families in Providence's inner city. In addition, Fleet has participated in several neighborhood revitalization projects and sponsors everything from local fairs to sports clinics. According to the bank, "The current management group is, without question, the strongest in the history of the organization. Performance is at optimum levels, and the dedication and loyalty of the staff unparalleled. . . . Being part of a forward-thinking, results-oriented organization is both challenging and stimulating, and offers opportunities for the advancement and rewards demanded by today's banking professionals." It sounds good, but what do trainees think? "It's not an easy program, but you'll never be bored," says one liberal arts graduate. "The bank really does let you participate. When some of my friends were still sitting through credit training classes, we were already working on real assignments. If you want to get out of school and have responsibility early on, this is a great place to be."

GREY ADVERTISING INC.

Contact Info:

Edward H. Meyer, Chairman of the Board and President

Dr. James T. Brink, Personnel Manager
777 Third Avenue
New York, New York 10017
(212) 546-2000

Financials (1985):

Billings: $1,514,263,000
Net Income: $10,061,000

The Organization

Grey is a worldwide company based in New York whose primary business is creating and placing advertising. Founded in 1917, Grey is one of the ten largest agencies in terms of worldwide billings and is the largest advertising agency in New York City. Its U.S. clients include Beecham, Canon, General Foods, Inter-Continental Hotels, Procter & Gamble, Revlon, and Timex. The company has developed expertise in such related areas as marketing, consultation, direct response, research, packaging, product publicity, public relations, sales promotion, catalog design, and television program syndication. The company creates advertising, recommends media purchases, and places advertising in the media. These actions are guided by an advertising and marketing plan, which the company develops after studying a client's business, the distribution or utilization of a client's products or services, and the media choices suitable to achieve the desired market performance.

The Jobs

While Grey Advertising does hire for its creative, media, marketing and research, promotion, and production areas, the best pathway into the company is through the account management function. In fact, it's known as a blend of science, art, and people management, as the place where information is evaluated and articulated, where the ideas and human needs that flow from research into the creative process are moved from the world of science into the world of art. The belief at Grey is that to inspire the right advertising—brilliant, breakthrough advertising that builds clients' businesses—the right account manager must possess a full range of people-management skills and keen instincts about the trends and life-styles that motivate consumers.

The first year at Grey is a learning process, a time when people with "strong educational backgrounds and innate talent" become advertising professionals. Account management proficiency grows on the job, through working with experienced account professionals in a team system. The first year includes on-the-job training, seminars, continual feedback, and senior management involvement.

More specifically, you'll be placed on one of the best training accounts, which means that you'll join the team serving one of Grey's blue-chip, long-term, multinational packaged-good clients, such as General Foods, P&G, or Revlon. Serving this calibre of client is tough and makes you a professional quickly. Concurrently your on-the-job training—your title is assistant account executive—includes teamwork with two people who were where you are not too long ago: the account executive and the account supervisor. The more senior level people in your life—the management supervisor and the senior and executive vice presidents—also participate in your care and grooming, for the success of the account genuinely depends on the whole team pulling together.

The agency runs seminars with senior executives that are in-

tended to familiarize newcomers with the agency, its departments, and the other Grey subsidiaries. Seminar topics include
broadcast production; the international network; Grey subsidiaries; and the legal, creative, media, marketing and research, and
financial departments.

Formal evaluations happen after a year. What matters most at
Grey are performance and progress, as measured by strategic
thinking skills; contribution to creative excellence; and communication and organizational skills. And with the "godparent" program, each assistant account executive is getting good guidance
from day one. Every assistant account executive is matched with a
veteran account exec or management supervisor on a different
account; your godparent provides you with guidance and perspective in a nonjudgmental atmosphere. At worst, what you have is an
unofficial guidance counselor for your first nine or ten months on
the job; usually what happens is that lifelong friendships grow out
of this give-and-take.

The Payoff

Grey's starting salaries are competitive with what you'll make
anywhere up and down Ad Alley. Its benefits are also competitive
with all agencies and with all industry. One additional bonus is that
while Grey stock is traded over the counter, more than half of it is
held by Grey's employees—and it has averaged a 45 percent annual growth rate. That means that the agency's profits go into the
pockets of the people who make its success happen.

The Word

If the adage is true that advertising is one of those industries in
which the inventory gets on elevators and goes home at night,
Grey's inventory stays around longer, coming in earlier and leaving later, than the inventory at most of its competitors. While
critics claim that entry-level life is sweat-shop living, no one can
challenge Grey's claim that the agency invests in its people and
that it develops the best account managers.

Take, for example, the career path of one liberal arts graduate
who joined the firm in 1974 after earning a B.A. in sociology from

the University of Pennsylvania. Today she is vice president and management supervisor, with responsibility for General Foods' Kool-Aid line and Post Cereals. She had served as assistant account exec, account exec, account supervisor, and management supervisor over the course of the past twelve years—and is a working mom who claims that "a working mother is only as good as her housekeeper!" When asked what the truest stereotype about advertising is, she responded, "That it's enormous fun." One of her colleagues, a graduate of Stanford University who earned his B.A. in economics, has been with the agency since 1980, and is now account executive on General Foods' Baker's Coconut & Chocolate New Product Development. He said that the truest stereotype is that it's never boring. And his identification of the most annoying stereotype was that advertising is "mostly superficial hype."

Don't forget that Grey's leader, Ed Meyer, is an English major from Cornell. Meyer leads the drive to create outstanding advertising that captures the hearts and minds of consumers around the world—*and* grows this agency with great business savvy. His influence is felt in Grey offices worldwide. This means that like client Church's Chicken Sandwiches, Grey's smart people are "on a roll." And also like its advertising, Grey's success and track record as a leading trainer do the talking.

HALLMARK CARDS, INCORPORATED

Contact Info:

Irvine O. Hockaday, Jr., President and Chief Executive Officer

Sam Willett, College Relations Manager
2501 McGee
Kansas City, Missouri 64141
(800) 821-2118

Financials (1985):

Sales: more than $1.5 billion

The Organization

Hallmark Cards, Inc., is the world's leading creator and manufacturer of social expression products—greeting cards and a host of other products that people use in expressing feelings for and to one another. Some of these products are designed as gifts and remembrances, others as home and special occasion decorations.

Hallmark, a privately held company, produces more than 12,500,000 products each day in eighteen major product lines. Merchandise is distributed in one hundred countries and in twenty languages. In every phase of its operations, the constant emphasis is on quality.

The dedication to quality makes the Hallmark name synonymous with excellence. Its corporate slogan, "When you care enough to send the very best," has been found by independent researchers to be believed by more consumers than that of any other corporation.

Hallmark Cards, Incorporated, was founded in January 1910 by Joyce C. Hall. The company's name was Hall Brothers, Inc., until 1954. The firm manufactures greeting cards and other products under the brand names of Hallmark, Ambassador, Springbok, Crayola, Liquitex, Trifari, Burnes of Boston, and Heartline.

Hallmark Cards, including subsidiaries and international operations, has more than twenty thousand full-time employees, including about six thousand employees at its Kansas City headquarters. Hallmark and Ambassador share the world's largest creative staff, numbering about seven hundred persons who work as artists, designers, stylists, editors, and photographers.

The Jobs

Hallmark Cards is a mecca for liberal arts superstars. Its president is an English literature major from Princeton; the chairman of the board, Donald J. Hall, is a graduate of Dartmouth.

Meg S. Owens, corporate communications coordinator, recommends three pathways into Hallmark for liberal arts grads: product management, field marketing, and production.

The first job in the product management career path is as planner. The planner's primary responsibility is product development. This includes planning and controlling the content and design balance of a particular product line while meeting profitability goals. Two major processes are involved: First, the planner must determine which items in the product line should be replaced or redesigned. In order to make this determination, the planner researches the sales of the products for which he or she is responsible and makes competitive comparisons. Cost and market research information is also examined. Second, the planner coordinates the development of new items. This involves working with members of the creative department to generate new and innovative ideas. While generating these product ideas, the planner ensures that they are compatible with the Hallmark quality standards, that they meet profitability goals, and that Hallmark has the capability of producing or purchasing the products and designs. Once a new product is designed and approved, the planner works with a variety of departments to ensure that products meet established production and profitability goals.

Hallmark field marketing representatives provide merchandising counsel to retailers in department stores, drugstores, and specialty shops. Ambassador Cards, a subsidiary of Hallmark Cards, markets products through mass merchandising outlets, including supermarkets, discount stores, variety stores, and drugstores. Representatives in either organization participate in a nine-week training program consisting of both classroom and field training. Upon completion of this program, the representative is assigned a territory of thirty to seventy-five accounts and begins working under the guidance of a district marketing manager. As a representative, you are expected to increase each account's volume and open new outlets within your territories. The responsibilities of the field marketing rep extend beyond sales. You assist in planning store layouts, organizing display and inventory controls, and developing individual advertising programs. You also train retail personnel in sales and merchandising techniques.

Within the production function, the entry-level job is section manager. The principal responsibility of a section manager is to supervise ten to thirty employees involved in one or more production processes. This includes assigning work to department personnel and verifying that production standards are met. You also handle routine personnel problems, including counseling, interviewing, training, and evaluation. In addition, the section manager ensures that proper maintenance is performed, good housekeeping practices are followed, and safety regulations are followed.

For really artistic smart people, there is one more pathway to consider: editorial and design. Hallmark recruiters visit colleges and universities and professional art schools in search of excellent young artists. During on-campus interviews, art portfolios are evaluated according to how well they demonstrate an applicant's basic creativity, conceptual ability, and thorough knowledge of the fundamentals: drawing, design, color, and painting skills.

Based on portfolio content, artists are placed in the design studios where their particular abilities are most needed and assigned supervisors who provide the requisite attention, encouragement, and guidance to ensure that you advance and grow.

The Payoff

Hallmark offers salaries competitive with similar positions in a variety of American businesses; a profit-sharing plan; a retirement plan; a thrift savings plan; insurance; tuition reimbursement; and paid vacations. One additional perk is discounts on the purchase of company products and on a variety of other quality merchandise at company-owned department stores.

The Word

An Indiana University graduate said, "Hallmark is a large, sophisticated corporation, yet still has a relaxed family atmosphere. One thing that impresses me is the team attitude." A graduate of Notre Dame added, "Many companies hire 'brand assistants' and give them specific products that are virtually unchangeable and already have a well-established market. Here, though, it's 'product management' and it's different. You can study the market needs and create or modify a product. . . ."

Hallmark is a renaissance company, and its senior executives, especially CEO Hockaday, are renaissance people, men and women who see both the forest and the trees. In a *Business Week* profile in 1984, Hockaday told his interviewer, "My philosophy for succeeding in business is that you have to develop relationships." He explained that this was behind his decision to study literature at Princeton and that "literature deals with relationships, people-to-people and people-to-society. That has much more significance than numerical formulas. It never occurred to me to concentrate on finance."

Hallmark is on the move, into crayons, broadcasting, maybe even financial services. Regardless of where the company goes, its headquarters are likely to remain in Kansas City. Kansas City, Missouri, the site of the company's international headquarters, is a city built on more hills than Rome, Italy. The Missouri River sweeps through the area, which is also checkered with lakes and ponds. Parks abound. Quality of life is high. But it's still Kansas City and less than two hundred miles from the geographic center of the United States. One advantage, therefore, is that "Kansas Citians can fly to any one of twenty-one cities—from New York to Los Angeles—spend at least four hours there, and return home, all in one day."

HOLIDAY CORPORATION

Contact Info:

Michael D. Rose, Chairman of the Board

Jeffrey M. Cava, Corporate Manager, College Relations
1023 Cherry Road
Memphis, Tennessee 38117
(901) 762-8600

Financials (1985):

Sales: $1,804,472,000
Profits: $150,023,000

The Organization

Holiday Corporation is a multiple-brand hospitality company specializing in hotels and hotel/casinos. In addition to its Holiday

Inn brand established in 1952, the company now has four other hotel products serving distinct hotel market segments and, in the hotel/casino business, Harrah's. Together these brands offer business and vacation travelers more than eighteen hundred hotels with over 340,000 rooms in fifty-three countries and hotel/casinos in the four major U.S. gaming markets.

Through an ongoing commitment to customer service and product quality, each of the company's new brands expects to achieve a leadership position within its individual market segment equal to the flagship Holiday Inn hotel brand and Harrah's gaming casino brand.

The company consists of six brands:

Holiday Inn Hotels—the lodging industry's recognized leader in the full-service mid-price market, serving guests worldwide at approximately 1,700 locations

Holiday Inn, Crowne Plaza Hotels—hotels that offer extra amenities and personalized services at a superior price/value to a growing number of travelers

Embassy Suites Hotels—the world's largest all-suite hotel system, offering spacious suite accommodations and extra services at the single-room price of an upscale hotel

Hampton Inn Hotels—a new limited-service hotel chain providing high-quality guest rooms and selected services at an excellent value to price-conscious travelers

The Residence Inn Hotels—a unique system of residential-style, all-suite properties designed for guests who typically stay five days or longer

Harrah's Hotel/Casinos—a leader in the casino gaming industry, recognized for the superb quality of its service, entertainment, facilities, and fine dining

The company traces its beginnings to a Tennessee entrepreneur's elegantly simple business concept—one that caught fire, grew explosively, and transformed the lodging industry. The idea, a galvanizing first in the early 1950s, was to found a chain of standardized, reasonably priced, reliable hotels across the nation. The entrepreneur was Memphis businessman Kemmons Wilson, and the company was Holiday Inns of America, Inc. From the beginning, growth was impressive, fueled by the new mobility of people in the postwar era. Twelve years after ground was broken for the first Holiday Inn hotel in 1952, there were five hundred in the United States. Four years later, there were more than a thousand, and the eye-catching orange-and-green signboard had become a fixture on the American scene.

Now in its fourth decade, there are more than 314,000 Holiday Inn hotel rooms, and on a given day, 70 percent of them are occupied. Holiday Inn is the core brand; the company's new name, Holiday Corporation, reflects the wider range of lodging choices it provides. The company, which is the largest hospitality enterprise in the world, employs more than fifty thousand people.

The Jobs

About 80 percent of the professionals who are employed by Holiday Corporation are involved in the management of individual hotel properties, as food and beverage managers, chefs and executive chefs, guest services managers, or general managers. Other professionals work in various regional, divisional, and corporate headquarters staff groups and are concerned with many of the functions common to any business—accounting, finance, systems, logistics and supply, and so on. Some professionals are also employed in such areas as development of new properties and in franchise relations, supplying franchisees with the services that support their own management teams.

For the majority of its operating and staff professionals, the fundamental building block of a Holiday Corporation career is experience in hotel management. The best way to acquire the essential knowledge of the technical side of the business is by gaining hands-on experience. In several years, you can become intimately familiar with the basics of hotel operations and can rise to general manager of a small- or medium-size property.

When you become a general manager, or an assistant general manager in a larger hotel, you develop a broad understanding of the profession and see your role as that of total asset manager, devoted to making the most of the property under your supervision. You keep close tabs on such key components of success as customer satisfaction, employee satisfaction, community image, financial performance, and the condition and appearance of the hotel property.

Improved performance may rest primarily on fine-tuning internal systems for higher efficiency—reducing waste in food preparation, for example, or planning meeting and banquet functions for optimum staff utilization. Maybe you can find a way to trim a day from the credit card reimbursement cycle, or make the case to upper management for a revenue-boosting capital improvement. Perhaps your promotional skills will be of key importance as you host important events, open attractions, and take other steps to increase the visibility of your property.

Every hotel is different, and as a manager, you will face entirely new challenges as you move to new properties. Types of locations, size of facilities, services offered, the interpersonal dynamics of the staff—all must be taken into consideration as you set your performance goals and take steps to meet them.

Various divisions of Holiday Corporation sponsor programs to help you begin in hotel management. These programs are tailored to the individual needs of a given brand or region. They have in common the objective of getting you started fast—giving you a real job to do and as much responsibility as you show you can handle while learning the fundamentals. You might begin as the assistant to a department manager at a larger hotel, then rotate among various functions: housekeeping, food and beverage, customer service, sales. Or you might start as assistant manager at a smaller property, taking an active part in overall administration and decision making.

The Payoff

Holiday Corporation offers competitive entry level salaries and benefits that encompass competitive insurance, savings, and retirement plans. Successful managers can expect periodic relocation as part of their advancement. Certain professional jobs with the company can provide the opportunity for extensive travel, both domestically and internationally.

The Word

Holiday Corporation may have hotels in fifty-three countries, but it is very definitely committed to its Memphis base. For one thing, the company gives big chunks of money to a few projects in the city, including Memphis Partners, created to help prepare youth for jobs. A welcome outcome of this giving activity is that the company is identified with its projects, such as its 1986 Scholarship Program. The company awarded full two- and four-year college scholarships, including tuition, books, and lab fees, to local students wishing to attend any of six Memphis-area schools. The company's goal is to be providing full financial assistance to a maximum of 119 students by 1989, at an annual cost of about $260,000. With this much emphasis on education, and with growth that screams "opportunities," how could you go wrong by choosing to start your career on Holiday?

E. F. HUTTON & COMPANY, INCORPORATED

Contact Info:

Robert Fomon, Chairman

Elizabeth S. Lasdon, University Relations Manager
One Battery Park Plaza
New York, New York 10004
(212) 742-5385

The Organization

If asked to recite the most famous slogan on Wall Street, we'd expect four out of five people to say, "When E. F. Hutton talks, people listen." Despite several hardships over the past few years, having primarily to do with a defrauding scheme run by middle managers, Hutton remains one of the most important and impressive major brokerage houses in the United States. Founded in 1904 by Edward F. Hutton in San Francisco, one of the firm's earliest claims to fame was operating a telegraph wire between New York and California. During the great earthquake of 1906, one hard-working Hutton manager supposedly recovered the firm's records, found his way to a nearby telegraph office, and continued placing customer orders. In 1920, Hutton married Marjorie Merri-weather Post, the Postum Cereals heiress, and he left the firm to run Postum. While there, he engineered the merger of more than a dozen companies that ultimately became General Foods. The firm continued to grow and prosper without him, eventually becoming one of the top ten brokerage houses in the country.

Over the eighty-odd years of its existence, Hutton has maintained steady profitability and has increased its capital position to more than $1 billion. Under the rule of Robert Fomon, the firm became a financial supermarket offering a vast array of investment products and services. Today Hutton's brokerage subsidiary is the second-largest independent securities firm in the country, and the firm has some seven thousand account executives located in more than 410 offices around the world—as well as more than 1.5 million clients. In addition to selling and trading stocks, bonds, futures, and commodities, Hutton has pioneered Treasury bond receipts, zero coupon municipal bonds, and universal life insurance. The firm has also dedicated its considerable resources toward establishing an ever-increasing role in assisting corporate and public entities in the capital formation process. In the corporate finance area, Hutton structures its clients by industry—for example, natural resources, technology, utilities, transportation, telecommunications—and by product—private placements, mergers and acquisitions, general industry. The public finance group is organized along geographic and specialty lines, including airport construction, hospital and health care, higher education, state housing, industrial development, resource recovery, and public power. In addition to its headquarters at the southernmost tip of Manhattan, Hutton has major regional offices in Boston, Charlotte, Chicago, Houston, Los Angeles, and San Francisco.

The Jobs

Perhaps because of its high-visibility ad campaigns, Hutton attracts thousands of applicants for entry-level positions each year. The firm employs over seventeen thousand people and hires several dozen liberal arts grads annually. According to Hutton, "We're interested in people who want to get right into the business and take responsibility, to enter the marketplace and compete." The firm looks for "risk takers," "entrepreneurs," "innovators," and "achievers." While a background including course work in accounting and finance may be an advantage, good grades, extracurricular leadership, and a strong interest in investment banking will get you in the door.

Hutton hires liberal arts grads into most divisions, including institutional and capital markets, operations, and auditing. Each area has its own character, requirements, and training system. The most talented students are generally hired for the corporate financial analyst program, which covers a two-year period. In this program, you're actively involved in the firm's investment banking activities. You'll do plenty of number crunching, particularly cash flow analysis and statistical data maintenance. The program begins with classroom training and rotational general assignments. After an initial period of exposure lasting several months, you'll begin handling more specialized assignments. You might work in corporate finance, on a range of industry and product groups, or in public finance, where you'll gain expertise in either general municipal finance or in a specialty group. Since you'll have the chance to work on several major projects, you'll learn from a large number of senior managers. When required, on-the-job training is supplemented with in-house seminars and rotations through other areas of the firm. After two years, you'll have the option of returning to graduate school or remaining on and choosing a specialty area.

The Payoff

While Hutton doesn't pay the highest salaries in the industry, the firm claims it's "fully competitive with other investment banks." Most liberal arts grads start in the high-twenties range, although some with relevant experience earn more. The firm's comprehensive benefits package includes life, health, and accident insurance, as well as reduced stock commissions and stock purchase opportunities.

The Word

Recently Hutton has gotten a whopping share of bad press. In 1985, the firm pleaded guilty to federal charges of defrauding a number of small banks. Essentially Hutton executives operated a check-writing scheme that provided several million dollars in interest-free loans. However, with the explosion of Wall Street's insider trading scandal, many other investment banks have been implicated in unethical or illegal operations, and consequently Hutton isn't alone. Within the firm, employees don't seem to find much wrong. They say the atmosphere is still friendly, relaxed, and challenging. "I don't think people are too disillusioned," says one analyst. "Of course, it's disappointing to find the firm's been in trouble, but the opportunities are still there." Overall, Hutton is trying a bit harder to earn public esteem and to alter its business mix. The new tax laws have reduced the demand for tax shelter products, which have been a big portion of Hutton's business. So management is beefing up trading operations and increasing the number of products manufactured in-house. Lately Hutton's stock has been hitting new highs due to persistent rumors that the company may be a takeover candidate.

JOHNSON & JOHNSON

Contact Info:

James E. Burke, Chairman and Chief Executive Officer

Michael Longua, Director, Corporate College Relations
1 Johnson & Johnson Plaza
New Brunswick, NJ 08933
(201) 524-0400

Financials:

Sales (1985): $6.42 billion
Profit (1985): $613.7 million

The Organization

The Johnson & Johnson credo—a statement of corporate social responsibility—spells it out: "Everything we do must be of high quality." And whether it is in manufacturing a product or in developing human resources, quality is the Johnson & Johnson way.

Johnson & Johnson is a diverse international health care concern comprised of 165 companies marketing products in more than 150 countries. Many of these companies and the products they manufacture don't bear the Johnson & Johnson name and aren't readily identified by the public as being Johnson & Johnson.

More than seventy thousand employees help produce a variety of products that serve a broad segment of health care needs. They range from baby care, first aid, and feminine hygiene products to ethical pharmaceuticals and products for hospitals and medical professionals, dental care, dermatology, and family planning.

The diversity makes J & J a leader in the health care field. Few companies offer such a broad assortment of consumer, pharmaceutical, and professional health care products.

Johnson & Johnson is organized on the principle of decentralized management. Business is conducted through operating subsidiaries that establish their own objectives and develop and implement strategies to meet those goals. Direct responsibility for each company lies with its operating management. Decentralization offers many management development opportunities and the rapid assumption of responsibilities in the autonomous companies.

Continual product improvement and new product development is the Johnson & Johnson way. Although the average consumer product in the United States has a life span of less than ten years, many from J & J have sold successfully for over half a century. Johnson's Baby Powder—some say it's the best recognized fragrance in the world—was introduced almost one hundred years ago.

The company's professional products enjoy the same reputation. Surgical sutures and ligatures were included in the first Johnson & Johnson price list in 1887. Modern technology has improved sutures and today some are ten times finer than a human hair. J & J remains the world leader in sutures and in many other fields.

The Jobs

Johnson & Johnson employees are part of relatively small, highly autonomous units. Whatever discipline you're hired for—most liberal arts graduates begin in sales—you'll train on the job and have an early opportunity to contribute to the excitement of providing products that help mankind. For those of you with a background in science and a bent for research, there are also career opportunities in the research areas of most of the Johnson & Johnson companies.

Johnson & Johnson serves a broad range of customers in four major business segments: consumer, professional, pharmaceutical, and industrial. Your potential employers in the consumer area are Advanced Care Products; Johnson & Johnson Baby Products Company; Johnson & Johnson Products Inc., Health Care Division; McNeil Consumer Products Company; and Personal Products. Your potential employers in the professional area are Codman & Shurtleff, Inc.; Critikon, Inc.; Ethicon, Inc.; Iolab; Johnson & Johnson Cardiovascular; Johnson & Johnson Dental Products Company; Johnson & Johnson Hospital Services; Johnson & Johnson Products Inc., Patient Care Division, Orthopedic Division; Johnson & Johnson Ultrasound; Ortho Diagnostic Systems Inc.; Pitman-Moore, Inc.; Surgikos, Inc.; Technicare Corporation; Vistakon, Inc.; and Xanar. Your potential employers in the pharmaceutical area are Janssen Pharmaceutica Inc.; McNeil Pharmaceutical; and Ortho Pharmaceutical Corporation. Your potential employers in the industrial area are Chicopee and Devro, Inc.

Although the diversity of the company's business offers a broad range of sales opportunities, Johnson & Johnson sales professionals share a number of common attributes: intelligence, drive, resilience, the ability to be a self-starter, and the desire to work hard in pursuit of above-average goals.

Those starting with pharmaceutical or professional companies will be trained to converse about products with physicians, nurses, hospital administrators, and other health care professionals. Armed with the ability to talk intelligently about the products and ways in which they can be beneficial to patients, as a Johnson & Johnson sales professional, you will serve as an essential link between the research and development organization and the end use of those health care products.

The consumer business also has distinct markets. With a consumer products company, you deal with the various distribution channels—drug, supermarket, discount, syndicate or department stores. This can be done directly or through wholesalers. Consumer products sales reps provide advice on promotion and placement in an effort to help individual retailers build volume and profits.

A sales career begins with an intensive training program to learn about your employer and its products, and to acquire effective sales techniques. To learn firsthand about the business, time is spent with an experienced sales rep before your territory is assigned. Although there is J & J support, success depends on strong individual effort because you are actually running your own business.

The Payoff

Starting salaries are competitive, as are benefits programs. Salaries are reviewed periodically and merit increases are administered based on performance.

The Word

Johnson & Johnson is unique for three primary reasons: its form of decentralization; its adherence to the principles embodied in its credo; and its commitment to manage the business with a focus on long-term results.

The authors of *Rating America's Corporate Conscience* (considered "the best guide to corporate social responsibility by America's leading public interest research organization" by consumer advocates) notes that Chairman Burke "believes that social responsibility should be a tenet of good management and integral to running a profitable company." Johnson & Johnson has been tested twice by crises with Extra-Strength Tylenol capsules that had been tampered with once they were on retail shelves. The company's reaction to both events was consistent with its "general pattern of thorough and broad-reaching approaches to its social initiatives." In its annual report, Burke and president David R. Clare reported, "Upon careful examination, we came to the reluctant conclusion that we could no longer guarantee the safety of capsules to a degree consistent with Johnson & Johnson's standards of responsibility to its consumers. Consequently, we have removed from the market all of our capsule products directly available to the consumer and have no plans to manufacture or sell these products for the foreseeable future."

The letter to shareholders outlined the cost of this decision—$100 to $150 million after taxes—and then noted that McNeil Consumer Products, producer of the Tylenol capsules, was being helped in its turnaround effort by "their sister companies."

That's what J & J is, one big family, happy most times, supportive all the time. Father Jim sets the tone and all the siblings band together on the big issues and run their own kingdoms on the small ones.

JORDAN MARSH—NEW ENGLAND
(a division of Allied Stores Corporation)

Contact Info:

Elliot J. Stone, President

Janet Fisher, Recruiting Manager
Box 9159
Boston, Massachusetts 02205-9159
(617) 357-3286

Financials (1985):

Sales: about $600 million

The Organization

Jordan Marsh is the largest full line department store in New England and one of the largest department stores in the country. The company was established in 1851 through the partnership of Eben Jordan and Benjamin Marsh. It has since grown to a nine-teen-store complex encompassing over four million square feet, located in both urban and suburban markets. It has plans for expansion throughout the Northeast. Jordan Marsh employs over ten thousand people in Massachusetts, New Hampshire, Rhode Island, Connecticut, Maine, and New York. Its corporate headquarters is at The Downtown Crossing in Boston.

Jordan Marsh is the flagship division of Allied Stores Corporation, one of the largest retailing organizations in America. Allied operates 597 stores located in forty-five states, the District of Columbia, and Japan. There are 21 department store divisions nationwide—of which Jordan's is the largest—and 6 specialty store divisions, including Brooks Brothers, and Bonwit Teller.

The Jobs

Jordan Marsh—New England maintains a year-round college relations effort with schools throughout the Northeast. The company actively recruits on thirty campuses and participates in a multitude of career fairs, recruiting consortiums, and campus-related activities. Candidates are also screened and interviewed in Boston on a year-round basis.

Karl Sparre, Director of Recruitment and Placement, reported, "In all prospective candidates, the company looks for a variety of qualities, including enthusiasm, strong quantitative ability, a positive record of achievements demonstrated in campus activities and/or prior work experiences, strong interpersonal skills, leadership potential, adaptability and stress tolerance, and the maturity and confidence to make spontaneous, high-risk decisions on a daily basis." He was quick to note that many "smart people" with these types of qualities lead Jordan Marsh Company. They include William Goodlatte, Senior Vice President, Human Resources (B.A., history, Bates), Daniel England, Vice President and General Merchandising Manager (B.A., English, University of Pennsylvania), John Hancock, Jr., Vice President, General Merchandise Manager (B.A., economics, Dartmouth), and dozens more.

The typical entry level position for all graduates is in the Executive Training Program. This program lasts twelve weeks and is a combination of on-the-job training and classroom seminars. Trainees progress through four specific assignments: two weeks in sales systems; four weeks in sales management; two weeks in buying; and four weeks in advanced sales management. Training is performed by experienced executives, most of whom are graduates of the Executive Training Program themselves. Classroom seminars are taught once a week and cover a wide variety of topics ranging from management and buying techniques to the latest in computerized merchandise analysis.

After successful completion of the Executive Training Program, training continues throughout your career via the Jordan Marsh Management Development Program. Seminars are offered periodically for each position on the career path and cover topics such as negotiating skills and conflict management. Courses are taught by Jordan Marsh merchandising and management executives as well as corporate personnel administrators.

The standard career path at Jordan Marsh is as follows: executive trainee, sales manager, assistant buyer, divisional sales manager, buyer, assistant store manager, store manager/divisional merchandise manager, and then into the senior management ranks.

Karl Sparre emphasizes that alternative career paths exist in finance/control, operations, personnel, and sales promotion. You are encouraged to complete the first two steps of the career path—sales manager and assistant buyer—prior to pursuing other interests.

The Payoff

The starting salary for all executive trainees is currently $20,000. The entry-level compensation package includes health and accident insurance, short- and long-term disability insurance, profit-sharing and retirement plans, liberal vacations and holidays, and a generous store-wide discount. The salary range for the organization's most senior level executives often exceeds $100,000. And, best of all for when you're just getting started, salary is reviewed semiannually below the buyer level.

The Word

Jordan Marsh may not be unique as far as the retailing industry is concerned, but its management is very proud of its decision to change its strategy with regard to the changing demands and needs of the New England marketplace in the 1980s. This change in direction began in 1979 and 1980, under the leadership of Elliot Stone, who was convinced that New England demographics were changing dramatically and thus required an immediate reaction if Jordan Marsh was to maintain and increase its market share. The rest is history, so to speak. Jordan's, or JM as it's known, in the 1980s is an upgraded, updated department store with a commitment to providing the best merchandise selection and customer service for a new generation of New England consumers. The transition was a complete success and continues to be the overwhelming reason Jordan Marsh consistently has outperformed its New England competitors. Although a number of retailers have recently made the effort to try to change their strategy and improve their market position, few have effected the transition as quickly and successfully as this company.

One other great thing about JM is its people-conscious environment. In an industry notorious for high rates of executive turnover, Jordan's has maintained a company-wide commitment to training, developing, and supporting its executives throughout their careers. The well-developed Management Development Program for execs, as well as the awareness about treating smart people right, make JM special. This is evidenced in a dramatic reduction in executive turnover, especially at the entry level, in recent years.

Its commercials feature a jingle that sums it up: "Jordan Marsh! This is the place!" If you want a business career in New England, Jordan Marsh—this is the place.

KIDDER, PEABODY & COMPANY, INC.

Contact Info:

Ralph D. DeNunzio, President and Chief Executive Officer

Sharon Henning, Recruitment Coordinator
10 Hanover Square
New York, New York 10005
(212) 510-4016

The Organization

In 1985, Kidder, Peabody celebrated its one hundred and twentieth anniversary. Founded in Boston near the close of the Civil War, the firm has grown into one of the largest private international investment banking firms in the securities industry. Kidder, Peabody's origins lie in the brokerage house founded in 1824 by John E. Thayer, the son of a Boston minister. Several years later, Thayer's younger brother sold the firm to the brothers Francis and Oliver Peabody and their associate, Henry Kidder. The trio reorganized the firm into three primary areas of service: banking, brokerage, and foreign exchange. By the turn of the century, Kidder, Peabody was well established as one of the nation's leading financial firms. Following the stock market crash of 1929, it was revived by a new group of partners, Edwin Webster, Jr., Albert Gordon, and Chandler Hovey. At that point, they moved the firm from Boston to New York and began competing head-on with their peers. During World War II, the team managed to preserve capital, and Kidder, Peabody emerged from the wartime years in a stronger financial condition than before. In the 1950s, following the opening of its London office, the firm became the first major American firm to open an office in Hong Kong. Later, Kidder, Peabody expanded to Switzerland, and then to Tokyo. Throughout Albert Gordon has remained active in the firm; today, at eighty-seven, he is still chairman.

In June 1986, Kidder, Peabody sold 80 percent of its shares to General Electric Financial Services, a subsidiary of the General Electric Company, retaining a 20 percent ownership through its existing shareholder group. By combining the resources and skills of the two organizations, Kidder, Peabody hopes to reposition itself as a more competitive force in the global financial marketplace. The firm is looking to realize "synergies" in four particular areas: acquisition financing, asset securitization, energy project financing, and emerging growth company financing. Currently Kidder, Peabody has seventy-three offices worldwide and offers individuals and institutions a full range of services encompassing the following areas: investment banking, research, market making, and tax-exempt financing. Since 1976, the firm has enlarged its sales force from eight hundred people to two thousand and the number of domestic offices from forty-three to sixty-two.

Over the past few years, intense competition and deregulation initiatives in the investment banking industry have changed the size and scope of many firms. Kidder, Peabody prides itself on "resisting the temptation to diversify into a 'financial supermarket' offering a variety of unrelated items to an ever-changing client base." Instead the firm has "focused on offering value-added products and service to a sophisticated group of clients." The firm's efforts have been geared toward maintaining and enhancing its competitive position across the major segments of traditional investment banking and penetrating new markets for greater profitability.

The Jobs

Kidder, Peabody employs six thousand people around the world and hires about fifty undergraduates each year for its Associate Intern Program. This program is designed to introduce talented hires to the firm's investment banking department, which handles underwriting, private placements, mergers and acquisitions, financial restructurings, and tender defenses. Known as one of the better programs in the industry, admission is highly competitive. Kidder, Peabody's recruiting philosophy focuses on "pursuing select individuals who demonstrate a strong desire to achieve individual excellence while maintaining an established appreciation for the importance of teamwork." Good grades, extracurricular leadership, and analytical ability are important. In addition, creativity, a sense of humor, and a high energy level are desired.

Although you'll find plenty of Ivy Leaguers at Kidder, Peabody, many other institutions are represented.

The two-year Associate Intern Program, begun in the mid-1960s, has turned out some of Wall Street's top managers. Approximately 80 percent of the group work in New York, with the balance located in Chicago, Dallas, Los Angeles, and San Francisco. There's little formal education, since the firm believes in putting you on an account team immediately and offering you up-front responsibility. Typically your team will consist of a vice president, an assistant vice president, and an associate or an associate intern. Once you're assigned to a specific team, you'll remain on it throughout your two-year stay. That way you'll have ongoing exposure to client relationships and senior executives. About half of the investment banking department's professionals serve as generalists, while the rest focus on specialized industry and product groups. Current industry groups include financial services, health services, life sciences, media and entertainment, natural resources, retailing, technology, and utility finance. In addition, Kidder, Peabody has groups that handle corporate consulting, capital markets, high yield finance, mergers and acquisitions, project and lease finance, marketing, and new product development and private placements.

The Payoff

To attract the best and brightest, Kidder, Peabody offers a highly competitive salary and benefits package. Most liberal arts grads entering the Associate Intern Program start in the high-twenties to mid-thirties range. Bonuses, based on both individual and firm performance, tend to be generous. Benefits include medical, dental, and life insurance coverage, as well as reduced commissions on stock transactions and discounts on several other financial services.

The Word

Will joining forces with General Electric make a difference? That seems to be the major question facing Kidder, Peabody these days. Long known as one of the most distinguished old-line houses on Wall Street, the firm is fast shedding its clubby image. Liberal arts grads say it's a great place to work. Sure, you may pull a few all-nighters, but the overall attitude seems a bit less uptight than at some other firms. From what we heard, Kidder, Peabody has an open, friendly work environment. Although the individual is encouraged to excel, there's not much of a "star system." Said one recent hire, "I'm not the type who thrives in a cutthroat atmosphere, so it was really important to me that I find a firm that was both dynamic and supportive. The opportunities are definitely good here, but you don't have to step all over everyone to grab them." That seems to fit in with Kidder, Peabody's goal of creating "an environment in which one's competitive instinct is channeled outward toward the industry, rather than inward toward one's peers."

LIBRARY OF CONGRESS

Contact Info:

Daniel J. Boorstin, Librarian

Recruitment and Placement Office
James Madison Memorial Building
101 Independence Avenue, S.E.
Washington, D.C. 20540
(202) 287-5000

The Organization

If you've always liked to wander around libraries, you'll be in heaven at the Library of Congress, which has the world's largest collection of books and related materials. Founded on April 24, 1800, for use by members of Congress, the library was originally a small reference area for men who needed to research a broad array of issues. Over nearly two centuries, the library has extended its services to other government agencies and to other libraries, as well as to scholars and to the general public. Today, while the library's primary mission is still to serve Congress, it is used by more than two million people annually. The library has three buildings on Capitol Hill: the Thomas Jefferson Building, the John Adams Building, and the James Madison Memorial Building. The facilities house approximately 80 million books, maps, manuscripts, tapes, discs, motion pictures, music material, photographs, microforms, and other items. On the library's five hundred miles of shelves, you'll find everything from thousand-year-old manuscripts to yesterday's newspapers, all cataloged by the now-famous National Union Catalog, which lists books in libraries all over North America.

The Library of Congress is organized into several departments, whose responsibilities are administered by three management entities: The Office of the Librarian (administrative direction), the Office of the Associate Librarian for Management (automation, general management, and personnel direction), and the Office of the Associate Librarian for National Programs (national program direction). Specialized activities are carried out by the following departments: Congressional Research Service, the Law Library, Processing Services, and Research Services. The Congressional Research Service performs research and provides reference services for members and committees of Congress through a staff of specialists, research analysts, and reference librarians. The Law Library, established in 1832, has the largest collection of legal material in the world, covering both American and foreign law. It serves Congress by conducting legal research in any area of foreign, comparative, and international law. The Research Services department brings together major areas of scholarly, informational, and Congressional services not provided by the other divisions. The Processing Services department acquires, catalogs, classifies, and prepares books, government documents, serials, audiovisual materials, and other items for addition to the Library's collections.

Beyond its services to Congress, other libraries, and scholars, the library also protects the rights of the creative community through the Copyright Office. Since 1870, the library has been entitled to two free copies of all material copyrighted in the United States. The Copyright Office examines claims to copyright in a wide variety of literary, artistic, and musical works; registers those claims that meet the requirements of the law; issues certificates of copyright registrations; and catalogs all registrations.

The Jobs

The Library of Congress employs more than five thousand people. Because the activities of the library are highly diverse, there are career opportunities in a variety of professional, technical, support, and management positions. The largest number of vacancies usually occur in the library science field, including the positions of librarian, library technician, and library aid. The next largest number of openings are generally administrative. While a good liberal arts background will qualify you for many entry-level positions, the library believes that "relevant experience can often be substituted for educational requirements and pertinent education can often be substituted for required experience." In other words, most people may apply for most positions. While a graduate degree from a library school may be useful in obtaining some jobs, appropriate experience in a reference or research library can be substituted for formal training in library science.

Since the Library of Congress is part of the legislative branch of the federal government, appointees must be U.S. citizens and over eighteen years old. In some cases, you may be required to pass a specific qualifying test for employment. You'll also have to complete an SF-171, the Application for Federal Employment, fully and accurately. You may also be asked to submit additional materials such as writing samples or transcripts. Once your application is received, it'll be evaluated by a Recruitment and Placement specialist, and you'll be ranked according to your experience, education, training, self-development, outside activities, awards, and commendations. You should take care to describe your qualifications in depth, so that the reviewer sees as broad a picture of you as possible.

The Payoff

Positions at the Library of Congress are subject to the same general job classification and pay systems as those in the executive branch of the federal government—which means you'll be well taken care of. During your first three years of service, you'll receive thirteen paid vacation days; after that, it rises to twenty days. You'll have thirteen sick days and nine paid holidays a year. In addition, you'll receive full health insurance, life insurance, retirement coverage, and workers' compensation. You'll also have scheduled salary increases and be eligible for a variety of cash incentive awards.

The Word

From what we've heard, the Library of Congress can be a great place for liberal arts grads to work. If you've specialized in a subject ranging from medieval literature to African music, there may be a department that needs you to do research, write catalogs, or develop programs. Like many government agencies, there is a certain amount of bureaucratic red tape to wade through; however, staffers don't seem to find it overwhelming.

R. H. MACY AND COMPANY, INC.

Contact Info:

Edward S. Finkelstein, Chairman of the Board and CEO
R. H. Macy and Company, Inc.
151 West 34th Street
New York, New York 10001
(212) 560-3000

Joseph Maiorano
Manager, College Relations
Macy's New York
151 West 34th Street, 17th floor
New York, New York 10001
(212) 560-4174

Noel Nugent
Manager of Executive Recruitment
Macy's New Jersey
131 Market Street
Newark, New Jersey 07101
(201) 565-4175

Scott Ridgeway
Manager, College Relations
Macy's California
Stockton Street at O'Farrell Street
San Francisco, California 94108
(415) 393-3319

Pat Pennardo
Executive Recruiting Manager
Macy's Atlanta
180 Peachtree Street
Atlanta, Georgia 30303
(404) 221-7221

Financials (1985):

Sales: $4,368,386,000
Profits: $189,315,000

The Organization

In a time when many department store operators are cutting their losses and complaining of lowered profits and oversaturated markets, Macy's four operating divisions are earning record profits and expanding into markets others shun as "overstored." By doing careful market research and canny merchandising, and by generating excitement among the shopping public, this national company is beating the odds and confounding the experts. They must be doing something right.

One of the nation's largest department store companies, Macy's sells women's, men's, and children's clothing and accessories; furniture and home furnishings; and housewares and electronics. Macy's four regional store groups—New York (21 stores), New Jersey (23 stores), California (25 stores), and Atlanta (14 stores)—operate eighty-three stores in twelve states, more than three-quarters of them in major shopping centers. Founded in 1858 by an enterprising Nantucket sea captain, the corporation is now almost 130 years old.

The interiors at Macy's stores look like a series of independent shops. Through the use of individualized presentation and stylish decor, shoppers are attracted to fashionable, high-quality merchandise. The total store space of the eighty-three stores is approximately 21 million square feet. With its management-led leveraged buyout completed in 1985, it's no wonder that observers expect to see increasingly higher profit margins and increased productivity throughout Macy's ranks. As *Fortune* noted in a May 1985 market analysis, "Overstoring does not much bother what industry observers like to call power retailers—those confident merchandisers such as R. H. Macy & Co. . . . that have such financial strength, marketing skills, and reasonably-priced quality merchandise that [they] can bull their way into many markets, however saturated, and make a profit."

No explanation of the dramatic resurgence of Macy's as a national retailing force would be complete without mentioning the tremendous roles played by CEO Ed Finkelstein and his team of hand-groomed managers, the majority of whom are graduates of Macy's legendary executive training squad. *Fortune* reported, "Macy's hasn't made many mistakes under Finkelstein, who became chairman and CEO in 1980 after turning the chain's flagship store on Manhattan's 34th Street from a tacky relic into one of the country's most innovative department stores."

The Jobs

Each division recruits, hires, and trains its own professionals. Most divisions feature two entry-level executive training programs, one for merchandise executive trainees and one for management trainees. The former program prepares merchandising trainees for future assignments as store-line and buying-line executives. The latter, designed to introduce sales-support executive trainees to the principles of retail management, prepares college grads for eventual placement within specific store functions, such as control, finance, and human resources.

Merchandising executive trainees are recruited from all backgrounds. Sales-support (nonmerchandising) executive trainees usually possess more directly applicable qualifications, such as training in accounting or finance.

R. H. Macy's training programs, which have been lauded by *The Wall Street Journal* as the Harvard of retailing, were initiated more than sixty years ago and are continually being refined. The company's training programs have been designed to take bright liberal arts grads and develop them into complete executives. The company's training "squads" are designed to teach recent grads the fundamentals of the business. Through a combination of classroom and on-the-job training, all trainees learn about Macy's managerial and merchandising philosophies and technologies. The programs, which vary slightly in length by division, last for about three months.

Those who choose the merchandising career path move from the training program to early career rotations between store-line and buying-line positions. The first two positions are those of sales manager and assistant buyer. The next positions are, in order, those of group manager—which involves managing a merchandise area within a store—and buyer. This total exposure is essential to the development of effective senior level merchandising executives.

Sales-support executives receive similar classroom and on-the-job training. After newly hired execs complete their classroom training, they are assigned to the functional areas for which they were hired.

The Payoff

The divisions offer salaries that are competitive with those for similar positions in all industries. Offers in the high teens to mid-twenties are usual, and the benefits package is among the most comprehensive available. Life insurance, a pension plan, and health insurance are standard; liberal vacation policies acknowledge the demands made on retail executives to keep unconventional work hours and calendars. And, of course, there's *the* killer —the employee merchandise discount—which makes the paycheck seem so much smaller by the time you get home with what you haven't left behind in the store!

The Word

Women's Wear Daily, the industry rag, summed it up in a 1984 article: "The out-of-town retail view: 'We watch Macy's because we think that, in many ways, Macy's has the best retail minds in the country at work. They have combined class and mass retailing in the best way I can think of. Everything is new, but everything is solid. Everything is exciting, and everything is buyable.'" A *Wall Street Journal* article titled "Macy's Executive Training Squad Teaches Future Retailers the Intricacies of Selling" noted, "The fact that training-squad graduates *have* become presidents of Macy's and other stores is a big plus for Macy's recruiters."

And, for those of you who are interested in joining a prestigious alumni club à la Harvard, Princeton, and Yale, consider the following: Where else would a Farrell, a Lauder, or a Strawbridge train? Graduates of the training squad include Walter Hoving, Robert Sakowitz, and Marvin Traub, not to mention three-quarters of Macy's top executives.

Just bear in mind that prestigious or not, entry-level life isn't easy. "High pressure is a given," said a New Jersey assistant buyer, "so that by the time I get home, I can't handle anything which is too intense." The first job assignments can be in slightly out-of-the-way locations, which gets some sales managers crazy. "I worked sixty hours per week and then I went home to an apartment in Bay Shore," complained a Georgetown graduate. "Was I ready to be promoted to assistant buyer so that I could return to Herald Square and live in the city!" Life-style varies slightly from division to division, and some say that you should make your choice based upon where you see yourself settling.

For those of you who want a combination of fast-paced retailing and great business training, Macy's is a good career bet. And if you're undecided about which division is right for you, take the time to become acquainted with each of the four regions.

I. MAGNIN

(a division of Federated Department Stores, Inc.)

Contact Info:

Steven M. Somers, Chairman

Pauline Roothman, Manager, Executive Placement and
    Recruitment
Union Square
San Francisco, California 94108
(415) 362-2100

Financials (1985):

Sales: $319 million

The Organization

I. Magnin's twenty-six famous stores stretch from Seattle, Washington, in the north to La Jolla, California, in the south, and eastward to Washington, D.C. The first store began in San Francisco in 1876 as the idea of Mary Ann Magnin. She was the store's founder and its guiding inspiration. The principles she established—of style, fine quality, and taste—have been followed faithfully for more than a century.

The San Francisco store prospered, and I. Magnin built up the most fashionable clientele of the day. In 1906, while a new building was being constructed, the great San Francisco earthquake and fire wiped out the entire business district.

As a result, I. Magnin operated from temporary quarters for three years. The store then moved to a new shop on Grant Avenue, where it remained until 1948, when the present ten-story marble structure on Union Square was complete.

Probably the first American retailer to see the potential in branch stores, I. Magnin opened its first branch in Los Angeles in 1893.

I. Magnin was acquired by Bullock's, Inc., in 1944 and became part of Federated through the Bullock's merger in 1964. At that time, fifteen of the present stores had been opened, including the stores in Seattle, Portland, and Phoenix. The San Francisco store completed the final phase of renovation in 1983.

Under Federated, eleven stores have been added and a number of the older stores extensively remodeled and enlarged. Besides seven California locations, these stores include three in Chicago and one in the White Flint Mall in suburban Washington, D.C. A replacement store in Palm Springs opened in 1985.

I. Magnin has added a unique and exciting fashion catalog business that has gained acceptance nationwide. Today it operates twenty-six stores in northern and southern California, Chicago, Seattle, Portland, Phoenix, and the District of Columbia.

The parent company, Federated Department Stores, Inc., is a diversified retail firm serving customers across the nation through its department stores, mass merchandising stores, supermarkets, and other retail divisions. By the end of 1985, Federated had sixteen operating divisions and 604 stores in the major retail markets of thirty-six states.

The Jobs

The I. Magnin Management Training Program is designed to prepare you for a career in store or merchandise management. To give you a balance of practical experience and technical knowledge, the program combines on-the-job training with workshop instruction. Your performance is frequently evaluated and your career path charted; the overall purpose of the program is to foster your development as a well-rounded I. Magnin exec.

As a member of the Management Training Program, you move through a series of job assignments designed to give you hands-on experience in many areas of retail management. After completing the initial orientation program, you'll be placed in an assistant department manager's position, moving on to department management, with an option to pursue a career in store or merchandising management.

In each of your early assignments, you will work with a manager who will help you develop your skills and who will evaluate your performance. During a two- to four-year period, you will progress through a number of assignments:

assistant department manager—You will develop the managerial and technical skills necessary to assume department manager positions.

department manager—You will be responsible for supervising sales staff and building a profitable daily sales base; concurrently, you will master customer service skills, inventory control, merchandise presentation, buying office protocol, and staff motivation techniques.

assistant buyer—You will have responsibility for supporting the buyer in all aspects of merchandise analysis and selection, financial planning and forecasting, and store relations.

buyer—At this point, you'll be expected to run a profitable business, including identifying trends; selecting merchandise; financial planning; maintaining communications with stores, vendors, and the distribution center; and analyzing and identifying advertising opportunities.

The Payoff

As a former I. Magnin exec who now buys for Filene's noted, "Salaries are all pretty much the same, so are the benefits. What you have to evaluate when you get an offer from I. Magnin is the fit. Do you have what it takes to succeed in an environment that is both aggressive and refined, that is one part merchandising circus and one part *Town and Country* magazine?" Health and life insurance, dental insurance, disability, profit-sharing, retirement benefits, paid holidays and vacations, and a generous merchandise discount come along with the package.

The Word

If you want to begin your retailing career in an environment where analytical skill and creativity are a must, and good breeding is a must, too, then I. Magnin offers an exciting business possibility. Think of the company as the Morgan Bank of retailing; while it's not right for everyone, it is the third largest specialty store in the country, and this success means great opportunities for the fittest.

MANUFACTURERS HANOVER TRUST COMPANY

Contact Info:

John F. McGillicuddy, Chairman

Heather McGaughey, Assistant Vice President
270 Park Avenue
New York, New York 10017
(212) 286-6000

Financials:

Assets: $75.7 billion
Deposits: $44 billion
Loans: $57.6 billion

The Organization

Manufacturers Hanover Trust—or Manny Hanny, as it's known to its employees—is one of the five largest banks in the United States. Over the past five years, as the banking industry has undergone rapid change and consolidation, MHT has fought to keep up. With over $5 billion in loans to companies involved in the energy industries, the bank has spent a good deal of time and money working out problem loans. In addition, MHT's $7.6 million in loans to five struggling Latin American countries has dragged down earnings. However, the bank has begun a serious tightening and realigning effort. By laying off excess staff and pursuing high-margined small business and consumer lending, MHT is expected to get back on track. More and more the bank is attempting to be aggressive and innovative.

MHT's worldwide presence is impressive. The bank has 840 consumer offices in forty-three states and more than 100 branches in forty-one countries. It has major nonbank subsidiaries engaged in leasing, factoring, and commercial and consumer finance, and is increasing its commitment to these areas. Since 1970, the bank has been transformed from a single bank in a single city with only a limited presence abroad to an international financial power. MHT is divided into more than a dozen divisions and departments. The bank's major subsidiaries include Manufacturers Hanover Leasing Corporation, Manufacturers Hanover Financial Services, CIT Factoring and Commercial Finance Group, Manufacturers Hanover Mortgage Corporation, and Manufacturers Investment Corporation.

The Jobs

MHT is an excellent place for liberal arts grads to work. The bank employs some 32,000 people and hires one of the largest groups of college graduates in the industry each year. MHT recruits the cream of the crop from dozens of colleges and universities across the country. While the majority are from prestigious private schools, there's a good sprinkling of "state" students. But be forewarned: MHT generally hires one in fifteen or twenty candidates. MHT offers career opportunities in the auditing department, the treasury division, the real estate and mortgage department, the operations division, the special finance division, the private banking and securities industry division, the energy division, the retail banking division, and the North American division. Some positions are filled by direct placement, with training completed on the job.

Most liberal arts grads enter MHT's Credit Training Program, which is approximately eight months long for domestic areas and ten months for international. The program utilizes the lecture format, on-the-job training, and case studies. University professors are contracted to teach the academic portions of the program, while other "modules" are taught by MHT staff. The program begins with an orientation seminar, which provides a management-level overview of MHT and the banking and financial environment. The next seven weeks consist of full-day accounting, money, and banking classes. Following completion of this phase, a week is spent conducting credit investigations, and then you spend the next month or so on a line assignment within your employing division, applying the skills learned in class to the job. Then you return to the classroom for seven more weeks of full-day classes in corporate finance and business law. In addition, you'll attend seminars on noncredit bank service, international finance, and marketing analysis. Finally you'll study credit analysis, to understand how to analyze the credit worthiness of customers. Following credit analysis, you'll write a credit review, and if this is satisfactory, you're ready for placement in your permanent division or department.

The Payoff

Salaries are reported to be highly competitive at MHT. Most liberal arts grads hired for the Credit Training Program are paid in the mid-twenties range. The bank's complete benefit plan includes medical insurance, dental insurance, long-term disability, short-term sick leave, travel accident insurance, and group life insurance. In addition, MHT offers profit-sharing and retirement plans. You'll also be eligible for free checking accounts and discounted credit cards, personal loans, and residential mortgages. Paid vacation time is plentiful, as are holidays.

The Word

Training at MHT is extremely challenging, and many rate the program as the most prestigious in the industry. One trainee compares it to boot camp: "I never worked as hard in college as I did during the training program. You really have to pay attention all the time, or you'll start failing exams and falling behind." All along, you have to maintain a 75 percent average on tests—and tutors are available to help. Even though the program is tough, few trainees don't make it through. MHT has one of the lowest attrition rates in the industry, due to careful planning by management. Trainees are encouraged to take responsibility and to make themselves visible. If you distinguish yourself during training, you're likely to advance rapidly up your career path.

People-wise, MHT has a reputation for hiring good-looking athletes, the type who look as if they should be carrying a bag of golf clubs or a squash racket wherever they go. However, in recent years, the stereotype has changed significantly. Women, minorities, and non–Ivy Leaguers have all found a place at the bank. The "good old boy" network still holds strong, but MHT has increasingly become more of a meritocracy. Trainees frequently socialize after hours, and several months or years out of the program, they maintain an informal alumni network. There's not the feeling of constant activity you'd find at a Citibank or Chase, or the stuffy, traditional atmosphere of a Morgan or Bankers Trust. MHT occupies its own niche, and it's not nearly as conventional and complacent as it once was.

MARINE MIDLAND BANK

Contact Info:

John R. Petty, Chairman

Lyne Hawkins, Undergraduate Recruitment
140 Broadway
New York, New York 10015
(212) 440-1884

Financials:

Assets: $22 billion
Deposits: $15.7 billion
Loans: $15 billion

The Organization

Marine Midland Bank's origins date back to a summer morning in 1850, when a group of eight businessmen gathered at the shores of Lake Erie in Buffalo to organize a bank. Buffalo was the largest grain port in the country then, and the group wanted to develop finance arrangements that would keep the trade growing. They called the bank Marine, because of the importance of shipping. Later, the name "Midland" was added, as a reflection of the company's expansion along the railroad routes into the heartland of New York State. Over the years, Marine Midland acquired numerous banks throughout the state, eventually adding more than eighty subsidiaries. On New Year's Day, 1976, the bank undertook what was then the largest bank merger in history, consolidating all its regional outlets into a single statewide bank. Four years later, Marine Midland became the first multinational U.S. bank to align itself with a major foreign institution. It entered a partnership with The Hongkong and Shanghai Banking Corporation, one of the oldest British banks of Asia. Today Hongkong Shanghai owns 51 percent of the bank, and the organizations' joint resources put them among the top twenty-five banks in the world.

Today Marine Midland is an international financial services corporation providing banking, trading, investment, and securities services across the world. It deals with everyone from small businesses and municipalities to large corporations, governments, and other banks. In addition, Marine Midland currently serves one out of every five households in New York State. Recently the bank reorganized its basic lines into five sectors and moved aggressively into the development of new technology and products. Marine Midland maintains some three hundred branches, along with an extensive electronic banking network. Outside New York, the bank has offices in twenty-four locations overseas and in ten different states, including a separately capitalized subsidiary in Delaware.

The Jobs

According to Marine Midland, "Banking expertise isn't born, it's made." To this end, the bank recruits several dozen liberal arts grads each year for its variety of opportunities. Although recruiters say they "find the academic background most frequently compatible with our needs includes course work in accounting, money and banking, economics, and corporate finance," French and art history majors aren't discouraged from applying. The bank describes its ideal candidate as possessing "maturity and potential—a special balance of reason and creativity that makes an original thinker."

Most liberal arts grads undergo a training program, which consists of rotational on-the-job assignments, exposure to various divisions and departments, and formal courses and seminars. The Management Associate Program trains candidates for assignments in corporate/institutional/international banking, national commercial or middle-market banking, asset-based finance, credit policy administration, or capital markets. Core training is conducted in the New York City credit department and lasts about a year. The program begins with a review of accounting principles and exposure to the techniques used in statement spreading, credit investigations, and financial analysis. On-the-job assignments in credit analysis give you a chance to apply what you've learned. Next comes course work in intermediate accounting, money and banking, and corporate finance, taught by university professors. To supplement this training, periodic economic update seminars are conducted by Marine Midland's economic department. The final phase of the program is comprised of formal and informal lectures and seminars given by line and senior managers, as well as departmental training assignments. Permanent assignments for associates are determined at the end of the credit training period and are based on three factors: the bank's staffing requirements, your preference, and your performance.

The Payoff

While Marine Midland isn't known for offering stupendous starting salaries, the prospects for promotion and raises are good. Most liberal arts grads start off in the low- to mid-twenties range and are given reviews every six to twelve months. Marine Midland offers a complete benefits package, including medical, dental, and life insurance. In addition, staffers are eligible for free checking accounts and discounted credit cards, personal loans, and mortgages.

The Word

Marine Midland may not be the biggest, the most aggressive, or the most prestigious bank in New York—but trainees say it's a great place to work. Increasingly, the bank has attempted to recruit better and brighter candidates, for a mix of schools and backgrounds. Marine Midland is definitely not a clubby, stuffy, ingroup place. It's among the most democratic of the large money center banks, and women and minorities are visible at most levels.

THE MAY DEPARTMENT STORES COMPANY

Contact Information:

David C. Farrell, Chairman and Chief Executive Officer

Timothy W. Plunkett, Director, Executive Recruiting
611 Olive Street
St. Louis, Missouri 63101
(314) 342-6700

Financials (1985):

Sales: $5,079.9 million
Profits: $235.4 million

The Organization

Given its recent acquisition of the properties of Associated Dry Goods Corp. (ADG), The May Department Stores Company is now: May Co., California; Hecht's; Famous-Barr Co.; Kaufmann's; May Co., Cleveland; G. Fox & Co.; Meier & Frank; O'Neil's; May D & F; May Cohens; and the discount stores Venture and Volume Shoe; as well as Lord & Taylor; J. W. Robinson Co.; L. S. Ayres and Company; Sibley, Linsay & Curr Co.; The Denver Dry Goods Company; Goldwater's; Hahne & Company; and the discount stores Caldor, Inc., and Loehmann's, Inc.; and the specialty store Sycamore Specialty Stores. While newspapers such as the St. Louis *Post-Dispatch* predicted a "tricky path in melding two empires," the purchase, which was the largest ever by a company based in St. Louis, seems to be smoother than expected. So far, David Farrell and his cadre of executives have begun to meld two far-flung retail companies that employ a total of 145,000 people in nearly every state in the Union and several foreign countries.

In the letter to shareholders in its third-quarter report for 1986, chairman Farrell and president Thomas A. Hays reported record sales and earnings for the third quarter and for the year to date. The acquisition was reported completed, having become effective on October 4, 1986. "May's approaches and processes will benefit Associated, and Associated will provide a number of important growth vehicles. The job of assimilating these two companies could not be off to a better start. The entire organization is energized and working together."

The Jobs

The May Company offers opportunities—great opportunities—from sea to shining sea. Whether you join G. Fox and begin your career in New England, May Cohens and start in Florida, L. S. Ayres or Famous-Barr and begin in the Midwest, or Robinson's or May California in the Golden State, what you're joining is a company poised to lead its industry now and in the future. And unlike some companies of this magnitude that don't emphasize recruiting, hiring, and training, May is a company committed to excellence, especially to bringing excellent college grads into the business.

May recruiters are a special breed, a classy breed, and they comb campuses such as Berkeley, Brown, Cornell, Dartmouth, Duke, Indiana, Notre Dame, Stanford, Virginia, and the like to find the best and the brightest, to persuade you smart young folks that what they have to offer is better than the Manny Hannys and the Procter & Gambles of the working world. The May Company is credited with having been the catalyst for the great boost in entry-level salaries for liberal arts graduates who weren't headed to Wall Street. In fact, for the classes of 1983, 1984, and 1985, May created quite a stir by presenting a well-paying alternative that didn't require you to know that two years hence, you'd be heading back to school for an M.B.A.

The company has an official party line on liberal arts grads. "We hire men and women who can become future leaders of our company. Because our industry mirrors the world, we look for students of social trends as well as business trends. Retailing does not operate in a vacuum; it is a creative response to American consumers' lives. A liberal arts background is excellent preparation for a retailing career."

The first career steps in May companies are as executive trainee, department manager, and assistant buyer. In the executive trainee program, new associates spend several months building a foundation of technical retail knowledge and supervisory skills. Combining classroom study with in-store experience, topics such as selling skills, merchandise presentation, advertising preparation, shortage control, statistical analysis, and supervisory skills are introduced.

In most instances, your first assignment is as a department manager. Just a few weeks after you've enjoyed the graduation party scene, you could be responsible for a million-dollar-plus department. The technical skills developed during the training program become a daily way of life as you study merchandise flow, monitor inventory levels, analyze sales trends, budget, perform merchandise analysis, and create product presentations.

As a department manager, you determine what sells, who your customer is, and, in liaison with the buyer, monitor the content and assortment of merchandise. You are responsible for merchandise presentation—not just creating product displays but establishing the most efficient and effective use of floor space through dramatic fixturing and department arrangement.

The people skills introduced during supervisory training are now used as you deal directly with customers, sales associates, store management, and vendors supplying the products. As department manager, you have responsibility for staffing needs, performance appraisals, training, and motivation.

From department manager, your next career step is generally to assistant buyer, where emphasis is on the basics of buying: developing seasonal planning skills, controlling stock shortages, learning open-to-buy, analyzing reports, and evaluating advertising. Other important elements in this position include short- and long-term planning, forecasting, and developing marketing strategies to match economic conditions.

Once you've mastered merchandising principles and people management skills, you're ready to assume the position of buyer. This can happen anytime from three years after you join the company. One of the most familiar aspects of the buying job is the actual buying—visiting the markets in Los Angeles, Chicago, and New York City every four to six weeks to preview merchandise offered by vendors. In addition, May buyers sometimes travel overseas in conjunction with May Department Stores International's network of buying offices.

Selecting merchandise is part of the buyer's job, but as buyer, you're the total product manager of a merchandise category.

You're a financial manager, responsible for budgets totaling into the millions. You plan and work with vendors, obtaining products at the most advantageous price. A buyer is a marketing manager, tailoring merchandise to targeted customer segments, analyzing sales trends, and developing promotion and advertising activities. A buyer is an organizer, planning the timely arrival of products on the selling floor, and a researcher and forecaster, anticipating trends, predicting customer wants, and monitoring the competition.

Stated simply, each buyer is an entrepreneur, running a multi-million-dollar business within the larger framework of a store company. Thus, what May recruits is entrepreneurs who have the savvy to join and help build its dynasty.

The Payoff

No doubt about it, May is the retailing industry leader in salary and benefits and in total compensation, as well as in quality of entry-level life. For 1987, in the "old" May divisions of the company, offers should be in the $24,000 range, with top candidates getting slightly fatter offers. For 1986, the average salary offer was $22,600. In the "new" May divisions, the company is having to do some quick catching up, so first-job offers will be for less money. Have no fear, however: it's all May now and it will probably only be a matter of months before the company has solved the compensation dilemma caused by the acquisition.

Besides merchandise discounts, vacations and holidays, medical care programs, life insurance, disability coverage, travel accident insurance, and retirement and profit sharing and savings plans, May is somewhat unique in offering recent graduates relocation assistance—one-way transportation to the job location, plus an allowance for miscellaneous moving or temporary living expenses.

The Word

The company's mission is "Excellence in Retailing," and that means excellent opportunities for excellent people. Chairman Farrell is a liberal arts graduate of Antioch College who has spent his entire working career with the company and who is committed enough to its college recruiting program to make a few stops on campuses each year to interview prospective candidates for the several hundred openings the company has. With its purchase of ADG, May is the fourth largest retailer in America, and with chairman Farrell at the helm, this is probably one of the best employers in the country, whether you're looking for a job in business, in retailing, or in both. As Farrell said, "With a major, successful organization like May Company, retailing is one of the most challenging and rewarding careers available. . . . Career advancement is limited only by your skill and performance."

A University of Virginia grad working for G. Fox said, "The corporate culture is what makes the whole thing fly. I moved to Hartford and didn't know anyone. I joined a company softball team, worked long hours, and began making friends with the other trainees and with store executives. Soon the company becomes a way of life—a very pleasant way of life. When I introduced my fiancé to my colleagues and friends, he kept telling me how lucky I am, that most companies don't employ so many nice people who have so much in common." She added, "I have a sense that what they look for as much as anything is the in-common stuff, the zeal for life and living, the capacity to work hard and to play hard. You're either right for the business and the company and love it, or there's not a lot of chance that you'll make it through the half-dozen interviews that are pretty much the minimum when you're being considered as an executive trainee."

MELLON BANK

Contact Info:

J. D. Barnes, Chief Executive Officer

Judy Balmer, Manager of College Relations and Recruiting
One Mellon Bank Center
Pittsburgh, Pennsylvania 15258
(412) 234-4000

Financials:

Assets: $30.6 billion
Deposits: $19 billion
Loans: $19.4 billion

The Organization

Founded by Andrew Mellon, the son of an Irish potato farmer, Mellon Bank is the largest bank in Pennsylvania and one of the nation's top fifteen banks. Over the course of more than a century, Mellon has evolved from a small, private banking house into an international finance corporation. Mellon's history is closely intertwined with that of its parent city; the bank helped build Pittsburgh into the capital of industrial giants, helped it survive through the Depression, and now is helping with its revitalization campaign. Although there's not a Mellon at the top of the bank anymore, the family still controls 10 percent of the stock. In addition to its Pittsburgh headquarters, Mellon has representative offices in Atlanta, Boston, Chicago, Dallas, Houston, Los Angeles, New York, and San Francisco.

Today Mellon has over three hundred branches in Pennsylvania and Delaware and conducts business in more than sixty nations. Over the past five years, the bank acquired Philadelphia's Girard Bank, Central Counties Bank, and Northwest Pennsylvania Corporation. Mellon's principal areas of focus are worldwide commercial banking, domestic retail and wholesale banking, and trust and investment management services. Mellon's departments are organized into three broad areas: relationship, product, and support banking. The relationship departments—community banking, international banking, and national banking—deal directly with Mellon customers, individual and corporate alike. The product departments are concerned with specific specialties such as portfolio and funds management, real estate and trust, and investment. The support departments—corporate consulting, credit policy, finance, human resources, information management and research, marketing and communications, and operating services —are involved with every area of the bank.

The Jobs

As the largest bank in Pennsylvania, Mellon employs some fifteen thousand people. Although the bank states a preference for candidates with backgrounds in finance, economics, and accounting, "a limited number of outstanding applicants from undergraduate programs will also be considered." Since Mellon has lately taken a more aggressive stance in the management of its investment portfolio, this may be a good place to apply. Likewise, the bank plans to increase the national banking department, and that may be a good bet for liberal arts grads.

Mellon's training program involves three or four months of intensive classroom work, as well as credit reviews and an introduction to noncredit services. Once training is completed, you are given responsibility immediately. In addition to national and international banking, portfolio and fund management, and trust and investments, trainees can be placed in auditing, leasing, human resources, operating services, and real estate.

The Payoff

Although Mellon pays slightly lower salaries than the major New York money center banks, keep in mind the dollar's value in Pittsburgh. Most liberal arts grads start in the $19,000 to $25,000 range and are reviewed periodically and given raises. Mellon offers a comprehensive benefits package, which includes medical, dental, and life insurance coverage, as well as long-term disability insurance, complete vacation/holiday/sick day schedules, and tuition reimbursement. Mellon also offers a profit-sharing plan and a retirement plan. In addition, employees are eligible for free checking services and discounts on loans and other financial services.

The Word

You've probably heard that Pittsburgh is on the rise. In a much-publicized recent study, it was rated as one of the most livable cities in the United States. True, it's not as cosmopolitan as several of its neighbors to the north and east; however, you'll find the quality of life is surprisingly sophisticated. Cultural and recreational activities abound, and the city has an excellent cadre of universities and museums. In addition, Pittsburgh is an easy commute to Philadelphia, Washington, Chicago, and other urban areas.

Although you may not be as familiar with Mellon's reputation as you are with its competitors, Mellon is known for being one of the nation's most prestigious regional banks. While it continues to maintain the gentlemanly presence of its founders, Mellon has become increasingly creative and innovative. Lately it's had a few troubles; when LTV entered bankruptcy proceedings, Mellon's was disclosed as a primary lender to the steel company. Likewise, several energy related defaults have caused credit losses. However, management has tightened the reins on expenses, and the bank is expected to regain strength in its core businesses. With Pittsburgh's spreading renaissance of light industry and service companies, Mellon is seeing growing loan demand. "Even though the bank's history dates back over a hundred years, it feels like it's much younger. It's not a stodgy place, where the past seems to overshadow the present. The people here seem really excited about being part of the action," said one trainee.

MCKINSEY & COMPANY, INC.

Contact Info:

Ron Daniel, Managing Director

Chuck Farr, Director of Recruiting
55 East 52nd Street
New York, New York 10022
(212) 909-8400

The Organization

When many people hear the term "management consulting," they think of McKinsey. Since 1926, the firm has been handling problem solving and program implementation for corporate and government institutions across the globe. Many of the industry's standards were set by McKinsey, and most of the field's buzzwords were coined by it. The firm generally works at the top-management level to assist clients in improving the performance of their organizations, both by solving internal problems and by anticipating and responding effectively to external threats and opportunities. Part of McKinsey's strength lies in its history; many Fortune Five Hundred companies came to the firm for advice in the post–World War II generation, and a large number remain as clients. In addition, McKinsey has the most extensive global network in the industry. The firm has domestic offices in New York, Boston, Atlanta, Chicago, Cleveland, Pittsburgh, Los Angeles, Stamford, Washington, San Francisco, Dallas, and Houston. Internationally McKinsey is represented in London, Paris, Toronto, Brussels, Amsterdam, Zurich, Stockholm, Oslo, Copenhagen, Caracas, Mexico City, Osaka, Tokyo, Milan, Lisbon, Madrid, Hong Kong, Stuttgart, Munich, Hamburg, Frankfurt, Düsseldorf, Melbourne, and Sydney.

Currently about 56 percent of McKinsey's work is in the United States, while 34 percent is in Europe and 10 percent is divided among Japan, Australia, Canada, and Latin America. Although each office adapts to the cultural values and management practices of its own country, all share a common philosophy and adhere to a common set of standards. Unlike many of the newer consulting firms, which specialize in a specific area, McKinsey handles almost every kind of project imaginable. Nearly half the firm's work is in corporate strategy, overall organization, and related policy areas. The rest consists of direct efforts to improve clients' short-term performance by turning around profit declines, reorienting product/market strategies, cutting operating and overhead costs, and increasing productivity on all fronts. In addition, McKinsey handles research and development, finance, marketing, manufacturing and distribution, manpower development, executive compensation, computer systems, and planning and control.

As consulting has become an increasingly competitive business, with a host of aggressive young firms battling over the biggest and best clients, McKinsey has relied on a constant interchange of information, experience, and personnel. To provide the best possible mix of consulting skills and support services for a given project, any office can draw upon the firm's worldwide resources. In fact, more than 15 percent of McKinsey's work is performed by consultants loaned by one office to another for a particular assignment. However, since the firm does not avoid serving competing clients in the same industry, it maintains strict confidentiality about proprietary information.

Over the years, McKinsey has developed a unique approach to accepting and completing assignments. Before taking on a project, the firm makes every reasonable effort to ensure that there are opportunities for significant benefits to the client and that there aren't any real barriers to achieving these benefits. McKinsey refrains from entering into contracts with clients (except where required by law), so that at any time, the client is free to terminate the relationship. This also provides the firm with a safety valve, since it can choose to withdraw from an assignment if circumstances arise that make the agreed-upon objectives unattainable. In addition, McKinsey works very closely with members of the client organization, holding frequent progress reviews with individuals at all levels. This way the firm believes it can "usually overcome rather quickly the natural disturbance that may come with the presence of outsiders." McKinsey was one of the first major consultants to realize the effectiveness of using client personnel as members of the case team. By doing so, productivity is multiplied, costs are reduced, and implementation efforts are enhanced. In addition, client personnel can often apply what they've learned to other areas of the organization.

The Jobs

Competition for entry-level jobs at McKinsey is tough, and getting tougher all the time. The firm's training program for research analysts is considered tops by consultants inside and outside the firm. McKinsey employs more than a thousand consultants worldwide and hires a couple of dozen undergraduates each year, primarily for its domestic offices. The firm's recruiters are reported to be friendly but direct. They ask hard questions and expect well-thought-out answers. They're looking for students with excellent records of achievement, both in terms of academic credentials and extracurricular activities. Since you're going to be playing on their team, it's also important that you be mature, poised, and able to make sound judgments. The "ability to deal effectively with people at all levels" is how the firm puts it. In addition, you should be able to illustrate your analytical and quantitative skills with specific examples from your background. According to the firm, "Our personnel policies are designed to ensure that none but the best-qualified consultants are hired, and that only the ablest of these remain to make their careers with us." It's a tall order, but McKinsey fills it. Year after year, the firm hires blue-chip candidates from leading colleges and universities around the country.

Following a brief orientation to problem-solving methods and the firm's philosophy, research analysts are assigned to teams. Normally a team is headed by a director or principal who takes the lead in planning the assignment, maintains a close working relationship with client management, and bears full responsibility for the quality of results. As team leader, this individual participates personally in every phase of the project: gathering and analyzing information, formulating and testing hypotheses, developing and communicating recommendations, and preparing for implementation. Typically client assignments are three to six months long. During this period, research analysts essentially provide support for the project by performing financial analysis, compiling data, writing reports, and making presentations. As you gain experience and sharpen your skills, you'll be given increasing amounts of responsibility. Analysts are expected to work independently, and at a pace commensurate with their superiors.

After two years, most research analysts leave McKinsey to attend business or law school. However, a tiny minority who demonstrate a real knack for consulting may be asked to remain on. In addition, talented hires may be offered an interest-free tuition loan, which will be waived upon return to McKinsey after obtaining a graduate degree.

The Payoff

McKinsey offers an excellent salary and benefits package, which includes medical, dental, and life insurance. Most liberal arts grads can expect to start in the mid-thirties range, and many receive bonuses and raises that come close to doubling that amount.

Throughout your career at McKinsey, you'll be subject to frequent, rigorous performance reviews aimed at evaluating the quality of your problem solving and the results you've achieved for clients. Your compensation is likely to double within the first few years, and to continue rising as you advance. Perks are generous, particularly in the area of travel. Whether you go to a domestic or an international location, and stay two days or two months, McKinsey will take very, very good care of you.

The Word

From what we've heard, McKinsey is a rock-solid place to begin a consulting career. Over all, the training is excellent, the work is challenging, and the people are friendly and stimulating. However, several liberal arts grads complained that they were a bit further from the action than they'd like. Due to McKinsey's size and structure, most research analysts don't have much exposure to top management of outside organizations. You will be exposed to senior members of your own staff, but it's unlikely that you'll be actively involved in presentations to or discussions with clients. Once you've established yourself as a hot prospect, though, you'll begin interacting with a broader range of people.

Although McKinsey has become a corporation, it continues to operate as a partnership. Ownership and management are vested in some two hundred-odd directors and principals and a few key administrators. Membership in the ownership group is attained by election from the body of associates, who make up the majority of the consulting staff. Seniority is thus directly related to your professional achievement, and the firm operates as a meritocracy. Perhaps this explains McKinsey's success in keeping up with all the dynamic newcomers; the firm has persisted in giving opportunity to the best and brightest. "Some of the old-line firms have become dinosaurs," says one analyst, "but not McKinsey. It's got a real can-do spirit, and an entrepreneurial attitude."

MERCK & CO., INC.

Contact Info:
P. Roy Vagelos, M.D., President and Chief Executive Officer

Rodney Johnson, Manager of College Relations
P.O. Box 2000
Rahway, New Jersey 07065
(201) 574-6221

Financials (1985):
Sales: $3,547.5 million
Profits: $539.9 million

The Organization

From vaccines for newborns to advanced antibiotics, Merck products maintain and restore health. Merck is a global leader in its efforts to achieve a most critical goal: longer, more productive lives. Merck is a worldwide organization engaged primarily in the business of discovering, developing, producing, and marketing products and services to maintain and restore health.

Today around the world, Merck technologies are constantly at work and millions of people rely on the company every day. Standing behind its dozens of products are more than thirty thousand employees who make Merck the world's leading prescription pharmaceutical company. Headquartered in Rahway, New Jersey, Merck—which *Fortune* lauded as one of the most respected companies in America—is one of the nation's largest and strongest corporations. It is also an international concern, with some sixty facilities overseas and marketing networks in virtually every major nation. Merck ranks in the top quartile of the *Fortune* Five Hundred.

Merck is organized into a group of closely knit, interdependent divisions and subsidiaries. Every Merck organization has a specific charter and the resources to achieve the company's goals of being the premier ethical pharmaceutical company, of enhancing stockholders' values, and of keeping the company's financial position strong. Merck is Merck Sharp & Dohme Research Laboratories;

Merck Chemical Manufacturing Division; Merck Sharp & Dohme (MSD); Merck Sharp & Dohme International (MSDI); MSD AGVET; Calgon Corporation; Kelco; and Corporate Staff (which works with all these operations and encompasses executive management as well as professional groups devoted to financial control, analysis, and planning; computer resources; human resources; legal; public affairs; and other functions).

The Jobs

Merck was put in the top three by a cross section of executives polled by *Fortune* for its ability to attract, develop, and keep talented people. The company recruits liberal arts graduates for several functions, including marketing for MSD, MSDI, MSD AGVET, Calgon; sales for all divisions; and corporate staff in the computer resources, human resources, and public affairs areas.

Sales and marketing professionals bring the benefits of Merck technology to those who need them. The most common entry level position is with Merck Sharp & Dohme as a professional representative, working with physicians. MSD AGVET, Calgon, and Kelco also use marketing and sales professionals.

Once you're hired for these jobs, the company takes getting you prepared very seriously. Since Merck deals with physicians, the nation's most educated audience, all marketing and sales professionals are prepared to work successfully in that environment. Merck also stresses balance and expects its professionals to understand the correct applications of a product and to be able to explain in detail the efficacy and safety advantages as well as potential side effects. The company also emphasizes long-term relations, since it is a trusted partner in problem solving, not a short-term supplier. All sales professionals are provided with valuable resources in terms of training, marketing support, and tools for time and territory management. Finally, Merck offers you wide-ranging opportunities once you begin to show promise in the marketing and sales area.

As an MSD professional representative, you are the prime link between Merck and the health care community. You provide information about Merck products through direct consultations, serve specific geographic territories, and report to district managers. Reps spend their days arranging and having clinical conferences to review and discuss product or disease information. You work with physicians, hospital administrators, and other health care professionals, and may focus on specific diagnostic groups or medical specialties.

MSD provides an intensive training program for new professionals. Training, which takes place at regional offices and at West Point, Pennsylvania, includes self-paced study, lectures, case studies, videotaped presentations, interaction with Merck physicians, and on-the-job experience. The emphasis is on product knowledge and interpersonal communications skills.

Once you're successful in the professional representative position, you can move ahead to larger, more complex territories—district management, or to headquarters positions in marketing research, product management, and marketing communications.

Think about the following opportunities, which are just some of the jobs that are open to new grads:

MSD AGVET—You begin in a sales territory, calling on veterinarians, farmers, ranchers, and others involved in the care of farm animals and crops.
Calgon Commercial Division—You bring formulated products, such as antiseptic hand washes, to health care and industrial organizations.
Calgon Water Management Division—In a technical sales capacity, you consult with utilities and process industries and apply Calgon technologies to water management needs.

With the corporate staff jobs, several disciplines offer training. One example is the human resources associate program, which helps newly hired professionals gain experience in a variety of human resources functions. As an associate, you are provided with an array of line and staff assignments. With successful performance in the program, you should soon be in a position to move into human resources planning, compensation and benefits, training, recruitment, or employee relations.

The Payoff

The buzzword is "excellent," and in an environment known for its managerial excellence, it's no wonder that Merck rewards excellent performance appropriately. Entry-level salaries are above average and benefits are generous. Medical and dental plans, tuition assistance, life insurance, a savings and stock purchase plan, and a pension program are just starters.

The Word

Its slogan is "The World Expects Excellence From Merck." It's the Merck way of life, according to recruiters. The company pioneered some revolutionary new drugs such as Diuril, a diuretic that vastly improved the treatment of high blood pressure and congestive heart failure; Aldomet, another benchmark in the control of high blood pressure; and Sinemet, to treat Parkinson's disease. It also pioneered a fantastic corporate culture that encourages team spirit within companies, among companies, and throughout the company worldwide.

"With all the positive press the company has been getting for being well managed, let alone for its product innovations, it's becoming much more desirable as an employer," said one Ivy League placement director. "For a student who wants to work in the health care industry and isn't determined to be a doctor, Merck offers a unique opportunity to combine an affinity for business with an interest in medicine," he added.

MERRILL LYNCH & COMPANY

Contact Info:

Roger E. Birk, Chairman

Eva Taub, College Recruiting
One Liberty Plaza
New York, New York 10080
(212) 637-7455

The Organization

Merrill Lynch is known as the firm that brought Wall Street to
Main Street. Founder Charles Edward Merrill was an entrepreneurial genius with an uncanny knack for judging the nation's mood. During his youth in Jacksonville, Florida, he earned
pocket money by peddling newspapers to gentlemen on their way
out of a red-light district. After a brief stint as a bond salesman on
Wall Street, Merrill opened his own business in 1914. He took
Edmund Lynch, a soda fountain equipment salesman with whom
he shared a boardinghouse room, as his partner. During the 1920s,
Merrill Lynch mushroomed. The firm helped found several chain
stores, including Safeway, McCrory, K mart, and J. C. Penney. By
1930, Merrill decided to retire and sell his business to E. A. Pierce
& Company (formerly Burrill & Housman), at the time one of Wall
Street's largest brokerages. A decade later, following the Depression, Merrill returned to the business when his firm was merged
with Fenner & Beane, a New Orleans brokerage house. Thus the
company became Merrill Lynch, Pierce, Fenner & Beane. However, twenty years later, Alpheus Beane left the firm and was
replaced by Winthrop Smith—who had started his career as Merrill's office boy in 1916.

Over the years, Merrill Lynch grew and prospered, becoming a
broadly diversified financial institution. The firm's understanding
of chain stores no doubt helped in its expansion. Seizing the opportunity in the 1950s and 1960s, Merrill Lynch became the first
brokerage house to get John Q. Public to play the stock market.
Through an extensive mass advertising campaign, the firm convinced ordinary Americans that no matter how small their portfolios, they were worthy of Merrill Lynch's attention. One famous ad
was titled, "What Everybody Ought to Know About This Stock
and Bond Business." According to industry estimates, the firm
managed to get more than three times the number of people
involved in the stock market than were previously. In 1955, the
firm rented a Manhattan armory for a "How to Invest" show,
whose success led to a permanent Investment Information Center
located in Grand Central Station. Merrill Lynch also pioneered
the concept of the broker who worked for a salary, to help prove to

customers that they weren't simply trying to make as many commissions as possible.

Naturally, some of the more upper crust firms on Wall Street weren't thrilled with Merrill Lynch's rampant growth. In fact, many regarded Merrill Lynch as violating the privileged ranks by letting the average American have access to their territory. But when the stock market took an enormous dive in the late 1960s and many firms went bankrupt, Merrill Lynch kept on making money. In 1971, the firm went public and became one of the first member firms of the New York Stock Exchange to have its own stock traded on the Big Board. Today the firm is the world's largest securities broker, with some 550 offices across the globe, serving more than eighty thousand institutions and over five million individual customers. Among its main businesses are commodity futures, government and municipal securities, investment and merchant banking, real estate financing, relocation services, real estate brokerage, and mortgage insurance. The firm is organized into three departments: consumer markets, capital markets, and real estate and insurance.

Due to its massive size, Merrill Lynch has an enormous capital base that allows the firm to make investments and commitments that might not be possible in smaller firms. No deal or market is beyond its grasp, particularly because the publicly held firm controls over 10 percent of the brokerage market (which is more than twice the share of its nearest competitor). In recent years, Merrill Lynch has become known as the prototypical financial supermarket—a sort of one-stop-shopping location for customers desiring a galaxy of financial services. Despite the increasing globalization and institutionalization of its business, Merrill Lynch remains committed to a customer-oriented, rather than a product-centered, structure. The firm has regional branches around the country, with major centers in Chicago, Houston, Los Angeles, and San Francisco. The firm also does business in Canada, Europe, Japan, Asia, Latin America, Australia, and the Middle East, and maintains offices in most of those areas.

The Jobs

Merrill Lynch employs over 45,000 people worldwide, about 10 percent of whom work in the capital markets group. Every year several thousand college seniors apply for jobs and hundreds are interviewed across the country. Of these students, less than a hundred are hired for training programs in the capital markets division. According to the firm, "We are committed to recruiting a superior group of talented people—men and women whose goals match our own, people who are personally dedicated to providing first-class client service through innovation, creativity, and uncompromising standards of performance." While many Ivy Leaguers are hired, you'll find plenty of people who graduated from schools you've never even heard of. Good grades, extracurriculars, and personality count, as do maturity, energy, self-motivation, creativity, and integrity. Liberal arts grads are hired for most of Merrill Lynch's major divisions, including consumer markets, corporate systems, mortgage finance, and real estate.

If you're among the cream of the crop, you may be hired for Merrill Lynch's two-year financial analyst program. One of the industry's most prestigious, it allows you to work side by side with seasoned investment bankers, gaining exposure to a broad spectrum of business transactions. As an analyst, you perform detailed research on financial questions, developing extensive knowledge of information resources as well as technical mastery of sophisticated financial analysis methods. The job involves more than just number crunching, however; you can expect to be in direct contact with senior management, through meetings and presentations. In choosing applicants for this program, the firm looks for "a record of outstanding academic achievement, extracurricular involvement and work experience, and demonstrated leadership qualities. Analysts must be exceptionally articulate, able to write effectively, and able to work well with others." If you're selected, you enter a one-month full-time orientation program at Merrill Lynch headquarters in New York. In addition to an overview of the firm's varied operations, intensive training is provided in accounting, finance, securities, and computers. On completion of the classroom portion, you'll be assigned to an investment banking team. You may work for a product group, which focuses on a particular industry (e.g., transportation), or for a specialty area, such as mergers and acquisitions. In your second year, you may join another group or rotate through a regional investment banking office. At the end of your two years, you may return to business or law school and then return to Merrill Lynch to continue your career.

The Payoff

According to Merrill Lynch, "Financial analysts receive a substantial base salary as well as an annual bonus that reflects their own performance as well as that of the firm." In the past, analysts have been known to earn up to half their salary in the year-end bonus. Most liberal arts grads start in the high-twenties to low-thirties range. Merrill Lynch's comprehensive benefits plan includes health, life, and accident insurance, as well as pension programs, tuition refunds, and reduced commissions on stock transactions.

The Word

Most liberal arts grads who go to work for Merrill Lynch seem bullish on the firm. They say it's like a club—not a stuffy old men's club, but a dynamic young people's club. Merrill Lynch is truly "a breed apart" from its competitors, in that it's not interested in pursuing prestige for prestige's sake. Instead, the firm pursues power and performance. William Schreyer, who became chief executive in 1984, entered the firm's first junior executive training squad in 1948 and has never worked anywhere else. He's known as a gregarious, friendly type, although his detractors say he's not the most creative financier. However, his commitment to the business is intense; his father managed a brokerage office in Pennsylvania that later became part of Fenner & Beane, one of the firm's antecedents. From the time he was a child, Schreyer hung around the office and soaked up the atmosphere. In the Merrill Lynch annual report he stated, "Our mission is to be a client-focused, worldwide financial services organization, striving for excellence by serving the needs of individuals, corporations, governments, and institutions. Our objective is to be the acknowledged leader in the value we offer our shareholders and the rewards we offer our employees. This then will be our legacy of leadership." To know no boundaries. . . .

From what we heard, working for Merrill Lynch has more than a few things in common with working for Citibank. Both are monolithic organizations in which the individual has to shout a bit to be heard. And both offer tremendous opportunity for aggressive people to make a real contribution. Despite Merrill Lynch's size, liberal arts grads find management makes a serious effort to develop potential. However, some young staffers find the firm's magnitude overwhelming; they report that the firm can seem overly bureaucratic and political. "It's great to work for the biggest, but it isn't always the best," says one former analyst. "I found a real sink-or-swim mentality prevails. Nearly everyone is like a little fish in a gigantic sea."

If you can tough it out in a large organization (one way to tell is if you thrived at a 30,000-student university), Merrill Lynch may be an ideal home for you. Currently the capital markets side of the securities business is the fastest growing and most profitable—which means Merrill Lynch's position in the industry is rock solid. Increasing deregulation of the market has opened many possibilities, and the firm is eager to penetrate new areas. Although the firm doesn't take many huge risks, it has made some bad decisions. For example, Merrill Lynch entered the real estate business in 1980, believing that it could cross-sell real estate, mortgages, insurance, and other financial products. So far, the return on capital for the real estate segment is much lower than for Merrill Lynch's other businesses, and it looks like the firm will sell it off in the near future. However, most operations are enormously profitable, and Merrill Lynch is expected to see its earnings rise some 20 percent over the next few years—which means bonuses should keep growing.

J. P. MORGAN

Contact Info:

Lewis T. Preston, Chairman

Henry Bertram, Corporate Recruiting
23 Wall Street
New York, New York 10015
(212) 208-4622

Financials:

Assets: $64 billion
Deposits: $38.8 billion
Loans: $35.2 billion

The Organization

Morgan Guaranty Trust Company of New York—also known as the Morgan Bank—is the principal subsidiary of J. P. Morgan & Company. According to Lewis Preston, the bank's chairman, "J. P. Morgan & Co. is partly a commercial bank, and partly an investment bank, but neither label defines us accurately. Morgan is unique among financial institutions today, both in what we do and in how we do it." Morgan is currently among the top five U.S. banks, and its clients are the bluest of the blue chip. Its main customers are corporations, governments, correspondent banks, and other financial institutions, as well as high-net-worth individuals. In addition to domestic and international banking functions, Morgan's operations include the management of trust funds and other assets, financial and investment counseling, fiscal agency services, and dealing in money market instruments and foreign exchange. The bank is also a primary dealer in U.S. Treasury securities and is a leading underwriter of securities of states and local governments.

Back in 1933, J. Pierpont Morgan described the bank's goal as "doing only first-class business, and that in a first-class way." That year, under the Glass-Steagall Act, Morgan's firm was broken up into two divisions. One became Morgan Stanley, the investment bank, and the other merged with Guaranty Trust in 1959 to become the Morgan Guaranty Trust Company. Nearly three decades after the merger, Morgan Guaranty is generally regarded as one of the best-managed and most profitable banks in America. Its ratio of nonperforming loans is among the lowest, and its stock continually outperforms the market. Morgan is also the only U.S. commercial bank currently given the prized triple-A rating by Moody's.

Although Morgan has offices in many foreign countries, it doesn't have a multitude of domestic branches—three, to be precise. What Morgan does have is a major presence on Wall Street, due in part to one of the largest trust departments in the world. And if chairman Lewis Preston gets his way, the Glass-Steagall Act will soon be history. Along with several of his competitors, Preston is pushing for the Federal Reserve Board to allow banking companies to expand into several underwriting businesses, such as commercial paper, municipal revenue bonds, and securities backed by mortgages and consumer loans. Some on Wall Street say that Morgan may even consider giving up its commercial bank charter so it can become a full-service investment bank—and compete head-on with its former sibling. And unlike its peer Bankers Trust, whose major strength has been trading, Morgan is prepared to enter the underwriting business immediately.

The Jobs

Only the cream of the crop can cut it at Morgan. Liberal arts grads are welcome and are encouraged to apply. Although no major is best, grades *do* count. If your GPA is under 3.0—and you don't have significant experience in a relevant area—you might be better off looking to start your banking career elsewhere. Only a few dozen trainees are hired annually, so the bank screens prospects ultracarefully.

Although you'll find plenty of recruits from the West or Midwest, Easterners tend to dominate Morgan's ranks. We heard many stories about Chip this or Muffy that who got an interview through Daddy's tennis/golf/riding/rowing partner. All we can tell you is that while the old boy network may get Chip and Muffy into the bank for an interview, it won't get them a job. Morgan is after the very best and brightest, and no amount of back-slapping will get unqualified candidates a coveted position at the bank.

Morgan's management training program is reportedly tops in the field. Both B.A.s and M.B.A.s go through the program, but M.B.A.s are accelerated. The first six months are spent studying accounting, corporate finance, credit analysis, and economics. Morgan uses the case study approach, and from what we hear, a few of the cases make Harvard Business School look easy. There's plenty of homework, and frequent exams. At various times throughout the training cycle, senior bankers give seminars and workshops in their specialties. After mastering the fundamentals of banking and finance, trainees spend a couple of months completing several credit analyses. Finally, after a series of discussions with your manager and/or mentor, you're placed in your first assignment. Morgan makes every effort to locate trainees in areas they'll be comfortable with, assuming the bank's staffing needs are met. First assignments are generally at Morgan's New York City headquarters, although foreign nationals and other qualified individuals may be placed overseas. Wherever you go, it's likely that you'll be shifted around after two or three years. Morgan is big on developing expertise in more than one area.

The Payoff

Morgan sounds like money. And it does pay more than most commercial banks. Liberal arts grads generally earn starting salaries in the mid- to upper-twenties range, and most see that figure increase significantly at the end of training. One indicator of Morgan's generosity is the number of employees who can afford to live in New York City; out of Morgan's nearly 8,700 staffers working in New York, some 5,600 live in the city. Morgan offers a comprehensive benefits package, including medical, dental, health, and disability coverage. In addition, staffers are eligible for tuition reimbursement, profit sharing, and discounted fees on certain bank services. And there's one more perk: a free lunch. Each day the bank's corporate cafeteria feeds several thousand employees for nothing.

The Word

Classy. That's how most of the people we interviewed described Morgan. Upon entering the bank's offices, you might think you've stumbled upon some sort of private club. The plush carpeting, subdued artwork, and tasteful antiques are reminiscent of an exclusive, upper-crust establishment. Indeed, if there were a social register of corporate clients, Morgan would be keeping the score. Recently the bank announced that it would be leaving its sacred headquarters on the corner of Wall and Broad Streets, next door to the New York Stock Exchange, where it has been located since 1873. However, not to worry—it's only moving up the street, to number 60 Wall Street. The capital cost of completing its new headquarters, designed by world-famous architect Kevin Roche, is $550 million.

Back in 1973, according to one report, eleven out of fourteen of Morgan's top officers had gone to Harvard, Yale, or Princeton. Today there's plenty of ordinary blood along with the blue, although the Ivy League schools are well represented throughout the bank. If you've played on any sort of team, you'll be at an advantage, since Morgan puts an enormous value on teamwork. Most trainees find the program an intense setting that fosters close relationships. "Even though it's been a few years since I got out of the program, I'm still in touch with most of the people in my class," says one Morgan banker. "Perhaps it's made easier by the fact that almost all of them are still with the bank."

MORGAN STANLEY & COMPANY

Contact Info:

S. Parker Gilbert, Chairman

Patricia Lynch, Recruiting Coordinator
1251 Avenue of the Americas
New York, New York 10020
(212) 974-4736

The Organization

When you think investment banking, chances are Morgan Stanley comes to mind. For over half a century, the firm's name has been synonymous with its business. Morgan Stanley's roots lie in the Glass-Steagall Act of 1933, which forced J. P. Morgan to choose between commercial and investment banking. He chose the former, but soon after, three partners (Harold Stanley, William Ewing, and Henry Morgan) resigned to form the investment bank of Morgan Stanley & Co. On September 16, 1935, Morgan Stanley opened for business with seven officers and a staff of thirteen employees. The firm's certificate of incorporation stated that its purpose was to "underwrite, or participate in the underwriting of, the issuance, sale, distribution, purchase, exchange, extension or modification of any securities. . . . In addition, the firm may render advisory, investigatory, supervisory, managerial or any other services, excepting legal services, in connection with the underwriting . . . exchange or modification of any securities or interest therein."

From the start, the firm's clients were the bluest of the blue bloods. In 1936, Morgan Stanley's first full year of operation, it managed or co-managed $1.1 billion of public offerings and private placements. Fifty years later, the bank had expanded to include major divisions for asset management, equities, fixed income, investment banking, tax-exempt securities, real estate, corporate finance, administration, and operations. As it has grown, Morgan Stanley has earned a reputation as the most prestigious and exclusive firms in the industry. In 1985, when the bank celebrated its fiftieth anniversary, chairman S. Parker Gilbert wrote, "While the pace of change in our business will not diminish, we continue to believe that the quality of financial advice and services delivered by our firm should be defined not by the volume of business which we transact, but rather by the needs of our clients, the value of our services, and the judgment and integrity of the people who provide these services." Gilbert, a Yale graduate and former U.S. Army intelligence officer, had been with the firm for twenty-five years when he became chairman in 1984. He succeeded Robert Baldwin, who spent thirty-six years with Morgan

Stanley before retiring to head the firm's blue-ribbon Advisory Board.

Currently Morgan Stanley serves governments, corporations, and financial institutions in principal markets around the world. It manages, underwrites, and distributes public offerings; arranges private placements of securities; provides merger and acquisition services, and offers advice on special financial matters. In addition, the firm is a member of principal U.S. stock and commodity exchanges and plays a major role in investment research, investment management, brokerage, and secondary market trading of fixed income and equity securities. Morgan Stanley also is an important dealer in government and money market securities, mortgage-backed securities, foreign exchange, and precious metals. Outside of the firm's Manhattan headquarters, the firm has offices in Chicago, San Francisco, Toronto, London, and Tokyo.

The Jobs

Getting to be one of Morgan Stanley's four thousand employees is no easy matter. Each year thousands of college seniors solicit the firm, and hundreds are interviewed. Of the many qualified applicants, only a few dozen receive offers. The best and the brightest, the cream of the crop, whatever you call it—these are the people Morgan Stanley wants and gets. Among important attributes cited by the firm are innovativeness, creativity, intellectual capabilities, interpersonal skills, and willingness to assume responsibility. The firm's recruiters are reputed to be some of the toughest in the industry, and they can smell bull—— from a mile away. It helps if you've studied accounting, economics, and/or finance in school, but it's not essential. What's most important is that you have the right stuff. A high GPA is okay, but honors are better. Likewise, playing on a team helps, but being captain really counts. And belonging to an organization is nice, but serving as president will make a difference. Many, many talented students want to work for Morgan Stanley, so distinguishing yourself from the crowd is the name of the game.

Since Morgan Stanley aims to develop well-rounded generalists in the investment banking field, new hires are exposed to a wide array of the firm's products and services by rotating through various business groups. This introductory overview is supplemented by specific training programs provided by different departments. If you're assigned to the investment banking division, you may work in investment banking services, mergers and acquisitions, international finance, or corporate finance. New analysts in investment banking learn the basic skills of financial problem solving, negotiation, and execution. Once you're familiar with these fundamentals, you're assigned to a team, which consists of a managing director, a principal or a vice president, an associate, and an analyst. All Morgan Stanley professionals are on several teams concurrently, three or four of which will be active at once. How do they handle it? According to the firm's recruiters, "[We] place a premium on an associate's ability to assume the responsibility for as much of the workload as possible." At the end of the program, each associate is placed in a specific assignment. New associates in Morgan Stanley's real estate division work in one of the firm's two real estate subsidiaries: Brooks Harvey, which concentrates on real estate projects, and Morstan Incorporated, which advises clients and makes investments for them.

The Payoff

Each year starting salaries on Wall Street creep up, and Morgan Stanley is sure to keep on top of them. The firm is generally among the top two or three bidders for new talent, offering the most competitive salary and bonus packages. Most liberal arts grads start in the low- to mid-thirties range, and can expect up to half that sum in a year-end bonus. In a recent survey of major investment banking firms, Morgan Stanley's employee benefits program was ranked at the top in overall value. In addition to medical, dental, vision care, and hearing aid plans, the firm offers life insurance, disability coverage, business travel accident insurance, and a variety of other flexible benefits. Employees may also take advantage of the deferred profit sharing plan, the pension plan, and the tuition assistance program. Morgan Stanley's matching gift program matches gifts on a dollar-for-dollar basis to eligible educational institutions, and the firm's employee assistance program provides a resource for employees whose personal problems may have an impact on job performance.

The Word

Sometimes reputations are hard to live up to. While Morgan Stanley remains one of the most important forces in the financial industry, it's not nearly as innovative or creative as some of its competitors. However, the firm is reported to be solid as a rock—something you can't say about too many players in its league. As finance has changed, Morgan Stanley has scrambled a bit to keep up. Just as we noted that Morgan Guaranty handled the social register clients of the commercial banking business, so Morgan Stanley deals with the social register of investment banking. But increasingly the brash young turks of Wall Street aren't impressed by tradition. The new breed wants results, and they don't necessarily have to be served up on a silver platter. Apparently Morgan Stanley realizes this and is taking action. The firm is making an effort to develop new products (such as junk-bond financing), to improve its position, and to attract new customers.

If you're a high-powered person searching for some of the best all-around training in the industry, Morgan Stanley could be for you. Former and current analysts warn that it's an incredibly demanding program. Stories abound of all-nighters spent in conference rooms and month-long assignments squeezed into two-week periods. In addition, you may have to carry a beeper when you leave the office, just in case you're needed later. "You've got to be prepared to give up nearly all your free time, and to not mind breaking more dates than you make," says one analyst. "The rewards are big, though. I've made some really close friends, and learned an amazing amount."

NCNB NATIONAL BANK OF NORTH CAROLINA

Contact Info:

Hugh L. McColl, Jr., Chairman

Craig A. Buffie, College Recruiting
One NCNB Plaza
Charlotte, North Carolina 28255
(704) 374-8235

Financials:

Assets: $15.7 billion
Deposits: $11.3 billion
Loans: $9.5 billion

The Organization

In recent years, NCNB has become an aggressive regional power. It is currently the largest banking organization in the Southeast and among the top twenty-five banks in the United States. Due to a spate of recent mergers and acquisitions, NCNB has a presence across much of the region, with banks in North Carolina, South Carolina, Florida, and Georgia. It has more than five hundred domestic offices and international branches in seven foreign countries, as well as operations in New York, Chicago, Tennessee, California, and Maryland.

While NCNB is far from a stuffy, conservative Southern bank, it doesn't take big risks. Because of this, its loss ratios are much better than that of most of its competitors. In addition, NCNB is cautious in lending to the energy, agriculture, and shipping industries. Like most commercial banks, NCNB is testing the investment banking waters, developing a subsidiary that will provide a broad selection of financial services.

The Jobs

With approximately ten thousand employees, NCNB is one of the largest employers in the Charlotte area. Each year the bank hires a few dozen liberal arts graduates, as well as a number of accounting and finance majors. Although many new recruits are from the University of North Carolina, Duke, Vanderbilt, Emory, and other Southern institutions, many colleges and universities across the country send graduates to NCNB. Competition is stiff but a bit lower key than at most money center banks. "You've got to have the right stuff," says one trainee, "but you shouldn't give too hard a sell." Most liberal arts grads are hired for commercial lending, investment management, funds management, or investment banking. The commercial lending area offers a nine-month training program that combines on-the-job credit analysis with classroom instruction. In the investment management and investment banking divisions, most recruits spend several months doing short rotations before being permanently placed. The funds management area teaches trading and sales skills through six months of rotations.

The Payoff

While NCNB doesn't offer the highest salaries in the industry, it does stay in line with most of its competitors. Remember that the cost of living in Charlotte is at least 25 percent lower than in a major city, so your $25,000 salary might really be worth more like $30,000. And NCNB has well-structured reviews, so your compensation package is reexamined fairly often. NCNB's benefits plan includes medical, dental, and life insurance plans, as well as tuition reimbursement for job-related study. In addition, several banking services, such as checking and loans, are discounted for employees.

The Word

If you want to bank in Charlotte, NCNB is it. Analysts predict the bank's growth will continue, and the area is undergoing a rapid revitalization. People say Charlotte combines the best of urban, suburban, and rural living in one town. And as the Southeast develops, NCNB is likely to expand and diversify. Liberal arts students find the bank's aggressive development strategy attractive; according to one trainee, "There's an incredible amount of energy and enthusiasm. The officers are really gearing up for the future, and they're looking to blanket the Southeast."

NATIONAL SECURITY AGENCY

Contact Info:

J. Douglas Donald, Chief of Recruitment

William E. Shores, College Relations Manager
Attention M322
Fort Meade, Maryland 20755
(301) 859-6444

Brian W. Meddaugh, Manager,
   Southeastern Recruitment Office
(404) 688-9150

Terry L. McNair, Manager,
   New England Recruitment Office
(617) 451-5737

The Organization

The National Security Agency was established in 1952 as a Department of Defense agency to produce intelligence information and to safeguard our government's communications and computer activities. NSA is charged with collecting, analyzing, and assessing foreign signals to provide the federal government with critical intelligence information. Its second major function is communications security, which involves the protection of diplomatic, military, and other official communications channels from exploitation. In cooperation with industry, NSA also works to establish standards for computer security for use throughout the government.

In order to carry out these vital missions, NSA makes use of the most sophisticated technologies, often years in advance of their commercial application. For example, NSA's ongoing effort to make the government's telecommunications secure requires the development of standardized cryptographic chips that can be designed into emerging telecommunications systems. This is just one of the many tasks at NSA that involves work on the frontiers of technology.

Cryptography, the development of code and cipher systems, is the most unusual field at NSA. With the advent of new, increasingly sophisticated computer systems, cryptography has grown dramatically over the years. Scientifically devised, tested, and selected cryptographic systems are used to ensure the maximum degree of security for the transmission of military, diplomatic, and other sensitive information.

Because of the unique nature of its work, NSA sets its own job definitions, conducts its own aptitude testing, and recruits its new employees directly. The constantly increasing demands on the agency ensure that its employees will have increasing opportunities for individual achievement and professional growth. And due to the consistently high priority given the agency's contributions to the nation's defense, employees at NSA enjoy extremely stable job security.

The Jobs

A substantial number of liberal arts graduates are hired by NSA each year. Slavic, Middle Eastern, or Asian language majors are hired as linguists and liberal arts, including physical science, majors are hired for internships aimed at providing for a smooth transition from campus to NSA's major career areas. These grads are trained in such fields as intelligence research, traffic analysis, rare foreign languages, cryptography, communications security, and signals research and analysis.

If you majored in one of the key language areas, you may find that NSA offers a challenging opportunity to use your education. You will improve your language skills dramatically and apply your knowledge of culture and politics to the analysis of current intelligence information. Linguists at NSA are involved in the living language and their work is directly related to the real world and to the protection of our nation's security. Specific duties include translating technical materials into English; transcribing or summarizing spoken materials; and compiling linguistic aids such as glossaries and handbooks and the results of language analysis. Assignments could also include preparing grammars or courses for poorly documented languages, teaching foreign languages, or working in peripheral fields such as computer applications to linguistic problems. Fluency in the spoken language is generally not required, but familiarity with modern idiomatic speech and colloquial speech is essential.

Language instruction is usually given at the agency's National Cryptologic School, and special courses may be taken at the Defense Language Institute in California, the Foreign Service Institute, related government agency schools, and nearby universities.

NSA offers a limited number of positions outside the continental United States, and interested employees are invited to apply for these positions, which usually last for a couple of years.

One thing you should keep in mind if the NSA appeals to you is that due to the vital nature of the agency's work, it requires extensive procedures before an offer of employment can be made. These include personal interviews, a background investigation, and a medical exam. The rule of thumb is that it takes at least four months for this process to be completed. This means that you should contact the agency with plenty of lead time, whether you're still in college or if you're already in another job.

The Payoff

Starting salaries at NSA are competitive with those in private industry and are based on qualifications. If you join the National Security Agency, the benefits are extensive, including nearly three weeks of vacation; four weeks comes after three years on the job.

The Word

Several college placement officers told us that for students who can fit well into such an agency, NSA offers great challenges. A sticky aspect of considering the NSA is that nobody seems to know exactly what it is that the NSA does and does not do.

A very practical plus is the location of the headquarters, halfway between newly renovated Baltimore, Maryland, and exciting Washington, D.C. In its recruitment literature, NSA notes that it offers the "ideal location for access to the beach resorts of the Atlantic Coast and to the Allegheny Mountains. Almost any type of leisure activity—from backpacking and skiing to sunbathing and sailing—is an easy drive away."

OGILVY & MATHER WORLDWIDE

Contact Info:
Kenneth Roman, President

Julian Clopet, Director in Charge of Training
2 East 48th Street
New York, New York 10017
(212) 907-3400

Financials (1985):
Billings: about $3 billion
Net Income: $411 million

The Organization

Ogilvy & Mather Worldwide is advertising, direct response, public relations, sales promotion, health care communications, and related creative services. It has six purposes: "to serve our clients more effectively than any other agency; to maintain high ethical and professional standards; to run the agency with a sense of competitive urgency—to strive to excel in all disciplines; to earn a significant increase in profits each year; to make Ogilvy & Mather the most exciting agency in which to work, and to offer outstanding career opportunities; and to earn the respect of the community." Ogilvy & Mather Worldwide is the largest agency network in The Ogilvy Group.

While advertising is a service business, O&M's president Ken Roman likes to think of what the firm does in concrete terms, as suggested by the word "product." "We make things for our clients —advertisements and commercials, sales promotions and direct mail packages, strategies and plans—things that have down-to-earth functions and serve down-to-earth purposes."

David Ogilvy founded Ogilvy & Mather in 1948 with a staff of one and no clients. Today it is a network of 225 offices in forty-four countries, with a staff of 7,400 serving 1,800 clients. Some of the agency's U.S. clients are AGA, American Express, Avon, Chesebrough-Pond, General Foods, Parker Pen, Seagram, Searle, Shell, TWA, and Unilever.

The Jobs

Ogilvy & Mather is an industry leader in recruiting, hiring, training, and grooming professionals. According to the company, "Unlike lawyers or doctors, advertising men and women don't have to master a body of knowledge before they're allowed to practice. As a result, professional qualifications vary widely even among the most talented and the most able people in the business." Years ago, O&M recognized that it had to set its own professional standards, that it must hire the best. Management published standards to people and then trained people to meet these standards. Today Ogilvy & Mather has over thirty international and regional training programs in account management, media, creative, and direct response. They take place in Toronto, London, Melbourne, São Paulo, Srinagar, Hong Kong, and New York. In addition, more than one hundred offices run their own in-house training programs.

In all, O&M's investment in training is significant—in 1986, the agency spent $1.5 million. Top management is invested in this training; training is embraced as a direct responsibility, and most of the agency's directors "teach."

In New York, for example, about two dozen liberal arts graduates join the firm each year as assistant account executives and begin training with a weekend retreat, at which they become part of the Ogilvy family. This is one firm where learning the corporate culture is at least as important as mastering the technical aspects of the job. David Ogilvy explained that corporate culture is "a compound of many things—tradition, mythology, ritual, customs, habits, heroes, peculiarities, and values." Here's how he saw the O&M culture: "Some of our people spend their entire working lives in our agency. We do our damnedest to make it a happy experience. I put this first, believing that superior service to our clients, and profits for our stockholders, depends on it." He continued, "We do *not* admire superficial people. We despise office politicians, toadies, bullies, and pompous asses. We discourage paper warfare. The way up the ladder is open to everybody." Finally he added, "Our far-flung enterprise is held together by a network of personal friendships. We all belong to the same club." One peculiarity shared by all these friends is that they "like reports and correspondence to be well written, easy to read—and short."

Assistant account executives train on the job and attend weekly seminars that introduce all aspects of the business, including the other functional disciplines within the agency. William E. Phillips, chief executive, worldwide, pinpointed the key principles of account management. When college grads have mastered these principles, they are well on their way to great success. They are: stay involved in your clients' business; keep your clients' sales healthy; first earn your clients' respect; respect your clients; make your clients look good; stay ahead of your clients; ideas are your business; have guts; be responsible; work hard with competitive urgency; be task-directed rather than people-oriented; stay in touch with your market; inform and involve the agency in your account; build the faith with your creative partners; learn to be a good salesman; learn to be an excellent communicator; put it on paper, but be brief; you are speaking for the agency—not for yourself; and if you want to grow, learn to let go.

The Payoff

Ogilvy starts its assistant account executives at annual salaries in the mid-twenties, with periodic salary reviews. The agency offers a competitive benefits package that includes tuition reimbursement. After a few years on the job, you'll be eligible for profit sharing and a stock-purchase program.

The Word

In *Advertising Age*'s most recent survey of three hundred advertising managers, O&M was once again named "best agency" more often than any of its competitors. Jay Schulberg, creative head, New York, suggested, "I'm not big on dreamers who haven't the foggiest notion of reality. But I cherish those who dream dreams that never were and have the brilliance, the wisdom, the stamina and creativity to make them happen." That, in essence, is what Ogilvy & Mather is about: brilliance, wisdom, stamina, and creativity. If you think you have these qualities, run, don't walk, to whoever can help you—and it's mostly going to be you helping yourself—get in the door at O&M.

David Ogilvy held a variety of jobs before he formed the agency: cook in a Paris hotel, kitchen stove salesman in Scotland, and assistant to researcher George Gallup; if you can't land one of the highly coveted spots as assistant account executive, think hard and long about how else you could begin your career at Ogilvy. "What you learn matters much more than what your job title is," says an account executive who began her tenure in the illustrious job of fourth-floor receptionist. "I moved to New York and I wanted to work in advertising. I would have swept the floors if I had been asked to do so. All that mattered to me was getting in the door. I knew that over time, I could make my own breaks if only I was meeting the right people and getting the chance to understand the language of the business as well as the dialect peculiar to this agency."

THE PEACE CORPS

Contact Info:

Loret Miller Ruppe, Director

Bruce Cohen, Recruiting Director
P-301
Washington, D.C. 20526
(800) 424-8580

The Organization

Since its founding, America has had a long history of pooling individual human resources in the interest of collective progress. Starting in the eighteenth century, many private organizations and church groups began sending citizens abroad to help contribute to the global community. In 1957, Senator Hubert H. Humphrey first proposed a formal "program of national service in an international endeavor," and the federal government began to seriously consider an organized effort to send Americans abroad. Four years later, President John F. Kennedy established the Peace Corps by executive order. Within six months, both houses of Congress lent their enthusiastic support, and legislation formally inaugurated the Peace Corps as a government agency. The Peace Corps Act mandated three goals: to promote world peace and friendship by making available to interested countries Americans willing to serve overseas; to help promote a better understanding of the American people on the part of people served; and to promote a better understanding of other people on the part of Americans.

Naturally it's taken a great deal of time and experience to figure out how best to fulfill this mission. At first, the Peace Corps provided communities overseas with direct technical assistance, such as offering an engineer to design and build a bridge in Nepal, a nurse to inoculate the children of Colombian farmers, or a teacher to train Filipino vocational students. But as volunteers returned to the United States and related their experiences, it became clear that more permanent contributions were likely to come from "capacity building" efforts rather than from merely supplying "direct services" that could be enjoyed only as long as a trained American lived and worked in a community. Thus the Peace Corps modified its approach to promote institutions and programs that encouraged continuing self-help. As the Third World changed and new nations came into being, the Peace Corps has established new relationships and priorities. Over two and a half decades, nearly 100,000 Americans have served in more than ninety countries. In any single month, more than one million lives are directly affected by Peace Corps volunteers at work in more than sixty countries. They have fought to conquer illiteracy, hunger, poverty, and illness, and to replace fear and mistrust with goodwill and understanding.

The Jobs

The Peace Corps just may be the most prestigious agency you can volunteer for. And being invited to take on an assignment isn't easy. According to the organization, "Because the needs and expectations of both the host countries and the Peace Corps are great, while resources are limited, special care must be given to insure that the best individuals America has to offer are selected to assume the responsibilities of service." Although the minimum legal age for service is eighteen, very few people under twenty-one are selected. (Recruiting materials note that "Our oldest volunteer is 83 and going strong.") U.S. citizenship is required, and applicants must meet medical and legal criteria. The application (available at your campus placement office or from the area recruiting office) is the major source of information by which you'll be evaluated, so you should take special care in completing it. Detailed information about education, specific skills, life experience, and motivation is requested, and facts about previous volunteer activities, community work, and full- or part-time employment should also be included. Generally the Peace Corps receives requests for volunteers well in advance of the project assignment start date. You're encouraged to apply six to nine months in advance of your availability date, due to the processing time and the competition for assignments. However, you can't apply more than one year before you'll be available.

Once your completed application has been received, you'll undergo a suitability interview, in which your skills and motivation will be assessed. Following this, the recruiter will attempt to match you to a specific assignment. Every effort will be made to accommodate your preferences, but the final determining factors are the requests from host countries. According to the Peace Corps, "We will not send you to a country/area where you do not want to be a volunteer." However, if you indicate that you're only willing to serve in one country or area, your chances of being accepted as a volunteer will be substantially reduced. Once you've been matched to an area, the recruiter will nominate you to this particular assignment. In order for a final invitation to be issued, you'll have to provide eight references, who will be sent a standard form used to evaluate you as an applicant. If the reference responses are favorable, you'll then undergo a physical and dental examination. Finally, if you've made it through all this, you'll be issued an invitation to serve in the Peace Corps. Although you won't have a legal or contractual arrangement, you'll be expected to serve for two years.

The Peace Corps assignment areas most in demand by host countries include crop extension, agricultural education, mechanics, construction, physical/occupational therapy, forestry, fisheries, public health/sanitation, primary education, special education, and civil engineering. Several other areas are continually requested, such as community services, rural youth development, business management, economics/bookkeeping, health/nutrition, and nursing. In addition, a few areas are occasionally requested, such as veterinary medicine, communications/journalism, urban planning, architecture, computer science, arts and crafts, and mechanical engineering. You may be assigned to a broad array of regions; a partial listing of locations where volunteers live includes Guatemala, Costa Rica, Paraguay, Liberia, Cameroon, Togo, Sri Lanka, Nepal, Fiji, and Western Samoa.

Once you've accepted an assignment with the Peace Corps, you'll complete eight to fourteen weeks of orientation. This generally takes place in the host country. Depending on the skills necessary for your assignment, you'll receive technical, cross-cultural, and language training. Before you leave the United States, you'll be sent a list of suggested items to bring—or not bring—with you, according to the climate and availability of different goods. Depending on where you go, you'll live in a cement, brick, or adobe house. Mud huts aren't the norm, although many residences will be without running water and electricity. According to the Peace Corps, "Most volunteers live a comfortable but modest lifestyle."

The Payoff

All expenses related to Peace Corps service are taken care of by the Peace Corps. This includes travel, health care, and insurance, as well as housing, vacation (48 days during 2-year service), and monthly living expenses. Following your term in the Peace Corps, you'll receive $175 for each month of training and service. The final amount can vary from $4200 to $4725, depending on the length of training and service. You'll also receive round-trip airfare from your residence to the volunteer site, and food, lodging, and pocket money during the training period.

The Word

Clearly, the Peace Corps isn't for everyone. As the recruiting literature explains, "Successful Peace Corps service requires a high level of motivation, commitment, idealism, and flexibility. Thus, the decision to become a volunteer should not be made lightly. The Peace Corps recognizes that students have spent considerable time, effort, and money to acquire their educations, and wants to help students make their first post-graduate experience professionally and personally rewarding."

The most successful volunteers have the emotional stability and physical energy to maintain their roles under stress, and they have a strong sense of humor. Contrary to popular opinion, the most difficult part of the Peace Corps is not physical hardship—it's the slow pace at which change occurs. Usually volunteers see an enormous gap between the existing and the potential situation in a host country. Making a difference takes a great deal of time, and often results develop after the volunteer is no longer present. Peace Corps volunteers need motivation strong enough to sustain commitment during periods of frustration, and a high level of resourcefulness and flexibility. They also need to understand that no single volunteer can change the world overnight. "There's a place for idealism, in terms of affecting the lives of many people," says one former volunteer. "But you've got to be realistic and not set your sights too high. You've got to be comfortable with making a contribution that isn't immediately evident."

Over all, being a Peace Corps volunteer means accepting hard work, rigorous conditions, long hours, and personal sacrifice. From what we've heard, liberal arts grads tend to find serving in the Peace Corps both very demanding and very rewarding. In addition, those who've stuck it out for two years are in high demand by other profit and nonprofit organizations; former Peace Corps volunteers hold prominent positions in government, industry, and academia. The alumni represent some of the best and brightest individuals in the country, and they form a network that spans the globe.

THE PROCTER & GAMBLE COMPANY

Contact Info:

John G. Smale, Chairman of the Board and Chief Executive

Samuel H. Pruett, Vice President, Personnel
Box 599
Cincinnati, Ohio 45201
(513) 983-3788

Financials (1985):

Sales: $15.4 billion
Profits: $709 million

The Organization

Procter & Gamble is known primarily for its preeminent position in the consumer packaged goods field. Familiar brands such as Tide laundry detergent, Crest toothpaste, Pampers disposable diapers, Duncan Hines cake mixes, Ivory soap, Head & Shoulders shampoo, Folgers coffee, Crisco shortening, and Cascade dishwashing detergent are among its market leaders.

Recently P&G's consumer product base has been expanded to include soft drinks (Crush, Hines), orange juice and other citrus products, and pharmaceuticals (Pepto-Bismol, Encaprin, Macrodantin). In addition, institutional, industrial, and cellulose pulp products have contributed importantly to the business for many years.

The company's sales figures have consistently placed it among the top twenty-five U.S. industrial corporations. Importantly, more than 75 percent of this business is in new products introduced within your lifetime! Owen Butler, former chairman of the board of P&G, told *Career Insights,* "Part of the appeal of this industry is that the products we sell improve the quality of life for almost every family in America. Washing dishes is a lot less unpleasant than it used to be when the grease from dishes floated to the top of the water. And we're raising a generation that has 70 percent fewer cavities than the previous one. . . ."

Procter & Gamble has also increased in size through acquisitions. In November 1985, Richardson-Vicks Inc., a worldwide manufacturer and marketer of personal care products, was acquired and is now operated as a wholly owned subsidiary. In December 1985, P&G acquired the over-the-counter drug business of G. D. Searle & Co.

During 1986, the company also achieved significant growth in several core product categories that form a major part of its domestic business.

In the disposable diaper category, shipment volume and market share moved ahead strongly following major product technology changes made over the past two years. Market share significantly improved and P&G's position as dentrifice market leader was also expanded, led by strong consumer acceptance of new Crest Tartar Control Formula toothpaste.

In the highly competitive laundry detergent category, the volume and market share growth of Liquid Tide, and the expansion to national distribution of Liquid Bold-3, gave the company leadership in the liquids segment. This success was accomplished by overall growth in the company's laundry detergent business, a category in which it has long held the position of market leader.

The Jobs

Advertising genius David Ogilvy recommends that if you want a career in advertising, one great place to start is in brand management at Procter & Gamble. In fact, there are two common quick ways to success in the consumer products industry, and both meet in the marketing function: careers in sales management and careers in brand management.

It was P&G that pioneered the brand management system about fifty years ago, and today the company is still organized along these lines, with products grouped as follows: laundry products, cleaners and dishwashing products, foods, beverages, paper and personal hygiene products, skin care products, hair care products, oral care products, and health care products. Brand assistant is the first job for those who are invited into the elite world of brand management. While you're an assistant, you might handle the promotional budget for a brand, track the progress of a special test market, and develop display and sales promotion materials.

You'll be working as part of a team and you'll be collaborating with specialists in copy, media, and promotion, and with product development and sales executives.

Once you've shown that you've mastered these jobs, you'll be rotated into a sales district, at the company's expense, so that you're able to spend three to five months in the convenience store/supermarket jungle, observing how the sales promotion process actually works.

After sales training ends, you return to Cincinnati and are promoted to assistant brand manager and assigned to a new brand. During your three to four years in this capacity, you will be supervising advertising, media, and product development for the brand(s) in your charge and will be working alongside your team members to increase brand recognition and market share.

Sales careers at P&G are equally demanding. After a two-day orientation session when recent hires are introduced to each other, their accounts, their brands, the P&G sales procedures, and their territories, sales reps head for their territories and begin to learn the job by doing it. Most trainees work directly with managers and watch and listen to how business is analyzed, advertising and merchandising are negotiated, and the shelf-space war is strategized. During the first few months, you'll return to the corporate office for a weeklong training session.

When you're just starting, you'll be assigned a territory with a population of roughly a half-million people. Each sales rep manages two to five retail or wholesale accounts within his territory. This could mean that you are overseeing more than one hundred different stores. You're responsible for creating and implementing new merchandising plans, whether that means starting a special coupon offer or initiating a promotion by linking a product to a local or national sports event. And besides fighting the in-store wars (Butler pointed out that "sales people spend their days calling on businessmen, and from the beginning they are alone in the arena where marketing battles take place. They come face to face with competitors' products as they work with retailers on displays, pricing, and shelf position and can study which merchandising techniques succeed and why"), you're reporting back with analyses that will allow the company to fine-tune its marketing plans and strategy.

The next promotion, which is about sixteen months away, is to unit manager. As a unit manager, you have the added responsibility of building, managing, and training a staff, including new sales reps.

The Payoff

Excellent starting salaries, way into the twenties, are the tip of the compensation iceberg. Benefits are generous and include all the usuals, plus a company car if you've chosen the sales management route.

The Word

By everyone's account, Procter & Gamble is the best, offers the best, and hires the best (you should even expect to have to take a psychological battery as part of the interview process). "Responsible" and "traditional" are two appropriate adjectives to describe the P&G organization. Its executives are something like Boy and Girl Scouts in their communities, and the company encourages volunteerism and community spirit in all its employees, at all levels within the organization.

P&G was featured in *The 100 Best Companies to Work for in America,* and its employee benefits were worthy of special note. But the best benefit of all is that having P&G on your résumé is something like having earned your M.B.A. at Harvard Business School; at least that's how future employers are likely to regard the experience. And the contacts you'll be making are tomorrow's advertising and consumer products superstars. The alumni roster of P&G is something like a Who's Who and who's going to be who of Madison Avenue.

ROSS ROY, INC.

Contact Info:
Glen E. Fortinberry, Chairman of the Board and President

Jill A. Denman, Senior Account Executive
2751 East Jefferson Avenue
Detroit, Michigan 48207
(313) 568-6000

Financials (1985):
Billings: approximately $300 million

The Organization

Ross Roy, Inc., headquartered in Detroit, Michigan, is one of the twenty largest advertising agencies in the country. Some of its clients include Chrysler Corp., Florists' Transworld Delivery Assoc., K mart Corp., Texaco, Inc., and Upjohn Co.

The firm's breakdown of gross billings for 1984 was newspaper ($15,120,000), magazine ($17,640,000), point-of-purchase ($25,200,000), television ($126,000,000), radio ($40,320,000), and other ($15,120,000).

The Jobs

Ross Roy's management-training program has often been referred to as one of the best-kept secrets in the advertising industry. It is one of the oldest—if not *the* oldest—formalized on-the-job advertising training programs in the nation. Several hundred men and women who have graduated from this program hold respected positions in the advertising industry all over the world.

While in the early days, trainees frequently remained in the program for as long as four full years, today's trainees are usually out in half the time. Applicants are required to have earned a B.A., and important consideration is given to students with related work experience, involvement in student organizations, community activities, and/or academic internships related to the communications field. Recruiting is conducted regularly at leading colleges and universities, and more than five hundred of the fifteen hundred prospects who apply are interviewed for about fifteen spots.

A "class" of fourteen joined the agency in February 1986; these eight men and six women have an average age of twenty-four. Seven received their education in Michigan and seven are graduates of out-of-state institutions.

The program consists of formalized in-house, on-the-job training performed by Ross Roy executives. Although it is designed to be completed within two years, most trainees complete the program in about fifteen months. In combination with hands-on work experience, trainees attend thirty-five scheduled seminars taught by senior executives. All aspects of agency operations are explained, from account management to media planning. The management training program encompasses all major disciplines within the agency: account services, media, creative, new business, and research. Trainees enter the program carrying one of five titles: account administrator, assistant media buyer, research assistant, market planner trainee, or creative trainee. To further their appreciation and understanding of the agency's involvement with the community, all trainees are given the opportunity to work on a public service project. They are responsible for all aspects of the project, from research to the final presentation to the client.

Once they've been promoted from the training program, training doesn't end. Management training seminars specifically designed for these new young executives are conducted periodically to keep them updated on the agency's future direction and status.

Most often, trainees begin as account administrators or assistant media buyers. As an account administrator, you'll be assigned to one or several account groups. You'll work with your account group and with other departments in the agency, including creative, media, and production. It will be your responsibility to track and carry jobs through the agency, maintaining the proper communications to complete them on schedule. As an assistant media buyer, you'll learn the media side of the business by executing the decisions of the buyer to whom you will be assigned and by calling in orders for radio and television schedules. You'll be assigned your geographic market areas, for which you will be entirely responsible.

The Payoff

Ross Roy offers a competitive compensation package for trainees. Beware, however, of comparing it dollar for dollar with an offer from a Chicago or a New York agency. Cost of living in Detroit is much lower, and less may well buy you more.

The Word

Graduates of schools like Northwestern, Boston University, the University of Michigan, the University of Tennessee, the University of Missouri, and the University of Illinois report great satisfaction with this agency and the training they've gotten. "It's the trainees with a special flair for advertising who make their mark on Ross Roy," said one graduate. "The people in the training program serve as a support group that extends beyond the office," said another. Overall, the sense is that when you join this company, what you're getting is "something extra," a friendly atmosphere and a special camaraderie among trainees. While those who are living through the rigors of training claim that it's common adversity that brings them together, folks who know better (meaning they've lived through the experience) think it's the common background and common experience that create bonds where friendships bloom. Unlike competitive Ad Alley, this Detroit oasis offers agency-bound graduates a Midwestern alternative that feels a whole lot like home.

SALOMON BROTHERS INC

Contact Info:

J. H. Gutfreund, Chairman and CEO

Stephanie Asphar, College Recruiting
One New York Plaza
New York, New York 10004
(212) 747-5225

The Organization

Salomon—or Solly, as it's known on Wall Street—is one of the most aggressive financial institutions in the country, if not the world. Long known as a powerhouse in stock and bond trading, Salomon has a reputation for taking risks and succeeding. The firm was founded with $5000 of capital back in 1910, by the brothers Arthur, Herbert, and Percy Salomon. Salomon is the oldest and largest dealer in U.S. government securities, and for many years, the firm controlled Wall Street's institutional trading decisions. Over three-quarters of a century, Salomon has grown from a tiny partnership into one of the world's largest fully integrated investment banks. In 1982, when the firm merged with Phillips Brothers (a leading commodity trader) to form Phibro-Salomon, many partners became millionaires several times over. Salomon is now a public firm, under Phibro's auspices, but remains in the mold of a partnership. The merger made good sense, because Phillips's operations in the commercial and commodity markets dovetail neatly with Salomon's investment banking and securities businesses.

Over the past two decades, Salomon has opened offices in Chicago, San Francisco, Los Angeles, Boston, Atlanta, Dallas, and Houston, as well as in London, Tokyo, and Sydney. Along with this geographic expansion, the firm has developed several industry specialty groups in order to focus on communications, technology, energy, financial, public utility, and transportation clients. Salomon has also created "product" groups for mergers and acquisitions, private placements, project finance, equipment and lease financing, and interest and currency swaps. During the past decade, the firm has developed a number of innovative financing vehicles, such as debt-for-equity swaps; zero coupon Eurodollar notes; multicurrency hedging transactions; forward purchase agreements for equity; and original issue discount bonds. The firm is organized into four general departments: corporate finance, sales and trading, municipal finance, and research. Currently Salomon is the industry leader in managing domestic market issues as well as U.S. issues worldwide.

The Jobs

Getting a job at Salomon is tough on a number of counts. For one thing, the firm likes to maintain relatively lean staffing levels. Some six thousand people work for Salomon, but only a few dozen college seniors are hired annually. During recent years, when many other investment banks dramatically increased the size of their entry-level staff, Salomon kept tight reins on its growth. The firm prefers a small number of highly qualified and motivated professionals to a large group of employees. Because of this, new hires generally have more responsibility sooner and tend to stay longer. In addition to the lean staffing policy, Salomon looks for a particular type. You've got to be smart, aggressive, and tough. If you've proved your success in taking risks, that helps. Plodding, methodical, uncreative types need not apply. Liberal arts grads are welcome; according to the firm, "Competence in previous pursuits and serious interest in a financial services career are of greater significance than a specific academic major." However, the firm is known for sending out recruiters that play hardball; we'd suggest you don't make your Salomon interview your first.

Salomon's two-year financial analyst training program is one of the best in the business. Beginning analysts may work in a number of different areas, including corporate finance, financial institutions, and real estate finance. Your role as an analyst is to assist senior staff members in doing research, crunching numbers, organizing data, and preparing reports. Upon entering the firm, you'll undergo a rigorous training program for two months, which is taught by business school professors, public accountants, lawyers, and banking officers. You'll be taught the fundamentals of accounting and analytical techniques, including everything from government securities and equities to money markets and corporate finance. In addition, you'll learn about all aspects of Salomon and its products and services. Following completion of this extensive classroom work, you'll be assigned to a team, usually comprised of an analyst, an associate, a vice president, and a managing director. You may handle a specific transaction, client, or new product. Salomon prides itself on developing some of the best generalists in the field; consequently analysts are encouraged to maximize product and client exposure. This practice assures you the broadest possible spectrum of career opportunities within the firm—and it seems to work. Salomon has one of the lowest turnover rates among the major investment banks.

The Payoff

Like its peers, Salomon offers a very competitive salary and benefits package. Most liberal arts grads will start in the high-twenties to low-thirties range. Since Salomon's business has been booming, it's likely that you'll take home a substantial year-end bonus—perhaps as much as 40 percent of your pay. The firm's comprehensive benefits package includes medical, dental, and life insurance coverage, as well as a stock purchase plan, a pension plan, and reduced stock commissions. Salomon also offers a tuition reimbursement program for job-related study.

The Word

From what we hear, you can't go wrong with Salomon. The firm is one of the fastest-growing and most exciting in the industry. Time and again, Salomon's deals make news, either for sheer size or unconventional approach. While the firm is among the most prestigious on Wall Street, it's among the least stodgy and conservative. Under the rule of John Gutfreund, many of the business's top players have been wooed away from competing firms. For example, Gutfreund recently brought aboard former budget director David Stockman, considered one of the most brilliant financial wizards in the country. In addition, Salomon currently enjoys a strong capital base and is likely to remain a major power in the trading and underwriting markets. Gutfreund is known for being quiet but made of steel; he's a highly analytical type who rarely shows much emotion in the office. He was hired by Salomon in 1953 and has never worked for another firm.

Liberal arts grads generally find Salomon a great place to work. The atmosphere is charged with a certain dynamic tension that self-starters seem to enjoy. Over and over, analysts describe their environment as "fast-paced," "challenging," and "intense." However, there are some who find Salomon a bit much. "I'm just not the overcompetitive type," says one former analyst. "You really have to be incredibly aggressive. There's not a lot of room for people who want to sit around and crunch numbers for a couple of years." Indeed, taking the initiative is tantamount to success at Salomon. That's how the firm stays on the cutting edge.

SHEARSON LEHMAN BROTHERS INCORPORATED

Contact Info:

Peter A. Cohen, Chief Executive Officer

Amanda Brown, College Recruiting
American Express Tower
World Financial Center
New York, New York 10285
(212) 298-3187

The Organization

Shearson Lehman Brothers, a wholly owned subsidiary of American Express Company, is one of the world's largest investment banking and brokerage houses. The product of a furious series of mergers, the firm dates back to the nineteenth century. Henry, Emanuel, and Mayer Lehman founded Lehman Brothers in 1850 in Alabama, and moved the firm to New York in 1868. During the early 1900s, the firm entered the investment banking business, and until 1924, all the partners shared the name Lehman. Meanwhile Carl Loeb, a German immigrant, opened his own investment banking house in 1931, which several years later merged into Loeb, Rhoades & Company. The firm acquired Hornblower & Weeks in the 1960s and became Loeb, Rhoades, Hornblower. In 1977, Lehman Brothers acquired Kuhn Loeb (no relation to Carl Loeb) and became Lehman Brothers Kuhn Loeb. At the same time, Shearson Hayden Stone acquired Faulkner, Dawkins & Sullivan. Two years later, Shearson acquired Loeb Rhoades Hornblower, becoming Shearson Loeb Rhoades. In 1982, American Express acquired Shearson and renamed the combined firm

Shearson American Express. Three years later, Shearson acquired Lehman, and the firm was called Shearson Lehman American Express. So far, that's where it stands, but who knows?

Over the past few years, Shearson Lehman has become known as one of Wall Street's best-managed and most profitable firms. With American Express's backing, it has begun taking enormous trading positions, wielding its huge capital base with excellent results. Once dismissed as a boring, uncreative retail house, Shearson Lehman has emerged in the mid–1980s as a real power player. Today the firm serves the diverse investment and financial counseling needs of individual, institutional, corporate, and government clients. Shearson Lehman is a leader in capital markets activities and is active in private placements, project and equipment finance, mergers and acquisitions, industrial development finance, restructuring, and international finance. The firm is also well known for its extensive retail and institutional distribution network and operates as a major broker of domestic and foreign securities, options, commodities, and futures. In recent years, Shearson Lehman has also engaged in real estate financing and mortgage banking. Outside of its New York City headquarters, the firm has offices in major locations around the world.

The Jobs

Shearson Lehman is one of the hardest investment banks to crack. It's known for offering some of the best training on Wall Street and for having a hardworking, go-getter corporate culture. While some background in accounting, economics, or finance is helpful, it's not necessary. Shearson Lehman genuinely likes liberal arts grads and pursues them actively. Among current and former analysts, you'll find people who majored in everything from American studies and art history to Russian language and Renaissance studies. The one thing these people have in common is a very high GPA, and often a slew of academic honors. In addition, nearly all of them have captained a team, led a student organization, supervised a volunteer group, or run their own business.

Shearson Lehman employs twenty thousand people and hires a few dozen undergraduates each year, mainly into its prestigious analyst training program. The firm recruits at Harvard, Columbia, Wharton, University of California, University of Virginia, Stanford, New York University, Northwestern, Dartmouth, Yale, and the University of Chicago, among other schools. According to recruiters, the typical shopping list applies: intelligence, imagination, analytical ability, strong interpersonal skills, and a high degree of motivation and personal commitment. However, there's an extra twist. You have to be able to maintain an incredible level of energy and enthusiasm to make it at Shearson Lehman. New analysts are generally hired directly into the corporate finance or public finance departments. You begin with an extensive classroom training program, which provides a basic introduction to a career as an investment banker. You'll study accounting and analytical techniques, and learn about the firm's vast array of services. Following completion of the training program, you'll report to your assigned department and participate in a broad range of activities. In corporate finance, you might work on public and private issues of debt and equity securities; merger and acquisition transactions; financial advisory services; and leasing and project-related financing. In the public finance department, you might handle funding for capital projects relating to public power, water and sewer, pollution control and industrial development, health care, education, housing, transportation, or resource recovery. As an analyst, you'll undertake challenging assignments and meet demanding performance expectations—often under extreme pressure. At the end of two years, most analysts return to school for a business or law degree. A select few remain at Shearson Lehman and are promoted to the associate level.

The Payoff

Starting salaries at Shearson Lehman are at the upper end of the scale. Most liberal arts grads are offered a sum in the low- to mid-thirties range, while students with significant financial expertise and/or work experience earn a bit more. The firm pays performance-related year-end bonuses, which may be as high as half your salary, depending on how both you and the firm have done. Shearson Lehman's comprehensive benefits package includes medical, dental, and life insurance coverage, as well as relocation expenses, tuition refunds, and reduced commissions on stock transactions. Insiders tell of a variety of perquisites ranging from free cigars to free white button-down shirts given to employees who pull all-nighters. In addition, analysts tend to travel more frequently at Shearson Lehman than they do at most firms.

The Word

"One of the classiest acts in the business," is how one former analyst put it. Shearson Lehman is known for being creative, innovative, and aggressive, without being cutthroat. "It's a real people place," says another analyst. "You get the feeling you're not just another number cruncher." Employees, customers, and investors alike say the firm is "solid" and "responsible." That's because Shearson Lehman takes itself very seriously. Those who've completed the two-year training program say it was the most intensely demanding experience of their lives. Since Shearson Lehman believes in understaffing, there's always plenty of work to go around. "Ninety percent of the time, there's a ton to do," says one analyst. "Ten percent of the time it's overwhelming." But the rewards apparently justify the costs; alumni of the analyst training program are much in demand, by the best graduate schools and other financial institutions.

Many of Shearson Lehman's current managers are protégés of Sanford "Sandy" Weill, who has been called the firm's spiritual father. Under Weill's rule, the firm became increasingly adept at playing hardball with its competitors. Peter Cohen, the current chief, was known as Weill's right-hand man. As the youngest head of a major securities firm, he has continued much that his mentor began. Cohen is reputed to be incredibly smart and equally intense. He has infused the firm with a fighting spirit and entered several new and daring areas. Recently Shearson Lehman started leading competitive bids for the right to sell certain securities and —even more risky—putting its own cash into leveraged buyouts. And while the firm has brought in fresh talent to spur on its move into the big leagues, it's retained many of its finest executives. Indeed, much of Shearson Lehman's strength has to do with the continuity of its management. Although the mergers caused a few dropouts and defections, most of the staff has stayed aboard to sail with the firm into the future.

SMITHKLINE BECKMAN CORPORATION

Contact Info:
Henry Wendt, President and Chief Executive Officer

Jack Cummings, Director, Corporate College Relations
One Franklin Plaza, P.O. Box 7929
Philadelphia, Pennsylvania 19101
(215) 751-7679

Financials (1985):
Sales: $3,256.6 million
Profits: $515.4 million

The Organization

SmithKline Beckman is one of the world's leading health care companies, with products including Tagamet, a breakthrough product for gastrointestinal disease, ranked for more than five years as the largest-selling pharmaceutical product in the world; Dyazide, an antihypertensive diuretic that for year has been one of the most frequently prescribed medications; and Contac, a leading sustained release cough/cold product. SmithKline Beckman's diagnostic and analytical testing products, led by Beckman's pioneering ASTRA line of automated clinical chemistry systems and its extensive line of centrifuges, can be found in major hospitals and research facilities throughout the world. In 1985, the corporation invested more than $300 million in research and development to keep it in the forefront of innovation and to assure its continued leadership in global markets.

SmithKline Beckman is a technology-intensive health care company that markets worldwide a broad line of prescription and proprietary products for human and animal health care, as well as diagnostic and analytical products and services that facilitate the detection and treatment of disease and the advancement of biomedical research. The company competes in two major markets.

Therapeutics. This group includes Ethical Pharmaceutical Products, generally promoted to the medical profession, and Consumer Health Care Products, advertised to the consumer and not requiring a prescription. Animal Health Care Products consist chiefly of vaccines, pharmaceutical products, and feed additives. The Eye and Skin Care businesses consist mainly of products used with contact lenses and those for the treatment of ocular inflammatory conditions and other ophthalmic and dermatologic disorders.

Diagnostic/Analytical. A leading supplier of instruments, products, and services for the detection and monitoring of disease and the advancement of biomedical research, this group consists of Beckman's Bioanalytical and Diagnostic Systems businesses, SmithKline Bio-Science Laboratories, SmithKline Diagnostics (which specializes in physician office testing), and Geometric Data, which produces blood cell analyzers.

SmithKline Beckman has formed a corporate accounts organization to make the most of the full spectrum of the corporation's health care products and services. This organization coordinates and facilitates sales of diagnostic and therapeutic products and services to major corporate customers.

SmithKline Beckman today markets its products in more than 120 countries around the world and has manufacturing operations in 20 nations. Pharmaceutical research and development is conducted at two primary locations: near Philadelphia, Pennsylvania, and outside London, England, in Welwyn Garden City. The possibility of a third center in Japan is currently under serious consideration.

About a third of SmithKline Beckman's sales are generated outside the United States. Japan is the corporation's second largest market and is an important base for the corporation's new strategic thrust to strengthen its position in Eastern Asia. Western Europe, the home of many of the company's international operations, currently accounts for more than 20 percent of all sales and is expected to make a major contribution to sales in the coming years.

Approximately one-third of SmithKline Beckman's 33,000 employees are located outside the United States.

The Jobs

SmithKline Beckman is a decentralized organization and allows its subsidiaries to operate as separate, relatively autonomous work centers. Each business works independently within this framework while enjoying the benefits of a large corporation. Delegation of responsibility and accountability are shared at the various levels.

Management development at the company is considered as important as business development. State-of-the-art management-development programs and succession planning supply the management training needed to develop employees for critical positions. SmithKline Beckman's two-year Management Access Program attracts bright, *bright* liberal arts graduates and offers them wide exposure to the company's operations.

Those who are hired for decentralized training—management associates—are placed within a specific center but still enjoy many of the benefits associated with the larger organization, including high-quality training. During the approximately two year training period, you will be rotated as appropriate. If you're hired for the marketing function, you'll move through marketing development, market research, product management, and sales.

The best entry level jobs are spots in the "centralized" training programs. These management associates are provided outstanding access to senior management and high-quality on-the-job training. The expectation is that today's associates will be running SmithKline Beckman in subsequent decades. Centralized trainees are hired at the corporate level and over the course of up to twenty-eight months are exposed to a diverse group of business functions, through four different job assignments. While the first assignment is designed to ease the transition from college to the business world, say an English major placed in marketing or a physics major placed in research and development, subsequent rotations build your breadth as well as your depth. One of the four rotations takes you outside the Philadelphia area.

Remember that besides the competition for the program being stiff, SmithKline Beckman created this fast-track training program to meet its management needs, *not* as a two-year stint between college and the almighty M.B.A. program.

The Payoff

Salaries are in the high twenties and benefits are better than standard, including paid relocation and full tuition aid for graduate study.

The Word

In 1986, *Fortune* magazine ranked SmithKline Beckman first of all pharmaceutical companies in terms of ten-year earnings-per-share growth. It ranked second of eighteen companies in total return to investors, ten-year average. But, putting its successful numbers aside, what SmithKline Beckman dominates is promise for the future. SmithKline Beckman has been acting as an investor in venture capital partnerships for about seven years in order to have a "window" on new health care technologies. S.R. One Ltd. is its own venture capital fund and invests in companies such as GMIS Inc., a medical information systems company, and International Canine Genetics Inc.

If you're planning for your own future and think that you're someone who could stick with a first employer for as long as the challenges are there, SmithKline Beckman should be at the top of your prospective employer list. The thing to be sure of is your fit into the organization for the long haul. As the authors of *Rating America's Corporate Conscience* noted, this is a traditional pharmaceutical company that supports conservative public policy research centers. While there is a conservative political tone to the top ranks, management emphasizes the promotion of women and minorities—women constitute more than 20 percent of the managerial ranks and minorities make up almost 10 percent of the managerial ranks, which are *very* impressive statistics.

THE SMITHSONIAN INSTITUTION

Contact Info:
Robert McC. Adams, Secretary
1000 Jefferson Drive, S.W.
Washington, D.C. 20560
(202) 357-1300

The Organization

The Smithsonian Institution is one of the world's most famous historical, scientific, educational, and cultural complexes. It was founded in the early nineteenth century by James Smithson, a British chemist and mineralogist, who willed $500,000 to the United States for philanthropic activities. After much deliberating over what exactly to do with the gift, Congress formally established the Smithsonian Institution in 1846, with the help of former president John Quincy Adams. The institution is governed by a board of regents that includes the vice-president of the United States, the chief justice of the Supreme Court, three senators, three representatives, and nine private citizens. The head of the organization is called the secretary, and his job involves overseeing the Smithsonian as an independent federal agency—and handling the budget, which is currently around $300 million.

Today the Smithsonian is a mammoth operation. It includes a dozen museums, mainly in Washington and New York, which run the gamut from art and history to science and technology. You've probably been to at least one of them: The National Gallery of Art, the National Museum of American History, the National Museum of Natural History, the Cooper-Hewitt Museum, the Freer Gallery, and the National Air and Space Museum are just a few. In addition to these museums, the Smithsonian also runs a nature preserve on the Chesapeake Bay, an astrophysics lab in Arizona, and a marine station in Florida, among other activities. But perhaps the single most well known part of the institution is *Smithsonian* magazine, which has a circulation of two million.

The Jobs

There are dozens of jobs open to liberal arts grads at the Smithsonian, and competition is very stiff. Art history and fine arts degrees are common, but literature, science, history, and technology majors are also well represented. Each museum has its own hiring structure, and openings for liberal arts graduates vary from year to year. Generally, appropriate qualifications include well-developed writing, researching, and speaking skills, as well as expertise in a specialty area. In addition, the Smithsonian likes applicants who have demonstrated their commitment to the field through internships or volunteer work.

The institution employs more than six thousand people and hires several dozen liberal arts grads each year. Depending on your area of interest, you may work on anything from researching artifacts to preserving and cataloging insects. However, beneath all the scholarship that goes on at the curating level lies an intricate network of support positions. Entry-level jobs exist for people interested in administrative detail, from shipping and insuring items for an exhibit to rearranging files and entering information on computers. You may be hired in various departments, and your duties may range from assisting curators and technicians to doing independent research projects. You may also be involved in fundraising or budgetary development.

The Payoff

Keeping in mind that the Smithsonian is a nonprofit government institution, salaries are pretty good. Over all, you won't earn nearly as much as your friends who've taken jobs in private industry. However, you'll earn more than many individuals working in other nonprofit administrative positions. The benefits are excellent and include plenty of paid vacation, sick and holiday time, as well as health insurance and retirement coverage.

The Word

You've probably heard the Smithsonian referred to as the nation's attic. Like an attic, it serves as a repository for some 100 million items that have been donated to or collected by the institution. Indeed, just keeping track of the inventory can be a massive task. Most liberal arts grads start work at the Smithsonian as glorified "go-fers," doing anything and everything that needs to be done. High-level positions are usually assumed by individuals who have experience in other museums, galleries, or nonprofit organizations.

One of the best things about working for the Smithsonian is the people, and one of the worst is the bureaucracy. "It's a lot like going to an Ivy League school," says one administrative assistant. "The people are really bright and motivated. You learn an incredible amount from just soaking up the atmosphere." However, says another recent liberal arts grad, "The bottom line is that you're working for the government, and you have to deal with all sorts of red tape. I envy my friends who went to work for small museums or galleries, where everything doesn't have to be approved a dozen times to get done."

STEELCASE INC.

Contact Info:

Robert C. Pew, Chairman and Chief Executive Officer

Jeanne Wiest, Employment Representative
Grand Rapids, Michigan 49501
(616) 247-2710

Financials (1985):

Sales: approximately $1.3 billion

The Organization

Steelcase Inc., listed among the top fifty private companies in America *(Forbes,* November 19, 1985), is the world's leading designer and manufacturer of office furniture, systems furniture, and office lighting. Founded in Grand Rapids, Michigan, in 1912, Steelcase Inc. also develops computer-assisted programs for those who want to plan, provide, and manage effective office environments.

In 1985, Steelcase Inc. was selected one of the "100 best companies to work for in America" and one of the "100 top companies to sell for in America," according to two nationally distributed bestselling books. Steelcase Inc., cited for a prize in "managerial efficiency" in *Forbes* (October 7, 1985), has led the office furniture industry in annual sales volume since 1968.

In the United States and Canada, Steelcase Inc. has nine manufacturing sites, more than 11,000 employees, and more than 550 independent dealers. The company also has 50 percent joint-venture interests in France, West Germany, and Japan.

Worldwide, Steelcase Inc. and its joint-venture operations have a combined work force of more than fourteen thousand; more than seven hundred independent dealers; sales offices or dealerships in fifty-eight countries; fifteen million square feet of manufacturing or assembly facilities in nine countries, and twenty-one manufacturing/assembly sites—seven in the United States, six in France, four in Africa, two in Canada, and one each in West Germany and Japan.

The Jobs

Steelcase recruits on college campuses such as University of Florida, DePauw, Notre Dame, Boston College, Denison, Indiana, Michigan, and USC for its sales training program, known as PACE (Professional Accelerated Career Entry).

For new employees, especially liberal arts graduates just beginning their career, a thorough orientation to the organization is the first step. This is followed by systematic intensive training based on individual performance. Training is conducted in two phases. The first phase is corporate orientation. It provides the background for all trainees to function effectively. You will be introduced to Steelcase organizational structure and function, management philosophy and systems, management personnel, and corporate employee development programs, as organized and administered by the human resources development staff.

Phase two is job training. This structured program of tasks prepares the trainee to assume the full responsibilities of the job. Training is completed on the job under the guidance of department/divisional management, as well as the human resources development staff.

The primary responsibility and control of training is in the hands of the trainee instead of the trainer. Many people assist, but in the final analysis, you are accountable for your own development—you set your own pace. Feedback is provided frequently and from varied sources on a daily, weekly, and monthly basis. A final evaluation of your total performance will be reviewed by a panel of selected reviewers.

The sales career path, as well as paths in dealer development and product marketing, are most frequently chosen by liberal arts grads. Sales usually leads to a position in management in one of twenty-one regional offices across the country. Successful PACE graduates begin as sales assistants and, from there, progress into sales management or move into other career areas within the company.

The Payoff

The wages and benefits enjoyed by Steelcase employees are considered among the best in the nation. In this privately held company, all employees participate in profit sharing through bonuses and a trust fund that provides retirement income. A flexible program of medical, dental, and life insurance options enables Steelcase people to tailor benefits packages to their specific needs. At its Grand Rapids headquarters, the company offers a wellness program, family and personal counseling, and an innovative child care referral program that helps parents find appropriate day care. Tuition reimbursement for job-related study and paid holidays and vacations are other benefits for Steelcase employees.

The Word

All Steelcase facilities serve as "living laboratories" for testing and proving the company's ideas and designs for pleasant and productive offices. So if you're looking for a productive space, as well as a productive place, to work, Steelcase offers you the right environment. An Atlanta sales assistant who earned her B.A. from Indiana University concluded, "Steelcase is very employee-oriented; they realize that if they take care of their employees, their employees are going to take care of them, and continue to produce—or sell—quality products."

As the authors of *The 100 Best Companies to Work for in America* pointed out, almost 90 percent of the people who were working for Steelcase in 1975 were still with the company ten years later! That's the best proof that this is a "smart" place to choose for your first employer.

STRATEGIC PLANNING ASSOCIATES, INC.

Contact Info:

W. Walker Lewis, Chairman

Gigi Lorman, Director of College Recruiting
600 New Hampshire Avenue, N.W.
Washington, D.C. 20037
(202) 778-7000

The Organization

Founded in 1972, Strategic Planning Associates (SPA) is an international management consulting firm that specializes in helping clients develop and implement solutions to complex business problems. The firm's stated mission is simple: "to help our clients —some of the largest publicly held corporations in the world— increase their profitability, actualize their growth opportunities, and enhance their shareholder value." In short, to improve bottom line performance. Over fifteen years, SPA has grown at a compound annual rate of 40 percent, from a small group of consultants to nearly two hundred professionals. Today the firm engages in a wide variety of disciplines, ranging from strategy, organization, and marketing to operations, finance, and management information systems. It assists organizations that span a wide variety of both mature and growth industries, including general manufacturing, consumer products and services, financial services, oil and gas, agriculture, pharmaceuticals, health care, information and communications, retailing, and transportation. Among SPA's clients are three of the top fifteen worldwide industrial corporations; two of the top fifteen U.S. industrial corporations; one of the top three U.S. diversified service corporations; one of the top three U.S. life insurance companies; and one of the top three U.S. utilities companies. In 1983, an office was opened in London, and the following year one was opened in Geneva. In 1986, a third international office was opened in Singapore. Currently about a third of SPA's revenues come from engagements outside the United States.

The Jobs

Each year SPA hires a handful of research analysts, mainly for the Washington office. The firm looks for highly talented, aggressive, and motivated recruits at leading institutions across the country. The typical laundry list of qualifications applies: top grades, excellent communication skills, and strong analytical and quantitative abilities. SPA interviewers have also been known for asking for SAT and/or GMAT scores, so be prepared.

SPA prides itself on providing "intensive training in a competitive environment." As an analyst, you'll go through a brief orientation period, which introduces the basics of strategic planning. Following that, you'll work closely with clients on projects that usually last from one to six months. The firm describes the research analyst's work as "challenging, creative, and demanding"— and particularly well suited to people seeking two years of exposure to different types of industries and businesses. Your responsibilities as an analyst include carrying out essential research and data collection to conducting complex quantitative, strategic, and financial analyses of corporations and businesses. You might work on any number of services, including business strategy development, industry structure studies, competitive analyses, financial policy studies, planning process development, strategic information systems, and organizational studies. In recent years, the majority of people who completed two years as a research analyst at SPA have gone on to MBA programs at Harvard, Stanford, Yale, Wharton, and the University of Chicago. A few have gone to law school, and a few have elected to stay a third year with the firm. Some exceptional analysts have also been given offers to return to SPA as associates after business school.

The Payoff

SPA offers an excellent salary and benefits package, including everything from medical and dental coverage to travel and life insurance. Prior to 1985, SPA's compensation policy set no limits on annual cash bonuses for consultants. However, the firm's current cash bonus policy is to pay out an aggregate amount worth about a third of the firm's income before taxes. In 1986, SPA's bonuses equaled about 29 percent of its income.

The Word

SPA is widely considered one of the best places to work in the consulting industry—and one of the toughest. Since the firm believes analysts will work up to their potential, you're given as much responsibility as you can handle. The hours are long, and there's a fair amount of travel. "If you want a fast education in strategic consulting, I can't imagine a better place," says one former analyst. "But you've got to be able to deal with huge amounts of work and be a real go-getter. The people who do best are very competitive types."

W. Walker Lewis, who founded the firm in 1972, was president from 1976 to 1983 and has been chairman since 1984. A Harvard graduate, Lewis is known for being a brilliant strategic thinker—and for hiring some of the best people in the business. At forty-two, he is one of the oldest executives at SPA; the average age of the firm's officers is about thirty-five. Largely due to Lewis's leadership, SPA has one of the highest rates of repeat business in the consulting industry. During 1986, more than 80 percent of the firm's total projects and revenues were attributable to long-term clients. In addition, SPA has increased its revenues every year since incorporating in Delaware in 1976. Industry watchers think the future looks bright for SPA, since the firm is equipped to deal with rapid change, due to deregulation, technological innovation, corporate raiding, and other factors. The firm's philosophy: "In the end, the best defense is a good offense."

TEXAS COMMERCE BANCSHARES

Contact Info:

Ben F. Love, Chairman

Carolyn H. Humphries, Professional Recruiting
P.O. Box 2558
Houston, Texas 77002
(713) 236-5008

Financials:

Assets: $20.7 billion
Deposits: $14.5 billion
Loans: $13.3 billion

The Organization

Texas Commerce Bancshares is the largest bank in Houston, the second largest in Texas, and among the top twenty-five in the United States. TCB owns some seventy banks in the region and has offices in half a dozen foreign countries. The majority of the bank's loans are in the commercial area, particularly in energy and real estate. TCB's major lending divisions are: middle market, large corporate, international, real estate, and energy. During the 1970s and 1980s, the bank has sustained a rapid growth rate, and it currently has one of the strongest equity bases of the Texas banks. But due to trouble in the oil and gas market, TCB's recent performance hasn't been exceptional. Assuming the local economy picks up, and the bank tightens the reins on operating costs, loan losses are likely to shrink gradually. In addition, there have been several rumors about the bank being a takeover candidate; several out-of-state banks are reportedly interested.

The Jobs

Some eight thousand people work for TCB, and the bank hires a group of college graduates each year. Although an accounting or a financial background is helpful, TCB welcomes qualified liberal arts graduates. Grades matter; recruiters look for students who are in the top 10 or 15 percent of their class. Popular schools include the University of Texas, Baylor University, the University of Houston, Louisiana State University, Rice, Southern Methodist University, and Texas Southern University. Most new hires enter TCB's Commercial Banking Officer Development Training Program (CBODP), a highly individualized, self-paced program that begins several times a year. The program involves completing several "modules," or learning areas. Each module requires completing clearly defined objectives. TCB doesn't believe in month after month of classroom instruction; rather, the bank focuses on teaching actual banking responsibilities. Since trainees move through the CBODP at their own speed, only self-starters need apply. There's little hand-holding, although bank officers provide plenty of support. While most candidates spend a year in the program, some highly motivated individuals can complete it in nine months.

The Payoff

TCB offers undergraduates starting salaries in the low- to mid-twenties range. Since Houston's real estate market is depressed, you won't put a major portion of your paycheck into housing. You will need a car to get around, though. Overall, the cost of living in Houston is lower than in most Eastern cities; however, it's not as cheap as other Southwestern areas. TCB's comprehensive benefits plan includes medical, dental, and life insurance coverage, as well as discounts on several banking services, such as credit cards, personal loans, and mortgages.

The Word

From what we've heard, TCB offers one of the most unusual and flexible ways to learn the banking business. Unlike some programs that emphasize academic assignments, homework, and exams, the bank believes on-the-job training is most important. Trainees speak highly of the module system and the amount of direct responsibility it allows at an early stage. "After a lifetime spent in school, I really couldn't see spending my first year in the 'real world' sitting in class," said one trainee. "I wanted to see what being a banker was all about right away." Clearly, the hands-on approach makes for satisfied employees; TCB's attrition rate is less than 10 percent over the first three years.

YOUNG & RUBICAM INC.

Contact Info:

Alex Kroll, Chairman, President, and Chief Executive Officer

Steven B. Nisberg, Manager of Employment
285 Madison Avenue
New York, New York 10017-6486
(212) 210-5029

Financials (1985):
Billings: $3.6 billion
Net Income: $480 million

The Organization

Young & Rubicam is the world's largest privately held advertising agency and one of the very few that has maintained its name, identity, and mission since early in this century. Young & Rubicam pioneered many of today's accepted marketing fundamentals, such as consumer research and radio and television production.

According to *Advertising Age*, the Young & Rubicam network consists of about thirty-five agencies in about thirty countries, including majority or maximum-allowable interest in twenty-seven agencies, minority interests in four, and nonequity affiliations with two other agencies. Some of the agency's worldwide business includes Adidas, Air Canada, and Richard/Dubonnet. Its U.S. clients include American Home Products, Bristol Myers, Colgate-Palmolive, DuPont, Eastman-Kodak, Ford Motor Company, Johnson & Johnson, and Time Inc.

The Jobs

Liberal arts graduates who are "fast learners, flexible, high achievers, team players, good communicators, persevere, understand the advertising business, and exhibit empathy" are recruited through résumés, placement offices, school visits, and formal intern programs offered by the agency.

For starters, Y&R offers a competitive and very selective summer intern program for students who have completed their junior year of undergraduate study. It is a ten-week paid internship in which students are assigned to a particular department. The program is supplemented by weekly seminars that cover the range of agency functions. (Interested applicants can apply for this program by sending a cover letter and résumé to Steven Nisberg, manager of employment.)

There are four typical pathways into Young & Rubicam for liberal arts graduates. These include communications services/media; market research; account support; and creative. All entry-level professionals train on the job and through account assignment rotations. Each department has a customized training program that usually consists of seminars on the technical aspects of the department as well as on general agency topics that are interdepartmental.

In the communication services/media function, there are three specialty areas: planners, buyers, and research. For planners, the entry-level title is media planner, followed by senior media planner, media supervisor, and group supervisor, manager, and director. The buying group includes local and network specialists. Entry-level title and pathway for local broadcast buyers is purchase service assistant, followed by assistant supervisor, assistant manager, associate director, and director. Entry-level title and pathway for network buyers is network specialist, followed by network supervisor, manager, group supervisor, and director. In research, the entry-level job is analyst. The career steps are senior analyst, manager, associate director, and director.

In market research, the entry-level position is assistant research account executive, followed by research account executive and research account supervisor.

In account support, the two entry-level positions are traffic scheduler or traffic coordinator, and the career paths lead into the client services department as staff assistant, then assistant account executive.

The creative department is made up of two paths: art direction and copywriting. For those who choose art direction, the entry-level position is assistant art director, followed by art director, senior art director, creative supervisor art director, and associate creative director. For those who choose copywriting, the entry-level position is assistant copywriter, followed by copywriter, senior copywriter, creative supervisor copywriter, and associate creative director.

The Payoff

Young & Rubicam's starting salaries for liberal arts graduates seem to be consistent with the agency's emphasis on market research as the quick way to success. As further proof that market research counts at Y & R, Ivy League grads who are recruited off campus usually begin their careers within this function. The overall entry-level compensation package for all includes limited overtime compensation; medical and dental coverage; vacation time; and floating holidays. Salary is reviewed annually for everyone.

What follows are annual salary ranges for each of the four functions:

Media	$13,000–$14,000
Market Research	$18,000–$22,000
Account Support	$13,000–$14,000
Creative	$16,000–$18,000

The Word

The low starting salaries and the emphasis on working tons of overtime to cover basic living expenses may explain why environments such as the media department of Young & Rubicam are known as havens for the (Y)oung & (R)estless. Visit the media department at about 6 P.M. any weeknight and you'll get the feeling that you're popping in on the reading room at your college during the early part of semester. The camaraderie is there, and so are the innocent flirtations. Just like any collegiate group, the alumni network seems to be one of the best bonuses of having punched and crunched the numbers hour after hour, day after day. "There is great turnover," reported one media supervisor, "so I have ended up knowing people in all kinds of related jobs, as well as in most of the leading advertising agencies." He continued, "By sharing the trials and tribulations of being poor and of being in a service industry where the client is always right—and there's also the account executive with his fancy M.B.A. who makes you feel one cut above a domestic—you end up making great friends." If this supervisor's experience is any guideline, those who endure the first years end up doubling their salaries or better and end up getting a first-rate marketing education.

An assistant research account executive said that a common denominator among recent graduates is that they forget how lucky they are to be working for such a prestigious agency and get caught up in complaining about the long hours and low pay. "After about six months on the job, I suddenly realized that I knew what I was doing, that I was learning about more than consumer reaction to ice cream bars when I spent hours observing focus groups. My perspective began to change and I became more professional about what I was bringing to and expecting to get from work."

When asked about how many of its top executives come from the liberal arts, the agency forwarded a lengthy list. Chairman Kroll earned his B.A. in English; Peter Georgescu, the president of Young & Rubicam Advertising, earned his B.A. from Princeton in political science. Four executive vice presidents are liberal arts graduates—two English majors, a communications major, and a sociology major. And six senior vice presidents are liberal arts grads, including three English majors, from Berkeley, Fordham, and Dartmouth, respectively. What this means, then, is that smart people need apply. According to Steven Nisberg, "Y&R gives people with ambition and initiative the opportunity to combine business experience with creative challenges." What more could a smart, well-educated graduate ask for besides such exposure—except Wall Street–type perks!

Notes

Introduction

1. Allan Cox, *Inside Corporate America*. (New York: St. Martin's Press, 1986), p. 60.
2. John A. Byrne, "Let's Hear It for Liberal Arts," *Forbes*, July 1, 1985, p. 112.
3. Allan Cox, *Inside Corporate America*, p. 63.
4. John Wright, *The American Almanac of Jobs and Salaries, 1987–1988*. (New York: Avon Books, 1986), p. 668.
5. Ibid.
6. *Harvard Business Review*, January-February 1984, p. 146.
7. Myron Magnet, "Baby-Boom Executives Are Making It," *Fortune*, September 2, 1985, p. 22.

Chapter One

1. Edward N. Ney, "On Advertising," *Career Insights* (1982/1983), p. 40.
2. Edward S. Finkelstein, "On Retailing," *Career Insights* (1982/1983), p. 74.
3. David C. Farrell, "On Retailing," *Career Insights* (1984), p. 80.
4. Ibid.
5. Cynthia Burr, "The Pygmalion Principle," *Career Insights* (1984), p. 107.
6. Ibid.
7. Marian L. Salzman, "The Lacrosse Connection," *Forbes*, October 6, 1986, p. 172.
8. Ibid.
9. Heather Evans, "The Hedonist in the Grey Flannel Suit," *Management Review*, April 1985, p. 32.

Chapter Two

1. Elizabeth Fowler, "More Liberal Arts Grads Wanted," New York *Times,* January 1987.
2. Ibid.

Chapter Three

1. Richard Nelson Bolles, *Newsletter about Life/Work Planning,* January 1977, p. 3.
2. Jesse M. Smith, "Campus Recruiting Pays Off," *Management Review,* April 1985, p. 64.
3. Steven Prokesch, "Remaking the American CEO," New York *Times,* January 25, 1987, Section 3, p. 1.

Chapter Four

1. Betty Lehan Harrigan, quote from *The Woman in Management,* ed. by Jennie Farley (Ithaca, N.Y.: ICR Press, Cornell University, 1983), p. 16.
2. John A. Byrne, "Be Nice to Everybody," *Forbes,* November 5, 1984, p. 244.
3. Michael Jackman, ed. *The Macmillan Book of Business and Economic Quotations* (New York: Macmillan, 1984), p. 32.
4. John A. Byrne, "Careers," *Forbes,* September 10, 1984. [Page unknown]

Chapter Seven

1. *Wall Street Journal* (roundup), August 27, 1981, "Season Work: Summer Interns Receive High Marks from College Students," p. 1.

Appendices

SOURCES FOR SMART PEOPLE

Preparation is 90 percent of the job hunt, according to those in the know. "Like you or not, if you don't know your stuff, you probably won't meet a recruiter who will be ready to make you a job offer," says Barbara-Jan Wilson, the head of career planning at Wesleyan University. To help you to get prepared, the following annotated bibliography is broken down into three broad categories: *The Basics,* which includes general and job-search directories, and books about career planning and decision making; *News Items,* which includes periodicals that contain information about careers and jobs; and *Career Fields,* which includes specialized references to the fields that tend to interest smart people, as well as contact information for key professional and trade associations.

THE BASICS

Career Guides

The Berkeley Guide to Employment for New College Graduates, James Briggs, Ten Speed Press, 1984. This is the right choice for those of you who are unclear about what you're looking for.

The Career Finder: Pathways to Over 1,500 Jobs for the Future, Lester Schwartz and Irv Brechner, Ballantine Books, 1983. A four-part guide that helps you self-assess and then match your interests; contains career descriptions; features lists of information sources; and indexes possible job titles.

Career Paths, Bob Adams, Inc., 1984. This book explores scores of career possibilities.

Careers and the MBA, Bob Adams, editor, Bob Adams, Inc., annual. This annual magazine features chapters on specific careers, with advice from leaders in these fields.

Career Satisfaction and Success: A Guide to Freedom, 2nd edition, American Management Association, 1981. Are you looking for help identifying your interests and skills and in formulating appropriate job search goals? This book provides just that help.

Careercycles, John Caple, Prentice-Hall, Inc., 1983. Personal development is as a consequence of cycles of living and working.

Careers Tomorrow, Gene R. Hawkes, New American Library, 1979. This primer answers two questions: Which jobs will be in the greatest demand during this decade? What training is required in more than 100 popular professions?

The College Placement Annual, The College Placement Council, annual. This guide to the largest employers of college graduates is indexed by career category and by location of jobs.

College to Career: Finding Yourself in the Job Market, John Shingleton and Robert Bao, McGraw-Hill, 1977. An essential how-to book that helps you choose a career, prep for a job interview, and brace yourself for the first days on the job.

The College Graduate's Career Guide, Robert Ginn, Charles Scribner's Sons, 1981. Ginn, formerly head of career services at Harvard University, stresses the importance of career planning for liberal arts grads.

Discover What You're Best At, Barry and Linda Gale, Simon & Schuster, 1982. These authors offer a system that lets you evaluate yourself to uncover your best career bets.

Dream Jobs: A Guide to Tomorrow's Top Careers, Robert Bly and Gary Blake, John Wiley & Sons, 1983. This book tells what it takes to break into and stay in some of the most popular glamour professions: advertising, cable television, public relations, travel, and the like.

THE DUN & BRADSTREET BOOKS:

Million Dollar Directory, annual. More than 100,000 companies are featured in this easy-to-read directory.

Reference Book of Corporate Managements, annual. Biographical data on key officers and directors is included within this guide to the companies of greatest investor interest.

Everybody's Business, An Almanac: The Irreverent Guide to Corporate America, edited by Michael Moskowitz, Michael Katz, and Robert Levering, Harper & Row, 1982. Describes the management philosophies and personalities behind more than 300 large companies.

The Harvard Guide to Careers, Martha Leape and Charles Kovacs, Harvard University Press, 1983. Harvard College is *the* ultimate liberal arts institution. This guide was devised originally to help its students explore careers; the second half of the book features one of the best bibliographies in the field.

How to Choose, Change, Advance Your Career, Adele Lewis, William Lewis, and Steven Radlauer, Barron's Educational Series, 1983. What are the realities of job hunting in today's marketplace?

In Search of Excellence, Thomas J. Peters and Robert H. Waterman, Jr., Warner Books, 1982. Several top-notch organizations are featured within this seminal study of the art of management, American-style.

Inside Management Training: The Career Guide to Management Training Programs for College Graduates, Marian Salzman with Deidre Sullivan, NAL/Plume, 1985. This is the forerunner of *Wanted: Liberal Arts Grads* and profiles more than 100 training programs in a dozen-plus industries. If you want to know what it is really like to train at Bloomie's, Chase Manhattan, Salomon Brothers, and others. . . .

MBA Jobs! Marian Salzman and Nancy Marx, AMACOM, 1986. This is the M.B.A.s' guide to the companies that hire them. Once again, the inside word on what it's like to work at the Firsts (Boston, Chicago, Interstate, etc.) and the Morgans (Guaranty and Stanley), as well as other top M.B.A. employers.

Money Jobs: Training Programs Run by Banking, Accounting, Insurance, and Brokerage Firms—and How to Get Into Them, Marti Prashker and S. Peter Valiunas, Crown Publishers, 1985. This is another insider's guide to entry-level jobs; its emphasis is on employers in the financial services industry.

THE NATIONAL REGISTER PUBLISHING COMPANY BOOKS:

The Corporate Finance Bluebook, annual. Who are the financial decision-making personnel within more than 4,000 companies?

Corporate Summaries, annual. This one-volume update is published in mid-year to provide information about publicly held companies.

The Directory of Corporate Affiliations, annual. What are the corporate structures in more than 4,000 private and public American companies? This is a leading source of information about who owns who, including affiliated companies, divisions, and subsidiaries.

Standard Directory of Advertisers, annual. Companies are listed by product classifications, and key executives on both the advertiser and agency sides are listed.

Standard Directory of Advertising Agencies, three times per year. About 60,000 accounts are listed, including 4,000 advertising agencies and 27,000 key agency personnel by title.

90 Highest Paying Careers for the 80's, Anita Gates, Simon & Schuster,

1984. These ninety careers are profiled, including info on getting started and what you'll be paid once you're on the job.

90 Most Promising Careers for the 80's, Anita Gates, Simon & Schuster, 1982. This book, the forerunner of *90 Highest Paying Careers,* tells you what you need to get hired in the most promising career categories.

Occupational Outlook Handbook, Neal H. Rosenthal, editor, Bureau of Labor Statistics, Superintendent of Documents, U.S. Government Printing Office, annual. A directory that features broad overviews of career categories and specific job titles.

The 100 Best Companies to Work for in America, Michael Moskowitz, Michael Katz, and Robert Levering, editors, NAL/Plume, 1985. What are the career opportunities within the "best" employers in America?

PATH: A Career Workbook for Liberal Arts Students, 2nd edition, Howard Figler, Carroll Press Publishers, 1979. This workbook includes exercises intended to help liberal arts students establish their work priorities and values.

Self-Assessment and Career Development, John P. Kotter, Victor A. Fauz, and Charles C. McArthur, Prentice-Hall, Inc., 1978. This book was developed at the Harvard Business School and is directed at those with professional goals; the self-help aspect of the book is complete and straightforward.

Skills for Success, Adele Scheele, Ballantine Books, 1979. This book equips you to get ahead in whatever career you pick.

Standard & Poor's Register of Corporations, Directors, and Executives, annual. When you need basic information on a company and its executives, S & P is the standard reference.

The Three Boxes of Life and How to Get Them, Richard N. Bolles, Ten Speed Press, 1981. To lead a happy life, it's essential to balance education, work, and leisure.

The Two-Career Couple, Francine S. and Douglas T. Hall, Addison-Wesley Publishing Company, 1979. Two-career couples face major life/work planning issues.

What Color Is Your Parachute? Richard N. Bolles, Ten Speed Press, updated regularly. This career guide seems to be a permanent bestseller; it includes exercises to help you discover everything you ever wanted to know about your own career aptitudes—and ways to gain this insight through serious self-assessment and artful information interviewing to test your interests.

What to Do With the Rest of Your Life, Staff of *Catalyst,* Simon & Schuster, 1980. Are you confused about beginning to plan, change, or advance a challenging career? This book is mostly for women who also have questions about the great juggling act.

Who's Hiring Who? 3rd edition, Richard Lathrop, Ten Speed Press,

1977. Once you decide on a career plan, the next step is launching a job campaign, including cover letters, artful follow-up, and networking.

Who's Who in Career Planning, Placement, and Recruitment, College Placement Council, annual. This guide to employers that recruit college grads lists contacts, including telephone numbers, within more than 1,000 organizations.

Some Other Key Directories

All in One Directory, Amalie Gebbie, editor, Gebbie Press, annual. If you are looking for a media directory, including contact information at all magazines, newspapers, radio stations, television stations, and trade publications in the United States, this is your all-in-one source.

American Register of Exporters and Importers, updated regularly. More than 32,000 firms are organized by product category.

The Consultants and Consulting Organizations Directory, Paul Wasserman and Janice McLean, editors, Gale Research, updated regularly. When you look for consulting firms by location or by specialty, this is your best source.

The Encyclopedia of Associations, Denise S. Akey, editor, Gale Research, annual. This is the best guide to national and international associations.

International Jobs: Where They Are and How to Get Them, Eric Kocher, Addison-Wesley, 1984. Are you looking for a job in banking or international management, and would you prefer to be living and working abroad? This book answers these questions, plus more, for you.

Job Bank Series, Bob Adams Inc., new titles added regularly. These books are organized as directories of jobs within single markets, such as jobs in Atlanta; Chicago; New York City; Washington, D.C.; Pennsylvania; northern California; etc. The specific job listings include brief descriptions of the organization and contact information.

Petersen's Annual Guides/Business and Management Jobs, Christopher Billy, editor, Petersen's Publishing Co., Inc., annual. The best comprehensive guide to employers that hire liberal arts graduates, including contact information and a comprehensive directory of hundreds of job-search leads.

The Research Center's Directory, edited by Mary M. Watkins and James A. Ruffner, annual. There are thousands of nonprofit research centers in the United States and Canada; this directory cross-lists entries by location and specialty.

Thomas' Register of American Manufacturers, Thomas Publishing Company, annual. This directory features product listings by both manufacturer and trademark.

The How-to Books:
Cover Letters, Interviewing, and Résumés

The Complete Job Search Handbook, Howard E. Figler, Holt, Rinehart, and Winston, 1982. There is a second essential part of preparing for the job search, and that is preparing for the emotional roller coaster that job hunters usually ride. This book tells you everything you need to know to write great pieces to help you to sell yourself.

Dress for Success, John T. Molloy, Warner Books, 1975. The adage about books being judged by their covers rings true for job hunters. When you're looking for a job in banking, dress like the bankers do. (There is also a women's version of the same theme.)

Getting Hired: Everything You Need to Know about Résumés, Interviews, and Job Hunt Strategies, Edward J. Rogers, Prentice-Hall, 1982. For liberal arts students who seek jobs in more creative fields, and for those who want to express themselves during their job search, there is no better job hunt primer.

Go Hire Yourself an Employer, Richard K. Irish, Doubleday, 1978. This career counseling guru advises you on making your own job-hunt breaks.

How to Turn an Interview into a Job, Jeffrey G. Allen, Simon & Schuster, 1983. There are *right* ways to interview.

Job Résumés: How to Write Them, How to Present Them, Preparing for Interviews, rev. ed., J. I. Biegelesisen, G. P. Putnam, 1982. Which résumé format serves your purposes best? What questions should you expect at a job interview?

111 Proven Techniques and Strategies for Getting the Job Interview, Burdette E. Bostwick, John Wiley & Sons, 1981. There are various ways to get an interview, ranging from traditional to much more creative methods.

Professional Resume/Job Search Guide, Harold W. Dickhut, Prentice-Hall, 1978. Are you looking for some cover letters and résumés?

The Working Woman Report: Succeeding in Business in the Eighties, Gay Bryant, Simon & Schuster, 1984. The editors of *Working Woman* has compiled tips that are appropriate for women who are beginning their careers.

NEWS ITEMS

Certain business periodicals are key references for job hunters. These are included here, with addresses in case you wish to subscribe.

Barron's
200 Burnett Road
Chicopee, Massachusetts 01021

Business Week
P.O. Box 506
Hightstown, New Jersey 08520

Business Week's Guide to Careers
P.O. Box 506
Hightstown, New Jersey 08520

Equal Opportunity: The Minority Student
The Collegiate Woman's Career Magazine
Equal Opportunity Publications, Inc.
P.O. Box 202
Centerport, New York 11721

Forbes
60 Fifth Avenue
New York, New York 10114

Fortune
541 N. Fairbanks Court
Chicago, Illinois 60611

Harvard Business Review
Soldiers Field
Boston, Massachusetts 02163

Inc.
P.O. Box 2452
Boulder, Colorado 80322

Money
P.O. Box 2571
Boulder, Colorado 80322

Success
P.O. Box 3035
Harlan, Iowa 51593

Venture
P.O. Box 10774
Des Moines, Iowa 50349

Working Woman
P.O. Box 10131
112 Tenth Street
Des Moines, Iowa 50340

The Wall Street Journal is a key source of business information, as are the business sections of the major daily newspapers: Atlanta *Journal-Constitution*, Boston *Globe*, Chicago *Tribune*, Dallas *Morning News*, Denver *Post*, Houston *Post*, Los Angeles *Times*, Minneapolis *Star Tribune*, *New York Times*, *Philadelphia Inquirer*, St. Louis *Post-Dispatch*, San Francisco *Chronicle*, Seattle *Post-Intelligencer*, and Washington *Post*.

CAREER FIELDS

In addition, there are key trade publications in specific industries that tend to attract smart people. The list has been broken down by general subject area: advertising, public relations, and marketing; computers and information processing; financial services; general industrial; and retailing and merchandising.

Advertising, Public Relations, Marketing

Advertising Age, weekly
740 Rush Street, Chicago, Illinois 60611

Adweek, weekly
820 Second Avenue, New York, New York 10017

Business Marketing, monthly
220 East 42nd Street, New York, New York 10017

Creative, The Magazine of Promotion and Marketing, bimonthly
37 West 39th Street, New York, New York 10018

Madison Avenue Magazine, monthly
369 Lexington Avenue, New York, New York 10017

Public Relations Journal
845 Third Avenue, New York, New York 10022

Computers and Information Processing

Computers and Electronics Marketing, monthly
1050 Commonwealth Avenue, Boston, Massachusetts 02215

Computer Decisions, monthly
50 Essex Street, Rochelle Park, New Jersey 07662

Data Communications, monthly
1221 Avenue of the Americas, New York, New York 10020

Infoworld, weekly
530 Lytton Avenue, Palo Alto, California 94301

MIS Week, weekly
7 East Twelfth Street, New York, New York 10003

PC, monthly
One Park Avenue, New York, New York 10016

Wall Street Computer Review, monthly
150 Broadway, New York, New York 10038

Financial Services

ABA Banking Journal, monthly
345 Hudson Street, New York, New York 10014

American Banker, daily
One State Street Plaza, New York, New York 10004

Bank Administration Magazine, monthly
60 Gould Center, East Tower, Rolling Meadows, Illinois 60008

Banker's Monthly, monthly
601 Skokie Boulevard, Northbrook, Illinois 60062

Best's Review: Life/Health Edition, monthly
Ambest Road, Oldwick, New Jersey 08858

Best's Review: Property/Casualty Edition, monthly
Ambest Road, Oldwick, New Jersey 08858

Corporate Finance, monthly
163 West Seventy-Fourth Street, New York, New York 10023

The Financial Planner Magazine, monthly
5775 Peachtree Dunwoody Road, Atlanta, Georgia 30342

Institutional Investor, monthly
488 Madison Avenue, New York, New York 10022

Investment Dealers' Digest, weekly
150 Broadway, New York, New York 10038

Journal of Insurance, bimonthly
110 William Street, New York, New York 10038

National Underwriter, Life & Health Insurance Edition, weekly
One Marineview Plaza, Hoboken, New Jersey 07030

National Underwriter, Property/Casualty Edition, weekly
One Marineview Plaza, Hoboken, New Jersey 07030

Securities Week, weekly
1221 Avenue of the Americas, New York, New York 10020

Security Traders' Monthly, monthly
150 Broadway, New York, New York 10038

United States Banker, monthly
One River Road, Cos Cob, Connecticut 06807

General Industrial

American Industry, monthly
21 Russell Woods, Great Neck, New York 11021

High Technology, monthly
38 Commercial Wharf, Boston, Massachusetts 02110

Industry, monthly
462 Boylston Street, P.O. Box 763, Boston, Massachusetts 02117

Management Review, monthly
135 West Fiftieth Street, New York, New York 10020

Retailing/Merchandising

Department Store Economist, 8 times a year
48 East Forty-third Street, New York, New York 10017

The Discount Merchandiser, monthly
Two Park Avenue, New York, New York 10016

Discount Store News, biweekly
425 Park Avenue, New York, New York 10022

HFD: Retailing Home Furnishings, weekly
7 East Twelfth Street, New York, New York 10003

Inside Retailing, biweekly
425 Part Avenue, New York, New York 10022

Stores, monthly
100 West Thirty-First Street, New York, New York 10001

GLAMOUR JOBS IN THE BIG APPLE

There are glamour jobs and then there are glamour jobs, especially for smart people. While glamour doesn't necessarily imply big bucks at the entry level, what it does mean is being where the action is, being around deal making and influence. And since the deal-making capital of the world is New York City, a.k.a. the Big Apple, what follows is a guide to the most glitzy New York firms and publications in the advertising, magazine, and public relations businesses; to the most prestigious law firms (liberal arts graduates usually make up the bulk of the paralegal work force in such firms); and to the most active venture capitalists. While a few of the organizations cited in this appendix are profiled in the book, most hire only a few liberal arts graduates each year and are worth pursuing once you've established a game plan and know why you are the exceptional talent who can hit the ground running.

10 Largest Advertising Agencies

(in size order, ranked by local office billings)

Grey Advertising
777 Third Avenue
New York, New York 10017
(212) 546-2000
Edward H. Meyer, chairman and president
N.Y. billings (1985): $981 million
N.Y. revenue (1985): $147 million
N.Y. staff: 1,700

Young & Rubicam New York
285 Madison Avenue
New York, New York 10017
(212) 210-3000

Peter A. Georgescu, president, Young & Rubicam Advertising
N.Y. billings (1985): $830 million
N.Y. revenue (1985): $115 million
N.Y. staff: 2,051

Ted Bates Worldwide Inc.
1515 Broadway
New York, New York 10036
(212) 869-3131
Donald M. Zuckert, president, Ted Bates Advertising/New York
N.Y. billings (1985): $754 million
N.Y. revenue (1985): NA
N.Y. staff: NA

DFS Dorland/New York
405 Lexington Avenue
New York, New York 10174
(212) 661-0800
Gary M. Susnjara, chairman
N.Y. billings (1985): $732 million
N.Y. revenue (1985): $106 million
N.Y. staff: 1265

Ogilvy & Mather
Two East 48th Street
New York, New York 10017
(212) 907-3400
Norman Berry, president
N.Y. billings (1985): $675 million
N.Y. revenue (1985): NA
N.Y. staff: NA

Saatchi & Saatchi Compton Inc.
625 Madison Avenue
New York, New York 10022
(212) 754-1100
Edward L. Wax, president and chief executive officer
N.Y. billings (1985): $590 million
N.Y. revenue (1985): $77 million
N.Y. staff: 700

Doyle Dane Bernbach/New York
437 Madison Avenue
New York, New York 10022
(212) 415-2000

Peter Falcone, president
N.Y. billings (1985): $580 million
N.Y. revenue (1985): $87 million
N.Y. staff: 885

J. Walter Thompson U.S.A. Inc.
466 Lexington Avenue
New York, New York 10017
(212) 210-7000
Steven Bowen, executive vice president/general manager, New York
office
N.Y. billings: $580 million
N.Y. revenue: NA
N.Y. staff: 645

NW Ayer Inc.
1345 Avenue of the Americas
New York, New York 10105
(212) 708-5000
Jerry J. Siano, vice chairman and president, New York office
N.Y. billings: $555 million
N.Y. revenue: $72 million
N.Y. staff: 1032

William Esty Co.
100 East 42nd Street
New York, New York 10017
(212) 692-6200
Gordon Bushell, chairman and chief executive officer
N.Y. billings: $510 million
N.Y. revenue: $77 million
N.Y. staff: 520

Magazines and Newspapers Not to Miss

Business Week, weekly
1221 Avenue of the Americas
New York, New York 10020
(212) 512-2511

Esquire, monthly
2 Park Avenue
New York, New York 10016
(212) 516-8100

Forbes, biweekly
60 Fifth Avenue
New York, New York 10011
(212) 620-2200

Money, monthly
Time & Life Building
Rockefeller Center
New York, New York 10020
(212) 586-1212

Newsweek, weekly
444 Madison Avenue
New York, New York 10022
(212) 350-4000

New York Magazine, weekly
755 Second Avenue
New York, New York 10017
(212) 880-0700

Time, weekly
Time & Life Building
Rockefeller Center
New York, New York 10020
(212) 586-1212

Wall Street Journal, daily except weekends
200 Liberty Street
New York, New York 10281
(212) 416-2000

Top 5 Public Relations Firms

Burson-Marsteller (parent company: Young & Rubicam)
230 Park Avenue South
New York, New York 10022
(212) 614-5000
N.Y. staff: 750
Number of clients: 175
Fee income (1986): $46 million

Hill & Knowlton Inc. (parent company: JWT Group Inc.)
420 Lexington Avenue
New York, New York 10017
(212) 697-5600
N.Y. staff: 300
Number of Clients: 250
Fee income (1986): NA

Ruder Finn & Rotman
110 East 59th Street
New York, New York 10022
(212) 593-6400
N.Y. staff: 225
Number of clients: 100
Fee income (1986): $13 million

Doremus Porter Novelli (parent company: Omnicom Group)
120 Broadway
New York, New York 10271
(212) 964-0700
N.Y. staff: 190
Number of clients: 120
Fee income (1986): $12 million

Ogilvy & Mather Public Relations Group (parent company: Ogilvy & Mather Worldwide)
708 Third Avenue
New York, New York 10017
(212) 682-6350
N.Y. staff: 180
Number of clients: 100
Fee income (1986): NA

Wanted: Paralegals

(15 largest law firms, by number of area employees)

Wilkie Farr & Gallagher
153 East 53rd Street
New York, New York 10022
(212) 935-8000
Number of paralegals: 35
Specialties: litigation; corporate and securities

Skadden, Arps, Slate, Meagher & Flom
919 Third Avenue
New York, New York 10022
(212) 735-3000
Number of paralegals: 96
Specialties: litigation; corporate and securities; tax; banking and
commerce

Shearman & Sterling
53 Wall Street
New York, New York 10005
(212) 483-1000
Number of paralegals: 70
Specialties: litigation; corporate and securities; estates and trust

Davis, Polk & Wardwell
One Chase Manhattan Plaza
New York, New York 10005
(212) 530-4000
Number of paralegals: 114
Specialties: all types of corporate law

Hughes Hubbard & Reed
One Wall Street
New York, New York 10005
(212) 709-7000
Number of paralegals: 37
Specialties: litigation; corporate and securities

Simpson, Thatcher & Bartlett
One Battery Park Plaza
New York, New York 10004
(212) 483-9000
Number of paralegals: 73
Specialties: corporate and securities

Weil, Gotshal & Manges
767 Fifth Avenue
New York, New York 10153
(212) 310-8000
Number of paralegals: 59
Specialties: all types of corporate law

Kaye, Scholer, Fierman, Hays & Handler
425 Park Avenue
New York, New York 10022

(212) 407-8000
Number of paralegals: 59
Specialties: litigation; corporate and securities

Cravath, Swaine & Moore
One Chase Manhattan Plaza
New York, New York 10005
(212) 422-3000
Number of paralegals: 65
Specialties: corporate and securities

Milbank, Tweed, Hadley & McCloy
One Chase Manhattan Plaza
New York, New York 10005
(212) 530-5000
Number of paralegals: 46
Specialties: banking and commerce; corporate and securities

Cahill Gordon & Reindel
80 Pine Street
New York, New York 10005
(212) 701-3000
Number of paralegals: 53
Specialties: all types of corporate law

LeBoeuf, Lamb, Leiby & MacRae
520 Madison Avenue
New York, New York 10022
(212) 715-8000
Number of paralegals: 80
Specialties: litigation; corporate and securities; insurance

Mudge, Rose, Guthrie, Alexander & Ferdon
180 Maiden Lane
New York, New York 10038
(212) 510-7000
Number of paralegals: 56
Specialties: corporate and securities; municipal

Fried, Frank, Harris, Shriver & Jacobsen
One New York Plaza
New York, New York 10004
(212) 820-8000
Number of paralegals: 58
Specialties: corporate and securities

Cadwalader, Wickersham & Taft
100 Maiden Lane
New York, New York 10038
(212) 504-6684
Number of paralegals: 43
Specialties: litigation; corporate and securities

5 Largest Venture Capital Firms

(by amount of capital, [1]number of deals in 1985)

Citicorp Capital Investors Ltd.
153 East 53rd Street
New York, New York 10043
(212) 559-1127
Number of deals: 84[1]
Total amount of capital: $102 million

Welsh Carson Anderson & Stowe
45 Wall Street
New York, New York 10005
(212) 422-3232
Number of deals: 36
Total amount of capital: $35 million

BT Capital Corp.
280 Park Avenue
New York, New York 10017
(212) 850-1916
Number of deals: 10
Total amount of capital: $28 million

Alan Patricof Associates Inc.
545 Madison Avenue
New York, New York 10022
(212) 753-6300
Number of deals: 40
Total amount of capital: $27 million

Adler & Co.
375 Park Avenue
New York, New York 10152
(212) 759-2800
Number of deals: 22
Total amount of capital: $24 million

P.S. If all you know is that you want one of these jobs but you're not sure how to land it and Gotham City has you at least a little bit intimidated, sign on with a temp agency (there are dozens listed in the Manhattan Yellow Pages) and earn while you consider strategies for breaking in. Consider enrolling in courses at The Discovery Center, The Learning Annex, or the continuing education programs of New York University or The New School for Social Research. All these programs offer how-to seminars in landing jobs in the most competitive fields. One last caveat: don't let the other fish intimidate you. While New York City is a big pond and any recent graduate is more or less a little fish, all you have to get is one bite and your break is made. From then on, it's a matter of slowly building your confidence and your contact base, and beginning to contribute to the bottom line of your glamorous employer. After all, the most glamorous employers are usually among the smartest, and that means that entry-level hires work mighty hard for the privilege of being affiliated with the fast lane. "I work twelve-hour days," says an assistant editor at *Elle*, "and not for the highest rate of pay!" She continues, "What's worse is that I don't dare complain to my friends because everyone works hard in the beginning and I am lucky enough to be toiling at an 'in' place, at a place where others wish they were working. And so what if much of my day is spent fact checking and typing. . . ."

COMPANIES THAT HIRE SMART PEOPLE

(Organized by Industry)

Accounting

Arthur Andersen & Co., Chicago, IL
Arthur Young & Co., NY, NY
Coopers and Lybrand, NY, NY
Deloitte Haskins & Sells, NY, NY
Ernst & Whinney, Cleveland, OH
KMG Main Hurdman, NY, NY
Laventhol & Horwath, Philadelphia, PA
Peat Marwick Mitchell & Co., NY, NY
Price Waterhouse, NY, NY
Touche Ross, NY, NY

Advertising

Backer & Spielvogel, NY, NY
BBDO International, NY, NY
Darcy Masius Benton & Bowles, NY, NY
DFS Dorland, NY, NY
Doyle Dane Bernbach, NY, NY
Foote, Cone & Belding, Chicago, IL
Grey Advertising Inc., NY, NY
J. Walter Thompson Company, NY, NY
Leo Burnett Company, Chicago, IL
McCann-Erickson, NY, NY
N. W. Ayer Inc., NY, NY
Ogilvy & Mather International, NY, NY
Saatchi & Saatchi Compton Inc., NY, NY
SSC&B: Lintas U.S.A., NY, NY
Young & Rubicam, Inc., NY, NY
William Esty Co., NY, NY
Wells Rich Greene, NY, NY

Commercial Banking

American Fletcher National Bank, Indianapolis, IN
American National Bank & Trust Co. of Chicago, Chicago, IL

Amsouth Bank, N.A., Birmingham, AL
Bancohio National Bank, Columbus, OH
Bank of Boston, Boston, MA
Bank of Credit & Commerce International, NY, NY
Bank of New England, Boston, MA
The Bank of New York, NY, NY
Bank of Oklahoma, Tulsa, OK
Bank One, Dayton, OH
Bank South Corp., Atlanta, GA
Bank of The West, San Jose, CA
California First Bank, San Diego, CA
Centerre Bank/St. Louis, St. Louis, MO
Central Bank of the South, Birmingham, AL
Chase Manhattan Bank, N.A., NY, NY
Chemical Bank, NY, NY
Citibank, N.A., NY, NY
Commercial Federal Savings & Loan Association, Omaha, NE
Continental Bank, Chicago, IL
Dime Savings Bank of New York FSB, Brooklyn, NY
Federal Reserve Bank, Chicago, IL
Federal Reserve Bank of Kansas City, Kansas City, MO
Federal Reserve Bank of Minneapolis, Minneapolis, MN
Federal Reserve Bank of New York, NY, NY
Fifth Third Bank, Cincinnati, OH
First Bank of Minneapolis, Minneapolis, MN
First City Bank of Dallas, Dallas, TX
First Federal Savings Bank, Phoenix, OH
First Fidelity Bank, N.A., North Jersey, Totowa, NJ
First Interstate Bank of Arizona, Phoenix, AZ
First Interstate Bank of California, Los Angeles, CA
First Interstate Bank of Denver, N.A., Denver, CO
First Interstate Bank of Oregon, N.A., Portland, OR
First Jersey National Bank, Jersey City, NJ
First National Bank and Trust Co., Oklahoma City, OK
First National Bank of Atlanta, Atlanta, GA
First National Bank of Chicago, Chicago, IL
First National Bank of Cincinnati, Cincinnati, OH
First National Bank of Commerce, New Orleans, LA
First National Bank of Maryland, Baltimore, MD
First Union National Bank, Charlotte, NC
First Wisconsin National Bank/Milwaukee, Milwaukee, WI
Firstmark Financial Corp., Indianapolis, IN
Fleet National Bank, Providence, RI
GEM Financial Corp., Dayton, OH
Harris Trust & Savings Bank, Chicago, IL
Huntington National Bank, Columbus, OH

Indiana National Bank, Indianapolis, IN
Interfirst Bank Austin N.A., Austin, TX
Interfirst Bank Dallas N.A., Dallas, TX
Interfirst Bank Fort Worth N.A., Fort Worth, TX
Interfirst Bank Houston N.A., Houston, TX
Irving Trust Company, NY, NY
Key Bank, N.A., Albany, NY
Key Bank of Central Maine, Augusta, ME
MBank/Dallas, Dallas, TX
MBank/Houston, Houston, TX
Manufacturers Hanover, NY, NY
Manufacturers National Bank of Detroit, Detroit, MI
The Marine Corp., Milwaukee, WI
Marine Midland Bank, N.A., NY, NY
Maryland National Bank, Baltimore, MD
Mellon Bank/East, Philadelphia, PA
Mellon Bank Corp., Pittsburgh, PA
Mercantile Trust Co., N.A., St. Louis, MO
Meridian BankCorp Inc., Reading, PA
Michigan National Bank, Detroit, MI
Midlantic National Bank, Edison, NJ
National Bank of Detroit, Detroit, MI
New Jersey National Bank, West Trenton, NJ
Northern Trust Co., Chicago, IL
Northwest Bank Des Moines N.A., Des Moines, IA
Norwest Bank Minneapolis, N.A., Minneapolis, MN
Old Kent Bank & Trust Co., Grand Rapids, MI
Old Stone Bank, Providence, RI
Pacific Western Bank, Portland, OR
Philadelphia National Bank, Philadelphia, PA
Pittsburgh National Bank, Pittsburgh, PA
Republicbank Corp., Dallas, TX
Shawmut Corp., Boston, MA
Southeast Bank, N.A., Miami, FL
Southtrust Bank of Alabama, Birmingham, AL
Sovran Bank, Richmond, VA
Sun Banks, Inc., Orlando, FL
Sunbank Service Corp., Orlando, FL
Texas American Bancshares, Inc., Fort Worth, TX
Texas American Bank/Dallas, Dallas, TX
Union Bank, Los Angeles, CA
Union Planters National Bank, Memphis, TN
United Bank of Denver, Denver, CO
United States National Bank of Oregon, Portland, OR
United States Trust Company of New York, NY, NY
Valley National Bank, Phoenix, AZ

Wachovia Bank & Trust Co., N.A., Winston-Salem, NC
Wells Fargo & Co., San Francisco, CA

Computers

AT&T International, Basking Ridge, NJ
AT&T Technologies, Bernardsville, NJ
Activision, Inc., Mountain View, CA
Adage, Inc., Billerica, MA
Amdahl Corp., Sunnyvale, CA
American Management Systems Inc., Arlington, VA
Apple Computer, Inc., Cupertino, CA
Arrow Electronics, Melville, NY
Ask Computer Systems, Inc., Los Altos, CA
Atex, Inc., Bedford, MA
Automatic Data Processing, Inc., Roseland, NJ
BTI Computer Systems, Sunnyvale, CA
Burr-Brown Corp., Tucson, AZ
Burroughs Corp., Detroit, MI
Canaan Computer Corp., Trumbull, CT
Century Data Systems, Anaheim, CA
Comptex Research, Inc., Buffalo, NY
Computer Automation, Inc., Irvine, CA
Computer Consoles, Inc., Rochester, NY
Computer Products, Inc./Measurement and Control, Pompano Beach,
    FL
Computer Sciences Corp., El Segundo, CA
Computer Technology Associates, Inc., Englewood, CO
Control Data Corp., Minneapolis, MN
Cray Research Inc., Minneapolis, MN
Creare Inc., Hanover, NH
Cromemco, Mountain View, CA
Cybernex Corp., San Jose, CA
DBA Systems, Inc., Melbourne, FL
Daisy Systems Corp., Sunnyvale, CA
Data General Corp., Westborough, MA
Data Resources/McGraw-Hill Inc., Lexington, MA
Datagraphix, San Diego, CA
Datapoint Corp., San Antonio, TX
Dataproducts Corp., Woodland Hills, CA
Dataproducts SPG (Milford) Inc., Milford, NH
Decision Data Computer Corp., Horsham, PA
Decisions and Designs, Inc., McLean, VA
Delta Data Systems Corp., Trevose, PA
Digital Equipment Corp., Concord, MA
Digitech Industries, Inc., Ridgefield, CT

Dravo Engineers, Inc., Pittsburgh, PA
E-Systems, Inc/Garland Division, Dallas, TX
E-Systems, Inc./Melpar Division, Falls Church, VA
ESL, a subsidiary of TRW, Sunnyvale, CA
Educational Computer Corp., Orlando, FL
Electronic Data Systems Corp., Dallas, TX
Emhart Corp./VSM Machinery Div., Beverly, MA
Evans & Sutherland Computer Corp., Salt Lake City, UT
Excellon Industries, Torrance, CA
Eyring Research Institute, Inc., Provo, UT
Floating Point Systems, Inc., Portland, OR
Formation, Inc., Mt. Laurel, NJ
Foxboro Co., Foxboro, MA
GTE Communications Systems, Research & Development, Phoenix, AZ
GTE Data Services, Tampa, FL
General Datacomm Industries, Middlebury, CT
Gould AMI Semiconductor, Santa Clara, CA
Harris Corp., Nashua, NH
Harris Corp./Government Support Systems Division, Syosset, NY
Hayes Microcomputer Products Inc., Atlanta, GA
Heath Co./Zenith Data Systems, St. Joseph, MI
Hewlett-Packard Co., Palo Alto, CA
Honeywell, Inc., Minneapolis, MN
IBM Corp., Armonk, NY
ILC Data Device Corp., Bohemia, NY
IOCS, Inc., Waltham, MA
Iomega Corp., Roy, VT
ITT Courier Terminal Systems, Tempe, AZ
ITT Telecom/Columbus Technology Center, Columbus, OH
Intergraph Corp., Huntsville, AL
Intermetrics Inc., Cambridge, MA
International Computers LTD, Stamford, CT
Johnson Controls Inc., Milwaukee, WI
Kustom Quality Electronics, Inc., Tenexa, KS
Kyocera International Inc., San Diego, CA
LTX Corp., Westwood, MA
Logicon Inc./Strategic and Information Systems Div., San Pedro, CA
Loonam Computer Products/AVNET Computer Technologies, Eden Prairie, MN
Lundy Electronics & Systems Inc., Glen Head, NY
MAI Basic Four, Inc., Tustin, CA
Mead Data Central, Dayton, OH
Measurex Corp., Cupertino, CA
Megatek Corp., San Diego, CA
Micro Data Base Systems, Inc., Lafayette, IN

Mid-Continent Computer Services, Inc., Englewood, CO
Multiwire Div./Kollmorgen Corp., Hicksville, NY
NBI, Inc., Boulder, CO
NCR Corp./Engineering & Manufacturing, San Diego, CA
NCR Corp./Systems Engineering-San Diego, San Diego, CA
NEC Information Systems, Inc., Boxborough, MA
National Semiconductor Corp., Santa Clara, CA
Par Technology Corp., New Hartford, NY
Perkin-Elmer Corp., Norwalk, CT
Pertec Peripherals Corp., Chatsworth, CA
Precision Monolithics Inc., Santa Clara, CA
Qume Corp., San Jose, CA
R & D Associates, Marina del Ray, CA
Rolm Corp., Santa Clara, CA
Racal-Milgo Inc., Ft. Lauderdale, FL
Racal-Vadic, Milpitas, CA
Rapidata Div./National Data Corp., Fairfield, NJ
SDRC (Structural Dynamics Research Corp.), Milford, OH
STSC, Inc., Rockville, MD
Syscon Corp., Washington, D.C.
Kurt Salmon Associates, Inc., Atlanta, GA
Howard W. Sams & Co., Inc., Indianapolis, IN
Setpoint, Inc., Houston, TX
Softech Inc., Waltham, MA
Sperry Defense Products Group/Computer Systems Div., St. Paul, MN
Sperry Information Systems Group, Blue Bell, PA
Storage Technology Corp., Louisville, CO
Syncsort, Inc., Englewood Cliffs, NJ
Systems Research Laboratories, Inc., Dayton, OH
TRW Electronics and Defense Sector, Redondo Beach, CA
Taylor Instrument, Rochester, NY
Tektronix, Inc., Beaverton, OR
Textronix, Inc./Information Display Group, Wilsonville, OR
Telesciences, Inc., Mt. Laurel, NJ
Teletype Corp., Skokie, IL
Triad Systems Corp., Sunnyvale, CA
United Technologies/Mostek, Carrolton, TX
Wallace Computer Services, Inc., Hillside, IL
Xerox Corp., Rochester, NY
Xerox Corp./Electronics Division, El Segundo, CA
Xerox Printing Systems Division, El Segundo, CA
Zenith Electronics Corp., Glenview, IL
Zentec Corp., Santa Clara, CA
Zytec, Eden Prairie, MN

Education

Baltimore County Public Schools, Towson, MD
Baylor College of Medicine, Houston, TX
University of California/Davis Campus, Davis, CA
University of Chicago, Chicago, IL
Control Data Institute, Decatur, GA
Educational Testing Service, Princeton, NJ
Harvard University, Cambridge, MA
University of Maryland Cooperative Extension Service, College Park,
   MD
Pennsylvania State University/Housing and Food Services, University
   Park, PA
Pittsburgh Board of Education, Pittsburgh, PA
Purdue University/Business Office, West Lafayette, IN
Rockefeller University, NY, NY
University of Rochester, Rochester, NY
University of Texas/Medical Branch, Galveston, TX

Government

Aberdeen Proving Ground Installation Support Activity, Aberdeen
   Proving Ground, MD
Department of Agriculture, Office of Personnel, Washington, D.C.
Air Force Civilian Personnel Office, England Air Force Base, England,
   LA
Air Force Civilian Personnel Office, Langley Air Force Base, Langley,
   VA
Air Force Civilian Personnel Office, Shaw Air Force Base, Shaw, SC
Animal and Plant Health Inspection Service, Minneapolis, MN
Army and Air Force Exchange Service, Dallas, TX
Army Audit Agency, Washington, D.C.
Army Civilian Personnel Office, Ft. Leavenworth, KS
Army Communication Electronics Command, Ft. Monmouth, NJ
Army Engineer Center and Fort Belvoir, Fort Belvoir, VA
Army Engineer District/Mobile, Mobile, AL
Department of Army/Harry Diamond Laboratories, Adelphi, MD
Army Information Systems Command, Fort Huachuca, AZ
Army Material Command, Philadelphia, PA
Army Material Command/Intern Program, Alexandria, VA
Bonneville Power Administration, Portland, OR
Center for Disease Control, Atlanta, GA
Central Intelligence Agency, Washington, D.C.
Coast Guard, Washington, D.C.

Coast Guard Academy, New London, CT
Department of Commerce, Washington, D.C.
Comptroller of the Currency, Washington, D.C.
Consolidated Civilian Personnel Office, Bethesda, MD
Contra Costa County Personnel Department, Martinez, CA
City of Dallas Police Department, Dallas, TX
Defense Contract Audit Agency, Alexandria, VA
Defense Intelligence Agency, Washington, D.C.
Defense Logistics Agency, Alexandria, VA
Defense Logistics Agency/Civilian Personnel Management Support
    Office, Columbus, OH
Defense Mapping Agency, Washington, D.C.
Edward Air Force Base, Edwards Air Force Base, CA
Federal Bureau of Investigation, Washington, D.C.
Foreign Agriculture Service, Washington, D.C.
Forest Service, Atlanta, GA
General Accounting Office, Washington, D.C.
General Services Administration, Washington, D.C.
Georgia State Department of Natural Resources, Atlanta, GA
Georgia State Department of Transportation, Atlanta, GA
Georgia State Merit System, Atlanta, GA
Hanscom Air Force Base/Electronic Systems Div., Hanscom Air Force
    Base, MA
Houston Police Department, Houston, TX
Illinois Department of Transportation, Springfield, IL
Indiana Department of Natural Resources/Division of Water,
    Indianapolis, IN
Internal Revenue Service, Washington, D.C.
Iowa State Commerce Commission, Des Moines, IA
Department of Justice/Justice Management Division, Washington, D.C.
Department of Labor, Washington, D.C.
Department of Labor/Bureau of Labor Statistics, Washington, D.C.
City of Los Angeles, Los Angeles, CA
Los Angeles Air Force Station, Los Angeles, CA
Los Angeles Department of Water and Power, Los Angeles, CA
Marine Corps., Washington, D.C.
Maryland State Police, Pikesville, MD
Metropolitan Sanitary District of Greater Chicago, Chicago, IL
Michigan Department of Transportation, Lansing, MI
State of Michigan, Lansing, MI
City of Milwaukee, Milwaukee, WI
Milwaukee Count Department of Human Resources, Milwaukee, WI
Missouri Department of Conservation, Jefferson City, MO
Missouri State Highway and Transportation Department, Jefferson
    City, MO
Monroe County Library System, Rochester, NY

National Aeronautics and Space Administration, Washington, D.C.
National Credit Union Administration, Washington, D.C.
National Oceanic and Atmospheric Administration, Rockville, MD
National Security Agency, Fort Meade, MD
Navair Engineering Support Office, San Diego, CA
Naval Air Development Center, Warminster, PA
Naval Air Engineering Center, Lakehurst, NJ
Naval Air Rework Facility, Norwalk, VA
Naval Air Rework Facility, Cherry Point, NC
Naval Avionics Center, Indianapolis, IN
Naval Civil Engineering Laboratory, Point Hueneme, CA
Naval Coastal Systems Center, San Diego, CA
Naval Ship Weapon Systems Engineering Station, Point Hueneme, CA
Naval Surface Weapons Center, Silver Spring, MD
Naval Undersea Warfare Engineering Station, Keyport, WA
Naval Underwater Systems Center, China Lake, CA
Naval Weapons Support Center, Crane, IN
Naval Underwater Systems Center, Newport, RI
Navy Public Works Center, Honolulu, HI
Navy Recruiting Command, Arlington, VA
Navy Resale and Services Support Office, Staten Island, NY
New Jersey Department of Civil Service, Trenton, NJ
New York City Board of Education/Division of School Buildings, Long
     Island City, NY
New York City Transit Authority, Brooklyn, NY
New York State Department of Transportation, Albany, NY
Norwalk Naval Shipyard, Portsmouth, VA
Office of Administration, Washington, D.C.
Office of Personnel Management, Washington, D.C.
Patent & Trademark Office, Washington, D.C.
Peace Corps, Washington, D.C.
Pennsylvania Civil Service Commission, Harrisburg, PA
Pennsylvania Department of Transportation, Harrisburg, PA
Public Health Service/Engineering Programs, Rockville, MD
Bureau of Reclamation/Division of Personnel Management,
     Washington, D.C.
City of Raleigh, Raleigh, NC
City of Santa Monica, Santa Monica, CA
Social Security Administration, Baltimore, MD
Tennessee State Department of Transportation, Nashville, TN
State of Texas/Comptroller of Public Accounts, Austin, TX
Texas State Department of Mental Health and Mental Retardation,
     Austin, TX
Transportation Systems Center, Cambridge, MA
Utah State Division of Personnel Management, Salt Lake City, UT

Commonwealth of Virginia/Department of Personnel and Training, Richmond, VA
Virginia Department of Highways and Transportation, Richmond, VA
Warner Robins Air Logistics Center, Robins Air Force Base, GA
State of Washington/Department of Personnel, Olympia, WA
State of Washington/Department of Revenue, Olympia, WA
West Virginia Department of Highways, Charleston, WV
Western Area Power Administration, Golden, CO
Wisconsin State Government/Division of Merit Recruitment and Selection, Madison, WI

Health Care

Abbot Northwestern Hospital, Minneapolis, MN
ARA Living Centers/Rocky Mountain Area, Greeley, CO
Aultman Hospital, Canton, OH
Children's Hospital Medical Center, Cincinnati, OH
Community Hospital of Indianapolis, Inc., Indianapolis, IN
Community Hospitals and Health Care Systems Inc., Cheverly, MD
Hospital Corp. of America, Nashville, TN
Hospital of the University of Pennsylvania, Philadelphia, PA
Humana, Inc., Louisville, KY
Huron Road Hospital, Cleveland, OH
Mayo Clinic, Rochester, MN
Methodist Hospital, Houston, TX
Parkland Memorial Hospital, Dallas, TX
St. Anthony's Medical Center, St. Louis, MO
St. Joseph Hospital, Houston, TX
St. Luke's Hospital, Milwaukee, WI
University of Texas/Medical Branch, Galveston, TC4X
University of Texas System Cancer Center/M.D. Anderson Hospital, Houston, TX

Insurance

American National Insurance Co., Galveston, TX
Atlantic Cos., NY, NY
Automobile Club of Michigan, Dearborn, MI
Automobile Club of Southern California, Los Angeles, CA
The Bankers Life Co., Des Moines, IA
Blue Cross & Blue Shield of Alabama, Birmingham, AL
Blue Cross & Blue Shield of Massachusetts, Cambridge, MA
Blue Cross & Blue Shield of the National Capital Area, Washington, D.C.
Blue Cross & Blue Shield of Rhode Island, Providence, RI

Blue Cross & Blue Shield of Texas, Inc., Richardson, TX
Blue Cross & Blue Shield United of Wisconsin, Milwaukee, WI
Blue Cross of Western Pennsylvania, Pittsburgh, PA
CIGNA Corp., Hartford, CT
Century Companies of America, Waverly, IA
Chubb Group of Insurance Cos., Warren, NJ
Commercial Union Insurance Cos., Boston, MA
Employers Insurance of Texas, Dallas, TX
Equitable Life Assurance Society of the United States, NY, NY
Erie Insurance Group, Erie, PA
Farm Bureau Insurance Cos., West Des Moines, IA
Federal Home Life Insurance Co., Battle Creek, MI
Federated Mutual Insurance Co., Owatonna, MN
Fidelity Union Life Insurance, Dallas, TX
Firstmarch Financial Corp., Indianapolis, IN
Franklin Life Insurance Co., Springfield, IL
GAB Business Services, Inc., Parsippany, NJ
GM Acceptance Corp/Motor Insurance Corp., Detroit, MI
General Accident Insurance Co. of America, Philadelphia, PA
General Electric Credit Corp., Stamford, CT
General Reinsurance Corp., Stamford, CT
Great-West Life Assurance Cor., Englewood, CO
John Hancock Mutual Life Insurance Co., Boston, MA
Horace Mann Insurance Cos., Springfield, IL
IRM Insurance, White Plains, NY
Indiana Insurance Company, Indianapolis, IN
Industrial Risk Insurers, Hartford, CT
Integon Corp., Winston-Salem, NC
Kemper Group, Long Grove, IL
Liberty Life Insurance Co., Greenville, SC
Liberty Mutual Insurance Cos., Boston, MA
Life Investors, Inc., Cedar Rapids, IA
Life of Virginia, Richmond, VA
Lincoln National Life Insurance Co., Fort Wayne, IN
Metropolitan Insurance Cos., NY, NY
Michigan Mutual Insurance (Amerisure Cos.), Detroit, MI
Minnesota Mutual Life Insurance Co., St. Paul, MN
Monarch Life Insurance Co., Springfield, MA
Mutual Benefit Life Insurance Co., Newark, NJ
Mutual of Omaha Insurance Co., Omaha, NE
National Insurance Co., Montpelier, VT
Nationwide Insurance Co., Columbus, OH
New England Mutual Life Insurance Co., Boston, MA
New York Life Insurance Company, NY, NY
North American Company for Life and Health Insurance, Chicago, IL
Northwestern Mutual Life Insurance Co., Milwaukee, WI

Northwestern National Life Insurance Co., Minneapolis, MN
Old American Insurance Co., Kansas City, MO
Paul Revere Life Insurance Co., Worcester, MA
Peerless Insurance Co., Keene, NH
Penn Mutual Life Insurance Co., Philadelphia, PA
Phoenix Mutual Life Insurance Co., Hartford, CT
Protective Life Corp., Birmingham, AL
Provident Life & Accident Insurance Co., Chattanooga, TN
Prudential Insurance Co. of America, Newark, NJ
St. Paul Fire and Marine Insurance Co. of New York, Binghampton, NY
Sentry Insurance, Stevens Point, WI
Shelter Insurance Cos., Columbus, MD
Southwestern Life Insurance Co., Dallas, TX
State Auto Insurance Co., Columbus, OH
State Farm Insurance Cos., Bloomington, IL
State Mutual of America, Worcester, MA
Sunlife of Canada, Wellesley, MA
Transamerica Occidental Life Insurance Co., Los Angeles, CA
Travelers Insurance Co., Hartford, CT
U.S. Insurance Group, Basking Ridge, NJ
Washington National Insurance Group, Evanston, IL
Wausau Insurance Cos., Wausau, WI
Zurich-American Insurance Cos., Schaumburg, IL

Investments/Securities

Bear, Stearns, NY, NY
Brown Brothers Harriman & Co., NY, NY
The Capital Group, Inc., Los Angeles, CA
Chicago Board of Trade, Chicago, IL
Dean Witter Reynolds, NY, NY
Donaldson, Lufkin & Jenrette, NY, NY
Drexel Burnham Lambert Inc., NY, NY
The First Boston Corporation, NY, NY
E. F. Hutton, NY, NY
Fidelity Investments, Boston, MA
First Commodity Corporation of Boston, Boston, MA
Goldman, Sachs & Co., NY, NY
IDS Financial Services, Inc., Minneapolis, MN
Kidder, Peabody & Co., NY, NY
Lazard Freres, NY, NY
Louis Dreyfus Corp., Stamford, CT
Merrill Lynch & Co., NY, NY
Morgan Stanley & Co., NY, NY
PaineWebber, NY, NY

Prudential-Bache Securities, NY, NY
Salomon Brothers, NY, NY
Shearson Lehman American Express, NY, NY
Smith Barney, Harris Upham, NY, NY
Stein Roe & Farnham, Chicago, IL

Management Consulting

American Management Systems, Inc., Arlington, VA
American Water Works Service Co., Inc., Haddon Heights, NJ
Bain & Company, Boston, MA
Booz, Allen & Hamilton, NY, NY
The Boston Consulting Group, Boston, MA
Braxton Associates, Boston, MA
Buck Consultants, Inc., NY, NY
Charles River Associates, Boston, MA
Decisions and Designs, Inc., McLean, VA
A.S. Hansen Inc., Deerfield, IL
Hewitt Associates, Lincolnshire, IL
McKinsey & Co., Inc., NY, NY
Price Waterhouse, NY, NY
Saddlebrook Corp., Cambridge, MA
SRI International, Stanford, CA
Stanley Consultants, Inc., Muscatine, IA
Strategic Planning Associates, Alexandria, VA
Theodore Barry & Associates, Los Angeles, CA

Manufacturing

AC Spark Plug, Flint, MI
ADC Telecommunications, Inc., Minneapolis, MN
AEC Inc., Elk Grove Village, IL
AFG Industries, Inc., Kingsport, TN
AMCA International, Hanover, NH
AMF Inc., White Plains, NY
AMP Inc., Harrisburg, PA
AT&T International, Basking Ridge, NJ
AT&T Technologies, Bernardsville, NJ
AVX Corp., Myrtle Beach, SC
Abitibi-Price Corp., Troy, MI
Acme-Cleveland Corp., Pepper Pike, OH
Acme Electric Corp./Engineered Products Div., Cuba, NY
Aiken Advanced Systems, Alexandria, VA
Airesearch Manufacturing Co., Torrance, CA
Alberto-Culver Co., Melrose Park, IL

All-Steel, Inc., Aurora, IL
Allen-Bradley Co., Milwaukee, WI
Allied-Bendix Aerospace, Arlington, VA
Allied-Bendix Aerospace/Engine Products Division, Jacksonville, FL
Allied-Bendix Aerospace/Bendix Environmental Systems Div.,
    Baltimore, MD
Allis-Chalmers Corp., Milwaukee, WI
Alpha Industries, Inc., Woburn, MA
Aluminum Company of America, Pittsburgh, PA
Amcast Industrial/Newnam Div., Kendallville, IN
Amdahl Corp., Sunnyvale, CA
American Cyanamid Co., Wayne, NJ
American Edward's Technologies, Santa Ana, CA
American Hoechst Corp., Somerville, NJ
American Hospital Supply Corp., Evanston, IL
American Optical Corp., Southbridge, MA
American Roller Co., Bannockburn, IL
Amstar Corp., NY, NY
Amsted Industries Inc., Chicago, IL
Amway Corp., Ada, MI
Analog Devices, Norwood, MA
Anchor Hocking Corp., Lancaster, OH
Andrews Corp., Orland Park, FL
Anheuser-Busch Companies, Inc., St. Louis, MO
Appleton Papers Inc., Appleton, VT
Applied Magnetics Corp., Goleta, CA
Applied Solar Energy Corp., City of Industry, CA
Artesian Industries, Mansfield, OH
Avantek, Inc., Santa Clara, CA
Avco-Lycoming Div., Stratford, CT
Avery Label, Azusa, CA
Ayerst Laboratories, Inc., Rouses Point, NY
Babcock & Wilson, New Orleans, LA
Baker Instruments Corp., Allentown, PA
Ball Corp., Muncie, IN
Baltimore Aircoil Co., Baltimore, MD
Barker Coleman Co., Loves Park, IL
Barry Controls, Watertown, MA
Bausch & Lomb, Inc., Rochester, NY
Becor Western Inc., South Milwaukee, WI
Becton Dickinson & Co., Paramus, NJ
Belden Electrical Wire Products Division, Geneva, IL
Bell Helicopter Textrox, Fort Worth, TX
Bell & Howell Company, Skokie, IL
Beliot Corp., Beloit, WI
Benthos, Inc., N. Falmouth, MA

Bethlehem Steel Corp., Bethlehem, PA
Bidermann Industries, U.S.A., Inc., Secaucus, NJ
Bio-Rad Laboratories, Richmond, CA
Blonger-Tongue Laboratories, Inc., Old Bridge, NJ
Bloom Engineering Co., Inc., Pittsburgh, PA
Blue Bell, Inc., Greensboro, NC
The Boeing Co., Seattle, WA
Boise Cascade Corp., Boise, ID
Borg-Warner Corp., Chicago, IL
Borg-Warner Air Conditioning, Inc., York, PA
Bourns, Inc., Riverside, CA
Bowater Carolina Co., Catawba, SC
Brand Rex Co., Willimantic, CT
Branson Sonic Power Co., Danbury, CT
Brockway, Inc., Jacksonville, FL
Brown Shoe Co., St. Louis, MO
Brown & Williamson Tobacco Corp., Louisville, KY
Buick-Oldsmobile-Cadillac-GMC, Flint, MI
Bunge Edible Oil Corp., Kankakee, IL
Burlington Industries, Inc., Greensboro, NC
Burr-Brown Corp., Tucson, AZ
CD Medical, Inc., Miami Lakes, FL
Cabot Wrought Products Div./Cabot Stellit Div., Kokomo, IN
Calgon Corp./Commercial Division, St. Louis, MO
Campbell Soup Co., Camden, NJ
Carboline Co., St. Louis, MO
Carnation Co., Los Angeles, CA
Carpenter Technology Corp., Reading, PA
Carriage Industries, Inc., Calhoun, GA
J.I. Case Co., Racine, WI
Case Communications Inc., Silver Spring, MD
Caterpillar Tractor Co., Peoria, IL
The Ceco Corporation, Oak Brook, IL
Champion International Corp., Stamford, CT
Chemcut Corp., State College, PA
Chemineer, Inc., Dayton, OH
Chicago Pneumatic Tool Co./Tool Div., Utica, NY
Chicago Rawhide Manufacturing Co., Elgin, IL
Chrysler Corp., Detroit, MI
Church & Dwight Co., Inc., Princeton, NJ
Cincinnati Milacron/Heald Corp., Worcester, MA
Cincinnati Milacron Inc., Cincinnati, OH
Clairol Inc., NY, NY
Cleveland Pneumatic Co., Cleveland, OH
Clevite, Cleveland, OH
Clifton Precision Special Devices, Drexel Hill, PA

The Clorox Company, Oakland, CA
Coca-Cola USA, Atlanta, GA
Coleman Co., Inc., Wichita, KS
Colgate-Palmolive Co., NY, NY
Cone Mills Corp., Greensboro, NC
Conrac Corp., Stamford, CT
Consolidated Papers Inc., Wisconsin Rapids, WI
Container Corporation of America, Chicago, IL
Conwed Corp., St. Paul, MN
Cooper Industries/Energy Services Group, Mt. Vernon, OH
Cooper Tire & Rubber Co., Findlay, OH
Copeland Corp., Sidney, OH
Coopus Engineering Corp., Worcester, MA
Cordis Corp., Miami, FL
Corning Glass Works, Corning, NY
Coulter Electronics, Inc., Hialeah, FL
Craig Systems Corp., Amesbury, MA
John Crane/Houdaille, Inc., Morton Grove, IL
Cummins Engine Co., Inc., Columbus, IN
Cyclops Corp./Empire Detroit, Mansfield, OH
DSC Communications Corp., Richardson, TX
Dartco Manufacturing Inc., Augusta, GA
Databit Inc., Hauppauge, NY
Deere & Co., Moline, IL
Delco Moraine Div./GMC, Dayton, OH
Dexter Corp./Midland Div., Waukegan, IL
Diebold, Inc., Canton, OH
Diesel Recon Co., Memphis, TN
Digitech Industries, Inc., Ridgefield, CT
Dorsey Corp., Chattanooga, TN
Douglas Aircraft Co., Long Beach, CA
Dover Elevator Systems, Inc., Memphis, TN
Dow Corning Corp., Midland, MI
Drackett Co., Cincinnati, OH
Dranetz Technologies, Inc., Edison, NJ
Dukane Corp., St. Charles, IL
Duracell International Inc., Bethel, CT
Durkee Foods, Cleveland, OH
Edmont, Coshocton, OH
Elcor Corp., Midland, TX
Electric Machinery, Minneapolis, MN
Electro Scientific Industries, Portland, OR
Electro-Motive/GMC, La Grange, IL
Elkay Manufacturing Co., Broadview, IL
Elliott Co., Jeannette, PA
Emerson Government and Defense Group, St. Louis, MO

Emhart Corp./USM Machinery Div., Beverly, MA
Envirex Inc., Waukesha, WI
Ethyl Corp., Baton Rouge, LA
Exar Corp., Sunnyvale, CA
Excel Corp., Wichita, KS
Excel Industries, Inc., Hesston, KS
FMC Corporation, Chicago, IL
FMC/Ordinance Div., San Jose, CA
Fairchild Aircraft Corp., San Antonio, TX
Fairchild Camera and Instrument Corp., Mountain View, CA
Fasson-Avery International, Painesville, OH
Federal Mogul, Detroit, MI
Federal Products Corp., Providence, RI
Fieldcrest Mills, Inc., Eden, NC
Fischer & Porter Co., Warminster, PA
Fisher Controls International Inc., Marshalltown, IA
Fisher-Price, East Aurora, NY
Floating Point Systems, Inc., Everett, WA
Ford Aerospace/Aeronautic Div., Newport Beach, CA
Formation, Inc., Mount Laurel, NJ
Foster Wheeler Energy Corp., Livingston, NJ
Foxboro Co., Foxboro, MA
Fram Division, East Providence, RI
Frederick Electronics Corp., Frederick, MD
Freightliner Corp., Portland, OR
Fruehauf Corp., Detroit, MI
Fuller Co., Bethlehem, PA
Furnas Electric Co., Batavia, IL
GAF Corp., Wayne, NJ
GF Furniture Systems, Inc., Youngstown, OH
GTE Corp., Stamford, CT
GTE Government Systems Corp./Communications Systems Div.,
     Needham Heights, MA
Garrett Turbine Engine Co., Phoenix, AZ
Gates Rubber Co., Denver, CO
General Cable Co., Greenwich, CT
General Datacomm Industries, Middlebury, CT
General Instrument Corp./Optoelectronics Div., Palo Alto, CA
General Instrument/Jerrold Div., Hatboro, PA
General Motors Corp., Detroit, MI
General Railway Signal, Rochester, NY
Genesco Inc., Nashville, TN
Genrad Semiconductor Test Inc., Milpitas, CA
Genrad/Service Product Division, Phoenix, AZ
Georgia Kraft Co., Rome, GA
Georgia-Pacific Corp., Atlanta, GA

Gillette Co., Boston, MA
P.H. Glatfelter Co., Spring Grove, PA
Glidden Coatings & Resins, Cleveland, OH
Gold Bond Building Products, Charlotte, NC
Gold Kist, Inc., Atlanta, GA
BF Goodrich Co., Akron, OH
Goodyear Tire & Rubber Co., Akron, OH
Gould AMI Semiconductor, Santa Clara, CA
Gould Inc./Defense Electronics Div., Glen Burnie, MD
Gould Inc./Programmable Control Div., Andover, MA
Gould Inc./Recording Systems Div., Cleveland, OH
W.R. Grace & Co./Construction Products Div., Cambridge, MA
W.R. Grace & Co./Cryovac Div., Duncan, SC
W.W. Grainger, Inc., Chicago, IL
Graphic Controls Corp., Buffalo, NY
Great Northern Nekoosa Corp., Stamford, CT
A.P. Green Refractories Co., Mexico, MO
Griffith Labs USA, Alsip, IL
Haggar Co., Dallas, TX
Hamilton Industries, Inc., Two Rivers, WI
Hamilton Standard, Windsor Locks, CT
Hanes Hosiery, Inc., Winston-Salem, NC
Hanes Knitwear, Winston-Salem, NC
Harbison-Walker Refractories, Pittsburgh, PA
Harnischfeger Corp., Milwaukee, WI
Harris Corp./Business Information Systems Operations, Dallas, TX
Harris Graphics Corp., Melbourne, FL
Hartmarx Corp., Chicago, IL
Haworth Inc., Holland, MI
Hazeltine Corp., Greenlawn, NY
Hershey Foods Corp., Hershey, PA
Hexcel Corp., Dublin, CA
Hobart Corp., Troy, OH
The Hoover Company, North Canton, OH
Howmet Turbine Components Corp./Castings Div., Dover, NJ
J.M. Huber Corp., Borger, TX
Hughes Helicopters, Inc., Tempe, AZ
Hughes Tool Division, Houston, TX
Hydra-Matic Divisional Office, Ypsilanti, MI
Hydril Co./Mechanical Products Div., Houston, TX
Hyster Co., Portland, OR
IMCO Services, Houston, TX
ITT Avionics, Nutley, NJ
ITT Electro-Optical Products Division, Roanoke, VA
ITT/Gilfillan Division, Van Nuys, CA
ITT Marlow, Midland Park, NJ

Illinois Tool Works, Inc., Chicago, IL
Imperial Clevite Inc., Glenview, IL
Ingersoll-Rand Co., Woodcliff Lake, NJ
Inland Container Corp., Indianapolis, IN
Inland Div. of GMC, Dayton, OH
Inland Steel Co., Chicago, IL
Integrated Device Technology, Inc., Santa Clara, CA
Inteldex Inc., Corvallis, OR
Interlake Inc., Oak Brook, IL
International Harvester Co., Chicago, IL
International Jensen Inc., Schiller Park, IL
International Paper Co., NY, NY
Johnson Controls Inc./Control Products Div., Naperville, IL
Johnson Controls Inc./Systems and Service Div., Milwaukee, WI
E.F. Johnson Co., Waseca, MN
Johnson & Johnson, New Brunswick, NJ
Johnson & Johnson/Personal Products Co., Milltown, NJ
Kaiser Aluminum & Chemical Corp., Oakland, CA
Kayser-Roth Hosiery, Inc., Greensboro, NC
Kelthley Instruments Inc., Solon, OH
Kellogg Company, Battle Creek, MI
Kenner Products, Cincinnati, OH
Keystone Steel & Wire Products Co., Peoria, IL
Kinney Shoe Corp., NY, NY
Kohler Co., Kohler, WI
Kollmorgen Corp., Stamford, CT
Koppers Co., Inc., Pittsburgh, PA
Koret of North America, San Francisco, CA
Kroger Co., Cincinnati, OH
Kroy, Inc., Scottsdale, OH
Kustom Quality Electronics, Inc., Lenexa, KS
LNR Communications, Hauppage, NY
LTVAD-AM General Division, Tivonia, MI
Laclede Steel Co., Alton, IL
Ladish Co., Cudahy, WI
Lamb Technicon Corp., Warren, MI
Landis Tool Co., Waynesboro, PA
Lear Siegler Inc./Instrument Division, Grand Rapids, MI
Lecroy Research Systems Corp., Spring Valley, NY
Leeds & Nothrup, North Wales, PA
Libbey-Owens/Ford Co., Toledo, OH
The Lincoln Electric Co., Cleveland, OH
Lithium Corp. of America, Gastonia, NC
Lockheed Missiles and Space Co., Inc., Sunnyvale, CA
Longview Fibre Co., Longview, WA
Loral Electronic Systems, Yonkers, NY

Lord Corp., Erie, PA
Lukens Steel Co., Coatesville, PA
Lutron Electronics Co., Inc., Coosersburg, PA
M/A-Com Components Cos., Burlington, MA
MCC Center Line, Tulsa, OK
MPC Products Corp., Skokie, IL
Mack Trucks Inc./Engineering Div., Hagerstown, MD
Magnavox Electronic Systems Co., Fort Wayne, IN
Mallinckodt Critical Care, Glens Falls, NY
Manitowoo Co., Inc., Manitowoc, WI
Manville Corp., Denver, CO
Marathon Electric Manufacturing Corp., Wausau, WI
Martin Marietta Corp., Bethesda, MD
Masonite Corp., Chicago, IL
Maxon Corp., Muncie, IN
Maytag Co., Newton, IA
McDonnell Douglas Astronautics Co., Huntington Beach, CA
McDonnell Douglas Electronics, St. Charles, MO
McQuay Inc., Minneapolis, MN
The Mead Corporation, Dayton, OH
Mechanical Technology Inc., Latham, NY
Medtronic Inc., Minneapolis, MN
Micro Switch, Freeport, IL
Midland-Ross Corp., Cleveland, OH
Miller Brewing Co., Milwaukee, WI
Milliken & Co., Spartenburg, SC
Millipore Products Div., Bedford, MA
Minster Machine Co., Minster, OH
Mitsubishi Semiconductor America, Inc., Durham, NC
Mixing Equipment Co., Inc., Rochester, NY
Modine Manufacturing Co., Racine, WI
Molex Inc., Tisle, IL
Benjamin Moore & Co., Montvale, NJ
Moore Business Products Co., Springhouse, PA
Murata Erie North America, Inc., Marietta, GA
NCR Corp., Dayton, OH
NCR Corp./Engineering & Manufacturing, San Diego, CA
NCR/United States Data Processing Group, Norcross, GA
NEC America, Irving, TX
National Homes Corp., Lafayette, IN
Nekoosa Papers Inc., Port Edwards, WI
Niagara Machine & Tool Works, Buffalo, NY
Norchem, Inc., Omaha, NB
Nordam Systems, Norwalk, CT
North America Phillips Corp., NY, NY
Northern Electric Co., Laurel, MS

Northern Telecom Inc., Nashville, TN
Northern Telecom Inc./Cook Electric Div., Morton Grove, IL
Norton Co., Worcester, MA
Ohmeda, Madison, WI
Ohmite Manufacturing Co., Skokie, IL
Olin Corp., Stamford, CT
Omark Industries/Oregon Saw Chain Division, Milwaukie, OR
Omega Engineering, Inc., Stamford, CT
Optical Coating Laboratory Inc., Santa Rosa, CA
Ortho Pharmaceutical, Raritan, NJ
Outboard Marine Corp., Waukegan, IL
Owens-Corning Fiberglas Corp., Toledo, OH
Owens-Illinois Inc., Toledo, OH
Oxford Industries, Inc., Atlanta, GA
Paco Pumps/Div. of Baltimore Ancoil Co., Oakland, CA
PRC Systems Services/Aerospace Systems Div., Cocoa Beach, FL
Packard Electric, Warren, OH
Panduit Corp., Tinley Park, IL
Paradyne Corp., Largo, FL
Parker Hannifen Corp., Cleveland, OH
Parker Pen Co., Janesville, WI
Pepsi-Cola Company, Purchase, NY
Pet, Inc., St. Louis, MO
Philip Morris Companies, Inc., NY, NY
Philip Morris U.S.A., Richmond, VA
Piezo Technology, Inc., Orlando, FL
Pitney Bowes Inc., Stamford, CT
Plantronics Inc., San Jose, CA
Polaroid Corp., Cambridge, MA
Porta Systems Corp., Syosset, NY
Precision Castparts Corp., Portland, OR
Precision Components Corp., York, PA
Prestige, Inc., Neodeska, KS
Presto Products, Incorporated, Appleton, WI
Prestolite Battery, Toledo, OH
Procter & Gamble Co., Cincinnati, OH
Pure Industries, Inc., St. Mary's, PA
Quaker Oats Co., Chicago, IL
RTE Corp., Brookfield, WI
Ranco, Inc., Plain City, OH
Rapistan, Grand Rapids, MI
Raychem Corporation, Menlo Park, CA
Reed Tool Co., Houston, TX
Reliance Electric Co., Cleveland, OH
Rexnord Inc., Brookfield, WI
Reynolds Metals Co., Richmond, VA

Reynolds Metals Co./Listerhill Reduction Plant, Sheffield, AL
Richards Industries, Cincinnati, OH
Robbins & Myers, Inc., Springfield, OH
Roberts Corp., Lansing, MI
Rochester Instrument Systems, Inc., Rochester, NY
Rocket Research Co., Redmond, WA
Rockford Products Corp., Rockford, IL
Rohr Industries, Inc., Chula Vista, CA
Rolscreen Co., Pelia, LA
SCI Systems, Inc., Huntsville, AL
SCM Corp., NY, NY
SEEQ Technology, Inc., San Jose, CA
S.E.H. America, Inc., Vancouver, WA
SKF Industries, Inc., King of Prussia, PA
SPS Technologies, Inc., Jenkintown, PA
Saginaw Division, Saginaw, MI
Samsonite Corp., Denver, CO
Sangamo Weston, Inc., Atlanta, GA
Schindler Elevator Corp., Toledo, OH
Schneider Enterprises, Inc., Pittsburgh, PA
Scientific-Atlanta, Atlanta, GA
Scott Paper Co., Philadelphia, PA
Scovill Inc., Waterbury, CT
Sherwin-Williams Co., Cleveland, OH
Shley, Inc., Irvine, CA
Shure Brothers Inc., Evanston, IL
Siecor Corp., Hickory, NC
Siemens-Allis, Inc., Atlanta, GA
Signetics Corp., Sunnyvale, CA
Signode Corp., Glenview, IL
Silicon Systems, Inc., Tustin, CA
Siliconix Inc., Santa Clara, CA
Simplex Time Recorder Co., Gardner, MA
SmithKline-Beckman Corp., Philadelphia, PA
Snap-On Tools Corp., Kenosha, WI
Snyder's of Hanover, Inc., Hanover, PA
Solar Turbines Inc., San Diego, CA
Sonoco Products Co., Hartsville, SC
Spartanburg Steel Products Inc., Spartanburg, SC
Spectra-Physics Inc., San Jose, CA
Sperry Defense Products Group/Computer Systems Div., St. Paul, MN
Sperry New Holland, New Holland, PA
The Stackpole Corporation, St. Mary's, PA
A.E. Staley Manufacturing Co., Decatur, IL
Steelcase, Inc., Grand Rapids, MI
Sterling Drug Inc., NY, NY

J. P. Stevens & Co., Inc., Greenville, SC
Stewart-Warner Corp., Chicago, IL
Stride-Rite Corp., Cambridge, MA
Stromber-Carlson (A Plessey Telecommunications Co.), Lake Mary, FL
Structureal Metals, Inc., Seguin, TX
Sumitomo Electric Research, Research Triangle Park, NC
Sundstrand Corp., Rockford, IL
Superior Electric Co., Bristol, CT
Swedlow Inc., Garden Grove, CA
TRW Aircraft Components Corp., Euclid, OH
Tamko Asphalt Products, Joplin, MO
Taylor Instrument, Rochester, NY
Tektronix, Inc., Beaverton, OR
Teledyne Continental Motors/General Products Div., Muskegon, MI
Teledyne Geotech, Garland, TX
Teledyne Microwave, Mountain View, CA
Teledyne Wah Chang Albany, Albany, OR
Telesciences, Inc., Mt. Laurel, NJ
Teltone Corp., Kirkland, WA
Temescal Semiconductor Products, Berkeley, CA
Temple-Eastex Inc., Diboll, TX
Temple-Eastex Inc./Pulp and Paperboard Div., Silshee, TX
Tenneco Inc., Houston, TX
Teradyne Inc., Boston, MA
Texas Instruments Inc., Dallas, TX
Thilmany Pulp & Paper Co., Kaukauna, WI
3M, St. Paul, MN
Timeplex Inc., Woodcliff Lake, NJ
The Timken Co., Canton, OH
Trane Co., La Crosse, WI
Uarco Inc., Barrington, IL
UNC Resources/Naval Products Division, Uncasville, CT
USG Corporation, Chicago, IL
UTC/Carrier, Syracuse, NY
Ultratech Strepper, Santa Clara, CA
Union Carbide Corp./Battery Products Div., Rocky River, OH
Union Switch & Signal Division, American STD Inc., Pittsburgh, PA
Uniroyal Inc., Middlebury, CT
United McGill Corp., Inc., Groveport, OH
USX, Pittsburgh, PA
United Technologies Corp., Hartford, CT
Universal Instruments Corp., Binghamton, NY
The Upjohn Co., Kalamazoo, MI
Vallen Corp., Houston, TX
Valspar Corp., Minneapolis, MN
Vanier Graphics Corp., Santee, CA

Vapor Corp., Niles, IL
Varian Associates, Palo Alto, CA
Varian/Extrion, Gloucester, MA
Vetco/Gray, Ventura, CA
Vickers, Inc., Troy, MI
Viking Pump, Cedars Falls, IA
Volkswagen of America, Troy, MI
Vought Aeroproducts Div., Dallas, TX
Wabash Inc., Wabash, IN
Walker Manufacturing Co., Racine, WI
Wallace Computer Services, Inc., Hillside, IL
Jim Walter Corp., Tampa, FL
Warren Petroleum Co., Tulsa, OK
Wavetek Scientific Inc., Rockleigh, NJ
Jervis B. Webb Co., Farmington Hills, MI
Welch Allyn, Inc., Skaneateles Falls, NY
Westpoint Pepperell, Inc., Westpoint, GA
Westinghouse Air Brake Div./American Standard, Inc., Welmerding,
    PA
Westinghouse Electric Corp., Pittsburgh, PA
Weston Instruments, Newark, NJ
Westvaco Corp., NY, NY
Whirlpool Corp., Benton Harbor, MI
Willamette Industries, Inc., Portland, OR
Wolverine Worldwide Inc., Grand Rapids, MI
Woodward Governor Co., Fort Collins, CO
Wright Line Inc., Worcester, MA
Wm. Wrigley Jr. Co., Chicago, IL
Xerox Corp., Rochester, NY
Xerox Printing Systems Dev., El Segundo, CA
Zenith Electronic Corp., Glenview, IL
Zimmer, Inc., Warsaw, IN

Media

Atlanta Journal-Constitution Newspapers, Atlanta, GA
CBS Inc., NY, NY
Walt Disney Productions, Burbank, CA
Disneyland, Anaheim, CA
R. R. Donnelly & Sons, Co., Chicago, IL
Donrey Media Group, Fort Smith, AK
Doubleday, NY, NY
Dun & Bradstreet, Murray Hill, NJ
Encyclopedia Britannica USA, Chicago, IL
Gannett & Co., Inc., Arlington, VA
Knapp Communications Corp., Los Angeles, CA

McGraw-Hill Inc., NY, NY
National Broadcasting Co., NY, NY
Penton-IPC, Cleveland, OH
Taylor Publishing Co., Dallas, TX
Time, Inc., NY, NY
The United Methodist Publishing House, Nashville, TN
Video Applications, Inc., NY, NY
Western Publishing Co., Inc., Racine, WI

Nonprofit

Anser (Analytic Services, Inc.), Arlington, VA
Aerospace Corp., Los Angeles, CA
B'Nai Brith Youth Organization, Washington, D.C.
Boy Scouts of America, Irving, TX
Boys Clubs of America, NY, NY
Coro Foundation, San Francisco, CA
Institute of Gas Technology, Chicago, IL
International Voluntary Services, Inc., Washington, D.C.
Midwest Research Institute, Kansas City, MO
National Board of the YWCA of the USA, NY, NY
Rand Corp., Santa Monica, CA
Research Triangle Institute, Research Triangle Park, NC
Southwest Research Institute, San Antonio, TX
Worcester Foundation for Experimental Biology, Shrewsbury, MA
YMCA of the USA, Chicago, IL

Retailing

Abraham & Straus, Brooklyn, NY
B. Altman & Co., NY, NY
Ames Department Stores, Inc., Rocky Hill, CT
L. S. Ayres & Co., Indianapolis, IN
Batus Retail Group, NY, NY
Belk Stores Services, Charlotte, NC
P. A. Bergner & Co., Milwaukee, WI
Bloomingdale's, NY, NY
Bradlees, Braintree, MA
The Broadway/Southern California, Los Angeles, CA
Broadway/Southwest, Mesa, AZ
Brown Group, Inc., St. Louis, MO
Buffums, Long Beach, CA
Bullock's Department Stores, Los Angeles, CA
Bulluck's Fashion Island, San Mateo, CA
Burdines Department Stores, Miami, FL

Cain Sloan Co., Nashville, TN
Carson Pirie Scott & Co., Chicago, IL
Carter Hawley Hale Stores, Inc., Los Angeles, CA
Channel Home Centers, Whippany, NJ
Chess King, NY, NY
Children's Place, Pine Brook, NJ
County Seat Stores Inc., Minneapolis, MN
Dayton-Hudson Corp., Minneapolis, MN
Dayton-Hudson Department Store Co., Minneapolis, MN
The Denver, Denver, CO
Edison Brothers Shoe Stores, Inc., St. Louis, MO
Emporium-Capwell, San Francisco, CA
Famous-Barr, St. Louis, MO
Filene's, Boston, MA
Filene's Basement Corp., Wellesley, MA
Fisher's Big Wheel Inc., New Castle, PA
Foley's Department Stores, Houston, TX
G. Fox & Co., Hartford, CT
Frederick & Nelson, Seattle, WA
C. J. Gayfer & Co., Mobile, AL
Genesco Inc., Nashville, TN
Goldsmith's Department Store, Memphis, TN
Goldwaters Department Store, Scottsdale, AZ
Goudchaux/Maison Blanche Inc., Baton Rouge, LA
Hahne's, Newark, NJ
Hartmarx Corp., Chicago, IL
Hecht's Department Stores, Washington, D.C.
Hess's Department Stores, Inc., Allentown, PA
Higbee Co., Cleveland, OH
Hills Department Stores, Canton, MA
D.H. Holmes Co., LTD, New Orleans, LA
Jordan Marsh/Florida, Miami, FL
Jordan Marsh/New England, Boston, MA
K mart Corp., Troy, MI
K mart Apparel Corp., North Bergen, NJ
Kaufmann's Department Store, Pittsburgh, PA
KayBee Toy & Hobby Shops, Inc., Lee, MA
Kayser-Roth Hosiery, Inc., Greensboro, NC
Kinney Shoe Corp., NY, NY
Kobacker Co., Columbus, OH
Lady Foot Locker, NY, NY
Lazarus Department Stores, Columbus, OH
Lechmere, Inc., Woburn, MA
The Limited, Inc., Columbus, OH
Linens 'n Things, Inc., Clifton, NJ
Lord & Taylor, NY, NY

Maas Brothers, Tampa, FL
Macy's, NY, NY
I. Magnin, San Francisco, CA
Maloney Enterprises, Mt. Sterling, KY
Marshall Field's, Chicago, IL
May/Cohen's, Jacksonville, FL
May Co./California, North Hollywood, CA
May Co./Cleveland, Cleveland, OH
May D&F, Denver, CO
May Department Stores Company, St. Louis, MO
McAlpin Co., Cincinnati, OH
Meier & Frank, Portland, OR
Mercantile Stores Co., Inc., NY, NY
Miller & Rhoads, Richmond, VA
Millers Outpost, Ontario, CA
Neiman-Marcus, Dallas, TX
O'Neils, Akron, OH
Parisian, Inc., Birmingham, AL
Peebles Department Stores, South Hill, VA
J. C. Penney Company Inc., NY, NY
Pomeroy's/Levittown, Levittown, PA
Prange's, Green Bay, WI
Read's Inc., Trumbull, CT
Rich's, Atlanta, GA
Richway Stores, Atlanta, GA
Robinson's of Florida, St. Petersburg, FL
J. B. Robinson Jewelers, Cleveland, OH
J. W. Robinson, Los Angeles, CA
Roses Stores Inc., Henderson, NC
S & K Famous Brands, Inc., Richmond, VA
Sage-Allen & Co., Inc., Hartford, CT
Saks Fifth Avenue, NY, NY
Sanger Harris, Dallas, TX
Service Merchandise, Nashville, TN
Sheplers Inc., Wichita, KS
Shillito-Rikes, Cincinnati, OH
Shopko, Green Bay, WI
Sterns, Paramus, NJ
Stewart Dry Goods Co., Louisville, KY
Strawbridge & Clothier, Philadelphia, PA
Strouss, Youngstown, OH
Thalhimers, Richmond, VA
Venture Stores, Inc., O'Fallon, MO
Volume Shoe Corp., Topeka, KS
Wal-Mart Stores, Inc., Bentonville, AR

John Wanamaker, Philadelphia, PA
Weinstocks, Sacramento, CA

Utilities

AT&T Communications, White Plains, NY
Alabama Power Co., Birmingham, AL
Allegheny Power System/West Penn Power, Greensburg, PA
American Electric Power System, Columbus, OH
Appalachian Power Co., Roanoke, VA
Arizona Electric Power, Benson, AZ
Arizona Public Service Co., Phoenix, AZ
Arkansas Power & Light Co., Little Rock, AK
Atlanta Gas Light Co., Atlanta, GA
Baltimore Gas & Electric Co., Baltimore, MD
Bell Atlantic Network Services Company, Washington, D.C.
Bell of Pennsylvania, Philadelphia, PA
Bellsouth Corp., Atlanta, GA
Brooklyn Union Gas Co., Brooklyn, NY
Carolina Power & Light Co., Raleigh, NC
Carolina Telephone & Telegraph Co., Tarboro, NC
Central Illinois Public Service Co., Springfield, IL
Central Maine Power Co., Augusta, ME
Central Power & Light Co., Corpus Christi, TX
Chesapeake & Potomac Telephone Co., Washington, D.C.
Cincinnati Bell Inc., Cincinnati, OH
Cleveland Electric Illuminating Co., Cleveland, OH
Commonwealth Edison Co., Chicago, IL
Consolidated Edison Co., NY, NY
Consolidated Gas Transmission Corp./Hope Gas Inc., Clarksburg, VA
Consolidated Rail Corp., Philadelphia, PA
Consumers Power Co., Jackson, MI
Delmarva Power & Light Co., Wilmington, DE
Detroit Edison Co., Detroit, MI
Duke Power Co., Charlotte, NC
Duquesne Light Co., Pittsburgh, PA
EUA Service Corp., Brockton, MA
East Ohio Gas Co., Cleveland, OH
El Paso Natural Gas, El Paso, TX
Electric Power Board of Chattanooga, Chattanooga, TN
The Empire District Electric Co., Joplin, MO
Florida Power Corp., St. Petersburg, FL
Florida Power & Light Co., Miami, FL
GTE/Florida, Tampa, FL
GTE/Illinois, Bloomington, IL
GTE/Indiana, Fort Wayne, IN

GTE/Kentucky, Lexington, KY
GTE/Midwest, Grinnell, IA
GTE/Northwest, Everett, WA
GTE/Ohio, Marion, OH
GTE/Pennsylvania, Erie, PA
GTE/Southeast, Durham, NC
GTE/Southwest, San Angelo, TX
GTE/Hawaiian Telephone Co., Honolulu, HI
GTE Midwestern Telephone Operations, Westfield, IN
GTE Spacenet Corp., McLean, VA
GTE/Sprint Communications Corp., Burlingame, CA
Georgia Power Co., Atlanta, GA
Gulf States Utilities Co., Beaumont, TX
Houston Lighting & Power Co., Houston, TX
Illinois Bell Telephone Co., Decautur, IL
Indiana Bell Telephone, Indianapolis, IN
Indiana & Michigan Electric Co., Fort Wayne, IN
Indianapolis Power & Light Co., Indianapolis, IN
Interstate Power Co., Dubuque, IA
Iowa Gas Co., Des Moines, IA
Iowa-Illinois Gas & Electric Co., Davenport, IA
Iowa Power & Light Co., Des Moines, IA
Jersey Central Power & Light Co., Morristown, NJ
KN Energy, Lakewood, CO
KPL Gas Service Co., Topeka, KS
Kansas City Power & Light Co., Kansas City, MO
Kansas Gas & Electric Co., Wichita, KS
Kentucky Power Co., Ashland, KY
Kentucky Utilities Co., Lexington, KY
Laclede Gas Co., St. Louis, MO
Lincoln Electric System, Lincoln, NB
Long Island Lighting Co., Hicksville, NY
Lower Colorado River Authority, Austin, TX
Metropolitan Edison Co., Reading, PA
Michigan Bell Telephone Co., Detroit, MI
Minnesota Power, Duluth, MN
Mississippi Power Company, Gulfport, MS
Montana Power Co., Butte, MT
Mt. Fuel Supply, Salt Lake City, UT
Nebraska Public Power District, Columbus, NB
Nevada Power Co., Las Vegas, NV
New England Electric, Westboro, MA
New England Telephone, Boston, MA
New Jersey Bell, Newark, NJ
New Orleans Public Service, New Orleans, LA
New York Power Authority, NY, NY

New York Telephone, NY, NY
Niagara Mohawk Power Corp., Syracuse, NY
Northeast Utilities, Hartford, CT
Northern Illinois Gas Co., Aurora, IL
Northern Indiana Public Service Co., Hammond, IN
Northern States Power Co., Minneapolis, MN
North-West Telephone Co., Tomah, WI
Northwestern Bell, Omaha, NB
Ohio Bell, Cleveland, OH
Ohio Edison Co., Akron, OH
Ohio Power Co., Canton, OH
Orange & Rockland Utilities, Pearl River, NY
Pacific Bell, San Francisco, CA
Pacific Gas & Electric Co., San Francisco, CA
Pacific Northwest Bell, Seattle, WA
Pacific Power & Light Co., Allentown, PA
People's Gas Light & Coke Co., Chicago, IL
Peoples Natural Gas Co., Pittsburgh, PA
Philadelphia Electric Co., Philadelphia, PA
Philadelphia Gas Works, Philadelphia, PA
Portland General Electric Co., Portland, OR
Potomac Electric Power Co., Washington, D.C.
Public Service Co. of Colorado, Denver, CO
Public Service Co. of Oklahoma, Tulsa, OK
Public Service Electric & Gas Co., Newark, NJ
Public Service Indiana, Plainfield, IN
Public Service of New Hampshire, Manchester, NH
Puget Sound Power & Light Co., Bellevue, WA
St. Joseph Light & Power Co., St. Joesph, MO
St. Louis County Water Co., St. Louis, MO
Salt River Project, Phoenix, AZ
San Antonio City Public Service Board, San Antonio, TX
San Diego Gas & Electric Co., San Diego, CA
Savannah Electric & Power Co., Savannah, GA
South Central Bell, Birmingham, AL
Southern Bell Telephone & Telegraph Co., Atlanta, GA
Southern California Edison, Rosemead, CA
Southern California Gas Co., Los Angeles, CA
Southern Natural Gas Co., Birmingham, AL
Southern New England Telephone Co., New Haven, CT
Southwestern Bell Telephone Co., St. Louis, MO
Southwestern Public Service Co., Amarillo, TX
Tennessee Valley Authority, Knoxville, TN
Texas Utilities Company System, Dallas, TX
Toledo Edison Co., Toledo, OH
Tucson Electric Power Co., Tucson, AZ

UNC Nuclear Industries, Richland, WA
Union Electric Co., St. Louis, MO
Union Pacific System, Omaha, NB
United Illuminating Co., New Haven, CT
United Inter-Mountain Telephone Co., Bristol, TN
United Telephone Co. of Ohio, Mansfield, OH
Valero Energy Corp., San Antonio, TX
Washington Gas Light Co., Washington, D.C.
Wisconsin Electric Power, Milwaukee, WI
Wisconsin Gas Co., Milwaukee, WI
Wisconsin Power & Light Co., Madison, WI
Wisconsin Public Service Corp., Green Bay, WI
Wisconsin Telephone, Milwaukee, WI

Praise for *Newsroom Confidential*

"An opinionated but fair and accessible tour of the big debates roiling the 'reality-based press,' as she calls mainstream newsrooms . . . [Sullivan is] a veteran practitioner with street cred, still in touch with the 'unaccountable joy' of reporting and writing that continues to draw talented young people to the field."

—Steve Coll, *The New York Times Book Review*

"If Sullivan started out intending to write a memoir, she ended up with a manifesto. This is a book about the role of the press in a democracy that's in grave jeopardy."

—Kathy Kiely, *The Washington Post*

"Dogged, thoughtful, and unafraid." —*The New Republic*

"A beguiling memoir." —Charles Kaiser, *The Guardian*

"*Newsroom Confidential* might have been just another journalist's rehash of stories—literally old news—except that the story in front of Sullivan was the struggle of the U.S. press to save itself and, maybe along with it, American democracy."

—Karl Vick, *Time*

"The great newswoman takes a clear-eyed look at her own storied career and the troubled state of her much-loved profession." —*People*

"Margaret Sullivan's perspective on our increasingly cacophonous media ecosystem is invaluable. By detailing her personal and professional experiences in this wise and engaging memoir, she pulls the curtain back to reveal how journalism really works and the very human decisions behind it."

—Katie Couric

"Her voice is engaging, her frankness refreshing, and her call to action well worth heeding."

—Leonard Downie Jr., former executive editor of *The Washington Post*

"Diversity, male arrogance, journalistic thin skins, colorful newsroom characters—they're all here, along with a strong underlying warning about looming threats to democracy. This book is a remarkable achievement."

—Neil Barsky, founder of Pulitzer Prize–winning The Marshall Project

"Margaret Sullivan is a national treasure. You'll want to read this essential memoir."   —Rem Rieder, former *USA Today* editor at large and media columnist

"No public editor of *The New York Times* commanded more must-read attention or respect than Margaret Sullivan. No *Washington Post* media critic has proved more consistently astute in her examination of an industry in turmoil. Sullivan turns that same unflinching eye on herself as she shares the no-holds-barred details of her journey from schoolgirl intern to editor in chief of the same paper, and from there to further distinction on two coveted national platforms."

—Brooke Kroeger, author of *Nellie Bly: Daredevil, Reporter, Feminist* and *Undercover Reporting: The Truth About Deception*

NEWSROOM CONFIDENTIAL

Lessons (and Worries) from an Ink-Stained Life

—————————◆—————————

MARGARET SULLIVAN

ST. MARTIN'S GRIFFIN
NEW YORK

Published in the United States by St. Martin's Griffin,
an imprint of St. Martin's Publishing Group

www.stmartins.com

Designed by Steven Seighman

The Library of Congress has cataloged the hardcover edition as follows:

Names: Sullivan, Margaret, 1957– author.
Title: Newsroom confidential : lessons (and worries) from an
   ink-stained life / Margaret Sullivan.
Description: First edition. | New York : St. Martin's Press, 2022. |
Identifiers: LCCN 2022020121 | ISBN 9781250281906 (hardcover) |
   ISBN 9781250281913 (ebook)
Subjects: LCSH: Sullivan, Margaret, 1957– | New York times—
   History. | Washington post—History. | Women journalists—
   United States—Biography. | Journalism—United States—
   History.
Classification: LCC PN4874.S779 A3 2022 | DDC 070.92 [B]—
   dc23/eng/20220705
LC record available at https://lccn.loc.gov/2022020121

ISBN 978-1-250-90600-7 (trade paperback)

Our books may be purchased in bulk for promotional, educational, or business use. Please contact your local bookseller or the Macmillan Corporate
and Premium Sales Department at 1-800-221-7945, extension 5442, or by
email at MacmillanSpecialMarkets@macmillan.com.

First St. Martin's Griffin Edition: 2023

10 9 8 7 6 5 4 3 2 1

In memory of my parents, Jack and Elaine Sullivan,
with love and gratitude

Contents

AUTHOR'S NOTE   ix
PROLOGUE   1

1. The Long Arm of Watergate   7
2. Little Miss Lifestyles Breaks Out   23
3. Pulling Up Roots   44
4. "Welcome to the Fishbowl"   56
5. But Her Emails . . .   76
6. Jill Abramson and Dean Baquet   98
7. Small Victories   118
8. Moving On   132
9. The Joys of Style   143
10. "Venomous Serpent"   159
11. "Fake News," You Say?   176
12. Objectivity Wars and the "Woke" Newsroom   196
13. How to Clean Up the Mess We're In   226
14. About Those Lessons   245
15. Sweeney (and Other Legends), Reconsidered   253

ACKNOWLEDGMENTS   271

Author's Note

Sections of this book describe my experiences at *The New York Times* and *The Washington Post,* where I was writing blog posts and columns at a rapid clip, sometimes as often as three or four times a week. I draw on those published pieces here, sometimes by directly quoting from them and sometimes by summarizing or paraphrasing. I also rely on the scores of journals I have kept for more than five decades—starting at age ten, when my father handed me a blank 1968 datebook that I decided to use as a diary.

NEWSROOM CONFIDENTIAL

Prologue

On January 6, 2021, the Covid pandemic was still raging, and amid the lockdown, it had been months since I had set foot in the *Washington Post* newsroom or covered a story in person. That once bustling D.C. newsroom was largely shuttered, along with the smaller New York City office where I often worked, and most of us—reporters, editors, and columnists—were working from home. Like almost everyone else, I watched Donald Trump's "Stop the Steal" rally, and the horrifying riot at the Capitol that followed, on TV. What started out looking like just another raucous rally turned downright frightening as a violent mob stormed the barricades. Even though I was safe at home, I could easily imagine myself there because both the Ellipse, near the White House, and the Capitol were less than a mile from where I had lived as Trump's presidency began. And I know what I saw: one of the most appalling moments in all of American history. Unlike the attacks on 9/11, decades earlier, this was an attack from within—incited by a defeated president who demanded that his vice president, Mike Pence, do what should have been unthinkable in the world's greatest democracy: reverse the results of a legitimate presidential election and give the loser an unearned second term.

The news coverage, of course, was wall-to-wall, even on Trump's favorite and most dependably supportive outlets, Fox News and One America News. You couldn't live in America and fail to understand what was happening. But it didn't take long for denialism to take hold. On that very day, at the pro-Trump network One America News, a supervisor reportedly ordered his staff to ignore the obvious: "Please DO NOT say 'Trump Supporters Storm Capitol.' . . . DO NOT CALL IT A RIOT!!!" By the spring, a Republican congressman would describe the violent attack as something that looked like a "normal tourist visit." By October, even the former vice president was trying to sow doubt. The rioters may have been chanting "Hang Mike Pence!" and they may have erected a symbolic gallows, but when Sean Hannity interviewed Pence on Fox News, the vice president downplayed the insurrection as merely "one day in January." He accused the mainstream media of giving it too much attention and of trying to demean Trump supporters.

This revisionism is working. As I write this, many months later, public opinion polls continue to reflect the nation's ugly divide and the refusal of many Americans to accept reality. Most Republicans believe—or *say* they believe—that the election was stolen from Trump. They believe this despite the lack of evidence and against the outcome of every court challenge and every politicized "audit" of votes in states like Pennsylvania and Arizona. They believe it, in large part, because of the constant drumbeat from right-wing media: on Fox, on podcasts, on radio shows, all amplified enormously on social media, especially on Facebook.

The traditional media—what I call the reality-based press—was at fault, too, in creating this democracy-threatening mess. In a less obvious way, they worsened the harm. They did so by treating the denialists as legitimate news sources whose views, for the sake of objectivity and fairness, must be respectfully listened to and reflected in news stories. By inviting the members of Congress's "insurrection caucus" on the Sunday broadcast-TV talk shows week after week. By framing the consequential decisions being made in Congress, including Trump's second impeachment, as just another lap in the horse race of politics. Examples abounded. When House Speaker Nancy Pelosi, quite reasonably, refused to give seats on an investigative committee to two congressmen who had backed Trump's efforts to invalidate the election, many journalists framed it as a partisan feud, not as an effort to protect the integrity of the committee. Politico even called Pelosi's necessary decision a "gift" to Kevin McCarthy, the Republican minority leader of the House of Representatives, again depicting the investigation as little but a political game, complete with winners and losers.

The extreme right wing had its staunch, all-in media allies; the rest of the country had a mainstream press that too often couldn't, or wouldn't, do their jobs. Too many journalists couldn't seem to grasp their crucial role in American democracy. Almost pathologically, they normalized the abnormal and sensationalized the mundane.

These days, we can clearly see the fallout from decades of declining public trust, the result, at least partly, of so many years of the press being undermined and of undermining itself. What is that fallout? Americans no longer share a common basis of reality. That's dangerous because American democracy, government by the people, simply can't function this way. It's high time to ask how public trust in the press steadily plummeted from the years following the Watergate scandal and the publication of the Pentagon Papers in the 1970s—when seven of ten Americans trusted the news—to today's rock-bottom lows.

For me, this story of lost trust is personal. I was drawn into journalism as a teenager, partly by the intrepid and history-changing Watergate reporting at *The Washington Post*. Soon after, I became the editor of my high school's student newspaper. After part-time clerking jobs and reporting for college newspapers, my career began for real. Over more than four decades, I've worked at news outlets as tiny as the *Niagara Gazette,* with its handful of reporters covering a small Western New York city, and as large as *The New York Times,* with nearly two thousand journalists posted all over the world.

As a young reporter, I nearly choked on the smoke and fumes as I covered a propane explosion in downtown Buffalo that took the lives of five firefighters and two civilians. Years later, as the newly minted chief editor of my hometown *Buffalo News,* I raced up to a standing microphone in a packed Washington, D.C., hotel ballroom and asked President Clinton a question that infuriated him; his answer made front-page news all over the country.

On September 11, 2001, I approved the 120-point headline on an emergency "extra" edition of the *News* that hit Buffalo's streets just hours after the terrorist attack in our state. As the public editor of *The New York Times,* I watched from a balcony overlooking the vast newsroom as publisher Arthur Sulzberger stunned the gathered staff by announcing that he had summarily replaced the paper's first woman editor, Jill Abramson, with its first Black editor, Dean Baquet.

I thought I had seen a lot in my career, but I wasn't prepared for the ugliness that came next. As a just-hired columnist for *The Washington Post,* I stood inside the Cleveland arena where Donald Trump was about to become the Republican nominee for president and heard the raucous crowd shouting out vitriol against Hillary Clinton—"Lock her up! Lock her up!" Two years later, I was taking notes in a packed Senate chamber as Facebook founder Mark Zuckerberg testified before Congress for the first time, with empty apologies for his company's endless misdeeds, including the ones that spread lies and helped Trump get elected. His presidency would have as a central theme the disparagement of the reality-based press, and a bizarre symbiosis with the right-wing media. For many Americans, that constant drumbeat would erode still further their already diminished trust in journalism and would heighten their antipathy toward reporters.

Journalism has been my profession, my obsession, and—maybe more than has been strictly wise—my life's focus. I believe in the power, the absolute necessity, of good reporting. I've admired it at its best, as journalism uncovers wrongdoing and illuminates the best and the worst of our society. Journalism matters—immensely—when it sends serial molesters, like the former USA Gymnastics doctor Larry Nassar, to jail; when it uncovers the criminal insider trading of a local congressman; when it points out abuses at a U.S. Army hospital; when it shows how poor pilot training can crash airplanes; when it proves how Facebook maximizes profit over truth. Journalism matters, too, when it spotlights great music, theater, and art or shows us inspiring examples of human courage. We need journalism—and we need it to be at its best, to be believed, and to *deserve* to be believed.

Much as I love and value my craft, I'm worried. I am sickened at the damage done by the hyperpartisan media and distressed about the failures of the reality-based press. We're in deep trouble. How did we Americans become trapped in this thicket of lies, mistrust, and division? Can we slash our way out? I believe we can, and must, but first let's see how we got here. My journey is personal, of course, *and* it tells the larger tale. Won't you come along? It starts in a steel town along the shore of Lake Erie, just south of Buffalo.

1

The Long Arm of Watergate

At twilight, the sky over Lackawanna would glow electric coral, but we kids were savvy enough to know that this spectacle was no gorgeous sunset over Lake Erie. It meant, to use the neighborhood slang, that "they dumped the slag at the plant." The plant was Bethlehem Steel, the hulking factory covering more than thirteen hundred acres along the shoreline just south of Buffalo; the slag was the molten industrial waste that was poured nightly out of huge vats onto the shoreline or right into the lake. We took this environmental travesty for granted as another daily ritual—like fetching the morning newspaper, the *Buffalo Courier-Express*, from the side door, and, some eight hours later, doing the same with *The Buffalo Evening News*.

Just as we believed in steelmaking as a community good—union wages, after all, for more than twenty thousand workers who didn't need a second income to support a family—we believed what appeared on those front pages. All the explosive issues of the day came to us that way: the Vietnam War, second-wave feminism, civil rights protests, the assassinations of John and Robert Kennedy and Dr. Martin Luther

King, Jr., and the deadly National Guard shootings of student protesters at Kent State University. My whole family read the papers, and like many of our neighbors, we watched the nightly CBS newscast anchored by "the most trusted man in America," Walter Cronkite, whose pessimistic appraisal of the Vietnam War in 1968 dealt a death blow to the American government's decades-long involvement. ("It seems now more certain than ever that the bloody experience of Vietnam is to end in a stalemate," he told his millions of viewers after the surprise attacks known as the Tet Offensive rocked South Vietnam, and following his own reporting trip there.)

My parents subscribed to both dailies, each owned by a prosperous Buffalo family. One carried Ann Landers's advice column; the other published her sister, known as Dear Abby. One supported Richard Nixon until nearly the end of his ill-fated and corrupt presidency. The other wanted him gone much sooner. The news all seemed personal, close to home. In these pre-internet days, it didn't come to us immediately via iPhones in our pockets, but it reached us, and touched us, nonetheless.

When I was in first grade, I was sitting at my desk at Our Lady of Victory Elementary School when our teacher, Sister Romana, a diminutive nun of the Sisters of St. Joseph order, was called out of our classroom. She returned to tell us that President Kennedy had been shot to death in Texas and she was sending us home for the day. Our school sat next to the parish's grand European-style basilica, which dominated the Lackawanna skyline; here, the assassination of the first Roman Catholic president hit especially hard. My family members, like most of our Lackawanna neighbors, were observant Catholics; my father, a defense attorney, walked the short block to Mass at the basilica and received Communion every morning before heading to his firm's office in downtown Buffalo. Like my parents, most people in our blue-collar community were Democrats, with plenty of them members of the steelworkers union, though both of my mother's brothers, a doctor and a lawyer, were Republicans. At home, we talked and argued about all that was happening, with my father as the acknowledged expert on most subjects—everything from the seemingly endless Vietnam War to classic literature— but with opinions flowing freely from all five of us. I was the youngest, and always felt that I had less to contribute, but I was absorbing it all. I was reading the daily newspapers, too, or at least taking in the headlines.

Then came the Watergate scandal. Like most Americans and many Lackawanna residents, my family was glued to our one television set, a focal point of the living room, as we watched the Senate Watergate hearings, broadcast initially on every network, live and during the daytime hours. Later, the networks rotated coverage and public television replayed the hearings in the evening. You could hardly miss what was happening: 85 percent of households in the United States watched some part of the hearings. This high political drama played out for months as charges of corruption, even criminality, were leveled at Richard Nixon's administration, kicked off by a break-in at Democratic National Committee headquarters at the Watergate Complex in Washington, D.C. As the investigation unfolded, the players—Washington politicians—became as compelling and familiar to us as the characters of *The Sopranos*, or later still, *Mare of Easttown*, would be to generations several decades on. There was the folksy Sam Ervin, the conservative Democrat from North Carolina and chairman of the Senate Watergate Committee. There was the senator from Tennessee, Howard Baker, who, although a staunch Republican, put aside partisanship and embraced patriotism when he memorably asked, "What did the president know and when did he know it?" There was former White House counsel John Dean, the young preppie in his tortoiseshell glasses, who ultimately, and devastatingly, would characterize the scandal and its lie-filled cover-up as "a cancer on the presidency."

When the House of Representatives Judiciary Committee held its hearings, we were riveted by Barbara Jordan's soaring opening remarks about the Constitution, about being a Black woman in America, and about her obligation to her fellow citizens. It was a real-time lesson in civil rights, racial injustice, and governmental checks and balances. Her authoritative voice commanded attention as she talked movingly about her racial identity, and her mere presence as a Black woman was a stark contrast to the hearings' parade of white men. "I felt somehow for many years that George Washington and Alexander Hamilton just left me out by mistake," Jordan said. "But through the process of amendment, interpretation and court decision I have finally been included in 'We, the people.'" We could hear her conviction when she added: "My faith in the Constitution is whole, it is complete, it is total, and I am not going to sit here and be an idle spectator to the diminution, the subversion, the destruction of the Constitution." In 1974, a Black woman member of Congress was unusual enough, but Jordan was even more noteworthy because of this Judiciary Committee role that catapulted her onto the national stage. A lawyer in her late thirties, she was a first-term congresswoman who had grown up in segregated Texas and become the first woman and the first African American elected to Congress from her state.

My mother, in particular, seemed captivated by her eloquent passion. This admiration affected me. Barbara Jordan was my homemaker mother's idea of a powerful and accomplished woman of integrity, someone worthy of emulating. At a subconscious level, I took note. I had heard confusingly mixed messages as I was growing up about what a woman should be and do: Get married as soon as possible and have children? Have a successful career, but quit it, as my mother had done when she married? Do some kind of work in the public interest? But now, through the Watergate scandal, of all things, I absorbed an unspoken, but also unmuddied, message: Be like Barbara Jordan. Be brave, be authentic, make a difference, and have the courage of your convictions.

I was far from alone in my youthful reaction to the hearings. Timothy O'Brien, who would become an investigative business reporter for *The New York Times*, was twelve years old, attending a science camp in Illinois, where a camp staffer encouraged the youngsters to watch the Senate hearings. The drama and the characters affected Tim, just as they did me. "I remember Sam Ervin saying [of Nixon], when he thought his mic was off, 'He's just a goddamn liar,'" O'Brien recalled many years later when I interviewed him for a piece in *Columbia Journalism Review.* "Those televised hearings gave me one of my first civics lessons about checks and balances and holding power accountable."

O'Brien and I, and countless other Watergate-era kids, were drawn into our careers—and not just in journalism—by this high-stakes spectacle on Capitol Hill. Sherrilyn Ifill, the prominent civil rights lawyer, recalled that seeing Barbara Jordan's Watergate appearance on TV changed her life, too: "A woman, a Black woman, with a voice of absolute moral authority . . . very, very powerful for me in thinking about who I could be as a woman." Ifill became the president of the NAACP Legal Defense and Educational Fund, founded by Thurgood Marshall, the first Black justice of the U.S. Supreme Court. In 2021, she told *Your Hometown* podcaster Kevin Burke that Barbara Jordan's televised prominence was part of "how gender roles . . . began to open up, particularly in the early seventies."

As a teenager, I was living through a period of huge societal change brought about by the civil rights movement, second-wave feminism, and the counterculture revolution. Journalism may not have been as high-profile as civil rights activism as a way to create reform, but as Watergate made abundantly clear, it certainly could be an effective way of holding power accountable.

After all, the dogged investigative reporting of two *Washington Post* staffers, Bob Woodward and Carl Bernstein, lit the kindling that led to Nixon's eventual resignation, as they revealed the White House cover-up of the break-in and all kinds of other government malfeasance. Granted, my juvenile understanding of this was somewhat murky; it wasn't until the movie version of *All the President's Men* came out in 1976 that it all came into sharper focus. Journalism began to look downright fascinating as Robert Redford and Dustin Hoffman, in the lead roles as the reporters, dashed from office to underground parking garage, or worked their sources on deadline in the newsroom. The ringing phones and clattering typewriters added to the ambiance of a movie set that uncannily resembled the real-life *Post* newsroom of that era. Journalism seemed not only crucial for the good of the nation's democracy but also enticingly glamorous. There were untold numbers of us, the budding journalists of the Watergate generation; we flooded into newsrooms large and small after seeing the movie and connecting it to the real-life history we had witnessed only a few years before.

How could we resist the intrigue? "I wanted to be Robert Redford moving that ceramic pot," O'Brien recalled, referring to Woodward's secret signal to his confidential source, jocularly known in the *Post* newsroom as "Deep Throat." (That moniker was a play on the reporting term "deep background"—an agreement between reporter and source that is not quite as restrictive as "off the record"—but also a bawdy reference to a then-current pornographic movie.) O'Brien remembers thinking, "Wow, these are the guys that set everything in motion." I knew exactly what he meant: These two young reporters not only revealed corruption at the highest level of government and played a part in bringing down a corrupt president but also kicked off an intense new era of investigative journalism. And, despite the mostly male newsroom staff on display in the film, it never occurred to me that being a woman would be an impediment to joining this ultra-cool club. Maybe that was another Watergate-era message from seeing Barbara Jordan's strength and authenticity: *Seize your power.* It's certainly notable that a twenty-six-year-old Hillary Rodham also had a Watergate role, though I wasn't aware of it at the time. Not long out of Yale Law School, she worked on the impeachment inquiry staff of the House Judiciary Committee. Sitting in a windowless hotel room across the street from Congress, Hillary was one of the first to hear the Oval Office tapes that would bring Nixon down. Yes, Watergate's tentacles reached far and wide.

During the summer of the Senate hearings, my eldest brother, David, home from college, asked me what I thought I might like to do as a career. We were sitting in his bedroom, which, like my brother Phil's, featured curtains with a ships-and-maps pattern that evoked Magellan's circumnavigation of the globe. (Another unspoken gender message, that boys should be adventurous and set off to see the world? My room, by contrast, featured girly pink gingham, and—what's galling to me now—it lacked a desk like the big sturdy ones both of my brothers had. In adulthood, I've always made sure I had a substantial desk.) I told David what interested me, and what I thought I might be good at. Reading. Words. Knowing what's going on. Communicating. In one of my life's more significant moments, my brother looked me in the eye and offered a single word of advice, as if it were perfectly obvious and preordained: "Journalism." I wasn't quite sure how to move forward on the suggestion, or even fully sure what it meant.

Luckily, my all-girls high school, Buffalo's Nardin Academy, had a student newspaper and an inspiring advisor, Joanne Langan. She was married to the school's headmaster, Michael Langan, who shared my Lackawanna roots and became a mentor, too. Mrs. Langan was an enlightened English teacher who, long before most schools had diversified their reading lists beyond the canon of dead white men, had us reading Anne Moody's *Coming of Age in Mississippi,* Joyce Carol Oates's *them,* and the poems of Maya Angelou. Apparently, she saw something promising in me, and pushed me to put my name forward to edit the student newspaper, *Kaleidoscope.* The year after Nixon resigned the presidency in disgrace (escaping inevitable impeachment and likely conviction), Nardin's faculty and newspaper staff named me the editor in chief. Classroom 210 became my first newsroom—the first of many—and one of my best friends, Sheila Rooney, was my second-in-command. (We also shared the captaincy of Nardin's varsity basketball team.) As editor, in addition to making story assignments and ferrying the pasted-up newspaper pages to an off-campus printing plant, I wrote editorials on serious subjects. One reluctantly supported President Gerald Ford's decision to pardon Nixon, thus sparing the country endless turmoil and division. Another considered the merits of the court-ordered busing to integrate Buffalo's schools; this was a controversial topic locally and in many parts of the country.

All the while, I was looking ahead. I had asked my uncle,

the managing editor of *The Cleveland Press,* the evening paper at the other end of Lake Erie, how to get started for real as a working journalist. I was lucky to have a close family member showing me what a career in journalism could look like; even better, it was obvious that Bob Sullivan enjoyed his job, which contrasted with my father's observation that his own profession, the law, too often was nothing but "drudgery." My uncle insisted that the best foundation for journalism was a liberal arts education, not an undergraduate journalism degree; I could follow that with a master's degree in journalism like the one he had earned at Columbia University. I took his advice to heart.

The gender issues at play in the late 1970s for an ambitious girl like me were complicated, though I never stopped to think about them too hard since I was busy listening to music, playing sports, and hanging out with my friends. Maybe I didn't have the internal language to grapple with the role of women in American life. I knew this much: My mother had given up a promising future as a women's fashion buyer for a department store to get married and start a family in the 1950s; she was a rising star, scheduled for her first buying trip to Paris and Milan, when she resigned at age thirty to marry my father. Growing up, I was aware that she had some regrets about abandoning her career; but, as an American whose parents were born in Lebanon (soon after immigrating, her father opened a men's clothing store in Lackawanna, which became the family's livelihood), she channeled her urges for upward mobility into her children's lives. She propelled my older brothers toward academic achievement and careers in respected professions. Taking heed, they became a doctor and a lawyer. But she thought I might be best suited to become, as she put it, an "executive secretary." What she *really* wanted, it seemed clear, was for me to marry well (someone like my brothers would do fine) and to have children. This double standard, however, had a hidden advantage: Since she was pressing no specific vocation on me, I was forced—and also free—to imagine my own path. My brothers went to prestigious colleges in Massachusetts; I was initially restricted to someplace closer to home. I spent freshman year at Le Moyne College in Syracuse, a Jesuit school with a fine reputation, but one that I was determined to outgrow. I yearned for a major city and a big-name school. After earning close to perfect grades at Le Moyne, I persuaded my parents to let me transfer as a sophomore to Georgetown University; it would appeal to them, I calculated, in that it was also run by Jesuits, the scholarly order of Roman Catholic priests to which my family had close ties.

My plan worked. Suddenly, still a teenager, I was living in a Georgetown University dormitory only a few miles from the sites of those dramatic Capitol Hill scenes that had mesmerized me just a few years earlier during the Watergate hearings. And the big-journalism world of Washington was right there for the taking. Soon I was riding the city bus from campus to a part-time clerk's job downtown at Gannett News Service. Like a smaller version of the Associated Press, the service provided news to the chain's newspapers around the country. I did whatever tasks were sent my way, mostly typing articles from the bureau's Washington correspondents into the computer system for national distribution. Back at school, I was a reporter covering the medical-school beat for

The Hoya, the more traditional of Georgetown's two student newspapers; later, I became the arts editor of *The Georgetown Voice*, an alternative student newspaper that styled itself after *The Village Voice*, where I assigned theater and music reviews to student critics.

After my junior year, the Gannett connection paid off. My mentor in the Washington bureau, a generous editor named Anita Sama, helped me get a summer internship at the *Niagara Gazette* in Niagara Falls, New York, one of the papers in Gannett's national chain. I might have spent the summer writing concert reviews and feature stories from the compact newsroom, almost within view of the cascading waters of the natural wonder. That's how my *Gazette* internship started out. I was having fun, answering to the encouraging young editor for features, Susan LoTempio, and finding it hard to believe I was collecting a paycheck. Getting bylines and hanging around with the *Gazette*'s wisecracking wordsmiths suited me well.

But then disaster struck, quite literally. In mid-summer, President Jimmy Carter declared the city of Niagara Falls a national disaster area. An environmental calamity was unfolding in the Love Canal neighborhood, where for decades local chemical companies had dumped huge quantities of toxic waste. The long-buried poisons had begun bubbling up in residents' basements and yards. Children and adults were getting sick, as *Gazette* reporter Michael Brown had been reporting for years without garnering much attention. Once the chemical leaks and the residents' illnesses became too obvious to ignore, Love Canal became a huge national news story, and maybe the biggest story ever for the *Gazette*. The paper's small staff was so overwhelmed that the paper's city editor, Dave Pollack, had little choice but to assign me, an inexperienced intern, to cover some aspects of it. He must have been desperate; I didn't have much confidence, but I stumbled through whatever assignments came my way.

A journalism axiom dictates that there's "no crying in newsrooms," but I shed tears that summer. The formidable reporting duo of David Shribman and Paul MacClennan from our big-city competition, *The Buffalo Evening News,* had scooped us *again* on yet another important part of the fast-developing Love Canal story. (Shribman, then only in his mid-twenties, was a big talent, and eventually a Pulitzer Prize winner.) I was a competitive person, whether on the basketball court or in the newsroom, so it hurt to have our head handed to us, day after day, at the *Gazette.* Apparently, my tears of frustration didn't alienate my bosses or make them think less of me. At the end of the summer, the *Gazette*'s top editor, Fletcher Clarke, someone I had barely spoken to all summer, called me into his office. He startled me by offering a full-time reporting job—to begin immediately. Since that would have meant dropping out of college, I decided against it, an easy enough call, and went back to Washington for senior year.

After that summer, I knew that I was in the right field. The *Gazette*'s job offer and my front-page stories had boosted my confidence. I had an affirming sense, too, that journalists were held in high regard. Not by everyone, of course. Nixon had kept an enemies list that included media people, and his vice president, Spiro Agnew, famously had ranted about journalists as "nattering nabobs of negativism." Roger Ailes, who would help found Fox News two decades later, had given Nixon and his cronies advice on how to depict journalists as out-of-touch liberals, not quite "the enemy of the people" yet, but getting there. The nativist populism that would help elect Donald Trump was festering. With its growing resentment of the press and other supposedly elite institutions, it bubbled under the surface of American society like the toxins at Love Canal. Still, that mindset wasn't yet pervasive.

Gallup, the public opinion polling company, began measuring trust in the national press in the 1970s. The trust number, already high, ticked upward in the years after Watergate and the publication of the Pentagon Papers, the secret history of the United States' disastrous involvement in Vietnam, first by *The New York Times* and then by *The Washington Post*. The national newspapers were ably performing their watchdog role, the TV networks were following suit, and the vast majority of citizens seemed to appreciate it. In 1976, two years after Nixon's forced resignation, an impressive 72 percent of Americans had a great deal or a fair amount of trust in the press—and the numbers would never again reach that height. Of course, this was also an era in which other institutions were held in relatively high regard, too: schools, churches, business, law enforcement, even government to some extent.

Journalism certainly wasn't despised; far from it. When I told friends and family members that I was planning to be a reporter, that I'd been the top editor of my high school paper, and that I had gotten paid to write stories about the Love Canal disaster, they seemed impressed. After being wait-listed at Columbia's graduate school of journalism (a crushing blow, since I had assumed for years that I would get my master's degree there), I accepted a scholarship at Northwestern University's highly regarded Medill School. Was journalism school a necessity? Definitely not, but I've always been glad I had a master's degree, had formal education in media law and ethics, and had the chance to spend time in the Chicago area. During one semester, I got to do some reporting from Washington, D.C., for two small newspapers as part of the Medill News Service, in which students worked as national correspondents and had their work published on a near-daily basis. After an internship at one of my hometown dailies, *The Buffalo Evening News,* turned into a full-time reporting job, I covered hard-news beats—business, county government, public education—and broke my share of stories, including an investigation of financial malfeasance in Erie County government.

By the end of the 1980s, I had been named an assistant city editor, supervising a six-man (yes, all-male) team of politics and government reporters. That was stressful at times; the veteran politics reporter, in particular, didn't much like taking guidance from an editor barely in her thirties with much less experience than he had. We worked it out, though, and supervising this group meant that I had started my climb up the newsroom management ladder.

Not only was I mostly having fun, reveling in the newsroom atmosphere, but I also felt the reporting and editing work was important for my city and region. We were keeping powerful institutions honest, or at least helping to do so. I got no sense that I had entered a field that most people mistrusted. As the 1990s approached, many local newspapers were financially successful; profit margins well above 30 percent were nothing unusual. And the press was undeniably important in the United States, perhaps not beloved but recognized as vital to the way American democracy functioned. What's more, journalism offered a viable career path: not a great way to get rich but certainly a way to earn a living wage. As a bonus, it struck me as exceedingly cool.

Little Miss Lifestyles Breaks Out

t's 1995, and I am sitting in an auditorium at the offices of *The Buffalo News,* watching in horror as my boss takes credit for my idea. To make matters worse (or possibly comical), it's an idea he hates. He is Murray Light, the top editor of the paper. And at this moment I am the assistant managing editor for features, which is a typical job for an ambitious woman in newspaper journalism in the mid-1990s. The features department, sometimes known as "lifestyles," is where arts criticism and some of the most creative writing reside, and it's often a place for experimentation, since the *serious* people in the newsroom are all preoccupied with City Hall corruption and national politics, and therefore not paying attention. But, as a place for this "softer" journalism, the features department doesn't get nearly as much respect as the centers of hard news: the city or metro desk, the Washington bureau, the statehouse bureau in Albany, or, at larger papers, the foreign bureaus in Paris, London, or Beijing.

I enjoyed my job and loved my thirty-person staff of talented critics and features writers. But, after a few years, I found myself itching for a wider role at the paper. I had told Murray that I wanted to be put on the publisher's small committee assigned to think outside the box, as the management cliché went, about "reinventing" the paper. Circulation was falling, and something needed to be done to stem the losses. Murray agreed readily enough. So I immersed myself in research about readership trends and brainstormed with colleagues. Soon, along with my friends in the graphic design department, I cooked up a radically redesigned front page. There were no stories on it, just teasers to what was inside the paper. It was flashy and engaging, and it looked nothing like the stodgy, traditional *Buffalo Evening News* where I had come to work fifteen years earlier as a summer intern, and where many of the news stories I'd written as a hard-news reporter, covering business, education, and government beats, had appeared on the front page. The top editors of the paper were appalled by my redesigned atrocity, as they saw it. But they had a problem. The paper's publisher, Stan Lipsey, who outranked them, had heard something about this buzzy thing, asked to see it, and, heaven forbid, he loved it. So did his wife, Judith, who was the paper's marketing guru, though she was not on staff. Stan demanded that Murray and his top deputies present it to the newsroom and move toward rolling it out to the public—which is why my boss was standing on a stage taking credit for my idea, which he hated. Privately, Murray had chastised me: The redesign was a "concept car," he fumed, a crazy idea never meant to leave the auto dealer's showroom. Nevertheless, at this moment—in front of about

150 journalists who worked for him, and under duress from *his* boss—he was trying hard to sound as if he believed in it and had come up with it himself.

At one point during his presentation, a sports columnist not especially noted for his respect for corporate authority piped up: "I understand Margaret Sullivan had something to do with this project. I'd like to hear her vision." I was more than willing, and halfway out of my seat, thinking of how to sell the merits of this approach, when Murray shut it down in seven words: "Margaret has nothing to do with this." I sank back down. As I wrote in my journal: "A punch in the gut would have felt considerably less jarring." He tried to soften his brusqueness with a vague remark about my possible involvement in the future. That didn't help, since he had already uttered the all-too-memorable sound bite. He did, however, ask me to describe for the assembled staff a new section for kids that was being planned—a safe and appropriate use of my skills, from his viewpoint. I ranted in my journal about "the Little Miss Lifestyles Syndrome—the warm and soothing feeling that no doubt comes from seeing me firmly in my place as the talented and docile editor of the former women's section."

The Buffalo News never did roll that concept-car redesign out of the showroom. More traditional ideas prevailed, and maybe that was for the best. But a couple of years later, I finally reaped the benefits of that venture: After a fierce competition, I was named the paper's first woman managing editor, the number two job in the newsroom, and therefore the clear heir apparent to Murray as chief editor, who was due to retire the following year. What had hurt in the moment served me well in the long run, because I acquired a reputation for thinking creatively and taking risks.

Murray had been good to me most of the time I worked for him. He and his managing editor, Foster Spencer, had hired me straight out of school, which was unusual at the time. Over the years, Murray tolerated rookie mistakes I made as a reporter, gave me several promotions, and encouraged me to work a flexible schedule when my children were infants and toddlers. He was a person of integrity and a capable top editor who clearly recognized that I had something to offer. But when Murray announced he was going to retire in a year or so, it was clear that he wanted one of his longtime deputies, Ed Cuddihy, to be his successor. A no-nonsense former city editor, and a fine newsman who had spent his entire career at the paper, Ed would have built on everything Murray had done without turning anything on its head. He also had the advantage of being a middle-aged man with decades of experience, whereas I was significantly younger and a woman. The paper had never had a woman editor or managing editor. I had to figure out how to maneuver around that, since Murray would have a role in naming the next editor. Luckily for me, he wouldn't be the one to make the final choice. That was Stan Lipsey, the publisher, along with the *News*'s president, Warren Colville. I wanted the top job badly. Looking back, I don't think my reasons were particularly lofty. I was motivated by a desire for growth and advancement; I wanted to have a wider influence at the paper and in the city; and I thought that I would be the best choice for the paper's staff and for the readership.

I knew, though, that this promotion could cause problems at home. My then-husband was the editor of the paper's Sunday magazine; we had met in the newsroom when we were both reporters. He was less than enthusiastic about my quest to become the paper's editor. Mostly he opposed the idea, in part because our children were young and by its nature the job would be consuming. Even before I became top editor, it wasn't uncommon for us both to be awakened at night by a phone call from the on-duty editor to tell me about some major breaking story and to consult about where it should be displayed or what the headline should say. I had felt for years the difficulties of balancing motherhood with my job; I was always dashing from the pediatrician's office or the school Halloween parade to an editorial board meeting or the latest staff disruption, often feeling that I wasn't giving enough to either role.

Still, this was the opportunity of a lifetime, one that I felt called to pursue. So I campaigned for the job, making the case to the decision-makers that I would bring a fresh approach that would benefit the paper and serve its readers. I wrote memos, some serious, some lighthearted—even a meant-to-amuse "Ten Reasons Why I Should Be the Next Editor"—and relentlessly talked about my vision for the paper. I wanted to make the journalism more enterprising and public-spirited, and the presentation more appealing; I wanted more direct engagement with our readership. I wanted to establish the paper's first investigative team and do more watchdog journalism. *The Buffalo News* was a well-respected paper, but it also was a little dull, with a lot of attention to established institutions in the region. Our longtime rival, the *Courier-Express,* was livelier and more informal in its tone and presentation. But after 1982, it was out of business. I thought it was high time for the *News* to be edgier, to have a more conversational tone when appropriate, and to pay much more attention to the diverse communities we served.

Apparently, I persuaded them. When my appointment as editor was announced in 1999, much was made of my becoming one of the few women to run a regional newsroom; at just over forty, I was one of the youngest, too. At the one hundred largest newspapers in the United States, only thirteen chief editors were women. In Buffalo, this was a history-making first, and local women's groups took note. My office filled up with congratulatory floral arrangements; one, from a group of women lawyers, came with a small card that read, "We hear the sound of shattering glass."

At a *Buffalo News* picnic shortly after my appointment was announced, I stood on a stage, addressing the company's employees, not just journalists but advertising, production, and circulation staffers, too. A newsroom photographer captured an image that I cherish: My six-year-old daughter, Grace, stands at my side, looking adorably cute and right at home, leaning forward to peer at the audience while I speak into a standing microphone. For that moment, at least, all the elements of life seemed to be in harmony.

My twenty-year marriage came to an end in 2007, something that was painful for all of us. These days, many years later, I'm grateful that the family relationships have endured, and extremely proud to see my son and daughter thriving in their lives as they both pursue careers in public interest law. I've often asked myself if my ambition was a contributing factor in the marriage's demise. The answer, unavoidably, is yes, though our problems certainly were broader and deeper. And when I've stopped to wonder whether a man would have had a very different experience in similar circumstances, I get the same answer: an unequivocal yes.

I spent three decades at *The Buffalo News,* the last dozen as top editor. I certainly never intended to stay that long, but there was always another challenge: a new beat to cover, a great story to write, another step up the management ladder. And the final chapter—getting to lead my hometown paper as top editor—was one of the great privileges of my life. Every day, after parking in an outdoor lot within view of Lake Erie (sometimes covered with ice, sometimes sparkling in the summer sunshine), I would walk up the three flights of stairs to the newsroom. I liked to use the back door, the one closest to where the massive presses churned out hundreds of thousands of papers every day. I could smell the ink and hear the clanking of the freight elevator. As I emerged from the stairwell into the newsroom, I often thought of the J. D. Salinger character Buddy Glass, who came to regard *his* workplace, a small-college classroom, as a "piece of holy ground." I felt the same.

The top editor's position certainly had been a long time coming. When I graduated from Northwestern in 1980, I had internship offers at both of my hometown papers in Buffalo:

the *Courier-Express* and the *Evening News*. I asked my father which he thought I should take, and he replied without hesitation that the *Evening News* was "the dominant paper." I took the *News* internship and was hired at the end of the summer. My father had certainly called it right. In 1982, the *Courier* would announce that it was going out of business; once the investor (and eventual billionaire) Warren Buffett bought the evening paper, a fierce newspaper war—a battle for survival—was joined. In that era, there was enough ad revenue and reader interest for only one newspaper in most American cities. Second newspapers were going out of business all across the country. Buffett and his Buffalo representatives struck a death blow when they started a Sunday paper to siphon off some of the advertising revenue from the *Courier*'s most lucrative day of the week.

It turned out to be a tough year for the Buffalo area, since not only did its beloved morning paper go out of business, but Bethlehem Steel decided to shutter its huge steel mill in Lackawanna, the small city just south of Buffalo where I had grown up. Both events were devastating news for the region, and in both cases they were portents of what was ahead: the sharp decline of American manufacturing, along with the loss of blue-collar, union jobs that could support a family on one income; and the decades-long decline of local newspapers, a downward spiral that continues to this day. I felt both events deeply. My mother and father still lived in Lackawanna, so the steel-plant closing felt very personal. I had many friends at the *Courier,* one of the two papers I had grown up reading. The journalists there scattered all over the country, part of a Buffalo diaspora that went on for many years. I lost my chief competitor, Joan Verdon, who covered the education beat, and whose scoops I lived in fear of, as I hoped she did mine.

I lived in a second-floor apartment in Buffalo by then, and would race down the stairs every morning as soon as I woke to grab the morning paper and scan the front page for a Verdon byline. One of those above the fold on the front page made for a bad start to my day; it meant that I would be playing catch-up, and that the pressure would be intense to find some piece of education news that she didn't know about. By reporting it, I could then make *her* life miserable. And so it went.

I also wrote longer features, ones that had nothing to do with education. At one point I went to Washington to report a profile of Daniel Patrick Moynihan for our Sunday magazine. The Harvard professor turned New York senator spoke in eloquent riddles as I interviewed him; I scribbled furiously, and later realized I had next to nothing comprehensible to quote him on. At one point, I retreated to the bathroom in his Senate chambers and looked at my notebook in despair. My tape-recorded interviews with him didn't yield much more that was useful. I somehow wrote a cover story for the magazine, but it relied heavily on background reporting about the senator, whose intellectualism and originality of political thought made him both widely admired and polarizing. Decades later, as my train would arrive at the new Moynihan

Train Hall at New York's Penn Station, I'd conjure the erudite senator in his trademark bow tie and remember all the trouble I had interviewing him.

In 1998, Moynihan announced that he would be retiring from the Senate after twenty-four years, and he tapped Hillary Clinton—still the First Lady at that point—as his preferred successor. Not everybody agreed that this was a good idea. Plenty of New Yorkers, along with the Clintons' many political enemies in Washington, depicted her as an opportunistic carpetbagger. After all, she had grown up in Illinois and spent her professional life in Arkansas and Washington, D.C. The Clintons had only recently bought a house in Westchester County's Chappaqua, north of New York City. To try to counter this criticism, which could have been a political death sentence, she started what she called a listening tour across New York State. The tour brought her, among other places, to our editorial board meetings in Buffalo, a few months after I had been named editor. When she entered the third-floor conference room, where we held the daily meetings to plan the next day's front page, I cringed when Stan Lipsey, the publisher and my direct boss, greeted her with a kiss on the cheek. That was too cozy a relationship between newspaper publisher and politician for my taste, but Stan always did things his own way. (He once passed around a photocopied list of "dumb blonde" jokes at the weekly lunch meeting, where there were only two women, including me, at a table of a dozen newspaper executives; I complained afterward, and it didn't happen again.)

I hadn't met Hillary before, but I wondered with some trepidation if she was aware that only a few months earlier I had made national news by asking then-President Bill Clinton a most unwelcome question at the annual conference of the American Society of Newspaper Editors in Washington. President Clinton, who had been impeached in 1998 and acquitted the following year, had been trying to change the subject as he spoke to hundreds of news editors. I conferred with our Washington bureau chief, Douglas Turner, and we came up with a provocative question for me to pose: If his vice president, Al Gore, was elected later that year, would Clinton ask for a pardon for any possible crimes committed during his presidency?

I raced up to one of several standing microphones in a huge hotel ballroom so I could ask one of the first questions, identified myself as the editor of *The Buffalo News,* and fired away. The president reacted angrily, smacking the lectern in apparent frustration; this was clearly something he didn't want to address, since it put the attention of the nation's newspaper editors—and thus the nation—squarely back on his impeachment for perjury and obstruction of justice; that sordid saga had begun with his affair with a White House intern, Monica Lewinsky. But he had no choice under the circumstances, and he answered the question: No, he wouldn't ask for, or accept, a pardon.

This was news. Not only did the story about his answer appear on the front pages of *The New York Times, USA Today,* and *The Washington Post* the next day, but some of this national coverage identified me as the questioner—as if it were truly remarkable for a feisty woman editor from the provinces to challenge the president of the United States. My journal entry from April 14, 2000, jotted down at Reagan National

Airport as I left Washington, began: "Well, it looks like I've used up a few of my fifteen minutes of fame." I noted that I hadn't slept much: "I kept seeing myself at the microphone. Rehearsing after the fact."

If Hillary had any recollection of my encounter with her husband—I think she must have—she didn't give a hint in that *Buffalo News* editorial board meeting. She was cordial and businesslike. After it concluded, she asked me quietly if I could point her to the ladies' room; we were, after all, almost the only women in the room. Rather than just point, I accompanied her across the newsroom. We chatted as we went, a walk-and-talk scene out of *The West Wing,* and I could feel the newsroom staff's eyes on us. (She would go on to win the Senate seat in 2000, and again in 2006, but wouldn't finish her second term because, soon after the 2008 election, President Obama named her secretary of state.) Hillary, always well prepared and knowledgeable, made a point of observing to me that there weren't many top newspaper editors in the nation who were women. I appreciated that she knew such a thing, and her observation accomplished what perhaps it was intended to do: give me a sense that we had something in common as groundbreakers.

Often portrayed as cold or unlikeable, she came off to me as quite the opposite. She was personable and easy to identify with, as well as in complete command of Western New York minutiae. She could talk in detail about the region's bridges and water treatment facilities, and about its economic troubles stemming from the loss of manufacturing jobs like the ones, years before, at Bethlehem Steel in Lackawanna. But she also was willing to speak personally, and even in that short chat as we walked to the ladies' room, we mentioned our children; mine were in grade school at the time, while her daughter, Chelsea, was at Stanford University. It went unexpressed, but seemed understood, that we both had had the experience of being the first woman to do a particular job or be the only woman in a roomful of decision-makers.

The morning of September 11, 2001, was a sunny, almost cloudless day in Buffalo, just as it was across the state in lower Manhattan. It started off as a slow news day. In our regular morning news meeting, we editors scraped around for how to put together the front page of the afternoon editions. But when the second plane hit the World Trade Center, I stood in the middle of the newsroom and mentally flipped through the file cards of past news events, looking for a way to measure this. The Columbine school massacre in 1999? The Oklahoma City bombing in 1995? There was nothing to compare. I hadn't been alive when Pearl Harbor was attacked, but that was the only comparison I could come up with. The editors jumped into action, tearing up the front page of the afternoon editions, and immediately began planning special coverage. This was, of course, a huge national and international story, but for us, as New Yorkers, also a local one. Crews of Buffalo-area firefighters and emergency workers were headed downstate to help—and there were local people missing and presumed dead. I soon found out that among them was Sean Rooney. He was the brother of my close friend Sheila Rooney, who had worked on the Nardin *Kaleidoscope* with me. We quickly sent journalists to the scene in downtown

Manhattan. Chaos reigned. Life, and journalism, were never the same. At home, we talked to the children about what had happened. Alex, still in grade school but always an old soul, had a characteristic answer when we asked if he was scared: "I don't feel immediately threatened."

Not long afterward, my childhood hometown dominated the national headlines, as the Justice Department identified what it called a "sleeper cell" of potential terrorists only a mile from where I grew up. The Lackawanna Six were a half-dozen men of Yemeni descent who had traveled to Afghanistan for training, some of them reportedly even meeting with Osama bin Laden, and then returned to the United States. Under the Patriot Act, which was railroaded into existence mere weeks after 9/11, all sorts of previously forbidden snooping on American citizens was suddenly allowed, and this helped to ensnare these locally born and raised men. They all pleaded guilty and went to prison, and the Bush administration touted this as a legal and intelligence triumph that may have avoided another terrorist attack.

Perhaps it did, but the Patriot Act was government overreach with a serious downside, like the perfectly legal but morally suspect warrantless wiretapping of American citizens that would eventually make big news. But in the wake of 9/11, everyone—including the press—was expected to get on board the patriotism express without asking too many questions. For the most part, journalists did just that, to their eventual shame. At *The Buffalo News,* the arrests, prosecution, and sentencing of the Lackawanna Six were a huge continuing story that dominated our front pages for weeks and months. And for me, it was literally close to home—the very place where my childhood friends and I had watched the sky turn orange each evening as they dumped the slag at Bethlehem Steel.

In the years that followed, during my time as editor, our newsroom did crucial work, even as the newspaper business started to experience financial troubles, both locally and nationally, because of the loss of print advertising revenue. I had established the paper's first investigative team, and we embarked on many projects, including one called "The High Cost of Being Poor." Buffalo was one of the poorest cities in the nation, and its children suffered the worst; two of every five children in the city lived below the poverty line, and the public schools were, in the words of another series we did, "Halls of Inequity." Rich kids could get a good education in Buffalo; poor kids struggled for meager resources. Maybe we couldn't fix that problem, but at least we could show people how bad it was.

The Buffalo area's strong disagreements over abortion rights dominated these years as well. In this heavily Roman Catholic city and region, contentious protests outside local abortion clinics were a common sight; in 1992, Mayor Jimmy Griffin, a conservative Democrat, invited the anti-abortion activists Operation Rescue to put on a major event. Thousands of out-of-town protesters, representing both sides of the controversy, showed up for an event called the Spring of Life, attracting national attention and resulting in nearly two hundred arrests as anti-abortion protesters tried to block access to clinics. Then, in 1998, a local physician and abortion provider, Barnett Slepian, was assassinated in his own home by a sniper. Slepian was making soup in his kitchen after returning from a memorial service for his father when he was shot through a window; he died almost immediately. It was a huge national story, one whose developments and repercussions we would cover for years, including when the killer, James Kopp, gave a jailhouse confession to two of our reporters, claiming he had only wanted to wound Slepian to keep him from performing more abortions. Kopp was found guilty of murder by a Buffalo-area judge; his sentence was twenty-five years to life in prison. Everything about this coverage was fraught with high emotion and subject to extreme criticism, including within the newsroom itself, where conservative Catholics sat side by side with progressive feminists.

Among the biggest stories was the 2009 crash of a commercial airliner in which fifty people died; our Washington and Albany reporters, Jerry Zremski and Tom Precious, were indefatigable in digging out the causes. Their reporting on the role of pilot fatigue and training helped bring about national reforms that were credited with making flying safer for everyone. As they learned of the causes, the families of the Colgan Air Flight 3407 victims relentlessly pushed Congress to pass sweeping legislation designed to prevent future disasters, including the creation of a pilot-record database and the requirement that flight crews get adequate rest time between flights. Those reforms were tremendously effective. In the two decades before the Buffalo disaster, U.S. airlines had experienced a major crash, on average, every seventeen months. By contrast, in the decade after reform (the 2010 passage of an aviation safety law), they haven't suffered a single such accident. In terms of human lives, the difference is dramatic: 1,186 people died in those commercial plane crashes in the earlier two decades. The following decade saw only one such death and it was caused by a jet window that shattered.

This was the essence of local journalism with lifesaving impact: a Buffalo-area catastrophe, deep sorrow over hometown victims, and crucial national reforms rooted in the dogged journalism that followed over many months. Our journalism had helped make flying safer for everyone. Again, I couldn't help but take it personally. In a sickening twist of fate, one of the Flight 3407 victims was Beverly Eckert, the widow of Sean Rooney, who had died in the World Trade Center attack and who was the brother of my high school friend, Sheila Rooney. More bizarre still, Beverly was flying to Buffalo to award a scholarship in her late husband's name at his alma mater, Canisius High School—the same school from which my father, my brothers, and my son had graduated. At least I knew that we at *The Buffalo News* had done everything in our power to prevent something similar from happening again.

For many consecutive years while I was in charge, the New York News Publishers Association recognized the *News* with its top award for distinguished public service journalism; we competed in the same large-circulation category as the big papers in New York City and on Long Island. It made me incredibly proud of the staff to win that recognition year after year; journalism in the public interest, after all, is our highest calling. This recognition meant that, at least some of the time, we were fulfilling our mission. After the brilliant political cartoonist Tom Toles left *The Buffalo News* for *The Washington Post*, I hired Adam Zyglis, a twenty-two-year-old illustrator and summer intern, who in time would win our paper a Pulitzer Prize.

Amid the triumphs and satisfactions, of course, we made mistakes. Sometimes they were largely my fault, as with one aspect of our coverage of a mass shooting in downtown Buffalo in 2010. Eight people had been shot, four of them killed, outside City Grill, a restaurant where a wedding anniversary was being celebrated. A fifth man would die years later after being paralyzed as a result of his injuries. All the victims were Black. For days after the shooting, no one knew who the shooter was or what the motive was. As alarmed city residents tried to piece together what had happened, the paper published and prominently displayed a story detailing the criminal backgrounds of some of the victims, on the grounds that this information could be a part of the puzzle. The Black community was furious, accusing the *News* of deepening the pain of family and friends who were mourning and burying their loved ones. They were right. The story unintentionally put the blame in precisely the wrong place. I tried to make amends by arranging with a Black minister, Rev. Darius Pridgen, to come out to his church, True Bethel Baptist, to speak with some of his congregation.

It was not the small gathering I had sought; instead, seven hundred community members, some carrying accusatory signs, were there to confront me, not only about this story but also about the way the paper had covered their neighborhoods and communities for decades, long before I was editor. Our story and the placement of it had been harsh and insensitive. I learned a lot that evening from Buffalo residents like Cheryl Stevens, whose son-in-law was among the dead. "I feel that we were victimized twice," she told me in that public forum. "What you did to us was you poured salt on the wounds that had not even healed."

If anything provided a measure of solace on that difficult evening, it was the racial diversity of our newsroom staff, something that I had set out to improve through aggressive hiring and promotion. Many of the journalists of color in the newsroom decided of their own accord to come to the meeting, in part to show moral support for me since they knew I would be under fire. I was deeply touched by their presence; I can hardly imagine how much more difficult that evening would have been without it. Rev. Pridgen later told me that this made a difference to him, too: "I quickly scanned the staff, and when I saw diversity, it started to change the narrative in my mind." All of these events together turned into what he called "a healing moment." Chastened, I went back to the paper to put some reforms in place: training for our journalists on reporting more equitably and sensitively; covering the city's East Side in more thorough and considerate ways; forming a citizens council to bring complaints and ideas to the forefront.

Painful as the whole chapter was, it helped me understand the turmoil in newsrooms and around the country a decade later when George Floyd was murdered in Minneapolis and protests erupted everywhere. Far too often, as we had done in

Buffalo, the news coverage had the effect of blaming the victims. Black men who had died at the hands of police were described in news stories as "no angel," with their criminal records or personal flaws emphasized. I had learned the lesson once and for all, and was able to write about it with more empathy and insight when the issues came up again and again, particularly in the deaths of Trayvon Martin in Sanford, Florida, or Michael Brown in Ferguson, Missouri, as well as George Floyd's. "By seeking and blundering, we learn," wrote Goethe. Luckily for me, I got a chance not only to learn but also to move forward with what I knew. I'm not sure an editor today could have a similar opportunity for growth amid the heated rhetoric of Twitter.

The following year, I got an unexpected phone call from Ann Marie Lipinski, the former top editor of the *Chicago Tribune*. We had met briefly, and I admired her immensely, but we didn't know each other well. As the incoming co-chairwoman of the Pulitzer Prize board, she was calling to tell me that she and her board colleagues were inviting me to join them on that rarefied committee. This is the group that each year makes the final decisions on journalism's highest honors and on the coveted awards for fiction, nonfiction, poetry, drama, and music. I was thrilled, and a little disbelieving, at the invitation. Soon after, a veteran *News* copy editor, someone with plenty of strong opinions about journalism, surprised me when we crossed paths in the newsroom by proclaiming my Pulitzer appointment "overdue" and by offering some pointed advice: "Go knock some heads together."

Three decades earlier, as a college senior, I had cried bitter tears when Columbia University's graduate journalism school didn't immediately admit me. Now, many years later, I would have an exalted seat at the table within Pulitzer Hall inside the Columbia Journalism School.

In early 2012, I thought that being the first woman editor of my hometown daily and a member of the Pulitzer Prize board would be my most notable professional accomplishments. Both were beyond what I had dared to hope for. And now that I was over fifty, I assumed that I knew perfectly well what the first lines of my obituary would say. But life was about to take a radical turn.

Pulling Up Roots

was driving on Chapin Parkway, the leafy Olmsted-designed boulevard near my house in Buffalo, when a phone number flashed onto the dashboard display: (212) 556-1234. "Margaret, this is Arthur Sulzberger," came the disembodied voice. I pulled over to the curb. For weeks—or, if you looked at it another way, for years—I had been waiting for this moment, and I preferred not to commemorate it by smashing my car into a tree. The publisher of *The New York Times* was about to offer me the job that had been created a decade earlier after a combination of scandals (a rogue reporter's fabrications and the misleading reporting in the run-up to the Iraq War) had caused the leadership at the newspaper to establish some reforms. One of these was to hire an internal critic and reader representative, or in other words, an ombudsman. But the *Times*'s grander title for this position was "public editor." The concept: An experienced, independent-minded journalist would come to work at the paper for a limited period (limited so that this outside perspective didn't become an inside one), in order to hold reporters and editors to high standards and to field complaints from readers. This journalist would investigate when things went wrong, would be given full access to the decision-makers, and would then use that reporting to inform the readership. He or she (it had always been a he) would write about the findings in a column that the *Times* itself would publish. In the years after it was established, the handful of journalists who held the job had brought varying styles to it, some more aggressive or critical than others, some who leaned more heavily on commentary, others who emphasized reporting. Always, though, the *Times* public editor's work drew a great deal of outside attention; it was a high-profile position, to say the least. Some people went so far as to call it "the worst job in journalism," given the big egos and the inherent tension of reporting critically on one's own colleagues. I didn't see it that way. The role had fascinated me ever since the first *Times* public editor, Dan Okrent, started writing his pointed columns in late 2003, and even before that when *The Washington Post*'s various ombudsmen had published their work. Most memorably, at the *Post*, Bill Green wrote a tour de force investigation of reporter Janet Cooke's made-up story about an eight-year-old heroin addict; her feature story won a Pulitzer Prize in 1981 that then had to be ignominiously returned. At my desk in the newsroom of the *Buffalo News*, I had read Okrent's columns hungrily, and with a growing sense of a calling. When I read the news that the fourth public editor, Arthur Brisbane, would be finishing his tenure and that the position would be open, I decided to pursue it and did so aggressively, diving into the application process with a single-minded focus. I really wanted the job, in part because I was itching for a life and career change, and in part because I thought that being the public editor of *The New York Times* was something I would be good at. I knew I was smart, had good judgment, and would not be afraid of evaluating the journalism at a big national paper. I certainly had plenty of experience. Three decades of reporting, editing, and leading an urban newsroom had provided that. Over the past twelve years as editor, I had steered the paper through lawsuits from angry businessmen claiming defamation or libel, without ever settling or losing a case. I had dealt with community complaints about racist news coverage, and agreed with some of them, admitting error and putting reforms in place. And I had made consequential judgments on what news to publish and how to present it to our readers—for example, whether to honor a defense lawyer's objections over when to publish the jailhouse confession of his client James Kopp, regarding the murder of abortion provider Barnett Slepian. (We published the confession on our schedule, not his.) In other words, I felt ready.

On that phone call, I asked Sulzberger about the salary, something that hadn't come up in my various interviews for the public editor job over the past two months. After all, I would be moving to a much more expensive city, had a daughter in college and a son in law school, and after a twenty-year marriage, I'd been through a draining divorce. "Don't worry about that," he responded, and I pictured him in his thirteenth-floor office, high above the fray of Midtown Manhattan, dismissing my salary question with a magnanimous wave of the hand. (In fact, it took some negotiating later with the *Times*'s budget-keepers to match and even improve upon my executive editor's salary, but I had Sulzberger's airy promise to remind them of, and that carried considerable weight. I got what I asked for.) But, in the moment, his specific response about money really didn't matter; I was prepared to accept. In the dappled sunshine of that summer day in 2012, sitting in my parked car, I told Sulzberger I'd take the job. It had happened. I would be the fifth public editor of *The New York Times*, and the first woman.

I went home to start dismantling my life to prepare for the move to New York. Within a day or so, a crick developed in the left side of my neck, reaching down into my left shoulder. Having run a robust newsroom while raising young children, I had experienced plenty of stress and anxiety in my life. The scheduling conflicts and adrenaline rushes never stopped, and I had shouldered a lot of responsibility. But now, as I moved to the *Times* to take on this new role, the stakes were higher. Would I be up to the journalistic challenges ahead? Could I even manage to sell my house and get rid of all the accumulated possessions of having lived for decades in one city? By the time I reported for duty at 620 Eighth Avenue a few weeks later, the shoulder pain and I had settled into a long-term relationship. It was part of the price of this adventure, this chance for a growth spurt in middle age, and I was more than willing to pay it.

Within weeks, I had rented an apartment in the Flatiron District, three times as expensive as the monthly mortgage I had been paying in Buffalo. But I could walk to the *Times*

from there, or take a short subway ride, and I had a spec-
tacular view of the Empire State Building just a few blocks
north. The constant, dominant presence of that Art Deco
skyscraper, lit with different symbolic colors each night, began to seem personal—almost familial—and I would introduce the building to visiting friends as "my uncle." I arrived
in the city on Labor Day weekend, arranged a few things in
my new space, and rode my bicycle to Central Park, where
I gazed at the lake and felt a spiritual connection with the
New York writers I loved, some from the past, others very
much alive and living right on this island with me: Anna
Quindlen, Toni Morrison, E. B. White, James Baldwin, Nora
Ephron, J. D. Salinger, Joan Didion, David Halberstam, Gay
Talese. I was thrilled, and I also felt curiously at home. I once
again read E. B. White's classic essay "Here Is New York,"
published in 1949, and smiled at one of its first lines: "No
one should come to New York to live unless he is willing to
be lucky."

A few days later, I was in a fired-up mood for my first day at
work as I walked into the Renzo Piano–designed skyscraper
with its transparent walls, glass-enclosed garden, and multi-
level newsroom, lined with exposed staircases where editors would gather the staff to celebrate their endless Pulitzer
Prizes. An editorial assistant showed me to my office on the
third floor, not far from the obituary writers, which may have
been a subtle statement about my status in the newsroom.
My desk was piled with boxes of freshly printed stationery

and business cards featuring my name and my new title on ivory stock with black letters in the *Times*'s distinctive font. But I would barely touch them in the years ahead. Unlike the four previous public editors, I would be doing the job mostly online.

I started off by tweeting to my four hundred followers (I had joined Twitter less than a year before) something about being dedicated to serving the readers of the *Times*. In retrospect, this was far too earnest a tone for snarky Twitter; a friend had suggested I simply tweet: "The public editor is in the house." That would have been immeasurably cooler. And I settled down to write my first post on the *Public Editor's Journal* blog. I wanted to set the tone for my stint by advocating for rigorous adherence not just to the facts but to the truth, and away from the defensive, performative neutrality that some were beginning to call false balance or false equivalence ("Some say the earth is round; others insist it is flat" or, more pertinent, "Some say climate change is real and caused partly by human behavior; others insist it doesn't exist"). Before the day was over and just before my post was published on the *Times* website, my twenty-five-year-old assistant, Joseph Burgess, who had been the assistant to the last public editor, saved me from an embarrassing error. He popped in to ask me a question as he prepared to put my post into the content-management system for publication. He wanted to know if I was sure that *Times* reporter Michael Cooper, whom I had described as being at the Democratic National Convention, was really still in Charlotte. I realized that was only my assumption after interviewing Cooper by phone, and removed the reference to his location. Later that day, I saw the reporter right there in the New York newsroom, and chatted with him in a hallway. Burgess, bless him, had prevented me from having to append a correction to my first piece of public editor writing. It wouldn't be the last time that my young assistants—five of them would hold the role during my stint—would prove their worth.

I soon found out that anything written in *The New York Times* gets an immense response. Immediately after my initial blog post went online, media writers criticized or praised me, a press ethics expert called to disagree with what I'd written, and hundreds of readers responded in the blog's comments section, by email, and on Twitter. The topic of avoiding false equivalency, pegged to the convention where Barack Obama was being nominated for reelection, had clearly hit a nerve. One commenter wrote: "I sincerely hope Ms. Sullivan is serious when she asks, 'What is the role of the media if not to press for some semblance of reality amid the smoke and mirrors?' and will use her position to push the media to do this job. There's a whole lot of smoke to clear." People seemed to like the direction I was taking and the brisk pace I was keeping, responding to issues in real time.

When *New York* magazine put "The Rapturous Reception of Margaret Sullivan" into a headline and wrote that I had "gained something of an Internet fan club" after one month on the job, I began to think that this might turn out to be fun. Still, my neck and shoulder tension hadn't gone away. For good reason: The inherent difficulty of the job—being an outsider with inside access, complete independence, and a big platform—made itself known quickly a few days later when I met with a group of senior *Times* editors. With the purpose of getting to know me, about twenty editors, mostly white men (with a few notable exceptions), gathered in a big conference room, the same place where they made consequential decisions every day about which articles and photographs deserved to be on the front page. Jill Abramson, the first woman to run the newsroom as executive editor, was sitting in one of the grass-green swivel chairs that were placed around the gleaming table. So was her second-in-command, Dean Baquet. The standards editor, Phil Corbett, was there, as was his deputy, Greg Brock, who was in charge of correcting errors. So were the heads of Metro, National, and other sections. The group was welcoming, even friendly. But I noticed a tense undercurrent. Fully aware that I could make their lives miserable if I called out their misjudgments or errors, some seemed eager to let me know they wouldn't be pushed around by an unknown editor from a place that many of them could not have pointed to on the map. (Even though Buffalo is the second-largest city in the state, at holiday time I was often asked by well-meaning *Times* people if I would be "heading up north," as if I were going to Montreal; a map of New York State suggests that my route was mostly west.) The culture editor, Jonathan Landman, asked

me a question that brought a hush to the room: "Did *you* have
an ombudsman when you were the editor in Buffalo?" And
when he followed up with "Why not?" I stumbled, explaining that I had tried to be an accessible chief editor, quick
to respond directly to reader complaints, so an ombudsman wasn't needed. This seemed to satisfy no one. Another
editor asked what subjects I expected to concentrate on,
and someone called out, "Anonymous sources, right?"—
suggesting that I would probably join my predecessors in
criticizing how much the *Times* allowed government officials to get out their message without the accountability of
having their names attached. Knowing how much the paper had hurt its own credibility in the past because of this
overused practice, I agreed that that was a good bet.

The editors were clearly trying to get a handle on how I
would approach the job, how tough I planned to be, whether
I would treat them fairly and understand their decision-
making. They asked me which of the paper's previous public
editors, in my opinion, had done the best job. A couple of
them pointedly put forward the name of *their* favorite: Clark
Hoyt, the former Washington bureau chief for the Knight-
Ridder newspaper chain, who had held the public editor job
a few years earlier. I agreed that I admired Hoyt's thorough
and fair-minded reporting. When I mentioned my admiration for Okrent, who had been particularly fearless as well as
an elegant writer, I got some sour looks. (Okrent was remembered particularly for writing a column in 2004 that posed
the rhetorical question of whether the *Times* was a liberal
newspaper, and answering memorably at the top of his col-

umn: "Of course it is.") After about an hour, the grilling was over—none too soon for me.

On that late summer day in 2012, I had plenty of worries about the news business. I had spent the last several years cutting the newsroom budget at *The Buffalo News,* mostly by offering buyouts to veteran reporters and editors; the staff of 200 was down to 140 by the time I left. That was painful because, after my three decades at the paper, many of these journalists felt like family members to me, and because I knew very well that a smaller staff meant we couldn't do as much reporting on the city and region we served. This was true not just on hard-news topics; when our full-time theater critic retired, for example, we combined the roles of drama and art critic, but we still had a crack movie critic, Jeff Simon, who doubled as the books editor, and two music critics in Jeff Miers and Mary Kunz, both of whom I had hired. After the announcement that I would be leaving Buffalo for the *Times,* lots of people asked me if I felt guilty, as if I were a captain deserting her ship. The answer was simple: I didn't. I had given my hometown paper three decades of my life and career, had done my best, and was fully ready to move on.

When the 2008 recession hit, the *Times* went through the same kind of newsroom cost-cutting, reducing its much larger staff through buyouts and layoffs while trying to figure out how to make up for the loss of print advertising revenue that had long been the paper's lifeblood. It was a tough time for newspapers, big and small. I worried about that.

But one thing I wasn't too concerned about was whether

most Americans *believed* the news, whether they trusted the essential truth of what they read and heard from the mainstream press. Granted, trust had declined sharply since the 1970s. Soon after the Watergate scandal and the publication of the Pentagon Papers, when public trust was at its height, Americans seemed to feel that the national press was doing its watchdog role, keeping powerful people and institutions accountable. But over the next several decades, many factors would come along that—fairly or not—began to slice away at that positive feeling and that sense of trust. Some of this was the fault of journalists and news organizations themselves, and some of it was the result of outside forces. A perception of liberal bias, coupled with well-publicized ethical failures like the *Post*'s Janet Cooke disaster, caused Americans to feel that the national media was out of touch with their concerns. This was fed by relentless criticism from conservative politicians, from Nixon to Newt Gingrich; they fanned the flames of mistrust, as did the bashing from right-wing pundits like Rush Limbaugh on the radio or Bill O'Reilly on Fox News, which had been founded in 1996 and called itself "fair and balanced," but which was actually meant to help the conservative cause and to make billions by stirring up public outrage. Practices like the overuse of anonymous sources, especially prevalent in the flawed reporting about supposed weapons of mass destruction that helped lead America into the disastrous Iraq War, made things even worse. There were plenty of warning signs of this declining trust: charges of blatant media bias, anger at the *Times* and other mainstream news outlets for being leftist, legitimate disgust over the reporting in the run-up to war. The storm was building. In 2012, though, as I began settling into my new job, the level of Americans' basic trust in the news—in truth itself—didn't feel to me like anything close to a full-blown disaster. But over time, from my front-row seat at *The New York Times,* I would watch the crisis develop. I would do what I could, at this powerful institution, to fend it off.

"Welcome to the Fishbowl"

A scientist named Yvonne Brill had died, and the *Times*, in its wisdom, had decided she was worthy of an obituary. That was the normal part. The not-so-normal part happened almost as soon as the obituary was posted online. Brill was a rocket scientist with remarkable accomplishments, but the obituary's first paragraph focused on her domestic life, and its second paragraph seemed to mention her professional achievements almost an afterthought. It began like this:

> She made a mean beef stroganoff, followed her husband from job to job and took eight years off from work to raise three children. "The world's best mom," her son Matthew said.
>
> But Yvonne Brill, who died on Wednesday at 88 in Princeton, N.J., was also a brilliant rocket scientist who in the early 1970s invented a propulsion system to keep communications satellites from slipping out of their orbits.

Well before the obituary appeared in the printed newspaper, the Twitter universe was ablaze with mocking criticism of the *Times* for writing the obit in a way that downplayed Brill's scientific work. Some were angry, calling it outright sexism: Would any official account of a man's life read this way? Others were sardonically entertained and wanted to propose the cooking accomplishments they would like included in the first line of *their* obituary. "Dear NYT, just in case you're pre-writing obits of obscure book critics, everybody says I make delicious chocolate chip cookies," tweeted *The Washington Post*'s book critic Ron Charles.

When I interviewed the obituaries editor, William McDonald, he made it clear that he didn't see why there was a problem. As he explained it, the early references to cooking and being a mother served as an effective setup for the "aha!" of the second paragraph, which revealed that Brill was an important scientist. "I'm surprised," he told me. "It never occurred to us that this would be read as sexist." And the writer of the obit, Douglas Martin, saw the negative reaction as unwarranted, the whining of shallow people who didn't read the obituary fully but reacted only to what they saw on Twitter about the opening paragraph. It hadn't changed his mind about how he wrote it. Even after all the criticism, he told me, "I wouldn't do anything differently."

Martin was upset, though, at being attacked online, and he vented his anger in heated tones as he sat in my office—only a few yards from his desk—giving me an on-the-record response that I would use in a blog post. McDonald and Martin, both of whom I had had some pleasant conversations with since starting the job a few months earlier, seemed to think I should be defending them against what they saw as the Twitter mob. I got the feeling that they wanted me to use my column to explain and justify their decisions. The problem was that I didn't agree with their thinking, as I wrote in my post. After quoting the critics, as well as McDonald and Martin, and noting that the online version of the obituary was edited before it published in print to address the complaints (the beef stroganoff reference disappeared entirely), I ended the post like this:

> Here's my take: It was fine for the obituary to point out how unusual it was for a woman to be a successful rocket scientist at midcentury and what the obstacles were.
>
> And the way she handled her role as a wife and mother certainly had a place, given the era in which she did her work. Cultural context is important.
>
> But if Yvonne Brill's life was worth writing about because of her achievements, and all agree that it was, then the glories of her beef stroganoff should have been little more than a footnote.
>
> The emphasis on her domesticity—and, more important, the obituary's overall framing as a story about gender—had the effect of undervaluing what really landed Mrs. Brill on the Times obituaries page: her groundbreaking scientific work.

In some ways, the Yvonne Brill dustup was, as I acknowledged in my post, "a tempest in a Crock-pot"—certainly not an earth-shattering matter. It wasn't even in the top one hundred controversies I had to deal with. It was a telling episode, though, because it featured so many of the elements that would characterize my stint as public editor: Intense criticism that began on Twitter. Defensive reaction from the *Times*. Discomfort for me because of the physical proximity to the journalists whose work I was criticizing. And, in general, appreciation from the readership. Of course, not everyone agreed with my conclusions, but people did seem to like that I had taken up the mini-controversy immediately and conducted what they considered a fair-minded and thorough job of dealing with a complaint. To use my own regular tagline, here's my take on the Yvonne Brill episode: It was just another stressful day at the office. Not only stressful but very, very visible. "Welcome to the fishbowl," was *Times* spokeswoman Eileen Murphy's greeting when I began the job; she certainly had that correct.

In nearly four years in the job, I never had a completely comfortable day as public editor. If the people I worked next to were happy with me, I felt guilty for being too soft on the institution. (This didn't happen often.) If they were upset with me—sometimes even furious—I felt besieged and worried that I had made the wrong judgment or had been too harsh. If I hadn't written anything in a couple of days, I felt like a slacker since there were hundreds of reader emails to deal with every week. Thankfully, I didn't take the first cut at these endless complaints; that triage fell to a series of young "confidential assistants" who were assigned to me for roughly a year apiece; each one of them—Joseph Burgess, Meghan Gourley, Jonah Bromwich, Joumana Khatib, and Evan Gershkovich—was excellent and invaluable. Time after time, they saved me from mistakes, served as sounding boards, and suggested which subjects seemed to need taking up most urgently.

From the beginning, I pushed myself to give this singular job all of my energy and the best judgment I could muster. I knew what I had to offer: an outsider's perspective, my background as a top editor, and a clear sense of journalistic right and wrong. At times, I felt like Nick Carraway in *The Great Gatsby*—the visitor from the Midwest who had come east and so was able to observe the scene from an outsider's perspective. I took comfort in knowing that, unlike almost everyone at the *Times,* I had run a newsroom, albeit a smaller one. At *The Buffalo News,* for nearly thirteen years, my desk was where the buck stopped on unending problems and challenges. These included public-records fights with Buffalo's mayor and police chief, demands (often reasonable and constructive ones) from the union representing our journalists to change working conditions, and pressure from the publisher to tinker with stories he was personally involved with. I had dealt with all of this and so much more. With the help of the newsroom management team I had assembled and whose counsel I often sought, I had survived them all. When I arrived at the *Times,* I may have questioned myself or felt insecure occasionally, but underneath all of that, I had a sense of confidence that I knew a thing or two. At a deep level I trusted my own judgment and my own gut. Still, it could be a challenging situation, sometimes close to impossible. The *Times* newsroom was packed with reporters and editors who, having reached the starry heights of their profession, were not always inclined to be open to constructive criticism, especially when delivered publicly.

One of my first tests came with the Tesla controversy, which pitted the *Times*'s automotive journalists against Elon Musk, the billionaire entrepreneur and CEO of the famous electric car company, and his many devotees who felt he could do no wrong. The problem began with *Times* writer John Broder's test drive of the Model S Tesla and the company's new super-charging stations, which were supposed to allow Tesla owners to make long-distance trips. Broder's test drive, to put it mildly, didn't go well: The Model S ran out of juice along the way. "Stalled Out on Tesla's Electric Highway" read the headline of the test-drive story, accompanied by a color photo of the cherry-red car being transported, after the failed test, on a flatbed truck. The story was a black eye for Tesla—one that Musk had no interest in accepting with equanimity. The CEO hit back hard: The story was faked, he claimed, and Broder intentionally caused the car to fail. On his blog, Musk laid out the evidence, as he saw it, using the Model S's computer-generated driving logs. Broder and his editors couldn't really counter those claims effectively, since the reporter had merely taken conventional notes in a small notebook that sat next to him on the front seat. It amounted to conventional journalism going up against advanced technology.

Besieged by aggrieved Elon Musk superfans on one side and worried *Times* journalists on the other—and lacking a great deal of automotive expertise myself—I spent days investigating and trying to come to a conclusion. When I did, it made news in a number of publications, as my pronouncements often did. "*New York Times* Public Editor Margaret Sullivan has published her final word on the *New York Times* vs. Tesla saga, saying she does not think writer John M. Broder purposefully sabotaged the Model S test drive. But she isn't letting him off the hook completely," wrote Rebecca Greenfield in *The Atlantic*. The test drive was done in good faith, I concluded—I saw no reason to question Broder's journalistic integrity—but the reporter didn't use the best judgment along the way, which didn't help the car's performance. Nor was he precise enough in compiling his evidence of the drive's failures; that lack of precision left him and the *Times* vulnerable to attack.

The Tesla controversy was, at some level, unimportant. It centered on a test drive, after all, not a national security breach. But readers cared, some of them passionately, and I knew in my gut that anything that brought criticism of the paper's integrity had to be taken seriously. Still, there were far more consequential problems than obituaries and electric cars, ones that went to the heart of the paper's credibility and mission. Others touched on sensitive issues of race that were roiling newsrooms across the country as old-school practices and thinking ran up against the beliefs of a new generation steeped in the values of diversity, equity, and inclusion.

I agreed, for example, with readers who were outraged by television critic Alessandra Stanley's 2014 piece that opened with a racist trope: "When Shonda Rhimes writes her autobiography, it should be called 'How to Get Away with Being an Angry Black Woman.'" In the same article, Stanley referred to Viola Davis as "less classically beautiful" than other Black actresses; that phrase quickly became a mocking hashtag. After blaming Twitter for the viral blowback, Stanley told me that she had assumed her loyal readers would understand. "I didn't think *Times* readers would take the opening sentence literally," she said, "because I so often write arch, provocative ledes that are then undercut or mitigated by the paragraphs that follow." I didn't quite buy that, and privately thought that "arch, provocative ledes" might make a pretty good hashtag, too. More broadly, the episode gave me the opportunity to write about the importance of newsroom diversity and to point out that of the paper's twenty culture critics at that time, not one was Black.

One of the most stressful episodes came in 2015 when a talented young *Times* reporter, Sarah Maslin Nir, published her fascinating two-part investigation about the employee abuse rampant within New York City's hundreds of nail salons, many of which were owned and staffed by immigrants from China and Korea. Workers sometimes had their wages stolen by salon owners, and were constantly exposed to dangerous chemicals. The series, called "Unvarnished," hit like a bomb when it was published, thanks to an elaborate *Times* rollout similar to a high-end book launch. The praise for Nir's enterprising reporting, which had taken her more than thirteen months, was widespread and effusive. "This is why we need the *New York Times*. Thank you," wrote one commenter, with five hundred others chiming in to agree. Immediately, the project brought about governmental reform at the state level and was mentioned as a strong contender for a Pulitzer Prize, recognition that is extremely important at the *Times*. Soon, though, doubts arose about some of the investigation's conclusions. A former *Times* reporter, Richard Bernstein, who, along with his wife and sister-in-law, both originally from China, owned nail salons in the city, published a lengthy critique of Nir's reporting in a somewhat unlikely place, *The New York Review of Books*. Bernstein got in touch with me, too, wanting me to write my own critique that might amplify some of his points: that Nir's conclusions were overstated, that the salon employee abuses, while real, were not as widespread as depicted, and that some characterizations in the series were simply wrong. He used fighting words like "flimsy" and "wholly inaccurate."

Executive editor Dean Baquet had issued a persuasive point-by-point rebuttal, but I knew I had to take up the subject; it was far too hot to ignore. I also knew that what I would say would probably carry a lot of weight because of the intense disagreement and the high stakes. I felt like a referee at a cage fight. I interviewed many of the players; at one surreal point, two metro desk editors sat in my office as one of them, Michael Luo, translated into English Chinese-language classified advertisements for salon employees from neighborhood newspapers. What I ended up writing didn't fully absolve the *Times* of the outside criticism. I admired the investigation but called it overwrought in places and said that one piece of evidence of ridiculously low wages was overstated. The series probably needed to be dialed back about 10 percent before being published, seldom a bad idea with a big investigation. My conclusions didn't make me many friends on the staff. But then again, that's not what I was there for. (The investigation ended up as a Pulitzer finalist, but not a winner.)

What made criticizing the project even harder was that Nir had made efforts to cultivate, even befriend, me early in my tenure. She asked me to come speak to a group of young

Times women who called themselves the Old Girls Club and who got together occasionally to support each other's careers. They sought the advice of other experienced women journalists, including Gail Collins, the op-ed columnist and former *Times* editorial page editor. One day after work, on Nir's invitation, I met the young women—mostly reporters in their twenties—at Smith's, a bar on Eighth Avenue. I listened as they went through their regular opening ritual of going around the table and unapologetically bragging about some recent accomplishment; the exercise was supposed to overcome women's tendency to downplay their own strengths. Afterward, they asked me questions about how I had managed my own career and whether I had encountered sexism along the way.

That was all very flattering; these young women already were far ahead of where I had been at their age, just by virtue of having landed at the *Times*. So when I criticized Nir's "Unvarnished" investigation, I had the feeling of betraying the young sisterhood that had reached out to me. I reminded myself, though, that I hadn't come to the *Times* to be a mentor or a friend. I was there as the readers' representative and an internal critic. I gave Nir plenty of credit in my column for the virtues of her investigation, writing that the series "effectively and movingly does some of the core work of journalism: It gives voice to the voiceless, and by illuminating wrongdoing and suffering, it advocates for those who cannot do so for themselves." I couldn't find it faultless, however, no matter how much I might have liked its author personally.

Despite the seriousness of the job, I tried to have some fun along the way. Because I wrote an almost-daily blog, not just a weekly or bimonthly print column, I gave myself the freedom to take a lighter approach once in a while. I started a series of posts called "Perfectly Reasonable Questions," asking a *Times* editor to answer a query from a reader. For example, in 2015, I asked standards editor Phil Corbett to expound on whether the paper should quote public officials directly when it was really their public relations people providing the quotes in a written statement; Corbett urged transparency in the writing. At the end of each of those posts, I encouraged readers to send me other questions but noted—I hoped humorously—that *I* would be the one to decide what was perfectly reasonable.

When the Styles section published stories revealing dubious fashion or lifestyle trends (granny underwear, man buns, colorfully dyed underarm hair), I joined those in the reading audience who found them ridiculous. The silliness reached a peak with an amusing but far-fetched story about the supposed popularity of wearing a monocle as a fashion accessory (headline: "One Part Mr. Peanut, One Part Hipster Chic"), and this gave birth to my own whimsical invention, the Monocle Meter. In a blog post, I asked readers to contribute stories to be rated with 1 to 10 monocles: "Send me your goofy trends, your ridiculous interviews, your fatuous features, yearning to be mocked." In subsequent posts, I assigned monocle ratings, something like rating movies with varying numbers of popcorn boxes. By that point, my location in the newsroom had been shifted from near the obituaries desk to a place right within Styles, bringing me full circle to my days running the Life & Arts section in Buffalo. The section editor, Stuart Emmrich, was only one office away, and writers like Katie Rosman, Alex Williams, Jacob Bernstein, and Alexandra Jacobs had desks nearby. I saw them all every day, and they were good-natured about the ribbing I was giving to some of their pieces.

When the legendary media columnist David Carr died suddenly in early 2015, I attended his packed funeral at St. Ignatius Loyola Church on Park Avenue. After, I shared a cab across Central Park, back to the *Times* office, with Katie Rosman, who had come to the paper from *The Wall Street Journal* and, like many others, was devastated by Carr's loss. He had mentored her and a host of other young journalists. Moved by the ceremony and the eulogies, we talked about David and about our own lives and our families. Much as I enjoyed Rosman's engaging company and admired her work, I felt wary about becoming too friendly. I always had to keep myself a bit apart; I couldn't afford to become an insider or to feel that there were people whom I wouldn't want to criticize if the occasion should arise. Not being able to make friends at work was part of the isolation and inherent tension of the job. I told myself that it was a good thing that I had made lots of friends earlier in my life and career; I wasn't adding any at the *Times*.

Some staffers made it easy to keep my distance. I had no interest, for instance, in becoming friends with the sports editor, Jason Stallman, one of the few people at the *Times* who seemed to have little appreciation of the public editor's role and who was unusually defensive about even my mildest criticism. When I agreed with readers who wanted the *Times* to pay more attention to women's sports, especially college basketball, he made it clear that he found it ridiculous that I had mentioned in a post that I had played basketball in high school and college and so had particular interest in the topic myself.

A bigger disturbance with Stallman arose over a story that the sports department saw fit to do about tennis superstar Serena Williams's body type. It was published during the 2015 Wimbledon tournament and just before her championship win. I started hearing angry criticism of the story, which carried the headline "Tennis's Top Women Balance Body Image with Ambition." The idea of the story was that despite Serena's remarkable success, some other tennis players had decided not to emulate her power game by becoming more muscular. For example, it quoted the coach of Agnieszka Radwanska: "It's our decision to keep her as the smallest player in the top 10. Because first of all she's a woman and wants to be a woman." The feminist writer Roxanne Gay tweeted: "That NY Times story on Serena's body is so misguided and racist and utter trash." I decided to write about it, quoting the critics and interviewing its author, the well-respected freelance writer Ben Rothenberg, as well as Stallman.

My post was critical of the piece but not harshly so: It gave both of them their say in defending it. I knew that Rothenberg felt remorseful about presenting the ingrained societal ideas about ideal women's bodies as a given and not sufficiently challenging them. I knew he was stunned by the vociferous criticism that was coming his way. That couldn't have been easy. Stallman seemed much more self-satisfied, though both of them acknowledged that the story could have been better. It was just another day at the office until I heard about what Stallman had told an interviewer for *The Takeaway,* a program on WNYC, the New York City public radio station, who had asked him not only about public reaction to the story but also about my fault-finding. Insisting that it was absurd to see the article as the *Times* taking a position on the subject of women's body types, he was not only dismissive but disrespectful. Regarding my view that the story was a missed opportunity to dig deeper into why such stereotypes exist and to challenge them, Stallman had this to say: "The public editor's piece was met with a lot of laughter and eyebrow-raising in the newsroom." He was still digging through the emails from his colleagues making fun of my absurd stance, he said. Some radio listeners felt like I did about this; one of them, Ann McIndoo, copied me on a letter to the editor she had written, one that was never published. "Your paper employs an editor who seems to think that since female athletes were interviewed for the article, that the author and the paper have essentially no responsibility for conveying sexist attitudes and expectations," she wrote. Was Stallman really so ignorant of the role that journalists play in framing issues? she wondered. McIndoo added that "when he shared that he and others had a good laugh over the public editor's feedback, I was stunned. To err is human; to laugh off the feedback of your public editor (and the public at large) is unforgivably arrogant."

Stallman seemed to be a popular, well-respected editor at the *Times,* and he's undoubtedly smart and skilled. But the episode left a bad taste in my mouth. When we spoke in person, he was perfectly polite, but in these public remarks, Stallman's behavior was unseemly—whatever his private feelings may have been or how much fun he was having sneering with his colleagues. All of this ran against the whole idea of the constructive role that the public editor was supposed to play.

For the most part, though, even those editors and reporters whose work I put a critical spotlight on were accepting, sometimes even appreciative. The columnist Joe Nocera actually thanked me after I rapped him for factual errors in a column about the famed investor Warren Buffett. (I had to disclose, in my column, that I had worked for Buffett, who owned *The Buffalo News* during my time there.) It couldn't have been fun for Nocera when various publications wrote pieces about my criticism, like one in Politico that carried the headline "Times Public Editor Comes Down Hard on Joe Nocera." But he handled it with grace, publicly admitted his error, and treated it as an opportunity to learn something.

The *Times*'s top editors—Jill Abramson, Dean Baquet, Joe Kahn, Lydia Polgreen, Susan Chira, Carolyn Ryan, Matt Purdy, and Andy Rosenthal—were generally cooperative with me and thoughtful about the issues I raised, if not always pleased with my conclusions. Those in the standards department, Phil Corbett and his deputy, Greg Brock (who calmly litigated the endless flood of demands for corrections), were particularly supportive—though, again, not always in agreement with my judgments. Corbett and Brock had roles that were somewhat similar to mine, in that they dealt with questions of accuracy and journalistic practices, but they were part of the newsroom hierarchy, reporting up to the executive editor, while the public editor was an external role; I was paid by the *Times* but was intended to be independent of the newsroom pecking order. I came to know all of these editors well, as day after day I fielded complaints, asked for their responses, and wrote my posts. I had access to them all; if I asked questions, I got answers. In general, the relationships were cordial. Over time, though, there certainly were some unpleasant disagreements. I seldom felt good about dishing out tough criticism; maybe to a fault, I could put myself in the place of the writers and editors. I could empathize, and at the same time I wanted to be as straightforward in my judgments as possible. I thought that the readers deserved that.

Throughout my tenure, just as senior editors had predicted when I first met with them, I was tough on the overuse of anonymous government sources by *Times* reporters, especially in the reporting from the Washington bureau. You would have thought that the paper finally would have learned its lesson about this after the embarrassment and damage caused by its reporting in the lead-up to the United States' invasion of Iraq in 2003. Reporters, most notably Judith Miller, wrote story after story that led readers to believe that Iraqi leader Saddam Hussein had developed "weapons of mass destruction," which helped to provide a pretext for going to war. That war would prove to be disastrous: extraordinarily deadly, lengthy, and largely pointless. But the stories were based on inaccurate information from unnamed sources in the United States' so-called intelligence community. When it became all too clear that the reporting had been flawed, the *Times* was forced to acknowledge what had happened in a lengthy and blame-accepting editor's note. It said, in essence, that some of these stories had not been reported with sufficient rigor or skepticism, and it pledged to do better.

After that, the newsroom's internal guidelines stated that anonymous sources were to be used rarely—only as "a last resort." My reading of the paper, day after day, suggested that there must have been a tremendous number of last resorts, since attribution to "a U.S. official" or "a Pentagon official" was an extremely common occurrence in the paper.

Readers despised this. The national security reporter Eric Schmitt told me that he had been appointed to a newsroom committee to look into the paper's reporting practices and thus was given access to readership data. Schmitt was surprised to learn that what bothered readers most wasn't factual errors or political bias: "The number one complaint, far and away, was anonymous sources." I constantly heard from readers like David Steinhardt of Hancock, Vermont, who railed against this practice, writing, "I beseech the *Times* not to facilitate government acting like the Wizard of Oz—behind a curtain." He made the point that such reporting "can easily serve to mask unaccountable half-truths and lies." It amounted, in the worst cases, to journalistic stenography, reporting that dutifully records what government officials say without appropriate skepticism or rigorous fact-checking. What's more, because the officials hide behind anonymity, there was no holding them accountable later if their information turned out to be bad.

So, one might ask, if this kind of reporting damaged credibility and if there were guidelines that discouraged it, why on earth did it continue unabated? Bill Hamilton, the national security editor in the Washington bureau and one of the most helpful and reasonable people I encountered, offered an explanation. Because of the Obama administration's crackdown on whistleblowers and on all kinds of leaks to the press, government officials had become even more wary of sharing information with reporters. "It's almost impossible to get people who know anything to talk," Hamilton told me. Getting them to talk on the record is even harder, but news gathering must go on. "So, we're caught in this dilemma."

Then, too, there's the competitive urge, and professional pressure, to break stories, something that's much easier to do when you can offer a source anonymity. This is what's known as "access journalism"—at its worst, a devil's bargain between reporters and their sources, in which each wins but the reader loses.

None of this is simple. Some of the most important journalism of the modern era (*The Washington Post*'s Watergate-scandal reporting, for instance, or Jane Mayer's stunning reporting on the CIA's "black sites") was accomplished, at least partly, through the use of confidential sources. It's a crucial, even indispensable tool in ferreting out information that's important to the public interest—especially when so much government information has been classified, often put in that category unnecessarily. The practice was being vastly overused, though, not just for ultra-sensitive reporting on the national security beat but also for all kinds of frivolous purposes—in gossipy entertainment pieces, in personality profiles, in real estate stories. What's more, the excuses given for relying on it were getting more and more strained, more and more absurd.

I went on a campaign in my blog against unnamed sources. I started an effort I called AnonyWatch, and asked readers to send me examples of anonymous sourcing and so-called blind quotes when they saw them in the paper. Many complied, and every once in a while I'd write a column rounding them up, or I would draw attention to them on Twitter.

Eventually, in early 2015, Matt Gross of *New York* magazine memorialized all of this in a piece titled "On the Condition of Anonymity: A Poem for Margaret Sullivan." It was introduced with a short setup, a passage from one of my recent columns: "For many months now, I've been keeping track of the overuse of anonymous sources in *The Times* as a way of discouraging a practice that readers rightly object to. The practice continues apace—as do ever more inventive reasons for granting anonymity." And then Gross's lengthy poem began, growing ever more bizarre with each free-verse line:

> *In keeping with diplomatic custom, with NATO practice,*
> *with a strong Vatican tradition of secrecy, with the peculiar conventions of Oscar publicity—*
> *In order to talk more freely about the campaign's internal thinking*
> *in order to protect her nephew's identity—*
> *To avoid drawing attention at her school*
> *to avoid upsetting past and potential future employers*
> *to avoid possible conflict with fellow executives in a rapidly changing situation*
> *to avoid antagonizing law enforcement officials*
> *to avoid disciplinary measures from the White House . . .*

The list went on for dozens more lines before its anticlimactic words: "He spoke."

The poem was clever and funny, and in every detail all too

realistic. Far from being treated as a last resort, anonymity was being handed out as generously as Snickers bars on Halloween. Eventually I would make some headway in getting the *Times* to change its ingrained bad habits on unnamed sourcing, habits that were so damaging to public trust. But it would take a journalistic disaster to make that happen.

5

But Her Emails . . .

*T*he *New York Times* has long prided itself on being the definitive news source. "All the News That's Fit to Print" is its longtime motto for good reason: The paper (whether in digital or print form) aims to be the first and last word on the tidings of the day. But how prominently a story is covered in *The New York Times*, the language in the headline, the framing given to a revelation or controversy—it all sets the tone for the way the larger news ecosystem, from the TV networks to social media, reacts. That's especially true in the first twenty-four hours after a big story breaks; it's been the case for a long time and remains so today. The Hillary Clinton coverage was particularly consequential.

The *Times's* coverage of Clinton seemed puzzling from the moment I started paying close attention to it in my first months as public editor. It took me a long time and a lot of thought—and plenty of complaints from *Times* readers—to figure out what felt wrong about the coverage. I kept trying to analyze the problem in a binary way. Was it too positive, too glowing? That didn't seem to be the case. Or was it too negative, seemingly intent on tearing her down? That wasn't really it either. Eventually I was able to put my finger on it—and to write a public editor column about it. There would be many more such Clinton-focused columns to follow, right up until I finished my stint at the *Times* in 2016, about six months before she lost the presidential election. Some of these columns would find their way into her 2017 book, *What Happened*, published after that crushing loss to Donald Trump, as she and many other Americans tried to grapple with that pressing question. Of course, there were many factors that resulted in Trump's victory, including the growing intolerance toward racial minorities in some parts of the country, the seeming inability of Democrats to articulate a vision that Americans could latch on to, and Clinton's flawed campaign, which nonetheless gave her a significant edge in the popular vote. But the media overall certainly played an important role, and like everyone else, Clinton clearly understood the power of *The New York Times*, which explained her book's inclusion of what a newspaper ombudswoman had written about her.

The implied question in her book's title was apt. What *had* happened in a campaign that was supposed to smoothly deliver her to the Oval Office as the first woman president? Almost everyone thought she would win—even Trump himself. The *Times*, because of its great influence, surely was one of the factors. When I hear people complaining about the supposedly liberal mainstream media, I like to remind them that it was *The New York Times* that broke the story about Hillary Clinton's emails and pursued it aggressively and, earlier, raised questions about the Clinton Foundation that gave a great deal of fuel to her opponents.

The reason the *Times*/Hillary problem (as I saw it) wasn't

obvious was that there was a confounding paradox at its heart. On the one hand, the campaign coverage treated her as the obvious next president. At times it felt like the prelude to a coronation. On the other hand, the coverage, which set out to be tough-minded, ended up also being extremely damaging, sometimes beyond what was reasonable.

In 2013—well before Clinton had even declared her candidacy for the Democratic nomination—executive editor Jill Abramson assigned a talented and fast-rising staffer who had been covering the news media, Amy Chozick, to report on Clinton full-time, although the beat was defined more broadly. That is, Chozick was to cover Hillary *and* the whole world of the Clintons writ large. But, in essence, this assignment meant that Chozick would focus largely on the would-be candidate. I interviewed her and her editor, Carolyn Ryan, soon after she was assigned to the beat, and soon after I started hearing from *Times* readers about their objections.

Chozick was forthcoming as she sat in my office, talking engagingly about her new assignment. In our conversation, which was on the record, she made it clear that she felt significant pressure from above to produce scoops and other coverage that *Times* competitors wouldn't have. Her editors, including Abramson, had told her to "own" the Clinton beat. Consequently, Chozick told me, "I live in constant fear" of losing even a single Clinton story to another news organization. And Ryan, a high-ranking editor who had been the *Times* Washington bureau chief and now was the senior editor for politics coverage, explained to me why there was such emphasis on Hillary Clinton at such an early stage. With Obama set to finish his second term, the *Times* leadership viewed Clinton, who was then secretary of state (and, of course, a former senator and First Lady), as "the closest thing we have to an incumbent" in the 2016 election. Ryan told me what the paper hoped to accomplish with this early coverage: "With the Clintons, there is a certain opacity and stagecraft and silly coverage elsewhere [but] Amy can penetrate a lot of that."

I always found Ryan, who had come to the *Times* from *The Boston Globe,* approachable; unlike some of her colleagues, she seemed to understand that we often wouldn't be in agreement, but she rolled with the punches, and any disagreement never lingered. Her outgoing personality served as a counterbalance to her ambition and finely tuned sense of internal politics. Almost as soon as I arrived as public editor, she suggested we go out to lunch. We walked over to Sardi's, that theater district standby of old New York, where she quizzed me relentlessly about my background, family, and journalistic views. I felt as if she were interviewing me, but it wasn't unpleasant; instead it seemed to arise both from her natural curiosity, certainly a good quality in any journalist, and— maybe, I thought—from a desire to protect herself in the future. Know thy enemy?

The all-in approach to covering Clinton at this early stage seemed ill-advised to me, as well as to some of the most astute observers I knew in journalism. I interviewed and quoted some of them for my column. Tom Rosenstiel, head of the American Press Institute and a former *Los Angeles Times* media critic, told me he doubted if it really was wise to "perpetuate the permanent campaign." He meant the kind of incessant national politics that never takes a year off but just keeps rolling. Brendan Nyhan, a political scientist at

Dartmouth College, pointedly wondered if a full-time Clinton beat would "cement the perception that she is the inevitable Democratic nominee and effectively serve to pre-anoint her."

As usual, these kinds of concerns, once aired in my column, didn't seem to penetrate the *Times*'s confident decision-making. Many readers, though, did seem to agree with these experts, and with my own reservations. One, commenting from Switzerland, offered this chillingly prescient comment after my column was published: "Promoting the candidacy of Hillary Clinton, as the NYT seems to be doing, is equivalent to campaigning for a Republican win in 2016." That was some accurate crystal-ball gazing, considering that it was written in 2013.

In my columns, I documented the many strange chapters of this coverage. For instance, Chozick's feature story in the *Times* Sunday magazine about Clinton's wide sphere of influence was titled "Planet Hillary." The magazine's cover image of her face as a fleshy globe in space drew remarkable amounts of feedback, almost all negative. "This makes me crazy," NBC News's Andrea Mitchell, one of the most prominent women journalists in the country, was quoted in Talking Points Memo, expressing doubt that the *Times* Sunday magazine would ever portray a male political figure like this. And a reader, Kevin Egan, emailed me: "The now-viral image is hideously ugly, demeaning, sexist, and completely premature for an election almost three years away." *Times* editors, right up through Jill Abramson, who had approved the image in advance and called it "very apt," couldn't understand the fuss. Deputy magazine editor Lauren Kern argued that "it might not be flattering in physicality but it is in concept. She is an icon. It shows her power." From my point of view, it also showed that when it came to covering Hillary Clinton, *Times* journalists often took things too far.

The dustup over the Sunday magazine cover took place in January 2014, a relatively innocent time in the saga of Hillary Clinton and *The New York Times*. As the months rolled by, far more fraught issues arose. When the Breitbart contributor and right-wing partisan Peter Schweizer published his 2015 book *Clinton Cash: The Untold Story of How and Why Foreign Governments and Businesses Helped Make Bill and Hillary Rich*, the *Times* was there to cover it. Schweizer's credentials included heading the benign-sounding Government Accountability Institute. It's actually a right-wing outfit funded by and closely aligned with the family foundation of Robert Mercer, the hedge fund manager and eventual major Trump funder. Mercer was also a principal investor in Cambridge Analytica, the infamous British political consulting firm that misused the private data of Facebook users to benefit campaigns, including Trump's. This was Schweizer's crowd.

Regardless, the *Times* made an "exclusive" deal to pursue one of the story lines in his book, as did *The Washington Post* and Fox News, which raised the question of how exclusive such an arrangement really could be. But that wasn't the major concern. That was what one reader wrote to me: "I'm very unsettled that the *Times* is hyping a book by an extreme partisan." The arrangement, said another, "lends Schweizer's overall body of work a legitimacy it does not deserve." This is what I meant about the confounding paradox of the Clinton coverage. The sense of a "pre-anointed" candidate again was coupled with negative coverage that seemed to go beyond normal vetting and that seemed to lack perspective about what really deserved to be considered of great importance.

In her article about the publication of the book, Chozick's lead paragraph was less about the book's substance and more about its likely political ramifications, seen through the eyes of Clinton's critics and rivals. "The book does not hit shelves until May 5, but already the Republican Rand Paul has called its findings 'big news' that will 'shock people' and make voters 'question' the candidacy of Hillary Rodham Clinton," she wrote. There's nothing wrong, of course, with deeply investigating— "scrubbing," to use the newsroom lingo—a presidential candidate's background; in fact, it's crucially important to do so, part of the watchdog role of the press. Sometimes the leads for doing that kind of investigation come from "opposition research," the practice by political campaigns of digging up dirt on a political rival for the purpose of discrediting them. Journalists don't need to ignore this kind of negative information when they learn of it (often through a confidential tip from a campaign staffer); the question is whether reporters can dig into the facts and independently determine if a damaging accusation is not only true but also newsworthy.

When the *Times* got around to reporting on the substance of the one aspect of the Schweizer book they had decided to pursue (their "exclusive" area of interest), the paper published a front-page story, "Cash Flowed to Clinton Foundation amid Russian Uranium Deal." It hit hard, and was delicious catnip for right-wing politicos and their media allies, who quickly distorted and exaggerated it. Sean Hannity of Fox News was one of many who transformed this story into something much more diabolical. Though his position was unsupported by evidence, he implied that this proved that the U.S. secretary of state was corrupt and that she had risked national security for a quid pro quo deal to benefit herself through the Clinton Foundation. *This* was the Russia scandal to end all Russia scandals, if you believed Hannity. That kind of credulity is never a particularly good idea, though he and the Fox News network have millions of true believers and set the tone for right-wing coverage across the media. Clinton wanted to portray herself as the people's candidate, but this development gave her political opponents more ammunition to portray her as greedy, deceptive, and venal, as they often had in the past. Not for nothing did Hillary popularize the phrase "a vast, right-wing conspiracy" to describe the forces aligned against her and her husband that were constantly trying to drum up scandals to destroy them politically.

Was it wrong for the *Times* to publish that Clinton Foundation story? No, it was deeply reported and germane, but it may have been overplayed, with its importance overstated. It was consequential in hurting her politically because it deepened the portrayal that Republicans were eager to circulate. Again, the *Times*'s promise seemed to be: Yes, never fear, Hillary Clinton *will* be the next president but our readers will have an exaggerated sense of her flaws when she takes the oath of office.

The most damaging Clinton reporting was yet to come. By 2015 the presidential campaign was in full swing, and the public editor's email queue was always jammed with readers' complaints about the coverage. Bernie Sanders was being dismissed or even mocked by the *Times*. (To some extent, I agreed with this, and wrote about it.) Donald Trump's appalling past business dealings weren't getting much attention. And Clinton? As always, she stirred strong emotions of all kinds, and I constantly heard from readers about the coverage of her campaign and of her past.

In March, the *Times* reporter Michael Schmidt broke the story about her questionable email practices: the ill-advised use of a private computer server during her stint as secretary of state. In print, it appeared on the front page under the less than explosive headline "Clinton Used Personal Email at State Department." No big deal, you might think. But soon all hell broke loose, and it never stopped for the duration of the campaign. The press, and Clinton's many haters, became obsessed with the email scandal, if that's what it really was. Then, in July, Schmidt and Matt Apuzzo, another Washington bureau reporter, wrote a story—sourced anonymously—about two inspectors general asking the Justice Department to open a "criminal investigation" into Clinton regarding her email practices. Again, it got front-page treatment. But almost immediately Clinton's people got in touch with the *Times* and protested, calling its wording inaccurate. Quickly, and apparently in response to these complaints, the language in the story was changed; now the inquiry was called a "security referral," and the Justice Department inquiry was described in less personal terms. It was about the email practices, not about Clinton herself, as the story originally had stated. Two corrections were appended to the story; later, an editor's note was published, addressing how readers might have been confused by the changes and the conflicting information.

I wrote a blistering blog post and then a more tempered Sunday column about all of this, quoting executive editor Dean Baquet calling what had happened "a screw-up." My main takeaway was that the *Times* had been too hasty in publishing the story, especially since it was based on anonymous sources. "We got it wrong because our very good sources had it wrong," a deputy executive editor, Matt Purdy, told me at the time. This statement angered the readers who wrote in the comments section of my post, as well as many others angered by the paper's article, who said that this sounded all too familiar; it brought to mind the disastrous media coverage in the run-up to the Iraq War as the *Times,* and others, misleadingly reported the likely existence of weapons of mass destruction in Iraq and the close connections between Saddam Hussein and Al-Qaeda. This, too, was reporting that was based on some supposedly very good (anonymous) sources who got it wrong.

"You can't put stories like this back in the bottle," I wrote. Especially when published by the influential *New York Times,* "they ripple through the entire news system." The coverage throughout the media was out of proportion to the supposed crime. Looking back recently at all the coverage of Clinton's email practices, I was struck—and had to laugh out loud—at a sentence from a 2015 news story in the *Times.* It stated that public opinion polls showed voters' opinions of Clinton hadn't been swayed much by these revelations. That certainly was no longer true by the fall of 2016. Exploited endlessly by Trump and right-wing media, and heavily covered across the media spectrum, Hillary's email seemed to be all anyone could talk about, and it was the pretense used by Trump to get his crowds chanting "Lock her up!"

Then it got even worse with the arrival of the infamous Comey letter, which has become the topic of countless reconstructions and analyses. In late October, after discovering a trove of Clinton emails on a laptop belonging to Anthony Weiner, the estranged husband of Hillary's top aide, Huma Abedin, Comey reopened the FBI investigation into her email practices. Before that, the media's attention had moved on, at least somewhat. But with the public release of his letter to Congress on October 28, made with significant fanfare that went against FBI strictures, the email contretemps was front and center again. And just days before the presidential election.

The *Times* again overdid its coverage, making Comey's overreach even worse. Editors devoted the entire top of the print front page to this admittedly startling development and its potential ramifications: three articles and a photograph, all "above the fold" in print, and similarly dominant in digital form. One of the headlines, under the bylines of Amy Chozick and another politics reporter, Patrick Healy, read: "With 11 Days to Go, Trump Says Revelation 'Changes Everything.'" There must have been rejoicing in the GOP camp over that; they couldn't have framed it better themselves.

Later, two researchers would publish a story in *Columbia Journalism Review* finding that in just six days "the *New York Times* ran as many cover stories about Hillary Clinton's emails as they did about all the policy issues combined in the 69 days leading up to the election." Did it matter? Without a doubt. The statistics guru Nate Silver at fivethirtyeight.com analyzed the effects of the Comey letter (and, implicitly, the media coverage, led by the *Times*) in a post-election article: "It might have shifted the race by 3 or 4 percentage points toward Donald Trump, swinging Michigan, Pennsylvania, Wisconsin, and Florida to him, perhaps along with North Carolina and Arizona." Silver stopped short of saying it made all the difference, or stating that Clinton would have won if this hadn't happened. It certainly contributed, though— especially in combination with the breathless coverage of WikiLeaks's release of Clinton campaign chairman John Podesta's emails, and the relative lack of attention to Trump's own misdeeds. Of course, the right-wing media went overboard with all aspects of the Weiner/Abedin story, the development that set off the entire endgame of the campaign—a disastrous one for Hillary Clinton. The Murdoch-owned *New York Post*, whose editorial page endorsed Trump in the primary and which was a dependable supporter of his campaign on the news pages, splashed its story on the front page. A tawdry photo of Weiner in his underwear accompanied a just-as-tawdry headline that screamed, "HARD COPY: Huma Sent Weiner Classified Hillary Emails to Print Out."

Abedin herself knew how devastating this development was for Clinton's campaign. In an interview with CBS News about her 2021 memoir, *Both/And*, she looked back at the anger she felt toward her estranged husband, who ended up going to jail for sending lewd text messages to a minor—the offense that opened up the emails to the FBI. "This man Weiner was going to ruin me. And now he was going to jeopardize Hillary Clinton's chances of winning the presidency," Abedin wrote in her book, describing how she called him when the news broke. "'Anthony,' I said, wanting to shake him through the phone, 'if she loses this election, it will be because of you and me.'" She had a point.

High drama, indeed, and consequential, too. With less than two weeks to go before the election, it looked like the Clinton campaign was embroiled—again!—in the worst kind of sordid scandal, and that it was only escalating. Within a few days, the story had changed, and of course the media covered that, too. Comey decided to wrap up the FBI investigation again, after determining that there really was no problem here after all. Eventually the FBI had to issue a correction about his original statement that "hundreds and thousands" of emails were involved. It turned out to be only a few.

After the election, Comey was defensive about publicizing his reopening of the email investigation while simultaneously *not* disclosing the FBI's investigation of the Trump campaign's ties to Russia. "It makes me mildly nauseous to think that we might have had some kind of impact on the election," he told the Senate Judiciary Committee, though he stood by both decisions, saying they were consistent with FBI policy. Not everyone agreed. Many in Washington—not just Hillary supporters—thought Comey had gone too far, and portrayed him as a showboat. They criticized how he had been so public about reopening the investigation and had spoken so freely about Clinton, describing her and the State Department's handling of emails as "extremely careless," though he brought no charges and said no reasonable prosecutor would do so.

The *Times* had certainly treated the FBI's two investigations of the 2016 presidential candidates very differently. It shouted one from the rooftops, and on Trump and Russia the paper used its quiet inside voice, playing right into the Republican candidate's hands. With a little more than a week to go before the election, the *Times* published a story with the headline "Investigating Donald Trump, F.B.I. Sees No Clear Link to Russia." If anyone was concerned about Trump's ties to Vladimir Putin, their fears might be put to rest by that soothing headline, though the story itself was considerably more nuanced. Even that reporting, not very damning for Trump, appeared on an inside page of the paper, a far cry from the emails coverage splashed all over the front page, day after day. We now know, of course, that Russia *had* set out to interfere with the election, and did so very effectively.

David Brock—the conservative turned liberal activist, who founded Media Matters for America, the progressive media watchdog organization—went so far as to say that the *Times*'s Clinton coverage deserved "a special place in journalism hell." Brock was brutally critical. His incendiary 2015 book, titled *Killing the Messenger: The Right-Wing Plot to Derail Hillary and Hijack Your Government,* pointed directly at Carolyn Ryan, the *Times*'s senior politics editor, as a leading culprit. Relying on anonymous sources within the *Times* (which, as always, should give the reader plenty of pause), Brock wrote that "experienced journalists in the *Times* Washington bureau, I've been told, are appalled at Ryan's unprofessionalism on the Clinton beat. 'She has a hard-on for Hillary,' said one source in the *Times*. 'She wants that coonskin nailed to the wall.'"

Maybe some *Times* people did feel that way. From what I knew and observed, I don't believe that the paper, as an institution, was trying to get Trump elected or cause Clinton to lose. Nor do I believe that Ryan was playing out a personal vendetta. So why *did* this hugely influential news organization keep portraying Clinton so negatively and inflict so much damage? I come back to the same maddening answer: that it was because her presidency seemed inevitable, and they wanted to be tough on her before she became the leader of the free world. Often accused of liberal bias, the *Times* wanted to show clearly that this was not true, in coverage that implicitly shouted, "Look how tough we are on Hillary Clinton (your next president)." In addition, the news media, including *The New York Times,* loves to cover politics as a horse race. Since journalists across the board seemed to be convinced that Clinton would win handily, it made for a more exciting horse race if the favorite was loaded with extra weight to slow her down.

By the late spring of 2016, I had departed from the *Times* and begun a new job as media columnist at *The Washington Post.* So when the presidential campaign was in its last days, I was no longer in a position to demand that *Times* leadership tell me why they made the decisions they did. But my successor as public editor, Liz Spayd, commented more than once on the mild coverage of Russian interference in the election, such a contrast to the paper's Clinton coverage. The headline of one of Spayd's columns referred to a "muted alarm bell" on the relationship between Trump and Russia. She wrote, "This is an act of foreign interference in an American election on a scale we've never seen, yet on most days it has been the also-ran of media coverage, including at the *New York Times.*" Executive editor Dean Baquet bridled at the charge that the *Times* had held anything back. "We heard about the back-channel communications between the Russians and Trump," he told Spayd for her column. "We reported it, and found no evidence that it was true. We wrote everything we knew—and we wrote a lot. Anybody that thinks we sat on stuff is outrageous. It's just false."

All of this highly consequential coverage became—and still remains—a sore spot with a number of the *Times* journalists involved with those stories. My harsh criticism over the "criminal inquiry" story in 2015 struck some of them as unfair. Even after I left the paper for *The Washington Post,* I heard from more than one suggesting I revisit this in my new role as media columnist, recanting my earlier criticism. They pointed to a new *Times* story, published in 2017, in which the Justice Department essentially stated that the original reporting had been right all along, that there was no substantial difference between a "criminal investigation" and a "security referral" or a "security matter." That was, expressed in the reporters' own words in the story, "a distinction without a difference." After all, the argument went, the FBI is not the Federal Bureau of *Matters;* what it *does* is investigate crimes. It was no surprise to me that Comey, the centerpiece of that more recent story, would think so, and say so, since he or his top aides may well have been among the main sources for the since-corrected story.

What's more, if the "criminal inquiry" story was right to begin with, why had the *Times* seen fit to publish those two corrections, which remain to this day? If they were right to begin with, would they have to correct their own corrections? That never happened, although in addition to the appended corrections, the archived version of the story now begins with an italicized editor's note from 2018 (more than three years after the story was first published). That note directs readers to the "distinction without a difference" article from 2017 and to Comey's book, published the following year, for "additional light" on the subject. Well, maybe, but I'm not too sure any additional light was cast.

A reader coming fresh to that story today, with all of its piled-on baggage—two corrections and a years-later editor's note—would need a user's manual, a field guide, and a compass to figure out what had happened and what it all meant. I still think that the original language of "criminal inquiry," used in a front-page headline, was misguided, if not technically untrue. There are all kinds of ways to frame stories and all kinds of language choices to be made, particularly in headlines. Clinton later described the effect of that original "criminal investigation" story: "Now my campaign had to deal with questions about whether I was being measured for an orange jumpsuit." And I maintain that the chaotic way the changes were made to the story and headline, apparently under intense pressure from the Clinton campaign, was improper, confusing, and lacking in transparency. This flawed coverage, and its dire consequences, angered and alienated many *Times* readers, a fair number of whom haven't forgiven or forgotten what happened. In this way, too, it is similar to what happened with the Iraq run-up coverage; it has become a long-standing grievance. The difference is that there was no public mea culpa for the Clinton coverage, and perhaps not even an internal admission that anything was really wrong. I believe that many readers sense that self-satisfaction and are offended by it.

In her post-mortem book, Clinton expresses her resentment of the media coverage of her campaign, particularly the way it equalized her flaws and Trump's when they weren't close to equal. "If Trump ripped the shirt off someone at a rally, and a button fell off my jacket on the same day," she wrote, "the headline 'Trump and Clinton Experience Wardrobe Malfunctions, Campaigns in Turmoil' might feel equal to some but it wouldn't be balanced and it definitely wouldn't be fair."

As for the way she was treated in the nation's most influential newspaper, she had a few complaints there, too. The original email story, the one that set off all the endless coverage and near-hysteria in right-wing outlets, had real problems, she said. For example, it wasn't until the eighth paragraph that the story included the rather important fact that she was not the first government official, or secretary of state, to use a personal email account to conduct official business. She observed, accurately, that whatever the *Times* does tends to affect the entire media and politics ecosystem: "The facts didn't stop the hamster wheel of Washington scandal from spinning into rapid motion, as other media outlets sought to follow a story that must be important, because the *New York Times* had put it on the front page."

Clinton had become a tough press critic—and for good reason, since she'd had so much experience with being covered over many decades. Later, in one of my media columns for *The Washington Post,* I wrote about Clinton's book and asked Carolyn Ryan whether she and other editors had any regrets about the campaign coverage. I wanted to know whether any soul-searching had taken place. She was circumspect and acknowledged no blame. Reviewing political coverage, Ryan assured me, is "something we engage in all the time and have done so after this election." That internal review was focused on the use of public opinion polling, the need for reporters to get beyond New York and Washington, and how to dig more effectively into policy and issues. Though I pressed her, Ryan—frustratingly—wouldn't say whether those high-level newsroom conversations had taken up complaints about unfair coverage of the candidates, particularly from Clinton, or whether any reforms had been put in place.

Nor did the majority of the news media acknowledge they had gone too far with the infamous email story or that they had made serious errors with the campaign coverage in general, except to say that they needed to get out into "real America" more. (Not a bad idea, though it ended up producing what I called the Endless Diner Series, in which coastal reporters interviewed Trump voters in their hometown eateries, all competing to find the most "average" Americans and to learn that they hadn't changed their minds.)

In my view, the 2016 campaign coverage exposed the worst tendencies of the mainstream press: its addiction to sensation and the horse race, its propensity for overkill, and its profit-driven desire for clicks or TV ratings. The numbers told the story dramatically. The major broadcast TV networks gave only 32 minutes during 2016 to covering policy, but the email scandal got 100 minutes, according to a Tyndall Report study. This reflected a steady, sharp decline in policy coverage over the years. In 2008 the same networks gave a relatively generous 220 minutes to policy; in 2012 it was less, only 114 minutes. Meaningful coverage was dropping at a rapid pace. But CBS president David Rhodes shrugged off any wrongdoing when he was interviewed by former *Face the Nation* host Bob Schieffer: "There's always a blame-the-media phase of any campaign."

Cable news might have been worse. CNN's Jeff Zucker was pilloried at a post-election gathering at Harvard for how much free airtime his network gave to Trump's rallies and speeches while simultaneously going wild with coverage of the email scandal. Zucker responded by employing an absurd logical fallacy in his network's defense. "Half the people want to blame us for Trump, and half the people want to say that we're terrible to Trump," he said. "That's how I always think we're doing the right thing." It's one of journalism's most annoying and most self-satisfied axioms: If both sides are mad at us, we must be correct. That's often simply false, and certainly was when it came to 2016 campaign coverage. Much more on point was an analysis from the *Times*'s former Washington bureau chief, David Leonhardt, who criticized media organizations for how they handled a different email-related story: WikiLeaks's publication, late in the campaign, of thousands of emails stolen by Russian agents from Hillary Clinton's campaign. Leonhardt (at that point a *Times* opinion-side writer) wrote that the "overhyped coverage of the hacked emails was the media's worst mistake in 2016." Fallout from the hacked emails did force the resignation of Debbie Wasserman Schultz from her post as Democratic National Committee chairwoman, because they showed DNC officials discussing how to undermine Bernie Sanders in the primary so that Clinton would be sure to win. Other than that, the hacked emails didn't produce much else of substance, and yet the gossipy revelations dominated many a news cycle and mixed with the *other* email scandal into a toxic, anti-Clinton stew. "I love WikiLeaks!" Trump crowed at a campaign rally, and he tweeted constantly about how the emails simply proved everything evil about "Crooked Hillary." Writing in *Esquire,* the astute politics blogger and former sportswriter Charles Pierce described the atmosphere around Hillary; he had seen it all before when her husband was president. "Any relatively commonplace political occurrence," Pierce wrote, "takes on mysterious dark energy when any Clinton is involved."

Whatever Hillary Clinton's complaints may have been about the *Times*'s coverage, she had to have been pleased to get their editorial endorsement, as she did at most newspapers in the United States. Only a handful of papers endorsed Trump. Many editorial boards issued warnings with what Jim Rutenberg, then the *Times* media columnist, described as a "collective sense of alarm" about what electing a dangerous demagogue, as *USA Today* put it, might portend. The *Times* editorial board— which functions separately from the newsroom, with its own staff and with many floors of physical separation—was almost effusive about Clinton. "Our endorsement," they wrote, "is rooted in respect for her intellect, experience, toughness and courage over a career of almost continuous public service, often as the first or only woman in the arena." The editorial made it clear that the *Times* endorsement was given on the candidate's own merits, not just in opposition to Trump, though the editorial described him as "the worst nominee put forward by a major party in modern American history." But, in my experience and observation, the editorial endorsements of newspapers—no matter how full-throated—rarely sway elections. However, relentless front-page political coverage can, especially when it's in the hugely influential *New York Times*. In this case, I believe it did.

There was a fitting coda. In the fall of 2019, almost three years into the Trump administration, Congress received a short report from the State Department that summarized its years-long investigation into Hillary's email practices while she was at the helm. Writing in *Vox,* Ian Millhiser described in shorthand the anticlimactic findings: "She shouldn't have done that. But it wasn't that big of a deal." The exculpatory study was received by the news media with a collective shrug. *The New York Times*—after all that—ran it on page A16.

6

Jill Abramson and Dean Baquet

The night before Jill Abramson's firing was announced, I sat across from her in a booth at a Lower Manhattan restaurant. Abramson knew what was about to happen the next day: She was about to be unceremoniously dumped as the first woman to hold the exalted position of executive editor of *The New York Times*. I, however, innocently eating my fancy pasta, had no idea what the next day would bring. Afterward, I found it remarkable that, knowing what she did, Abramson didn't cancel our dinner plans. Why would she spend her last evening in the most prestigious editorial post in American journalism by dining with me, someone who had been an annoying burr under her saddle? Why would she hang out with the public editor, the person whose job it was to critique *Times* journalism—and therefore, often, her decisions as its top editor—on behalf of the paper's readers? Jill and I weren't in the habit of socializing over meals, but she had recently turned sixty and I had suggested a dinner as a way to note that and to get past the tension that had developed in our relationship many months earlier.

The air had grown chilly between us ever since I started

to do research for a column that she vehemently objected to. I wanted to investigate how, roughly ten years earlier, *The New York Times* had withheld an important story—for thirteen long months—in deference to national security objections from the George W. Bush administration. Jill wasn't the top editor back then, but she was a ranking newsroom leader, high up in the Washington bureau, who was involved with the story. That withheld story, about the way the U.S. government was secretly wiretapping its own citizens, was a crucial early look at the American surveillance state that had developed after 9/11; after it was finally published, it won a Pulitzer Prize. It might never have been published at all if one of its authors, the prominent investigative reporter James Risen, hadn't held a metaphorical gun to his editors' heads by declaring that he would soon be publishing his reporting in his book *State of War.*

A look back was germane because of something that had happened more recently: The whistleblower Edward Snowden, a former National Security Agency contractor, had not brought his bombshell story, about a cache of inside information regarding government surveillance, to the *Times.* As he told a journalist, those who put themselves in danger to leak information to the press "must have absolute confidence that the journalists they go to will report on that information rather than bury it." He lacked that confidence in the *Times,* based on what had happened with the infamous thirteen-month delay, so he ultimately cooperated with *The Guardian* and *The Washington Post,* a big blow to the *Times.*

Learning of my intentions, Abramson summoned me and bluntly told me she didn't think it was in my job description to go digging around in the past, taking up things that had happened a full decade before I began my stint as public editor. (I had been sitting in Risen's backyard in suburban Washington, interviewing him for the column, when one of Abramson's deputies left me an urgent-sounding message to see her soon and gave me a hint of why.) I was stunned. After all, I didn't report to her, even indirectly.

To her mind, such a column simply wasn't fair game. My job, she insisted, was to critique *Times* journalism in the present tense and to deal with the concerns of readers as they arose in real time. This, she believed, was out of bounds. She told me that she also felt protective of her predecessor as top editor, Bill Keller, whose managing editor she eventually became; it was Keller who had decided to withhold the story, on the strong advice of then-Washington bureau chief Philip Taubman. For many reasons, Jill simply didn't want to dredge up that whole episode again.

In fact, she warned me that if I insisted on writing the piece, she might take an extreme step: she'd consider cutting off communication with me altogether. We had some tough words about it, a conversation that was gut-wrenching for me, by far the most upsetting encounter I had had at the *Times* so far. I still cringe to remember that while sitting in her spacious corner office—the pinnacle of editorial power in American media—I mortified myself by starting to cry as she made her strong objections known. (Despite the axiom "there's no crying in newsrooms," I've managed to shed embarrassing tears in most of the places I've worked, from the *Niagara Gazette* to *The New York Times*.) Still, my courage didn't fail me about what really mattered. I knew what I had to do: Go ahead with the column and let the chips fall where they may. I knew Abramson wouldn't go so far as to order it killed. That would be beyond the pale, especially since a number of staffers were already aware it was in the works, which I pointed out to her. There seemed to be no other choice but to continue, *especially* after she told me not to. As public editor, I was supposed to be completely independent; it was a central tenet of the job description.

As it turned out, nothing terrible happened to me, to Jill, or to Bill Keller as a result of the column. I reported it as rigorously and fairly as I could, even interviewing Michael V. Hayden, the former CIA director and former director of the NSA, and, of course, all the key *Times* figures, including the since-retired Taubman. Hayden made a little news for me by stating unequivocally that the government never would have attempted to keep the *Times* from publishing had editors chosen to go ahead: "Prior restraint was never in the cards."

I interviewed Keller, by then a columnist, who was forthcoming about why he made the decision to hold back the story on national security grounds. He talked about the atmosphere in the country after 9/11, saying that those kinds of concerns loomed large. "Three years after 9/11, we, as a country, were still under the influence of that trauma, and we, as a newspaper, were not immune," Keller said as we sat in his office several floors above the newsroom he had run. "It was not a kind of patriotic rapture. It was an acute sense that the world was a dangerous place." He advised me against judging something in hindsight without understanding the moment in which it occurred. I took his point, but I still thought it had been the wrong move, one far too deferential to the government. The delay meant that publication came *after* George W. Bush's reelection, not when it might have swayed some voters. Keller expressed doubt about whether publication would have made much of a difference politically: "It's become an unexamined article of faith" on the left, he said, that publication in the fall of 2004 might have given John Kerry the presidency.

My column was read appreciatively, perhaps adding something worthy to the historical record, but it certainly never went viral. After all that drama, its publication was anticlimactic and it was time to move on to other, more current subjects. Nevertheless, I look back on that column, "Lessons in a Surveillance Drama Redux," as one of the best pieces I did; it raises important questions and holds up well. I'm glad I had the guts to go forward with it over the internal resistance, despite my own trepidation.

The incident had left Jill and me on awkward terms (at least *I* thought so) for quite a while, and I hoped to change that. After all, it would be prudent to keep cordial relations with the executive editor, if possible, and not to let a permanent rift develop. What's more, I admired Jill in so many ways: her high intelligence, the journalism she had fostered, her strength of character, the book about Supreme Court justice Clarence Thomas she had written with *The New Yorker*'s Jane Mayer—and certainly her pioneering role at the *Times,* which was similar to my breakthrough appointment in Buffalo, though on a much larger stage. I was no fangirl, but I appreciated spending time in this storied newsroom, run for the first time by a woman. So I had suggested we get together for dinner, and she suggested the restaurant, a Soho favorite of hers: Raoul's. It seemed like a pleasant enough idea for a weeknight outing. Especially since I didn't know that the hammer was about to come down.

The next morning, the *Times* publisher—Arthur Sulzberger, Jr.—stopped by my office, asking if I was planning to be in the newsroom later. There would be an all-hands meeting, and he thought I would want to attend, even though I wasn't really a member of the staff in the usual sense. Something in his demeanor made me think this had some momentous consequence. My reporter's antennae went up. What's it all about? I asked him. He wouldn't say. I was so curious that, while he was standing in my office that Wednesday morning, I took a stab at it to see how he would react. Jill is stepping down, I guessed, and you're installing Dean Baquet as editor. Sulzberger looked stunned, and asked who had told me that. No one, I said, which was the truth. But something about Abramson's demeanor and remarks at dinner the night before, combined with a recent conversation I had had with *Times* media columnist David Carr about the contentious relationship between publisher and editor, gave me a flash of intuition. As it turned out, a few hours later, there would be no gentle "stepping down" from her lofty post. No pretense about wanting to explore other career options (as if there could be other career options for the top editor of *The New York Times*). Abramson—the first woman to run the *Times* newsroom— had been summarily fired after less than three years on the job. This was legitimately shocking.

But why was she fired? That's what everyone wanted to know. Was it, as some of her women supporters believed, that she was the victim of sexism—seen as "too pushy," when a man exhibiting the same behavior would have been seen as forceful and, at most, a tough, demanding boss? People started making comparisons to Howell Raines, another fired *Times* editor, but one who had been treated with more deference—he was given the chance to say goodbye to the staff, for one thing— and who had had a full-fledged journalism scandal happen on his watch: the Jayson Blair fabrication and plagiarism mess.

Was Abramson a poor administrator, prone to management mistakes, like the way she had moved to hire a second managing editor without getting buy-in from Baquet, the one already doing that second-in-command job? Or was something else going on—something that had a lot to do with the hierarchical structure of the *Times,* still run by the Sulzberger dynasty, and a lot to do with a vision for the future of the institution? Not long before Abramson's firing, the young man who would soon become publisher—Arthur Gregg Sulzberger, known as A.G.—had been the driving force behind a document that had become known informally as the Innovation Report. (In fact, Abramson herself helped choose A.G., who then was barely into his thirties, for that leading role.) After she was fired, a summary of the report was leaked to the news media, and eventually the full report was published. Meant to assess the *Times*'s ability to stay on top of evolving technology and tastes, the gist of the report was that the newsroom wasn't moving nearly quickly enough, or fully enough, into the digital age. *Print was over.* Discussions of which seven stories should appear on the next morning's front page shouldn't be the focal point of every day. Huge, seismic change was taking place in the media business, and the *Times* needed to be leading the way. Writing about it in Harvard's Nieman Lab, Joshua Benton commented on how raw its self-criticism was: "You can sense the frayed nerves and the frustration at a newsroom that is, for all its digital successes, still in many ways oriented toward an old model."

Inside the *Times,* the report was a huge topic of conversation and, mostly, agreement: We needed to break through the barriers and move forward more boldly. "The *New York Times* is winning at journalism," the report began. "At the same time, we are falling behind in a second critical area: the art and science of getting our journalism to readers. . . . We haven't done enough to crack that code in the digital era." The report said that the two major competitors, *The Washington Post* and *The Wall Street Journal,* were further along; it also mentioned admiringly the digital progress of other news organizations like *Vox, USA Today,* and *The Guardian.* And it said that, frequently, more traffic to *Times* stories was coming from news aggregators like Flipboard than from the *Times* itself. Here was a particularly devastating set of findings: "Over the last year, the *Times* has watched readership fall significantly. Not only is the audience on our website shrinking but our audience on our smartphone apps has dipped, an extremely worrying sign on a growing platform."

Abramson, who justifiably prided herself on encouraging digital projects such as the groundbreaking "Snow Fall," with its arresting graphic treatment of a deadly avalanche, objected to the idea that she wasn't pushing hard enough into the digital world. She and Baquet jointly issued a memo that said they approved of the report's major recommendations. There was some doubt, though, about whether she fully embraced them. Was she willing to work closely and cooperatively with the business side of the company, rather than trying to preserve the firm, traditional separation between the newsroom and the bean counters? Not enough, apparently, for the younger Sulzberger and those he trusted most. True, his father was still in charge, but probably not for long; A.G.'s opinion mattered tremendously.

And then there was the Dean Baquet factor. At the newsroom meeting where Abramson's firing was announced to a stunned staff, Sulzberger also announced, with a celebratory air, that Abramson's second-in-command would become the paper's first Black executive editor. Had Baquet given Sulzberger something of an ultimatum, along the lines of "Do something about Jill or I'll leave the *Times*"? Maybe, some speculated, it was even stronger: "It's her or me. Pick." Baquet denied in an NPR interview that he ever gave such an ultimatum to Sulzberger, though he said he did make it clear to the publisher that he was unhappy. I asked Baquet about it myself shortly after his ascent to executive editor, and he answered in words that acknowledged the Roman Catholic upbringing that we shared: "I've examined my conscience on this, and it's clear." (I didn't offer to help him examine it more closely.)

Given Abramson's various management missteps, both in managing up to her powerful boss and down to her staff—many of whom had become disillusioned with her sometimes brusque management style while still respecting her as a journalist—the choice apparently seemed fairly obvious to Sulzberger. He had already overseen the departure of a high-ranking Black editor, Gerald Boyd, who had been Howell Raines's managing editor and who had had a role in enabling Jayson Blair's wrongdoing, as he'd mentored the young Black reporter. In other words, it would look very bad to have Baquet leave the *Times,* especially if he did so unhappily.

Baquet's personality was very different from Abramson's, though they had some qualities in common. Like Jill, Dean was an accomplished and respected journalist; his investigative reporting for the *Chicago Tribune* back in the 1980s had earned him a Pulitzer Prize, and, like Abramson, he had run the *Times*'s Washington bureau. What's more, the New Orleans native was gregarious, always ready with a teasing joke or a just-invented nickname. The weather around Dean was perpetually sunny. Except, of course, when his notorious temper flared; in 2013, after a disagreement with Abramson, his boss, he slammed his hand against a wall in the newsroom and left the building for the rest of the day. Later, in an interview with Politico, Baquet admitted he hadn't behaved well: "I feel bad about that. The newsroom doesn't need to see one of its leaders have a tantrum." But the main thrust of the article in Politico depicted not Baquet but Abramson in the most negative light, anonymously quoting critics in the newsroom who called her impossible to deal with and said she frequently blew up at editors in meetings. Somehow, Baquet's temper tantrum came off as a poor reflection on *her*.

Another time, Baquet shot back at one of his critics, a journalism professor, in a Facebook exchange, calling him an "asshole." The professor, Marc Cooper, had slammed Baquet—charging "absolute cowardice"—for not publishing controversial cartoons from the French satirical magazine *Charlie Hebdo*, where twelve people had died after an attack by Islamic terrorists in early 2015. The Baquet-Cooper dustup turned into a media-news story for days. I happened to be in Baquet's office interviewing him the day that the exchange came to light. An editor popped her head in, carrying her open laptop, to warn Baquet with considerable alarm that his Facebook page had apparently been hacked; she had seen the nasty name-calling, and of course assumed that the executive editor of *The New York Times* would never utter such a word on social media. "Oh, yeah, I wrote that," Baquet told her, laughing; she nodded, looking stunned, and quietly backed out of his office. He could get away with almost anything be- cause of his charm and because he had the complete backing of the *Times* publisher, who, after all, couldn't fire two exec- utive editors in a row, or three in only fifteen years, counting

Raines. He also clearly enjoyed Baquet's company and admired his journalism.

Sulzberger's pride in naming the first woman executive editor had been real, but from his point of view it hadn't paid off in the long run. Now, though, he could brag about another groundbreaking "first" because of Baquet's race. And he clearly felt much more comfortable with the choice, one that would last into the next decade until Baquet reached retirement age. (At the *Times*, high-ranking editors traditionally step down at the end of their sixty-fifth year of age.) Abramson, for her part, endured after the crisis. After all, she had been through worse, having survived a terrible pedestrian accident: She was hit by a delivery truck in Manhattan in 2007 and, as a result, had been hospitalized for a long period as she recovered. After leaving the *Times*, she began teaching narrative writing at her alma mater, Harvard, and wrote a book about journalism in the digital age.

Although Jill and I had had some harsh disagreements, I was disturbed to see her unseated so abruptly as top editor. In retrospect, I've come to think that her response to the Innovation Report—something short of an unquestioning embrace—was the biggest factor. Abramson felt strongly about preserving the traditional strict separation between the newsroom and the business side of the paper. The idea that journalists and marketing or advertising people should be working closely together on projects didn't sit well with her. The report advocated for that wall coming down, although it acknowledged the need to preserve editorial independence. Journalism was changing fast, and the *Times* had no intention of being left behind. In her book *Merchants of Truth,* Abramson addresses in detail and with considerable honesty what brought about her firing. Although that section was not a major part of her book and was a bit off its main theme, *New York* magazine published it as an excerpt in early 2019, anticipating correctly the great interest of many who had wondered what on earth could have been behind her firing.

The Innovation Report was, Abramson wrote, "an epic defeat" for her and a terribly disappointing one because she had been "so determined and worked so hard to be the transitional editor who would succeed in making the newsroom digital-first without causing a cultural meltdown or letting the best traditions die, like protecting the news from being colored by the crass commercialism I saw on news sites across the internet." She described the report as "a call to arms" for something that *Times* CEO Mark Thompson wanted desperately: more collaboration between the news and business sides.

But Abramson also carefully and candidly went through the other factors: She had been clumsy in handling an important personnel decision, as she moved to hire a second managing editor without communicating with the one she already had. That, understandably, put Baquet's nose out of joint, since he was Abramson's second-in-command. She also pointed to her efforts to be paid as much as her predecessors in the editor's role. She both admitted her own weaknesses and made it clear she had been treated poorly. She also wrote that, as editor, she had felt "lonely and depressed" at work, something I found poignant because I always perceived her as confident to the point of being high-handed. During the end game of her tenure, her integrity shone through; she refused to sign off on a *Times* press release that said she was voluntarily resigning. Abramson's attitude was that she'd always been a truth-teller and wasn't about to change that now. Her attitude, in essence: I'm getting fired, so let's call it what it is.

As all of this unfolded in 2014, I wrote several blog posts about what was happening, and tried to explore the reasons. I'm not proud of those pieces; I wasn't able to shed much light, and my reporting didn't yield much of value. *The New Yorker*'s Ken Auletta did much better, as did the *Times*'s own David Carr. But I did try to evaluate Abramson's performance as executive editor. While acknowledging her management missteps, I gave her credit for a tenure that had been free of scandal; she had "kept the paper straight," which was one of her stated aims. She moved the journalism forward into the digital realm. She defended press rights and stood up for her reporters, most notably with the tough reporting on the Chinese government, which brought howls and threats from its subjects. And during her brief reign, the paper won eight Pulitzer Prizes. What's more, I wrote, "she wore her feminism on her sleeve in just the right way—not with overplaying stories about women's issues, but with the determined promotion of qualified women into top roles." She had moved several women into editorial positions that would position them to be at the very top of the *Times* newsroom when the next changing of the guard came.

I'd go so far as to say elite journalism was never the same. It's impossible to overstate, for one thing, the importance of having a woman in the top position in the *Times* newsroom, something that had never happened before and that, when she was named, had still not happened at *The Washington Post* or many other major news organizations. A decade later, that would change dramatically. Abramson brought other women up along with her, not only on the masthead but on major beats, with an eye to increasing women's bylines on the front page. From all I've heard, she was influential in my appointment as public editor, too. Although it was the publisher, not the editor, who had the final call, she had told Sulzberger that hiring a fifth white male public editor would be a bad look and a missed opportunity. Accordingly, the two finalists for the job were both women.

I owe her a debt of gratitude, and we've remained on good terms, though we're very different people. Abramson and I have a mutual friend: David Shribman, a former *Times* man who had a stint at *The Buffalo News* before I worked there and went on to an outstanding career. At one point, while trying to work through a period of tension with Abramson, I had talked to him, and to his wife, Cindy Skrzycki of *The Washington Post*. David, droll and incisive as always, characterized the difference between his two friends, and a possible reason for occasional misunderstanding. "Jill is an uptown girl," Shribman said. "You're not." I didn't like the sound of that; I thought it made her sound urbane and sophisticated and me like a rube. But when I mentioned Shribman's words to my daughter, then in college at New York University, she offered a perspective that changed the way I looked at it (a specialty of hers): "I wouldn't say that's such a bad thing." Perhaps there was a benefit to not being part of the coastal elite. Grace's view was wise, I realized, especially since I did see myself in that

Nick Carraway role: the midwesterner who comes east and, because he is an outsider, sees the world of Gatsby with a fresh perspective.

My public editor stint was almost evenly split between Jill's and Dean's editorships. My role was such that I had plenty of contact with both of them. As issues would arise that I thought deserved my attention, I would sometimes get in touch with section editors or, less frequently, with the reporters. Sometimes that would be enough, as was the case with the Yvonne Brill obituary controversy, in which I interviewed the writer and the obituaries editor. At other times, I would get a response from the standards editor, Phil Corbett, particularly on issues about possible ethics violations or about language use (for example, whether the *Times* should keep using the phrase "illegal immigrant").

However, there were some instances when only a response from the executive editor would be sufficient. Generally, once I decided to pursue an issue (there were always plenty to choose from and I could never get to them all), I emailed the editor I wanted a response from; almost always I got their attention quickly. At that point, they either responded by email or suggested I stop into their office to see them. They rarely came to see me. And, with few exceptions, any interaction with ranking *Times* editors was understood to be on the record; if it wasn't, there had to be a mutually agreed-upon understanding about that. Doing it any other way would have made me a part of the editorial team, which I never wanted to be. I had to keep some professional distance, and one way of doing that was to consider myself a reporter at all times and to behave like one.

As with Abramson, I had some rough moments with Baquet as well, though overall I found him more approachable. Sometimes, though, he was impulsive and temperamental. In one instance, he misread an email I had sent him about what I intended to say in a post, as I asked for his response. When he read my post online after publication a few hours later, he fired off an email to me, suggesting that I had misled him about the point of view I intended to take. He actually used the word "sleazy" to describe what he thought I had done. I was shocked and pushed back hard: For one thing, I told him, you're wrong on the facts; check my original email. For another, you cannot use that word with me. When he realized that he had misunderstood me, and that in any case his adjective was out of line, he apologized profusely and immediately.

With one of his deputies in tow, he soon showed up in my office to make his apology in person. As Baquet stood in the doorway, he uttered one of the strangest (and funniest) phrases I'd ever heard: "Can you hug the public editor?" I laughed, held up one hand with palm outward, and said, "No, thanks." I accepted his apology and we moved on.

At the drama-rich *Times*—no matter who was in charge— there was always another dustup, another controversy, to contend with. Baquet would suffer his share of these, including some of his own making; a number of these happened after I had moved on from the *Times*. He mishandled the departure from the paper (a resignation under pressure) of the revered science writer Donald McNeil, who had uttered a racial slur while on an educational trip with high school students. Mc-Neil defended himself by saying that he used the "*n*-word" only because he was in a conversation about whether a student who had used the word elsewhere should have been suspended from school; in my view, his saying the word at all showed terrible judgment. But the punishment—being pushed out of the *Times* after a forty-year career, following internal protests by his colleagues—seemed too severe.

Baquet was the one who made the call about how to display (or, I believe, vastly overplay) the consequential story of FBI director James Comey's reopening of the investigation into Hillary Clinton's email practices less than two weeks before the 2016 presidential election. It was on his watch, too, that the *Times* had to retract the core of its celebrated *Caliphate* podcast, because its main source had fabricated his story, and return the Peabody Award it had won. When these later controversies and others were exploding and the critics were in attack mode on Twitter (often for good reason), I would issue my standard tweet: "It's another good day not to be the NYT public editor."

For anyone in the top editor's position, some missteps are inevitable. At the *Times,* they tend to be very public and can get ugly fast. But, unlike Abramson, Baquet usually got the benefit of the doubt internally. Nothing stuck. That may have been the result of his sunny personality, or his understanding of how to handle the boss (whether the older or the younger Sulzberger), or his greater popularity with the staff. Whether through luck or skill, talent or timing, he has survived—and thrived.

As Baquet turned sixty-five in September 2021, the question of who would succeed him as executive editor became the topic of even more heated speculation than usual. Reading the tea leaves about succession is a never-ending obsession at the *Times* and in the broader media world. Joseph Kahn, who held the second-in-command role of managing editor and is a former China correspondent for the *Times*, was the obvious choice, and indeed did get the all-important nod in late April of the following year. I was glad to see it. Among all the senior editors I dealt with, Kahn showed some of the most consistent good judgment; he struck me as not only particularly intelligent but also open to criticism. Although his own background is eastern seaboard Brahmin (he grew up in Boston and was president of the *Harvard Crimson*), he clearly has a strong feeling for the less fortunate, winning a Robert F. Kennedy Journalism Award for reporting on labor conditions in China's export factories and a Pulitzer Prize, shared with Jim Yardley, for stories on the often-unfair justice system in China.

When I brought divisive issues to him in his role supervising the international news coverage, I found Kahn to be accessible, nonimpulsive, and nondefensive. He was particularly thoughtful when I decided to address the extremely thorny subject of the paper's coverage of Israel and Palestine, and made some suggestions in my column for improving that coverage. (The topic is so fraught, such an obvious no-win, that my first line was "This is the column I never wanted to write.") Kahn understood the role of the public editor, including the notion that I represented readers and that it might be wise to listen to them sometimes. I doubt, though, that he would ever advocate for reinstating the position, a decision that would be made by the publisher, not the editor; *nobody* wants that trouble. It will be surprising to me if he doesn't turn out to be an excellent executive editor who will bring less drama than some of his predecessors. I wrote in a *Post* column shortly after he was named that Kahn's success (or lack thereof) will depend on how he directs politics and government coverage at this crucial moment when American democracy is on the brink. My pressing questions: "Will the paper's coverage forthrightly identify the problems posed by a radicalized Republican Party that is increasingly dedicated to lies, bad-faith attacks and the destruction of democratic norms, or will it try to treat today's politics as simply the result of bipartisan 'polarization'? Will it try to cut the situation straight down the middle as if we were still in the old days—an era that no longer exists?" Ever-influential, the *Times* needs to show strong leadership, and, of course, that comes directly from the top.

Naturally, I would love to see another woman or person of color run the *Times* newsroom someday; there are a number of such editors a bit further down in the editorial hierarchy, and Kahn quickly named Marc Lacey, who is Black, and Carolyn Ryan as his top deputies. With their appointments, a new round of speculation—will one of them succeed Kahn?—began even before Baquet stepped down. Thankfully, a lot has changed since the days, not so long ago, of all-white, all-male newsroom leadership. And still more change is necessary.

Small Victories

After reading a column of mine that warned about the news media's role in the perilous state of American democracy, my sister-in-law Catherine texted me to ask if I ever felt like Cassandra: the Trojan princess in Greek mythology who was cursed to warn, accurately, of future disasters but who was never believed. "More like Sisyphus," I shot back, without having to give it any thought. I was referring, of course, to another figure from Greek myth, the one who was forced as a punishment to roll a massive boulder up a mountain only to have it roll down again, at which point he would start over again. For all eternity.

I often felt like Sisyphus during my stint as *New York Times* public editor. After hearing complaints from readers or through my own observation, I would identify repeated practices that seemed harmful to the paper's effectiveness, integrity, or credibility, and I would write about them. Occasionally I could get top editors to agree that there *might* be a problem or even that there had been a bad mistake. At other times, they would decline to acknowledge that something had gone wrong, though it clearly had. And then, either way, whatever it was would happen again and again.

For example, *Times* journalists sometimes failed to give due credit to smaller news organizations (and, remember, every other news organization was smaller, comparatively) that had broken a story first. In general, they were more conscientious about this with major publications like *The Washington Post* or *The Wall Street Journal,* and worse with academic publications, local or foreign papers, or small start-ups. This was maddening for editors and reporters elsewhere who felt as though their hard, often underfunded work had been inadequately acknowledged by the powerful *Times;* in many cases, all they really wanted was a phrase of attribution ("the *Belarusian Journal of Obscure Disorders* wrote about this last August"), or even just a hyperlink to their story. But too often that didn't happen, and I would hear back from *Times* reporters or editors, asserting wide-eyed innocence: They had never even *seen* that earlier work. Sometimes, I'm sure, this was true. And sometimes such assertions were a little hard to believe.

It certainly could be frustrating to feel I was doing no good while enduring the hassles of the job. By early 2015, with two and a half years under my belt, the strain was getting to me. One critic of my work had accused me of writing "pious sermonettes"—in other words, of having the nerve to point out faults and to do so in what he considered a holier-than-thou tone. (I don't think this was generally true; I tried to avoid lecturing.) Another one disparagingly called me—as if this were some kind of a wounding insult—"a truth vigilante." That was the kind of vicious putdown I could happily accept. One of my journal entries from this period reads like a cri de coeur: "I don't know how much more of this gig I can take." But then there would be a good day or two, and I would bounce back, ready for more and, on balance, glad to be doing this strange job to the best of my ability. Piously or not.

One of the worst repeating problems, as I've noted, was the *Times*'s overuse of unnamed sources, also known as "confidential sources" or "anonymous sources." There were instances when the reliance on that kind of sourcing created real problems, but—in keeping with the Sisyphus syndrome—my pointing this out had had little effect. The policy of using unnamed sources only as a "last resort," according to one *Times* editorial dictum, was widely ignored. Every day's edition of the *Times* seemed to have information attributed to "a U.S. official" or "a White House official." Sometimes even frothy feature stories featured quotations from someone who couldn't speak on the record for one obscure reason or another.

I had been at the *Times* for more than three years when this problem came to a head in late 2015 with the tragic San Bernardino massacre. It was the deadliest mass shooting since a gunman had slaughtered twenty schoolchildren and six adults three years earlier at Connecticut's Sandy Hook Elementary School. In San Bernardino, a married couple targeted a county-run training event and holiday party in a terror attack that killed fourteen people and seriously injured many more. Terrible in itself, but then came a serious *Times* reporting error. A front-page article stated that the U.S. government had missed something that should have been an obvious red flag, something that could even have prevented the attack by refusing to allow the perpetrators to enter the United States. The red flag, according to the story, was the jihadist social media activity by one of the San Bernardino killers. The article began:

> Tashfeen Malik, who with her husband carried out the massacre in San Bernardino, Calif., passed three background checks by American immigration officials as she moved to the United States from Pakistan. None uncovered what Ms. Malik had made little effort to hide—that she talked openly on social media about her views on violent jihad. She said she supported it. And she said she wanted to be a part of it.

It was appalling—or so it seemed—that the American national security and immigration apparatus had missed such a thing. The problem, though, was that the key element of the article was wrong. Malik had not "talked openly" on social media about her support of violent jihad. She had written emails; she had posted on a dating site; she had written private messages. But that wasn't the way it was depicted on the Sunday front page of the *Times*, under a headline reading "Visa Screening Missed an Attacker's Zealotry on Social Media." As usual, the *Times*'s reporting got picked up everywhere. And the reaction soon turned political. Ted Cruz, the Texas senator who hoped to get the Republican nomination for president, began trumpeting the failures of the Obama administration, charging it with putting political correctness—extended to terrorists—above safety and national security. At a Republican presidential primary debate in Las Vegas, he used that story for some performative rage against Democrats: The administration "didn't monitor the Facebook posting of the female San Bernardino terrorist because the Obama [Department of Homeland Security] thought it would be inappropriate. She made a public call to jihad and they didn't target it." Of course, Malik had *not* made a public call to jihad, though the *Times* reported that she had.

I took this on in a column, after the truth came out and the story was corrected. Even the usually *Times*-friendly James Comey had to admit the news report was "a garble," which was an understatement since its major premise was simply wrong. I came down hard and called for "systemic change." The article's publication, I wrote, "involved a failure of sufficient skepticism at every level of the reporting and editing process—especially since the story in question relied on anonymous government sources, as too many *Times* articles do." In this case, top editors were in agreement with me, though they defended the reporters for all the good work they had done in the past, pointing out that one of them had won a Pulitzer Prize. How did this happen? The explanation was embarrassing. The story's sources, Dean Baquet told me, didn't understand the difference between public posts on social media and direct messages that are not public. But, I pressed, if these messages were believed to be public, why hadn't *Times* reporters insisted on seeing them? That seemed like due diligence, especially for a story this important. Baquet responded that insisting on seeing the posts would have been unrealistic given the time pressures of a deadline, but he agreed that a problem had been exposed.

"This was a really big mistake," Baquet told me, "and more than anything since I've become editor, it does make me think we need to do something about how we handle anonymous sources." He called it "a system failure that we have to fix." However, he said, it would not be realistic or advisable to ban anonymous sources entirely. I didn't disagree with that. I knew that giving sources the cover of anonymity is sometimes the only way to get important information to the public.

To his credit, Baquet took action. In mid-March 2016—about twelve weeks after the San Bernardino debacle, and not long before I wrapped up my public editor stint—the *Times* rolled out a new policy on handling anonymous sources. Its major tenet required that one of three top editors (including Baquet) must review and sign off on articles that depend primarily on information from unnamed sources. This would particularly concern those stories that "hinge on a central fact" from such a source, deputy executive editor Matt Purdy told me. That had been the case with the San Bernardino story. I wrote about the new policy, quoting Purdy calling those stories potential "journalistic I.E.D.s"—in other words, they were bombs that could explode unexpectedly and damage the *Times* and its credibility. Given their danger, he had told me, they required special oversight, and a process that may result in slowing down before publication. *Times* editors were clear in saying that they had been working on some new rules for a while; they didn't credit me with making it happen. And that was fine with me; I didn't need a citation with a gold seal from Arthur Sulzberger to hang on my wall. But I do believe I played a role.

The reform of the policy on the use of anonymous sources felt like something of a bookend to the *Times*'s changed policy on "quote approval" that I had pushed hard for at the beginning of my time as public editor back in 2012. In that case, reporters were instructed to stop allowing sources and their spokespeople to review, in writing, quotations from a background interview. It had become the norm for reporters, not just at the *Times*, to interview a newsmaker "on background," meaning not for direct quotation. Then reporters would email quotes they wanted to use in their stories to the newsmaker's spokesperson or to the sources themselves. And the spokesperson, or source, would either approve the quotes or decline them—or, frequently, change them to make them more acceptable in some way. That meant that, in many cases, direct quotes used in news stories were never actually uttered in an interview. Quote approval gave sources—both in government and in business—far too much control over what the *Times* would publish. Even after the policy was changed, I have no doubt that the practice of quote approval continued at the *Times* to some extent, but at least reporters were able to push back on their sources by saying there was a newsroom policy against it. The Associated Press banned quote approval, too. As an AP spokesman put it, their journalists don't allow sources to say, in effect, "I want those three sentences you want to use sent over to me to be put through my rinse cycle." The *Times*'s own media columnist, David Carr, had written about the general practice by journalists, though he didn't take up his own employer's policy specifically: "Inch by inch, story by story, deal by deal, we are giving away our right to ask a simple question and expect a simple answer. It may seem obvious but it is still worth stating: The first draft of history should not be rewritten by the people who make it." Amen.

I applied pressure by urging that the *Times* ban the practice. My push to do so was magnified by articles in other publications about my effort. I was gratified to have had some kind of role in getting quote approval banned—though, just as with the reform measures on anonymous sources, *Times* editors were clear that they didn't do this because of me. It had been in the works before I came along. I just gave it a big public shove in the right direction.

Both reforms—quote approval and anonymous sources—were important. But the change on anonymous sources meant more to me. As I had learned through all my correspondence with *Times* readers over more than three years, they hadn't forgotten the damage wrought by the use of unnamed sources in the prelude to the disastrous Iraq War. Some of them, no doubt, had watched the powerful PBS program in 2007, "Buying the War: How Big Media Failed Us," in which the great Bill Moyers made it nauseatingly clear how the American press, again led by *The New York Times*, got on board with the patriotic fervor sweeping the nation after 9/11. It detailed how little skepticism mainstream journalists demonstrated regarding the claims being made by the George W. Bush administration about the supposed close connections between

Saddam Hussein and the terrorist group Al-Qaeda, which had carried out the 9/11 attacks, and about Saddam's supposed development of chemical, biological, and nuclear weapons. "There was a real sense that you don't get that critical of a government that is leading us in wartime." Moyers tells of how Walter Isaacson, then the head of CNN, had sent a memo (leaked to *The Washington Post*) prior to the Iraq invasion, instructing producers to "balance" any upsetting images of civilian casualties in Afghanistan with reminders about the horrors of 9/11; Isaacson would later acknowledge to Moyers that "we didn't question our sources enough" about the rationale for war. *Times* pundits, particularly Bill Kristol and William Safire, were pushing hard for "regime change" in Iraq, despite the country's lack of a direct connection to 9/11; it was long overdue, they wrote in op-ed columns and urged, endlessly, on TV talk shows. Editorial pages got behind the looming war, too, with *The Washington Post* taking a particularly hawkish stance.

Opinion journalism was one thing; hard-news reporting should have been another. But too often it wasn't. In story after story, at *The New York Times*, *The Washington Post*, and elsewhere, anonymous government sources confirmed this line of coverage. Any reporting that questioned it or applied due skepticism was given far less prominence. In his memoir, *All About the Story*, the former *Washington Post* editor Leonard Downie, Jr., admitted what he termed "my biggest mistakes as executive editor." He looked back at the news coverage from before the war and concluded that while there were some skeptical stories about the administration's hawkish claims, they were mostly relegated to the paper's inside pages. In newsroom parlance, they got buried. "Thinking like an editor, rather than as a reader, I too often assumed they could easily be found by readers in the multipage packages of prewar stories inside the newspaper's front—or 'A'—section each day," Downie wrote. "That was a mistake."

In the *Times,* one byline stood out and has become infamous as a symbol of the media's overall too-credible coverage: that of Judith Miller, a star reporter in the Washington bureau. Time after time, her articles appeared on the paper's front page, sourced anonymously and underscoring the administration's war-hungry justifications. In her 2015 book, *A Reporter's Journey,* Miller admits she got the weapons of mass destruction story wrong, but claims it wasn't because she was spoon-fed her conclusions by the administration; rather, it was because her high-level sources were wrong. (Although Miller's name is synonymous with some of the flawed prewar reporting, her career was varied, to say the least. Part of a Pulitzer Prize–winning team exploring the roots of terrorism in the wake of 9/11, she also spent months in a Virginia jail for refusing to reveal a source, left the *Times* in 2005, later contributed to Fox News and Newsmax, and became a fellow at the conservative Manhattan Institute.)

As Moyers pointed out in "Buying the War," the journalists in the Washington bureau of the Knight-Ridder papers were an admirable rarity; their reporting stood out for its dogged skepticism about the Bush administration's claims. Jonathan Landay and Warren Strobel got the story right. But because Knight-Ridder had no newspapers in New York or Washington, their reporting didn't resonate widely. It certainly didn't have anything close to the impact of a front-page article in the *Times*. Discussing it, Landay told CTV how lonely it was when he and Strobel were "questioning why no one else was reporting what we were reporting." Journalists, after all, are not supposed to be stenographers, just transmitting what an administration wants them to. Of course, eventually it became well known that these connections between Saddam and Al-Qaeda were a mirage, as was the existence of weapons of mass destruction. It was engineered by the war-hungry Bush administration and eagerly believed by a press that failed to do its basic job.

In a lengthy editor's note in 2004, the *Times* cast blame on itself for that pre-war coverage, saying in part:

> We have found a number of instances of coverage that was not as rigorous as it should have been. In some cases, information that was controversial then, and seems questionable now, was insufficiently qualified or allowed to stand unchallenged. Looking back, we wish we had been more aggressive in re-examining the claims as new evidence emerged—or failed to emerge.

It was quite a mea culpa, though it stopped short of an apology. The press's failure of skepticism took a toll on public trust. It was one of many factors—but an important one—in the way trust plummeted in the early years of the twenty-first century.

The numbers from Gallup, the opinion pollsters, tell the story vividly. In 2005, the level of public trust in the news media (those saying they trusted the media a great deal or a fair amount) dropped to 50 percent; it had been steadily falling from its height of 72 percent in 1976, in the post-Watergate era and, perhaps coincidentally, the year that *All the President's Men* came out. By 2007 (the year that Moyers's "Buying the War" aired on TV), public trust in the news media had dropped to 47 percent. It would continue to fall. Of course, the reasons are complicated; for one thing, trust in many other institutions was also on the wane. It's not possible to point to the misleading reporting in the Iraq War run-up and say definitively, "This is why." But it was certainly part of the problem, one that's been hard to recover from. Once public trust is betrayed, it's almost impossible to regain it.

Given all of this in the background, but far from forgotten, I was gratified by the reforms. My criticism of anonymous sources had been a years-long project—including my Anony-Watch gimmick on Twitter, in which I asked readers to keep track of the use of unnamed sources as they saw them and to tweet them out or point them out to me in an email. In March 2016, a couple of months after the San Bernardino debacle, when the changes were announced, I was nearly ready to wrap up my public editor stint. I allowed myself to think that, maybe, I had done some lasting good. Not only for *Times* readers, but for the health of the media ecosystem overall, which is so profoundly affected by the ever-influential *New York Times*.

Did the new policy stick or did the *Times* backslide? It wasn't encouraging to know that this wasn't the first time that the rules had been tightened, seemingly to no avail. As mentioned earlier, editors instituted stricter policies on the use of unnamed sources after the Iraq War lead-up. That had been more than a decade earlier, but based on what anyone could see, the crackdown had proved largely toothless. After the new reforms in early 2016, I continued to see reporting based on unnamed sources, which was no surprise—and not necessarily a bad thing. Such sourcing will always be necessary; it's a question of how widespread it is and how much rigorous skepticism is applied to what these sources are selling.

Since then, the *Times* endured a major reputation-damaging debacle, in which the main source for its acclaimed and award-winning podcast *Caliphate* was given a pseudonym and allowed to spin lies about his supposed radicalization by the Islamic State. The spellbinding podcast, which began in 2018, had made a superstar of its main reporter, Rukmini Callimachi, whose journalistic focus for years had been Islamic extremism. In 2020, the whole thing fell apart—the source's story was revealed to be largely a hoax—and the *Times* had to retract the core of the podcast's findings and return a Peabody Award. Callimachi was reassigned, but Baquet chose not to blame her publicly; he called it an institutional failing, not that of one reporter. Baquet was clear about what had happened internally, telling NPR's David Folkenflik: "We fell in love with the fact that we had gotten a member of ISIS who would describe his life in the caliphate and would describe his crimes. I think we were so in love with it that when we saw evidence that maybe he was a fabulist, when we saw evidence that he was making some of it up, we didn't listen hard enough."

This was a different kind of problem than the anonymous government reporting in the run-up to the Iraq War, but they had something in common: Proper skepticism was missing. Clearly this problem hadn't gone away. Nevertheless, even now, I allow myself to hope that the stricter rules I pushed for have prevented a journalistic disaster or two that would have cut further into public trust. One commenter on my 2016 column about the new anonymous-sources policy echoed the doubt I expressed about how thoroughly it would be carried out in the long run, writing: "Sadly, Sullivan's skepticism carries more weight than Baquet's proclamation. If the Judith Miller episode, and other serious failures due to anonymous sourcing from many years past, weren't enough to make the policy stick, I'm less than confident we'll be seeing it vigorously enforced a couple of years from now when this deep addiction's suppressed cravings rise up again. If this new resolve does last, however, it will be thanks to a combination of Ms. Sullivan's persistent efforts and the loud objections of readers over the years who have tried to save the credibility and effectiveness of the country's best paper, and will be this Public Editor's most important legacy." For a brief moment, I felt as if Sisyphus had managed to keep the boulder balanced—however precariously—at the top of the mountain.

8

Moving On

Well into my third year at the *Times,* with less than one year to go, Arthur Sulzberger asked me to come up to his office on the sixteenth floor. This was highly unusual, and I wondered whether there was something unpleasant to discuss. Was I being sued? Fired? Taken to the woodshed? But no, it was quite the opposite. The *Times* publisher was happy with my work and wanted to invite me to stay longer than the four-year term we had agreed upon in 2012. I wasn't completely surprised by this development. While the *Times* newsroom, its editors and reporters, may not have enjoyed my scrutiny and sometimes my criticism, the publisher—who was a step above and apart from the fray—actually liked it when I wrote tough columns, as long as he considered them fair. After all, he had agreed to start the position in order to hold the institution accountable to its own standards; in some ways, he felt the public editor role was his baby, if not his brainchild. Clearly, he thought I was doing what I'd been hired to do. Now he wanted me to stay for another term of perhaps two more years, for a total of six; we never got far enough in the conversation to iron out such details because I indicated fairly quickly that I didn't think it was a good idea. And I told him why I thought so: The whole notion of the public editor's role requires the person doing it to be something of an outsider. But after three years of arriving at 620 Eighth Avenue, seeing the same writers and editors every day—usually on a friendly and collegial basis— and eating in the same cafeteria, I was starting to lose the outsider's mentality. Or at least I feared I was. I tried to guard against it in my work. Even a four-year term would be longer than any of my four predecessors had stayed.

Another reason I thought it was getting to be time to go was that it was seductive being a part of this important news organization, even if my role was a peculiar one. Like few other institutions—Harvard comes to mind as comparable— the *Times* has a singular kind of cachet. People tend to be impressed when you say you work there. I had done my best to resist that, too. Still, four years would be more than enough; in fact, three might have been a wiser limit.

But the old how-to-make-a-living question soon arose: If not another term as public editor, then what? At this point, I was well into my fifties, and I knew that being an older woman isn't an ideal condition for job hunting, especially in the ever-more-digital media realm. The sooner I made a move, I thought, the better. So I started to put out some feelers. As soon as I did, I realized that the past three years as public editor had put me in a strong position for job hunting. I had been on the national stage, and people knew my name and generally liked my work. I started hearing about some jobs at regional news organizations, even a top editor's job at one of the largest newspapers in the country. That was a great opportunity for someone, no doubt, but it was not something that I found particularly appealing. After all, I had had the privilege, for more than twelve years, of running the single local newsroom that I loved, the one at *The Buffalo News,* where the staff seemed almost like my family. Maybe it was too sentimental, but it struck me as almost disloyal to go across the country to a similar job elsewhere.

And I hated the thought of leaving New York City, which, from the moment I moved there, felt like my spiritual home. I'd made new friends, developed a social life, even bought an apartment on the Upper West Side. How could I leave my book loft, my walks in Central Park, the sense of good fortune I had when I realized that I had become a New Yorker, sharing geography if not talent with so many of the writers—past and present—I admired? And, after all, there were certainly lots of opportunities in New York, the media home of the nation, if not the world.

I had started to think about going to *The Washington Post,* the legendary newspaper that had first piqued my interest in journalism through the Watergate reporting of Bob Woodward and Carl Bernstein. I knew and admired Marty Baron, who had been named the top editor there just a couple of years before; he arrived before Amazon founder Jeff Bezos bought the paper from the Graham family for $250 million. Baron was revered in the news business for the journalism he had led at the *Miami Herald* and *The Boston Globe* (later immortalized in the Oscar-winning film *Spotlight,* in which he was played by a taciturn but inspirational Liev Schreiber). He was well known at the *Times,* too, where he worked for several years. *Times* people tended to remember him as a particularly demanding editor, a stickler for quality and journalistic rigor, no matter who might be (unapologetically) inconvenienced or how late at night such an inconvenience might happen. Marty didn't seem to care whom he annoyed when he was dissatisfied with a piece of journalism. He had even been in touch with me in my role as public editor in early 2014 to complain about the *Times* not giving adequate credit to the *Post* for its reporting. I had quoted him in a public editor's blog post, sounding clearly dissatisfied with the lack of adequate response from *Times* editors. In his email to me, he detailed a number of instances that perturbed him, suggesting that getting in touch with me was something of a last resort: "In each instance, we informed key *Times* editors that our previous reporting, often many months in advance, went uncredited. We either never heard back or were dismissed." I took Baron's complaints to Phil Corbett, the standards editor, who gave me a detailed and thoughtful response, without quite saying the *Times* had been in the wrong. I later heard that this kind of public complaint from a colleague and a high-ranking peer didn't sit particularly well with Dean Baquet, who counted Baron as a close friend. It's hard to imagine too many other top editors making such a complaint to a *New York Times* ombudsman, but it was in character for Marty.

At the *Post*, Baron already had made his mark, and he did it quickly; in 2014, the paper shared journalism's highest honor, the Pulitzer Prize for Public Service, with *The Guardian* for their reporting on the Snowden revelations. It took guts to do that kind of consequential work.

I didn't consider Baron a friend, exactly, but we knew each other a bit, ever since the days when I was editor of *The*

Buffalo News. So I got in touch with Marty and asked him if he'd have lunch with me in Washington. I said I hoped to ask his advice about my next move after the *Times*. He readily agreed, and we met on a Saturday at a casual restaurant not far from where he lived. Over lunch, I told him about the various leads I had on jobs and revealed my ulterior motive for the lunch: I asked him if he'd consider creating a new position at the *Post*, that of media columnist, modeled after the widely admired column that David Carr had written before his sudden death. This would be a reported column, not pure opinion, and it would be, according to my pitch, housed on the news side of the *Post*, not in its editorial section with the prominent op-ed columnists like Eugene Robinson and E. J. Dionne. I made it clear that I no longer wanted to be an ombudsman or public editor, and I knew that that wasn't an option at the *Post*; the paper, like a growing number of other news organizations around the country, had eliminated that position a few years earlier, much to its readers' unhappiness. I also said I saw myself writing in the Style section, which is devoted to arts and culture, not in the business section, as Carr had done.

Baron seemed at least moderately intrigued by my idea, and asked me to write a proposal describing how I'd approach the job and what it might produce. I did so, and he said he liked it; for someone whose demeanor and style of communication is famously low-key, this seemed almost enthusiastic. It certainly was encouraging. But I soon found out there was going to be far more to the process than the executive editor merely waving his hand and making it happen. There were editors—lots of editors—to meet and be interviewed by:

Kevin Merida, Cameron Barr, Tracy Grant, Liz Seymour, and David Malitz. As things progressed, Baron even had me meet with *Post* publisher Fred Ryan, once the chief of staff to former president Ronald Reagan and the co-founder of Politico, the D.C.–based news organization. During our cordial chat, Fred mentioned that he trusted I wouldn't turn myself into the *Post*'s ombudswoman after I got in the door. I didn't; if I'd wanted to be a public editor, I would have stayed at the *Times*.

In other words, I ran the full obstacle course. Finally, though, I had a firm job offer from the *Post*. Editors there, including Baron, preferred that I move to Washington permanently, but I didn't want to make that commitment and they didn't force the issue. Instead, I agreed to live in Washington for the first year, and after that, I would be free to move back to New York City. I hedged my bets on that by arranging to rent out my New York apartment but not to sell it. I didn't see myself falling out of love with New York City any time soon.

I was apprehensive about telling Sulzberger about my decision to leave the *Times*, especially because my four-year term wouldn't be complete until the summer; I intended to start at the *Post* a few months before that. I made another visit to his thirteenth-floor office, and broke the news. (It reminded me of another elevator ride to another publisher's office four years earlier, when I told my longtime boss in Buffalo, Stan Lipsey, that I was headed to *The New York Times*.) Sulzberger was completely gracious, though I didn't know that right away, since his first words were, "That damn Marty Baron! I'll never forgive him for this." He was kidding, though, and seemed genuinely pleased for me—and for Marty, whom he knew well from his stint at the *Times*. This was in keeping with my whole experience with Sulzberger, whose treatment of me as public editor was close to ideal. He was supportive of my work, even when it was harshly critical of his paper, and he gave me complete independence, never trying to intrude or to suggest what I could or couldn't write about. I know he was less than happy about some very early columns in which I questioned the *Times*'s hiring of CEO Mark Thompson, who had been embroiled in the aftermath of a scandal at the BBC, where he had been director general. Just before Thompson started the *Times* CEO job, I wrote: "His integrity and decision-making are bound to affect The Times and its journalism—profoundly. It's worth considering now whether he is the right person for the job." One of the New York City tabloids referred to me, in a big headline, as the "Thompson Gunner." This business-side move was arguably none of my business as public editor, and caused plenty of raised eyebrows inside the newsroom. To his credit, Sulzberger never told me to knock it off, though he did mention, quite mildly, that he would have appreciated some notice about what I was planning.

As I prepared to leave in 2016, Sulzberger did make one request: Would I stay through the presidential election and into early 2017, when a new president would be inaugurated? He thought it important to have an experienced public editor at such a critical time. I told him that I would think about it. In the end, though, it seemed as though it would be awkward, and potentially a conflict of interest, to stay around for another nine months when I knew I would soon be going to work for one of the *Times*'s chief competitors. So I declined his offer with sincere thanks and made my plans to wrap up my public editor stint and move to Washington.

Later, though, especially given the extremely consequential news events near the close of the 2016 presidential campaign, I wondered if my decision had been a selfish one. Certainly, it was driven in part by my desire to move forward to the next challenge—and not to be unemployed for even a short time. Living in New York City was not something I wanted to do without a steady paycheck. But maybe I should have simply waited. I consoled myself with the knowledge that even if I had served every minute of my four-year term, I still would have been gone from the *Times* by October 2016, a particularly crucial moment in the presidential campaign news cycle. That was when FBI director James Comey decided to reopen the investigation into Hillary Clinton's email practices, and when the *Times* overplayed that story, giving over the entire top of its front page to it just days before the presidential election.

At any rate, I harbored no illusions about being irreplaceable. I knew there were plenty of journalists out there who could do the public editor job as well or better than I had. Still, it was gratifying, and humbling, to hear how much readers had appreciated my work.

My departure had brought what one of my *Times* assistants, Jonah Bromwich, called "a standing ovation." One reader, whose handle was Dotconnector, contributed a comment on my last column: "What readers want most from the *Times* is for it to be true to its oft-stated values, and no one has ever given voice to our concerns about that more effectively than Ms. Sullivan. There simply never has been a more devoted—or prolific—reader advocate anywhere." I smiled at Dotconnector's allusion to the Carly Simon song "Nobody Does It Better."

I was glad to see that the *Times* soon hired a well-qualified person, Liz Spayd—a former *Washington Post* managing editor who had become the editor and publisher of *Columbia Journalism Review*—to be its sixth public editor. Once she got started, I admired some of her columns and disagreed with others. Because I knew firsthand what a fraught relationship existed between the public editor and the *Times* staff, I wasn't shocked when, only thirteen months later, the *Times* announced that it was eliminating the public editor's position altogether. The *Times*'s leadership said that Twitter and other forms of social media were supplying plenty of outside criticism, making an internal voice to represent the readers no longer necessary. Instead, there would be a new "Reader Center" to serve as a clearinghouse for complaints and to respond to criticism.

I thought that ending the public editor position was a serious mistake. I knew from experience that the job wasn't just about criticizing the paper; it was also about investigating problems and complaints, and getting answers from the decision-makers to relay to the readers. Twitter can't do that. But by then, this wasn't really my problem. I was already immersed in my work at *The Washington Post*, where, given the state of national politics, there was no shortage of all-consuming drama. Still, I was sad about it and, to some extent, I took it personally. If I had really been effective, wouldn't the job have seemed too valuable to toss out? As public trust in the news media declined, I knew that the continuing loss of these reader representatives at news organizations all over the country was a step in the wrong direction.

Shortly before I left, and after my new job at the *Post* had been announced publicly, Arthur Sulzberger organized a farewell dinner for me in a private room at Barbetta, an elegant theater-district restaurant within walking distance of the *Times*. The attendees were many of the same *Times* editors whom I had been publicly criticizing for more than three years. Conversation didn't exactly flow, since subject matter was limited. They couldn't freely talk shop with me present, especially since I was about to become a media writer at one of their biggest competitors. With both the publisher and the public editor present, newsroom gossip was off-limits. And some of them, no doubt, were still stinging from things I had written about them or their staffs in the recent past, perhaps feeling I had treated them unfairly or embarrassed them publicly. I couldn't imagine they were sorry to see me wrap things up, though I think most of them liked me well enough on a strictly personal level. In short, it was a bit awkward. Sulzberger led a toast to me, and the editors' glasses were raised, whether reluctantly or enthusiastically. We all got through it somehow, but like so many of my *New York Times* experiences, the farewell dinner was more than a little uncomfortable. I looked forward to being a real part of a newsroom again, not a critical outsider.

Much more fun was a final dinner with the young assistants who had served me so well. Only one, Joseph Burgess, was missing, since he had moved to California. But the other four were there: Meghan Gourley, Jonah Bromwich, Joumana Khatib, and Evan Gershkovich. All, I knew, were headed for great things or already achieving them, and that faith has been borne out. (By 2022, Bromwich was a *Times* courts reporter, Khatib an editor in the *Times* book review section, Gourley at Microsoft in Seattle, Burgess a veteran of *Apple News,* and Gershkovich—remarkably—was reporting from Moscow for *The Wall Street Journal* as Russia invaded Ukraine.) In honor of my and Joumana's heritage, we went to Ilili, a Lebanese restaurant on Fifth Avenue in the Flatiron District, not far from where I had lived when I moved to New York in 2012. After dinner, I asked a bystander to photograph the five of us. The street scene in that image has a film-noir feeling that captured my melancholy mood. I loved these brilliant young people and I felt real regret to be leaving them, and New York City, behind.

9

The Joys of Style

Whatever my regrets were about leaving New York City, it was exciting to be working at *The Washington Post.* And it was especially thrilling to be in the Style section, which the legendary editor Ben Bradlee had invented decades before as a much edgier successor to the traditional and predictable "women's section" of the paper, devoted to society news and homemaking tips. I'd been reading and admiring Style for a long time, as far back as when I was in college at Georgetown and the *Post* was my local paper, along with the now-defunct *Washington Star,* whose gossip column, "The Ear," was always a delicious read.

I loved the section's clever, often daring, writers, who brought a literary sensibility—and fearlessness—to their work. Among them: Judith Martin (who later became "Miss Manners," the arch and addictively readable etiquette columnist), Henry Allen, Sally Quinn, Stephanie Mansfield, Martha Sherrill, and—perhaps the greatest of all—Marjorie Williams, a sparkling writer who specialized in subtly devastating profiles of politicians, and who died far too early of cancer.

I also loved the section's history of taking chances, turning phrases, and annoying the Washington establishment. That tension was memorably depicted in the 2017 Steven Spielberg movie *The Post*, about the fraught decision to publish the Pentagon Papers in the early 1970s after *The New York Times* was temporarily stopped from publishing by a restraining order from the Nixon administration. Gorgeously played by Meryl Streep, the newspaper's publisher, Katharine Graham, mildly scolds Bradlee about his brainchild of a new section after getting a complaint from none other than President Nixon himself, who, even well before Watergate, considered the *Post* his nemesis. "I'm not sure I entirely blame the president on this one, Ben," Streep (aka Graham) pointedly tells her editor. "Would you want Judith [Martin] to cover *your* daughter's wedding? . . . She compared Tricia Nixon to a vanilla ice-cream cone." Graham, a social doyenne as well as a powerful businesswoman, wondered whether this journalistic experiment of Bradlee's was really turning out to be such a smart idea: "Sometimes that stiletto party coverage can be a little mean," she rebuked him. Bradlee, played by Tom Hanks, found it necessary to push back and assert editorial independence. "Katharine," he responded, "keep your finger out of my eye." Ultimately, she did just that, and continued to give free rein and plentiful support to Bradlee and his journalists. The section and its writers endured, and its blend of arts criticism and scintillating feature writing set the standard for American newspapers.

One of the reasons the section meant so much to me was that, as a young editor at *The Buffalo News*, I had founded a new section myself—also a successor to the paper's women's section—that was modeled on Style. At the *News*, we called our new section Life & Arts. I was still on maternity leave with my first child when I started envisioning it, but I nevertheless made arrangements to spend a day visiting the *Post* to talk with the Style editors, including the top section editor, Mary Hadar. While visiting the newsroom, in the old building, which I had seen before only in *All the President's Men,* I had the chance to sit in on a front-page planning meeting with Bradlee at the helm. He was making wisecracks and looking just as dashing as I'd imagined, even though he was nearly seventy years old. He paid little attention to me, a fledgling editor from the provinces. It all made for a never-to-be-forgotten day, though not really a pleasant one. I had given birth to Alex just a few months earlier and was still breastfeeding him full-time. That meant we couldn't be separated for very long. So I brought him down to Washington, where a friend took care of him in her northern Virginia apartment while I spent the day at the *Post.* I remember trying to use a clear plastic breast pump in one of the restroom stalls between meetings with editors, but feeling so much stress in the unfamiliar surroundings that I finally gave up. This was awkward and physically uncomfortable, and I couldn't wait to leave the newspaper's office and get back to my friend's place. After our longest-ever separation, Alex was more than ready to see me, too. There would be many times over the years that my personal life and professional ambitions would conflict, or even collide, and this certainly was one of them.

Now, more than twenty-five years after that visit—Alex had graduated from law school—it was time to show that I belonged in Style as a full-time writer, not just as a random visitor from another paper. But *did* I belong? In my early weeks at the *Post,* I had my doubts. Sitting in story-brainstorming meetings with reporters and editors, I didn't feel like I had much to offer. These were journalists who had been at the *Post* for years, who had put the special Style spin on members of Congress, First Ladies, media types, lobbyists, and fixtures of Washington society, from JFK, Jr., to Barbara Bush. They knew all the gossip about who used to be married to whom, and why that famous Washington lawyer fell from grace. I was having some trouble adjusting. One would have thought that the much more difficult transition would have come four years earlier when I left Buffalo and my top editor's job for *The New York Times,* but that went swimmingly from the start. It wasn't easy, but everything just clicked. That wasn't happening in Washington, not at first.

I felt the pressure of high expectations; I was a marquee hire for the *Post*'s top editor, Marty Baron, which meant I had a lot to prove. He was watching, I knew, and so were all the people who had read my *Times* work over the past four years. My profile was high because of the very visible role of the *Times* public editor. When I was hired at the *Post,* one media website wrote about how the paper had hired me before my term was up, "in a pre-emptive move." Now that I was here, I had to perform. On my first day at the *Times,* I had written a successful blog post that set the tone for my entire stint there. But at the *Post,* I spent my first day in an hours-long meeting about a clunky, non-intuitive "content management system" annoyingly called Méthode. That training was the kind of thing I detested; it made my head hurt. I went home that first

night to my underfurnished studio apartment in a nonde-
script building near the National Mall and flopped face-first
onto my bed. What was I doing here, alone, starting a daunting new job well into my fifties? I was having serious doubts
about the choice I'd made, and I was feeling the pressure to
prove myself. Soon.

Even working in Style—that section I had admired for so long
and imagined myself a part of—had one drawback. If you
weren't a Washington insider and a regular reader of the print
paper, the name was confusing. It was hard, sometimes, to explain to readers who didn't know the history of Style why my
work, often sharply opinionated about politics and critical of
the media, appeared in a section that sounded like a fashion
magazine. Some of them wondered: Had I gone from being a
tough-minded public editor to writing froth about hemlines?
So I explained, over and over (as did my brilliant new colleagues
like Dan Zak, Monica Hesse, Paul Farhi, Ben Terris, and Ann
Hornaday), that the section was, and always had been, about
the arts, politics, media, and the broader culture. Our part of
the newsroom was abundantly populated with Pulitzer Prize
winners: the art critic Phil Kennicott, the dance critic Sarah
Kaufman, the fashion and social critic Robin Givhan. Political
cartoonist Tom Toles, who had been my colleague in Buffalo
before succeeding the *Post*'s legendary Herblock, was a regular
presence, and the book critic Carlos Lozada would stop by to
chat with the savvy Book World staff, like my podmates Steve
Levingston and Nora Krug.

Stimulating as all of this was, I felt out of place. All of a sudden, after being a top boss and then having an important role at the *Times,* I was a writer again—a "humble scribe," in the self-mocking parlance of the newsroom—although at a legendary publication that was having another moment in the zeitgeist. My new role meant that for the first time in more than twenty years, I was without an office of my own, without an assistant, and without a single person who reported to me. My desk was out in the newsroom, where I was elbow to elbow with other writers and editors, overhearing them on the phone, just as they could do with me if anyone wanted to bother. I wasn't completely comfortable with the sudden lack of privacy and hierarchical status, but I've always loved the ambiance of any newsroom, whether at the *Niagara Gazette* or the grand *New York Times:* the wised-up attitudes, the practical jokes, the shared history of past moments of glory or embarrassment, the sense of having a front-row seat for unfolding history. Sitting in on those brainstorming meetings with my new *Post* colleagues, I was daunted. I found one of the editors, Amy Argetsinger, downright intimidating because she seemed so breezily knowledgeable about Washington personalities and their history; she had been the author of the *Post*'s gossip column for a few years. (In time, she would become my direct editor, someone who sharpened my copy immensely.) But I didn't yet feel I had much to contribute, though they seemed happy to have me there. I kept hearing how much my new colleagues had admired my work at the *Times*—but that was then. For once in my life, I was mostly keeping my mouth shut.

———

For a journalist, this particular newsroom was an exalted place. The *Post* had moved into a glitzy new building just before my arrival. Gone was the cluttered 1970s-style newsroom that the movie version of *All the President's Men* had copied so faithfully, with its phones ringing and typewriters clattering. Instead, I saw acres of glass walls, quiet "huddle rooms," and, etched on the walls, inspiring quotations from people like Ben Bradlee, Katharine Graham, and, yes, the *Post*'s new owner, Jeff Bezos. The founder of Amazon and one of the richest people in the world, Bezos had bought the paper from the Graham family in 2013 and had ambitious plans for its resurgence and for national—even global—prominence and reach. I liked Bradlee's quote, in particular: "The truth, no matter how bad, is never as dangerous as a lie in the long run." The place was quiet—no loud typewriters or phones ringing off the hook—but still bursting with energy. It was palpable in the air, and for good reason. Unlike almost every other newspaper in the country in 2016, the *Post* was growing, not shrinking. It felt ambitious, urgent, forward-leaning. If the newspaper industry, in general, was in retreat because of failing finances, the *Post* was doing the opposite under its billionaire owner: charging determinedly ahead. Compared to the *Times* newsroom, which I had just left, the *Post*'s felt edgier, less self-satisfied, with a sense of seizing this moment by the throat and not letting go. It reminded me of the old advertising line from the car rental company Avis, always comparing itself to the market leader Hertz: "We're number two. We try harder."

Although it was hard for me to readjust to working in the trenches again, I was extremely lucky in one regard: the particular journalists who sat around me. The great book critic Ron Charles, whose reviews I had admired for years, was mere feet away, and he was as funny, kind, and charming as could be hoped. Across from me was Julia Carpenter, who—although she was thirty years my junior—turned out to be a kindred spirit; we shared a fervent admiration for writers like Joan Didion, Nora Ephron, and Laurie Colwin. Julia was a great help as I figured out how to function in this new environment. She was one of the digital-audience experts who had been strategically placed around the newsroom where they could have a subtle (or in my case, not so subtle) influence on how our work was presented to the public.

When I wrote my first media column for the *Post*—an argument that journalism, though troubled, was still a good field for young people to enter as a career—I was told to put my own proposed headline on it for an editor to consider and possibly change. Peering over the short wall between our desks, I asked Julia if she had any thoughts on a headline; she quickly took a read and then introduced me to the fine art of the one-two punch headline: two brief sentences or phrases meant to engage readers with a conversational tone and, by introducing an element of mystery, to lure them into reading an article. Not meant to be clickbait, but serving as an intriguing invitation. What she suggested ended up as the published headline: "Now, There's One More Reason to Be a Journalist—You Can Help Save Journalism." This first column of mine was not exactly a hard-hitting piece; it was far from the most provocative column I would write at the *Post* or what editors wanted from me, though they didn't complain. The entertaining and incisive media critic for Politico, Jack Shafer, took a good-natured swipe at it, tweeting that my first *Post* column was "marred by optimism." He needn't have been concerned about this rosy outlook enduring for long; my point of view—on journalism but also on national politics and the direction of American society in general—would get darker and darker as the months went by, particularly as 2016 presidential politics moved fully onto center stage.

It took me several weeks, which felt like centuries, to begin to hit my stride. I recognized that my first few columns, while not disastrous, had missed the mark. One longtime reader of mine, a fan of my *Times* writing, emailed to tell me of his disappointment: "You used to be funny. You're not funny anymore." He had a good point; I hadn't found my voice, something that had come so easily to me as public editor. And even though I had gone to college in Washington and had lived there briefly one other time, I wasn't feeling at home in the District. I adored New York. When I moved downstate in 2012 to become the *Times* public editor, I walked around feeling thrilled. New York City fed my soul. Washington had a lot going for it—arts and culture, a burgeoning restaurant scene, and hip neighborhoods—but somehow it didn't really suit me. The man I was madly in love with referred to it with the disparaging nickname of "SACT": sterile, anodyne company town. I missed the more eclectic, grittier, glamorous city I'd just moved away from. I missed my Upper West Side apartment with its book-lined loft and its proximity to Central Park. And I'd left a relationship behind—to be continued, or maybe not. As usual, I hadn't made my decisions with my personal life at the top of the agenda. All of this was wrenching. But the writing difficulties, at least, were short-lived.

I realized soon that I had underestimated—simply didn't *get*—how thoroughly *The Washington Post* was concerned with national politics. You could almost say that, for the *Post* and its readers, there really was no other topic. It was the subject on which the *Post* had long excelled, where it had the most expertise—consider Watergate and, more recently, the stunning revelations from the government whistleblower Edward Snowden. National politics was what readers everywhere came to the *Post* looking for. I quickly found out that writing about anything else simply wouldn't get the job done.

Eventually I got the drift. I saw an opportunity to hit hard when CNN made the terrible decision to hire Corey Lewandowski as one of their talking-head pundits. Lewandowski, the former Trump campaign manager, had repeatedly shown himself to be a bully and an opponent of the legitimate press. He had even been arrested by Florida police after a reporter covering Trump claimed he had roughed her up; Lewandowski denied it, but one of my colleagues had witnessed it firsthand. (The charges were eventually dropped after prosecutors said there was "probable cause" to move forward but insufficient evidence to get a conviction.)

Several weeks into the job, I finally wound up my fastball. My column began: "Even in the highly competitive, ratings-mad, hardball-playing world of cable television, there should be a bridge too far. In hiring Donald Trump's fired campaign manager Corey Lewandowski, CNN ran blithely across that bridge and plunged into a sea of muck." My journal for that day makes note, with some relief, of the positive reaction: that Marty Baron "actually emailed to call it spot-on" and that the NYU professor and press critic Jay Rosen had tweeted that *this* was what he was hoping for when I moved to the *Post.* The clear implication, a little tough to take in, was that the Lewandowski column was the first time that Jay, who had become a friend in New York, was seeing any evidence of those hopes coming to fruition.

From that point on, I recognized that I needed to write nimbly and with a harder, more critical edge. I needed to react quickly to the immediate news of the day as national politics intersected with the news media. A couple of weeks later, on July 5, 2016—shortly before the national political conventions—I took on Hillary Clinton with a column about how she had been stonewalling the press during her presidential campaign, especially since she had tried to defend her email practices in a news conference widely seen as a bust. I had written, of course, about the Clinton-email story line quite a bit at the *Times,* so this was familiar territory. This column began:

Remember Fort Dodge, Iowa? No? Well, that's understandable. It's been a long time—seven months—since an event in Fort Dodge that turned out to be historic: Hillary Clinton's last news conference. The candidate, famously opaque, answered a grand total of seven questions there on Dec. 4, 2015. Since then, although she's given individual interviews, she hasn't made herself available for general media questioning.

I concluded with a strong push for more transparency from Clinton, the woman whom just about everyone at that point—myself included—considered to be the president-in-waiting: "This can't go on. It's not just time for a full-length, no-holds-barred news conference. It's way past time."

As I made the rocky adjustment from public editor to media columnist, my direct editor, Richard Leiby, a newsroom character of the old-school variety, was a help. Well, mostly. A former Pakistan correspondent for the *Post*, Leiby is a word-smith with deep institutional knowledge of the *Post* and of Washington. A clever writer himself, he would sometimes suggest a pithy phrase for my column that ended up being quoted and admired; I tried not to take the credit even though it was under my byline. We got along well, but our metabolisms were radically different in a way that I sometimes found frustrating. I was revved up: I would file my column in the morning, reacting to some news event, and would want to get it published as soon as possible. Realizing how important timeliness was, I had a sense of urgency, maybe more than was strictly necessary. I knew that publishing early in the day would mean that more readers would likely see it, and I wanted to take advantage of that. Unlike a lot of newspapers, which were still adjusting to the decline of print, the *Post* was oriented almost entirely toward the online audience. The priority of engaging that audience was built right into the goals we were urged to meet in our work: to be nimble and innovative, always. It was *Post* policy that stories always published online first; the printed newspaper, while not exactly an afterthought, was definitely secondary.

Leiby, who had seen it all before, was much more relaxed

than I and would often interrupt our editing sessions to introduce off-the-subject questions or stories that made me dig my fingernails into my palms in frustration. "Did I ever tell you about the time I nearly led the Iraq army?" he would ask about once a month, while we were on deadline. He also made some gentle fun of my idealistic views about the role of the press in American society, teasing that I ought to have a special key on my computer to insert a few ready-made, often-repeated lines about how journalism exists to hold elected officials accountable to citizens and how the press is a bulwark of our democracy. The most important thing was that he was careful and wise, and on one occasion when a column of mine was unfairly challenged by a source, he was adamant—and successful—in defending it.

There were layers upon layers of editors. Leiby reported to one of my favorite people, David Malitz, a young former music critic with impeccable journalistic judgment. And Malitz, in turn, reported to the whip-smart Liz Seymour, who as the top editor of the features department had the same job I had held for a long time in Buffalo—except she supervised a much larger staff. All of this made me start to feel like I was in the right place.

I didn't have a great deal of contact with Marty Baron, but when I did, it could be memorable. One time I sent the famously rigorous editor a draft version of a column I was working on (he had suggested the topic) and asked if he had any thoughts. I got back an incredibly detailed note, with suggestions about sources to talk to, other angles to take, problems with what I'd written so far, and some copy editing, down to the errant semicolon. It was all on point and useful—Marty is a top-flight editor—but I didn't often go down the road of sending him a column in advance. Occasionally he would send me a complimentary email, or even recommend my column on his personal Twitter feed. When that happened, I felt as though I could take the rest of the week off. Luckily, I suppose, it didn't happen all that often.

The *Post*'s top editor had far bigger things to think about than his new media columnist. Under Bezos's ownership and Marty's leadership, the paper was thriving and finding some of the moxie, so abundant in the Watergate era, that had been far less apparent in recent years when it was laying off staff and trimming back its ambitions. In those years, revenue dwindled and circulation fell, though it was still making a profit. Now, with this billionaire owner and his high-flying goals for glory and success (both journalistically and business-wise), it was a new day altogether. Marty was an editor who had elevated the journalism at every place he'd worked, particularly when he'd led the newsrooms at the *Miami Herald* and *The Boston Globe,* picking up Pulitzer Prizes along the way like loaves of bread at the supermarket. He made his mark almost immediately at the *Post* by directing the reporting based on former NSA contractor Edward Snowden's top-secret revelations about how the government, in the wake of 9/11, was surveilling its own citizens. It was a major scoop (done in concert with the American arm of the British *Guardian*), one that was especially gratifying since *The New York Times,* the *Post*'s major competitor, often jokingly referred to in the newsroom as "Brand X," didn't have the Snowden story and had to play catch-up. In the competitive world of journalism, not much is sweeter than that.

Bezos wasn't the *Post*'s owner yet when Marty was hired by the Graham family member Katharine Weymouth in 2012. The Amazon founder bought the financially struggling paper the following year for only $250 million; the bargain price reflected just how besieged the newspaper industry had become. (For context, *The New York Times* had bought *The Boston Globe* in 1993 for $1.1 billion; those were still the days of fat profits for regional dailies. By 2013, when the *Times* sold the *Globe* to John Henry, owner of the Boston Red Sox, the price was only $70 million.) He had the good sense to recognize that he had precisely the right editor already in place. To his credit, Bezos didn't mess with success, and while some at the paper worried that such a dominant personality would intrude on editorial independence, he has—by all accounts I've ever heard—exerted his influence only on the business side of the operation, pushing the company to become ever more digital and to seek an ever-larger global audience.

Just a few months before I arrived, I watched from a distance as Bezos spoke to the staff at a celebration for the return of Jason Rezaian, the *Post* reporter who had been held captive for eighteen months in an Iranian prison; Baron had been a fierce and effective advocate for his release. Bezos had just flown Jason and his family home from Germany on his private jet, and everyone was in good spirits since there had been no guarantee that this happy reunion would ever take place. Some had thought Jason would never be released or might be killed.

The owner's words were memorable, and they established a tone for what he wanted the newsroom to be and do, a movement that was already well under way: "Even in the world of journalism, I think the *Post* is just a little more swashbuckling. There's a little more swagger. There's a tiny bit of *bad-assness* here at the *Post*." After some applause and laughs from the exuberant crowd, Bezos elaborated on those words with some context: "Without quality journalism, swashbuckling would just be dumb. Swashbuckling without professionalism leads to those epic-fail YouTube videos. It's the quality journalism at the heart of everything. And then when you add that swagger and that swashbuckling, that's making this place very, very special."

This was the *Washington Post* newsroom that I had just joined: a place that strived for both quality and swagger, with every chance of achieving that aim. I planned to do my part. And, as it turned out, I would get my chance, because the biggest story I had ever covered was coming at me like a speeding train.

10

"Venomous Serpent"

By the summer of 2016, the relationship between the American press and the American public had been deteriorating for many years. Trust had broken down; the general public's belief in journalism as a necessary good in society had plummeted since I fell under its spell as a teenager in the mid-1970s. I knew this, of course, after many years in local journalism and my stint at *The New York Times* fielding reader complaints.

Yet I was unprepared for the moment of no return that came on a hot July day in 2016, as a blazing sun beat down onto the streets of downtown Cleveland. I had a familiar anxious feeling as I walked around the grounds of the 2016 Republican National Convention, looking for a column idea. I had been working at *The Washington Post* as the media columnist for only a couple of months after my *Times* stint had concluded, and at this moment, as almost always in my life, I was experiencing the combined blessing and curse of my relentless internal drive to prove myself.

I was all too aware that I had started a new chapter of my life and career, and that the accolades I might have collected at the *Times* wouldn't last forever. Journalism is ephemeral, after all; even the best journalists of their day are quickly forgotten. (Just try asking a cross-section of today's journalism students about yesterday's greats, like the *Times* reporter David Halberstam, who distinguished himself with Vietnam War coverage in the 1960s, or Gene Roberts, who turned a regional paper, *The Philadelphia Inquirer,* into a Pulitzer Prize–winning machine in the 1970s and 1980s.) The reporter's bitter joke is that, even after the greatest scoop of all time, your editor will have only one thing to say: "What have you got for me today?"

I shouldn't have worried about finding material; the biggest story of my life was unfolding right there before my eyes. I just had to find my angle and a way to do justice to it. Wandering and observing in downtown Cleveland, I came upon a table of souvenirs, meant to appeal to the convention attendees who had arrived from all corners of the nation to cheer on the Republican Party's nomination of Donald Trump as their presidential candidate. I already had seen some nasty anti-Clinton signs and paraphernalia ("Hillary sucks but not like Monica" was one appalling meme.)

The gleeful misogyny was palpable. But nothing measured up to the horror I felt as I registered the meaning of a T-shirt featuring the image of a noose and these words: "Rope. Tree. Journalist. Some assembly required." The notion of death by lynching was meant to be funny, I guess, but the message was all too serious: We journalists were hated. Better off dead.

That ugly tone permeated the convention. Inside Cleveland's Quicken Loans Arena the next night, the crowd chanted, calling incessantly for the imprisonment of Hillary

Clinton—"Lock her up! Lock her up!"—as Donald Trump officially became the Republican nominee for president. Waves of disgust and anger came off the crowd, and Trump gloried in it. He hadn't invented any of this wretched emotion, of course, but he certainly emboldened, unleashed, and took advantage of it. As I started to write what I hoped were well-reasoned columns about Trump's relationship with the media, I continually felt that irrational anger like an unending blast of liquid poison from an industrial-strength hose.

On social media, and in phone messages and in emails I received, the sheer hatred from Trump supporters shocked and even frightened me. I had no choice but to send some of these incoming hate missives to the security department at *The Washington Post*. One, unsigned but from a "lifetime member of the NRA," informed me that people like me wouldn't be around much longer. Another, signed "A Real, True Patriot," was typical, and I think it's worth reproducing here at some length because it gives a sense of the tone, if not the volume, of what was coming at me.

> Though I would never read manure-laden pile of toilet paper like Washington Compost, I heard about your Nazi column about "reaching the masses" with your fake news to convince people that your leftist Nazi lies are truth. You are a well-trained serpent of the left, following communist orders as you were taught. "If you say and repeat a lie often enough, it will eventually be seen as truth"— Lenin . . .
>   Here's what you (slithering, fake-news/propaganda-generating slimy slug) should do: Go fornicate yourself

with a large, sharp knife, and then eat rat poison until your belly is stuffed.

For the first time in my life, I was being called the "*c*-word" on a regular basis. One reader suggested I have my breasts cut off. Again, the misogyny was overwhelming. I wasn't writing about gender issues, but somehow the mere notion that a woman was asserting strong opinions set off the haters in an inexplicable way. I tried to let it roll off my back and even found it amusing when a Trump supporter referred to me as a "venomous serpent," something that my friends told me to treat as a bizarre badge of honor. The *New York Times* reporter John Schwartz, one of the kindest and funniest people I got to know during my time as public editor, suggested I title my memoir *Memories of a Venomous Serpent*. The humor helped, and for a while I put the description in my Twitter bio with a tiny green snake image. All of this vitriol seemed to have little direct relationship to what I was writing—it mattered only that I was critical of Trump and his right-wing media allies. Of course, my experience was relatively minor compared to that of reporters, including those at the *Post,* who covered Trump on a daily basis. It may have been worst of all for broadcast journalists like NBC's Katy Tur, who covered the 2016 Trump campaign. Trump seemed obsessed with Tur, singling her out for public abuse at rallies or media appearances, calling her "Little Katy" and recommending she be fired for incompetence or dishonesty. Her network eventually had to provide her with a private security detail.

Trump's acceptance speech in Cleveland taunted his enemies in the mainstream media. "If you want to hear the corporate spin, the carefully crafted lies, and the media myths—the Democrats are holding their convention next week. Go there." And, as I wrote in one column from Cleveland, he cast himself as truth-teller-in-chief, all while lying incessantly: "I will tell you the plain facts that have been edited out of your nightly news and your morning newspaper." He lumped Hillary Clinton in with the rest of the establishment, as the very symbol of it: "Big business, elite media and major donors are lining up behind my opponent because they know she will keep our rigged system in place."

At that early point, I was still looking for common ground with the Trump crowd—the kind I had always been able to find with readers of all political stripes. Never during my years at *The Buffalo News* did I believe that I couldn't listen to or communicate with readers, no matter what their party affiliation. And I cultivated that. After I moved into a management position, I made sure that I had no political party affiliation; I was registered to vote as a "blank." So, at first, I sought this same open-minded connection with Trump's fans. At the Cleveland airport, I talked with one convention delegate, a concierge for a car dealership named Mary Sue McCarty, who wore a cowboy hat and pearls as she waited for her flight home to Dallas. She was friendly and personable, but certainly had her mind made up about the news media: "Journalists aren't doing their jobs. They are protecting a certain class." When I pointed out that it was *The New York Times* that broke the story about Hillary Clinton's email misdeeds, and that mainstream media organizations (including

The Washington Post) had aggressively investigated the financial practices of the Clinton Foundation, she shrugged off these facts: "If it's a Republican, it's investigated to death. If it's a Democrat, it's breezed over." McCarty could hardly have been more wrong. The media's endless emphasis on Clinton's email practices doomed her campaign perhaps more than any other factor—though there were many factors to choose from.

Stoking anti-press resentment wasn't new in 2016, of course. In fact, attacks on the press are as old as the United States itself, as the media scholars Michael Socolow and Jennifer Moore have documented. In 1775, New York newspaper publisher and British loyalist James Rivington was hanged in effigy—and nearly tarred and feathered by the Sons of Liberty. And after Ida B. Wells published reports in the 1890s about lynching, a white mob threatened her and destroyed her press. There were many more examples, some of them violent, throughout the eighteenth and nineteenth centuries. But in my four decades in journalism, I'd never seen anything like the fever pitch I first experienced in Cleveland and then for a long time afterward.

The longtime TV journalist Ted Koppel provided some perspective when I interviewed him immediately after the convention. In 1964, Koppel recalled, Barry Goldwater got the Republican presidential nomination in California's Cow Palace, where signs proclaimed, "Don't Trust the Liberal Media." And now he was seeing similar press-bashing words projected on huge screens at the Cleveland convention. In Koppel's words: "It's a fifty-two-year-old meme." But Trump had fomented a new level of intensity and anger. And Koppel observed that what made Trump different from those in the past who attacked the press "is that Trump has no shame—he'll say anything," no matter how demonstrably untrue.

Koppel was right. But, for a long time, members of the mainstream press didn't seem to want to use the word "lie" for Trump's constant barrage of falsehoods. It was a bridge they simply didn't want to cross. Top editors explained their reluctance. To lie, they said, means to intend to be untruthful. Since we journalists couldn't be inside a candidate's or a politician's head, how were we supposed to know if—by this definition—they were really lying? The logic eventually became strained, given that Trump blithely repeated the same rank falsehoods over and over. If that wasn't intentional, what was it?

Reporters and their editors couldn't seem to figure out how to cover Trump properly. They didn't even seem to want to. From the moment he descended the golden escalator at Manhattan's Trump Tower in June 2015 to announce his candidacy for president, the mainstream media was in his thrall. They couldn't stop writing about him, showing his image on TV, and even broadcasting the empty stage waiting for him to arrive and start a rally. Trump had described himself as "the ratings machine," and for once he wasn't exaggerating.

In my columns, I criticized the press's obsession with the former reality-TV star, but I was caught up in it, too. I knew that if I wrote a column about Trump, it would find a passionate audience: thousands of comments, thousands of retweets, hundreds of emails, requests to talk on TV and on the radio. And because I wrote about the news media, and Trump never stopped using the news media as a foil, there was so much to say. Some of it was about Trump's terrible treatment of the press and his willful lack of understanding of its role in democratic society. But I was also appalled by the mainstream press's frequently poor performance and the way it was enabling this utterly unsuitable candidate. Part of the problem was that Trump was such a magnet for audience attention. A month before the 2016 election, I pointed an accusatory finger at the head of a certain cable news network. My column began:

> Looking for someone specific to hold responsible for the improbable rise of Donald Trump? Although there are many options, you could do worse than to take a hard look at Jeff Zucker, president of CNN Worldwide. It was Zucker, after all, who as the new head of NBC Entertainment gave Trump his start in reality TV with "The Apprentice" and then milked the real estate developer's uncanny knack for success for all it was worth in ratings and profits.

It was worth plenty. Trump as reality-TV star had dramatically boosted NBC's ratings and Zucker's career. A decade later, during the Republican primary, Zucker's CNN led the way in giving Trump untold amounts of free airtime and reaped the benefits in soaring ratings and revenue. I concluded with a rhetorical question: "Twice, Zucker made Trump a winner. And twice, Trump made Zucker a winner. But what about the rest of us?"

Of course, CNN was far from alone in using Trump to boost ratings and advertising dollars. Les Moonves was talking about political advertising, goosed by Trump's primary campaign, when early in 2016, according to *The Hollywood Reporter*, he said the quiet part out loud: "It may not be good for America, but it's damn good for CBS. . . . The money's rolling in, and this is fun. It's a terrible thing to say. But, bring it on, Donald. Keep going." Donald Trump was more than happy to oblige.

The worst of the press's performance was the way it sought to normalize Trump's behavior. In every way, Trump was a deeply abnormal candidate, but the news media couldn't seem to communicate that effectively or even grasp the problem. Instead, his every unhinged, middle-of-the-night tweet was covered like legitimate news. Typical enough was the day he apparently woke up and decided to go after General Motors in a tweet ranting about a Mexican-made version of the Chevrolet Cruze being shipped across the border and sold tax-free. It came with his threat: "Make in U.S.A. or pay big border tax!" As GM's stock took a hit, the corporation responded that all the Cruze sedans sold in America were made in Ohio, but the episode made news, and gave Trump another attention boost to feed his insatiable appetite. On those rare occasions when he would read a speech with a veneer of seriousness or stick to a teleprompter script, TV pundits would solemnly forecast that a change was in the wind: Candidate Trump was becoming "presidential." Paradoxically, there was some excellent journalistic digging about Trump. *The Washington Post* produced a full-length book, *Trump Revealed*, in August 2016—months before the election—that detailed the candidate's business failures and described his shady character. But this kind of information didn't seem to make a dent.

The reason was the key to so much of the campaign coverage: *No one really thought Trump would win.*

And so, in the late afternoon of November 8, 2016, election day, I walked into the *Washington Post* newsroom with a column already started about Hillary Clinton's supposedly inevitable victory. A few hours later, I was scrambling, just like every reporter, editor, and commentator across the media. My colleagues and I watched the television screens placed all around the newsroom as one battleground state after another fell to Trump. The Rust Belt states that made up the supposed "blue wall" were tumbling into the Republican column.

Tossing away my useless column about Hillary Clinton, I wrote something quite different: that the media coverage of the 2016 race had been, as I put it, "an epic fail." I accused the mainstream press—college-educated, left-leaning, and coastal—of missing the story of what was going on in most of America. These reporters and editors couldn't believe that the nation they knew (or thought they knew) "could embrace someone who mocked a disabled man, bragged about sexually assaulting women, and spouted misogyny, racism and anti-Semitism." They employed a kind of magical thinking: A Trump presidency *shouldn't* happen, therefore it won't happen. And Trump, who delighted in calling journalists "scum"—or worse—alienated us so much that we couldn't see what was right in front of our eyes.

In that column, which I wrote on deadline with my hands shaking under the stress, I predicted that we in the media had some reckoning to do: "Although eating crow is never appealing, we'll be digesting feathers and beaks in the next weeks and months—and maybe years."

Part of that reckoning had to include acknowledging the way mainstream news organizations had covered the campaign, giving Trump untold amounts of free exposure and vastly overblowing the Clinton email story, making it into a scandal far beyond what it deserved, particularly when the *Times* splashed it all over the front page. And of course, other news organizations took their cues from the *Times*.

After I filed my column sometime before midnight on election day, I stood around with several of my *Post* colleagues, trying to process what had just happened. One editor, a young Black woman, was emotional. For her, the vast empowering of Trump's racism and misogyny that was about to occur when he took office as perhaps the most powerful man in the world amounted to an existential threat. It was hard to know just what this would mean, but she had a strong sense that it wouldn't be good for her, and tears welled in her eyes. Another colleague, an older white editor, tried to provide some perspective and give her a little comfort. He confidently predicted that we were all about to get what every journalist yearns for: "It's going to be a great story." They were both right, as it turned out, and their respective reactions speak volumes about how the coming years would affect Americans in widely varying ways, with media figures too often seeing politics as an entertaining game and a boon to business, but not always focused on the real-world effects, especially on vulnerable citizens.

I didn't get to stand around and talk for very long. Soon, the word filtered down from the boss, Marty Baron, that I should produce a second column before I left the newsroom that night. He wanted me to write my recommendations for how the traditional press should cover Trump in the weeks and months ahead. I hadn't given this a lot of thought previously, since I had been convinced, like most other people, that it would never come to pass. But there was no choice, and a new deadline loomed.

So I wrote a call to arms for American journalists. It started like this: "Journalists are going to have to be better—stronger, more courageous, stiffer-spined—than they've ever been." I filed it, not at all convinced that I'd written anything worthwhile on this momentous night, said goodnight to my editor, and headed out of the newsroom at about 3 A.M. Stunned and spent, I walked slowly through the deserted streets of downtown Washington. As I neared my apartment, only blocks away from the National Mall and the White House, I could see the U.S. Capitol to the east: lit from within, glowing an ethereal white in the darkness.

I slept for only three hours. The next day, I took a look at the thousands of comments on my first column from the night before, and I could see how disgusted the public, or at least the *Washington Post* readership, was with the news media's performance during the campaign. "Tragic stupidity," wrote one. In a reference to the high-speed train, the Acela, that runs between New York City and Washington, the reader criticized "the Acela elites who did not see this coming because no one they know would ever vote for a crude piece of work like Trump." Journalists are supposed to listen, not make assumptions. But in general, they had failed to do that enough or effectively. Other readers complained about the media's normalization of Trump and demonization of Clinton. The readers had it right.

A month after Trump was elected, campaign aides for both sides gathered at the Harvard Kennedy School for a traditional post-election debriefing. A Clinton aide, Robby Mook, tore into the media coverage. The press hadn't covered Clinton's policy positions seriously: "They were treating her as the likely winner and they were constantly trying to unearth secrets and reveal and expose. . . . And then you put on top of that Comey and you put on top of that WikiLeaks." He was alluding to something that had happened late in the campaign: Just after *The Washington Post* broke the story about Trump's bragging to an NBC *Access Hollywood* host about groping women (this briefly looked like a death blow for Trump's campaign), WikiLeaks started tweeting links to emails hacked from the personal account of Clinton aide John Podesta. It set off weeks of embarrassment for Clinton just before election day. "I love WikiLeaks!" Trump gloated at a Pennsylvania campaign rally.

Like sharks to chum, the press fed greedily on the hacked emails, not sufficiently providing context about where they might have come from—as it turned out, a Russian cyber-intrusion into the Democratic National Committee, meant to turn the election to Trump. Mook's analysis, though clearly partisan, was largely correct. Much of the campaign coverage had been not only tone-deaf but unfair. And that was separate from the right-wing media, led by Fox News, which long before election day had become Trump's best friend and gave a powerful boost to his quest.

In the weeks that followed, I wanted some deeper insight into what had happened and why, and what the role of the news media had been. So, in 2017, I made some decisions about travel that might have seemed crazy. I turned down invitations to speak in Moscow, Istanbul, and Paris (the whole world, it seemed, wanted to hear expert insights about what Trump meant for the United States and beyond), and instead traveled to domestic destinations, particularly in red states or those that had flipped red for Trump: Alabama, Arizona, Indiana, and Wisconsin. I resolved to listen more than talk.

Part of my determination to understand came from a hostile email I'd received from a *Washington Post* reader, Daniel Hastings, who wrote to me frequently, though he didn't like my work. He thought I was out of touch with real America. "No one outside your liberal bubble at the *Post* or the general DC area can take you seriously," he charged. And he used a favorite Trumpism to deliver an insult: "Ergo, fake news!" Hastings challenged me to go listen to people with a different viewpoint: "Take a visit to the heart of the country. Go to a diner or a flea market. Strike up some conversations. Come back and report without malice or deceit."

The month after the inauguration, I drove to Luzerne County in Pennsylvania, near Scranton and Wilkes-Barre. I had chosen the location carefully, since it was a place where voting registration was heavily Democratic, where voters had favored Barack Obama in 2008 and 2012, and which had flipped decisively to Trump. It wasn't an exaggeration to say that counties like Luzerne, all over the country, gave Trump the presidency. I wanted to understand people's news habits and their thinking about the new president. I found plenty of people to talk to—among them an army recruiter and a community-college student.

Toward evening, I stopped in at J. J. Banko's Seafood restaurant in West Nanticoke, where neon beer signs glowed and a classic song by The Band, "The Weight," was playing on the jukebox as bar patrons sang along. (The lyric "I pulled into Nazareth, was feelin' about half past dead" is a reference, appropriately enough, to a Pennsylvania town only seventy miles away, not to the biblical city.) I was the only woman in the place other than the bartender. After a few conversations I figured out that this was a heavily pro-Trump crowd, and people here were in particular agreement with his hard-line immigration stance and his America-first trade rhetoric. One man told me he read the local paper; several said they watched Fox News. But most memorable was a bearded and soft-spoken forty-year-old construction worker named Dave Kuniega, who described his news sources as local TV and "whatever pops up on my phone." He had followed the campaign but disliked both candidates, so he went against a life-long tradition that had been ingrained by his parents, who leaned Democratic—he stayed home on election day.

Trump inspired passion, however misguided. Clinton left many voters cold. I had no doubt that there was a big dose of sexism in the reaction of some, but it didn't change the facts. A lot of potential Democratic voters simply shrugged and abstained, rather than pull the lever for her. (Besides, everyone knew Trump could never win; the media had told them so.)

A few months later, I spent some time in New York State's most Republican congressional district, where I once again buttonholed local people, wanting to understand their news habits and their politics. I stopped at places like Paulette's Blue Collar Inn in Angola, a village near the shore of Lake Erie, and spent a day at the Erie County Fair in the Buffalo suburb of Hamburg. I didn't say this out loud, but I was looking for common ground—the sense that American citizens might have wildly different opinions but that we all understood that there was an agreed-upon basis of reality.

After talking to thirty-five people, I came away discouraged. I thought about Yeats's apocalyptic poem "The Second Coming," with its dire lines: "The best lack all conviction, while the worst / Are full of passionate intensity." Most people I talked to just didn't care much about the news, shrugged off the implications of a Trump presidency, and seemed uninterested in following the news closely or critically, except for those who hated the press. One of these was Jason Carr from Green Bay, Wisconsin, who was visiting his girlfriend in Western New York. He was wearing a "Born to Chill" T-shirt and sitting behind the wheel of his Ford F-150 pickup truck as he told me that the mainstream media is nothing but a "puppet show," one that is "filtered and censored" by big business. He spun out conspiracy theories: The United States government was responsible for the 9/11 attacks. And the 2012 massacre of small children in Newtown, Connecticut, never happened; it was staged, he was convinced.

As for the members of the traditional press—people like me, in other words—Carr scoffed, with real disgust in his voice: "I don't believe anything they say. They get paid to be wrong." I left conversations like this feeling almost sickened. I couldn't help but recognize that when it came to acknowledging basic truths, huge swaths of America were very far gone. As for my longtime belief that, as an independent-minded journalist, I could communicate with almost anyone and that we all shared a common basis of reality? Gone, too.

11

"Fake News," You Say?

O ne summer day several years after the 2016 election, I introduced myself to a store manager in rural New York State, someone I wanted to interview in this heavily Republican district dotted with pro-Trump signs. After I identified myself as a writer for *The Washington Post,* he responded with a grin and what he probably thought was a devilishly clever quip, "So, fake news, right?" I didn't find it funny, but I eked out a weak smile and got him to talk to me.

How had it happened that a reference to one of America's most prestigious news outlets would bring such a disparaging response? It was far from unusual in my experience. The distrust of the mainstream press seems to get worse every day. Like so many institutions—business, education, the police— the American news media is far less trusted than it used to be. In 2021, a global study by the Reuters Institute put Americans' trust in the media at a rock-bottom 29 percent, the lowest of any of the forty-six countries surveyed. What on earth happened to the United States as a beacon of free expression and democracy?

The country was splintering. You could no longer depend

on your neighbors functioning from the same set of facts as you were. There were many factors at play, but none more glaring than cable TV networks, especially Rupert Murdoch's hyperpartisan Fox News, which stoked its viewers' outrage, night after night. Local newspapers, although relatively well trusted in their communities, were going out of business or were bought by private-equity companies that cut their newsroom staffs to the bone. Opinions, not facts, were what the internet thrived on. Facebook alone was well on its way to being one of the chief enemies of democracy, as its algorithms favored the crazily false over the verifiably factual. People's news feeds were inundated with various posts from organizations and people passing along supposed "news" that was at best skewed and at worse just outright false. In the 2016 election, Facebook became a pawn in Russia's disinformation campaign in the United States; no problem, as long as profits kept soaring.

If I had to answer in two words the question of how we got here, they would come easily enough. Not "Donald Trump," though those might garner second place. The words would be "Fox News." From my observation, there's been no greater influence, and it is a terribly negative one, on America's ability to tell truth from lies, or even to care about the difference. The network is not the only culprit but, because of its wide influence and the number of Americans who see it as their primary, if not sole, news source, it's definitely in first place.

In 2019, the great investigative reporter Jane Mayer wrote a stunning eleven-thousand-word piece in *The New Yorker* called "The Making of the Fox News White House." Through deep reporting, Mayer explored the symbiotic closeness between Donald Trump and the conservative cable network, and strongly suggested that Fox had moved beyond mere partisanship to straight-out propaganda. It had become something close to state television. Her investigation was masterfully done, and it resonated widely. Everyone knew, of course, how much Trump had benefitted from the conservative network's support, but this piece nailed down how it had happened and what effect Fox was having on American society. Within days, Democratic National Committee chairman Tom Perez announced that Fox News would no longer be considered as one of the hosts of the upcoming Democratic primary debates. That decision set off right-wing howls of censorship, though it struck me as a reasonable business decision based on the latest information. Why play ball with your mortal enemy?

When I read Mayer's article, I was already well versed in Fox's methods. I had been the media columnist for *The Washington Post* for nearly three years, and Trump had been the president for almost all of this period. I had written many columns about the network. I was harshly critical of how it had misled its viewers about the death of Seth Rich, a twenty-seven-year-old staffer for the Democratic National Committee, who in the summer of 2016 was fatally shot in the back on a Washington street. Based on some dubious reporting from his own network, Fox's prime-time star Sean Hannity relentlessly spun the notion that this might well be an inside job by the DNC—retribution by Hillary Clinton's camp for Rich's supposed sharing of emails with WikiLeaks. In other words, Hannity came close to suggesting that Hillary or her people had ordered Seth Rich killed. This conspiracy-mongering was nonsense, and it was cruel to Rich's family, who first protested the coverage and then filed suit against the network. Meanwhile, the police had concluded Rich probably was the victim of a robbery gone sideways.

As a columnist, I had many other occasions to look askance at Fox's coverage and commentary. The network tried to present itself as "fair and balanced," but it often was nothing of the sort, and never intended to be. Fox was founded to fulfill its founders' vision to make oodles of profit by fostering conservative outrage, as addictively as possible.

Impressed by the scope and detail of Jane Mayer's reporting, I decided to take my writing a step further. I thought it was important to build on Mayer's work and raise awareness about how Fox News functioned, almost as an arm of the Trump administration. So I took a big swing in a column titled "It's Time—High Time—to Take Fox News's Destructive Role in America Seriously." Everyone ought to see Fox for what it is, I wrote. It shouldn't be treated as a normal news organization with mistakes, flaws, and commercial concerns that may get in the way of serving the public interest. It was something quite different: a shameless propaganda outfit, making billions each year even as it attacks core democratic values such as tolerance, truth, and fair elections. In addition to serving as a megaphone for the right, I noted, Fox rarely corrected or acknowledged its own errors, which is one hallmark of legitimate news organizations. (It did retract the Seth Rich reporting, but it took Hannity too long to stop his on-air disinformation campaign; the family's suit resulted in a settlement.)

I pointed out that Fox doesn't have the kind of ethics and standards department that most networks have, and it certainly doesn't make its news standards public, as many outlets do. However, since the network enjoys First Amendment protections for the most part, it can broadcast what it wants, no matter how many falsehoods are spread as a result. I noted that there were some legitimate news people at Fox, including Chris Wallace, Bret Baier, and Shepard Smith. (Smith later left the network; he told Christiane Amanpour that he couldn't countenance staying any longer because of all the lies disseminated on the Fox opinion shows. By late 2021, Wallace had left the network, too, headed for CNN's new streaming service.) I concluded with this line: "Despite the skills of a few journalists who should have long ago left the network in protest, Fox News has become an American plague." I was certainly pushing the limits of my role as a news-side columnist providing "perspective," as my column was labeled, but I heard no complaints from the *Post* brass. I was confident that Marty Baron—while he didn't always agree with me—supported my right to call things as I saw them.

The "Fox is an American plague" column went viral. It sped to the top of the most-read stories on the *Post* site that day and stayed there for a long time, attracting hundreds of thousands of readers. It found thousands more on social media. More than five thousand commenters added their thoughts on the *Post* site. One of them expressed the core problem well, and with considerable reserve: "It is a relief to see this brought out into the light of day, as I truly believe Fox 'News' to be a key force in undermining the fabric of our society, and a grave threat to our well-being. But in a nation that cherishes free speech, rightfully, the most effective response to such a scourge remains elusive." One of my editors, David Malitz, would later refer to this piece as my "Fox-is-the-actual-devil column."

If I'd had few friends at Fox before, I had none now. Even before this I knew that anything I wrote about the network would be picked apart by its aggressive public relations staff, searching for any mistake, no matter how inconsequential, that they could bring to my editors' attention. I had the sense that they were hoping to embarrass me by getting a correction appended to my column and that this kind of potential misery might give me pause before writing another such piece. I did write about Fox again and again, always trying to make my columns especially bulletproof.

All of this was uncomfortable. I was used to criticism, but the tone and level of vitriol had reached new highs, as I received nasty responses from right-wing readers who threatened and insulted me by email and voicemail. The security staff at the *Post* tried to determine if the writers were just nasty or whether they might actually be dangerous. Often these messages contained the worst kind of profanity and misogyny. Even the relatively mild missives began to disturb my peace of mind because they arrived in such volume. "It sickens me that people like you post lies and deception to the public," wrote one *Post* reader to me. "This article has no right to be printed to the public. You are what is wrong with this country. Shame on you!" Despite the downside, I didn't think I should stop. I knew all too well that Fox was doing harm, and, I figured, what was the point of having my bully pulpit as *Post* media columnist if I didn't try to bring such things to light?

Let's take a deeper look at the term "fake news." It was not really in use until late 2014 (when BuzzFeed's Craig Silverman started using it to describe published lies he was investigating), but it would come to define much of the problem. It had a double meaning: one literal and one more diabolical. Fake news could mean intentional lies dressed up to look like legitimate news stories that spread on social media like oil slicks. It was *that* kind of fake news that convinced millions of people, during the 2016 presidential campaign, that Pope Francis had endorsed Donald Trump's presidential bid or that Hillary Clinton was running a child sex ring out of a Washington, D.C., pizza joint. But then there were the cynical cries of "fake news" from politicians—with Trump leading the way—that really meant "this is a story I don't like." Trump famously told CBS News's Lesley Stahl that he disparaged the press purposefully: "I do it to discredit you all and demean you all, so when you write negative stories about me no one will believe you." Appallingly, it worked.

Another part of the problem was that traditional news organizations, "Big Journalism," didn't know how to handle this shifting ground. Should they call out the lies? Should they bend over backward to normalize political behavior that was blasting through every guardrail of democracy? Should they try to look even-handed and neutral at any cost, giving equal treatment to both sides of a political conflict, even if the two sides aren't equally valid? They didn't seem to know. And too often, they seemed to be in a defensive crouch, while right-wing commentators branded them as left-wing activists.

The metastasizing lies from Trump and his media allies became an inevitable theme of my columns. Every day brought fresh evidence that truth was roadkill for the new president and his surrogates. Some days were more vivid than others. One of these came in late 2016, a few weeks after the election, when I was a guest on Diane Rehm's syndicated radio show. I was in the studio at WAMU, the public radio station in Washington, sitting next to James Fallows, the respected *Atlantic* writer and former White House speechwriter, and Glenn Thrush, then at Politico. We all listened, wide-eyed, as Rehm interviewed a guest who had joined us remotely, Scottie Nell Hughes, a frequent media surrogate for Trump. The conversation spanned subjects from flag burning to Trump's evidence-free assertion that he, not Hillary Clinton, would have won the popular vote if millions of immigrants had not voted illegally. With remarkable directness, Hughes fended off Rehm's suggestions that there was a real problem with Trump's habitual lying.

"There's no such thing, unfortunately, anymore, [as] facts," she memorably declared at one point. Hughes, who had been a paid commentator for CNN during the campaign, kept defending that assertion and her own qualification as what she called a "classically studied journalist." None of us knew quite what that meant.

Truth, it was becoming clear, was of no particular concern to the new president. He ordered his press secretary, Sean

Spicer, to lie about the size of the inaugural crowd during the very first press conference of the new administration. It was a bad sign of things to come. "This was the largest audience to ever witness an inauguration—period—both in person and around the globe," Spicer, who had been a Republican National Committee communications director, told reporters just one day after Trump took the oath of office. *The Washington Post*'s Glenn Kessler gave this claim the worst grade, Four Pinocchios, in the "Fact Checker" column. He characterized the briefing as "an appalling performance by the new press secretary." Kessler also observed that Spicer managed to make a series of false and misleading claims in service of a relatively minor issue, rather than pushing back against the president's demands. "Part of a flack's job is to tell the boss when lies are necessary—and when they are not," he wrote.

But Trump's staff was not about to make such distinctions. Ari Fleischer, a former George W. Bush press secretary, characterized the Spicer performance from a position of experience, calling it "a statement you're told to make by the President. And you know the President is watching." MSNBC's Mika Brzezinski referred to it in more vivid terms as "Sean Spicer's first hostage video."

Then it got worse. Trump advisor Kellyanne Conway defended her colleague on *Meet the Press*. Spicer, she said, had been providing "alternative facts" to counter what the media had reported. It was a phrase that would live in infamy. I argued at the time that this should mean that "access journalism," taking official pronouncements at face value for the purpose of scoops, should be declared dead. Only real digging—investigative journalism, in other words—would provide value for the public now. "Spicer's statement should be seen for what it is: Remarks made over the casket at the funeral of access journalism," I wrote, but it would turn out to be nothing but wishful thinking. Access journalism was alive and well during the Trump administration. Reporters continued to seek and amplify whatever the White House had to say, often under the cover of anonymity. In time, letting Trump be Trump would prove not only unwise and undemocratic but actually deadly. A pandemic was on its way, and the president would be in full denial mode. Much of the mainstream media, by now fully in thrall to the president, would be along for the ride.

Of course, Fox News was far from the only media friend of the Trump administration, though it may have been the most influential. But there were others. Infowars, a home for dangerous conspiracy theories, even got a temporary credential to attend White House press briefings at one point. This was the same outfit where Alex Jones—the screaming radio host who founded it—had promulgated disgusting lies. He told his listeners things I'd heard when I talked to ordinary people about their beliefs and their media habits: that 9/11 might well have been planned and executed by the U.S. government, that he doubted that Barack Obama was an American citizen, and that the 2012 massacre of schoolchildren in Newtown, Connecticut, may have been a hoax performed by actors. Under pressure, Jones sometimes recanted: In 2019, during a deposition as part of a defamation suit brought by the Newtown victims' families, he blamed "a form of psychosis" for his belief that the massacre had been staged. But the falsehoods had already taken root for some members of the public.

Watching Fox News function as Trump's amplification system and best friend, I couldn't help but think back to my interest in Watergate, which had drawn me into journalism as a teenager. I had never heard of Roger Ailes back then, but he was already an influence on Richard Nixon, whose presidential run in 1960 had crashed after he compared poorly in televised debate with the more telegenic and charismatic John F. Kennedy. Ailes and Nixon met in 1967, and not long after, Nixon hired him as a consultant with an emphasis on television appearances. That partnership helped Nixon win the presidency for the first time in 1968.

Nixon, of course, would flame out after Watergate, but Ailes only grew more and more influential. He advised Ronald Reagan and George H. W. Bush, helping them get elected with ideas like the "orchestra pit" theory of political campaigning, quipping about the virtues of sensationalism during a run for office: "If you have two guys on a stage and one guy says, 'I have a solution to the Middle East problem,' and the other guy falls in the orchestra pit, who do you think is going to be on the evening news?" If you want to win the news cycle, in other words, create a diversion, a sensation, or an outrage.

By the time Donald Trump was elected, this would all be terribly familiar. Ailes took everything he had learned into his partnership with Rupert Murdoch, the Australian-born media mogul. As David Greenberg, the historian and author of *Republic of Spin: An Inside History of the American Presi-*

dency, wrote in a *New York Times* piece shortly after Ailes died, the media mogul's techniques and philosophy were forged in the Nixon era. Just as Ailes helped Nixon with his television image, the media mogul learned a few things from the thirty-seventh president. "The welter of crimes and abuses of power known as Watergate obviously remains [Nixon's] greatest legacy, as current events are again reminding us," Greenberg wrote. "But in second place would surely be his reshaping of the Republican Party to enshrine his brand of cultural populism as both doctrine and strategy." That couldn't have been done without Ailes and Murdoch, who founded Fox News together in 1996. The entwined roots run deep, and they could hardly be more influential. Like Nixon, Ailes, too, would resign in disgrace, though he lasted much longer. After Fox's parent company settled Gretchen Carlson's sexual harassment case against Ailes for $20 million, the co-founder left the network in 2016 and died the next year. Unfortunately, his legacy lives on.

The paradox of Trump's rise was how much of it he owed to the very media he loved to criticize—both the highly partisan right-wing outlets (he was seldom completely satisfied with their sycophancy) and the mainstream press. He should have sent them thank-you notes for the free advertising instead of blasting them with criticism. During the 2016 campaign CNN gave Trump endless "unearned media" by broadcasting his rallies and speeches live. Why? Because he reliably drew an audience and CNN's top boss, Jeff Zucker, knew that very well. But it wasn't only the cable networks or the extreme partisan sites like Breitbart who were obsessed with Trump. Even those of us at serious outlets like *The Washington Post* came to understand very well that putting Trump's name in a headline would attract readers. It was audience-enhancing magic at a time when news organizations were fighting hard for that big digital audience, tracked in real time on huge screens set up in newsrooms. To varying degrees, many in the overall media world were guilty of playing the "outrage for clicks" game. The more responsible insisted on staying within the realm of truth; others didn't seem to care about that.

One regrettable episode—no friend to mainstream media's reputation for truth-telling—came with the publication by BuzzFeed of the so-called Steele Dossier. It was, in essence, a collection of unprovable allegations dressed up as an intelligence report from a former British intelligence officer meant to damage Donald Trump.

To some on the left, and in left-leaning media, this was manna from heaven. Its most outrageous suggestions about Trump's behavior and connections, though unverifiable, were taken as evidence and gospel. Trump, of course, was all over it, using his Twitter account to brand the dossier "fake news" and to identify a political witch hunt. He wasn't entirely wrong. Its publication and the over-the-top nonsense that followed were a dark chapter for the mainstream press. I wrote about it in my *Post* column, criticizing BuzzFeed's decision to publish it. In an era when trust in the media was already in the gutter, this did absolutely nothing to help. But even that isn't the core point, I wrote, which is far simpler: It's never been acceptable to publish rumor and innuendo.

After several years, when most of the dossier was proven to be meritless, the whole episode became even more regrettable. It was used as a way to "prove" that all the talk about Russia's efforts to influence the 2016 election was also false. That the *Times* and the *Post* should give back their Pulitzer Prizes, won for digging into those connections. That Trump's endless talk about the "Russia hoax" perpetrated by the media was true. That was absurd. Anyone who bothered to read the report issued by special counsel Robert Mueller would know that Russia was guilty of illegal interference "in sweeping and systematic fashion," and that the Trump campaign was willing to receive the help. That the head of the Trump campaign, Paul Manafort, was so involved with Russian operatives that he represented a "grave counterintelligence threat" to the United States. That many of the connections were far beyond inappropriate.

But the overhyping of the dossier's "findings" meant that all of this truth was disparaged. And more broadly, cable news had given far too much attention to speculation about Trump's Russia connections and what the Mueller report might eventually say. A Harmony Labs study published in *Columbia Journalism Review* showed that from election day in 2016 to April 2019, all the cable networks (even Fox, to a lesser extent) became obsessed with the subject, with MSNBC giving 32 percent of its prime-time coverage to the Russia-Trump story. Anyone who watched Rachel Maddow's show might think that number was actually low. "Cable news channels systematically favored the Trump-Russia collusion scandal for nearly three years, clogging the information pipeline citizens depend on to ground their civic participation," the 2019 article noted.

Beyond depriving citizens of a wider spectrum of news, this overkill contributed to an environment in which nuance had no place. And so the cries of "fake news" merely gained traction. All of this was a failure of the reality-based press, and a consequential one.

Still, the damage that the right-wing media was doing was in a class by itself. By undermining reality and spreading misinformation, it was wreaking havoc on American politics and culture. Among Fox News's worst sins over the years: the "birtherism" conspiracy theory that spread the racist falsehood that Barack Obama was not born in the United States and therefore could not be a legitimate president. The hateful depiction of immigrants and refugees at America's southern border, especially the so-called caravan that was making its way through Mexico. The deadly lies downplaying the virus in the early weeks and months of the coronavirus pandemic. The disinformation about rampant fraud in the 2020 presidential election.

January 6, 2021, brought it all home. As I wrote the following day, it was clear to me that the mob that stormed and desecrated the Capitol could not have existed in a country that hadn't been radicalized by the "news" they consumed, day after day, and the spinning of that news by the likes of Hannity,

Tucker Carlson, and Laura Ingraham—the prime-time stars of Fox News.

I almost felt sorry for some of the rioters because they so clearly were the victims of a poisoned media system. I always paid particular attention to the Buffalo angle of any major news story. (Oddly, there almost always *was* such an angle; in Buffalo, we called it the Ann Odre Syndrome, after the local woman, a tourist at the Vatican, who was hit by a stray bullet in 1981 when Pope John Paul II was shot in St. Peter's Square.) So I noted with interest the comments of Jul Thompson, a right-wing activist who boarded one of the two buses traveling from Western New York to Washington for the rally, then gave an interview to *The Buffalo News* about being "absolutely justified" in urging on those who scaled a wall of the Capitol.

After all, Thompson claimed, there had been rampant fraud resulting in a stolen election. "We would like all the courts to see the evidence of massive fraud and election interference," she said. "If they saw the evidence they would have no choice but to rule for Trump." It didn't matter to her, or perhaps she didn't know, that these allegations had already been duly considered by the courts and by election officials, including Republicans, and had been thoroughly rejected. But if your news source was Trump's Twitter feed and Fox News, you might never come across these facts.

Sean Hannity certainly was doing his part on his prime-time Fox show to push the idea of rampant fraud. "I can factually tell you tonight," he informed his audience of millions shortly after the election, "it will be impossible to ever know the true, fair, accurate election results."

The constant misleading of the TV audience was a classic case of Trump projecting his own faults on his enemies. For years, even as he led the political leagues in lying, he charged the mainstream news media with misleading the public. "Fake news!" he cried whenever there was coverage he didn't like because it put him in a bad light.

"The speed with which the term became polarized and in fact a rhetorical weapon illustrates how efficient the conservative media machine has become," said the journalism scholar Nikki Usher when I interviewed her for a column in which I proposed retiring the term. I thought it was unwise to feed the beast of misinformation by adopting Trump's language. Clearly, there is such a thing as false news, meaning actual misinformation in the form of news stories. There are whole industries set up to do it. But the term "fake news" had become so tainted that using it did more harm than good.

It had crept—no, sped—into the lexicon of conservative politicians in a heartbeat. Examples abounded. "You can put all that under the category of fake news," charged Jim DeMint, the former senator and Tea Party member, when he wanted to disparage a TV interviewer's suggestions that Obamacare had merits as well as flaws. "Fake news," blasted the conspiracy theorist Alex Jones when he wanted to deny a news report that Trump's daughter Ivanka would occupy the East Wing offices traditionally reserved for the president's wife. When a right-wing website needed a putdown for ABC News's chief White House correspondent, Jonathan Karl, it called him a "fake-news propagandist." All of this had a clear purpose: shoot the messenger. The phrase quickly moved from the national to the local level, with small-town school board members crying "fake news" in order to delegitimize reporters from local TV stations or weekly newspapers trying to do their jobs.

Trump had a special gift for this kind of memorable language. It was easy to understand, easy to embrace, easy to remember. At the same time, Trump had nicknames for his least favorite news organizations, among them the "Failing *New York Times*" (even as the company's revenue and subscriptions soared to new heights) and the "Amazon *Washington Post*," an unsubtle reference to the paper's owner, Jeff Bezos, another nemesis. (Amazon, which Bezos founded and where he is executive chairman, doesn't own the *Post*.) Misleading, yes—lies, even—but these nicknames tended to stick.

As Trump's second impeachment trial got under way in February 2021, the issue of lies, "alternative facts," and truth came to the forefront immediately. "Democracy needs a ground to stand upon—and that ground is the truth," the lead House impeachment manager, Jamie Raskin, a Maryland Democrat, said in his opening statement, quoting his father, the political activist Marcus Raskin. Raskin, who led the prosecuting team trying to make the case that the forty-fifth president had incited the January 6 attack on the Capitol, urged that the Senate trial not be seen as about lawyers or political parties. No, the trial should be "a moment of truth for America."

Listening to Raskin, I had to wonder: Did truth matter

anymore? Would most Americans know it when they saw it, or would they turn away? How could anyone, I wondered, watch the opening presentation of that trial—particularly the stunning thirteen-minute video that assembled all the pieces of what had happened into a compelling and horrifying chronological narrative—and not acknowledge the importance of the truth? I wrote about the January 6 video footage, saying that it defied the thermodynamic law of the internet age—growing *more* compelling with time, not fading with repetition. How could it be denied? I got my answer: Some Republican senators who would be voting to convict or acquit literally looked away. Rand Paul was doodling on a pad of paper and Rick Scott was busying himself with paperwork, the *Post* reported. Tom Cotton and Marco Rubio, at various points, also turned away from what was on the screen: the truth that Congress had been attacked by a mob inflamed by the president of the United States.

All of this resonated throughout the impeachment trial that resulted in Trump's second acquittal, despite bipartisan support for his conviction; the 57–43 vote fell ten votes short of the two-thirds majority required by the Constitution. The questions remain, but I'm increasingly apprehensive about the answers. One thing I do feel certain of is what that rural store manager would have to say and exactly what phrase he would choose to say it.

The ugliness deepened. In late 2021, Fox News's chief propagandist, Tucker Carlson, put out what he called a documentary about January 6, called "Patriot Purge." It promoted a series of dangerous lies: That the insurrection had been brought about by left-wing agitators, not Trump supporters.

That it was orchestrated inside the government so that these Trump supporters could be persecuted by federal law enforcement. That the left is relentlessly targeting and persecuting "legacy Americans," which is coded language for white people. Shortly after it came out, two high-profile resignations from Fox News followed. Jonah Goldberg and Stephen Hayes, conservative commentators who had told the truth about Trump over the years, called "Patriot Purge" the final straw in their disillusionment. In a resignation post, they called it "a collection of incoherent conspiracy-mongering, riddled with factual inaccuracies, half-truths, deceptive imagery, and damning omissions." They said that it wasn't an isolated incident but "merely the most egregious example of a longstanding trend" which creates "an alternative history of January 6th, contradicted not just by common sense, not just by the testimony and on the record statements of many participants, but by the reporting of the news division of Fox News itself." Goldberg and Hayes removed themselves; they didn't want to be associated with this anymore. But the damage lives on and grows worse.

12

Objectivity Wars and the "Woke" Newsroom

Around the time Marty Baron retired as executive editor of *The Washington Post* in 2021, some famous words of his joined the many inspirational quotations displayed on the walls of the newsroom he had run for eight years, leading the paper to a slew of Pulitzer Prizes. The quote read: "We're not at war . . . we're at work." To those of us who had been in the *Post* newsroom during the Trump administration, this needed no explanation. From editorial clerks to the highest-ranking editors, we all understood what this meant. The words were a kind of shorthand for the *Post's* guiding principle during the tumultuous past five years as Donald Trump dominated the national conversation and headlines. To outsiders or non-journalists, though, they might have seemed cryptic.

The words came from an onstage interview with Baron during a media conference in California about a year into Trump's presidency. They were a response to Trump's portrayal of journalists as his enemy, and as scum and the lowest form of life. He had said he was in a "running war" with the media. His advisor Steve Bannon had been even more inflammatory in an interview with *The New York Times:* "The media here is the opposition party. They don't understand this country. They still do not understand why Donald Trump is the president of the United States." Bannon went even further: "The media should be embarrassed and humiliated and keep its mouth shut and just listen for a while." These were fighting words. And they were meant to be; Bannon knew exactly how maddening they would seem to members of a profession that sees itself as doing a crucial service for the public.

Baron firmly rejected the "opposition party" idea. The fuller form of what he said went like this: "The way I view it is, we're not at war with the administration, we're at work. We're doing our jobs." His paper's journalists were covering Trump not with animosity but with journalistic rigor and independence—the same way, in fact, that they would cover any administration, and the same way they would have covered Hillary Clinton had she been elected. Baron's words were widely quoted and largely agreed with by journalists, and they played well with the public. But for some critics, they came to stand for something else: a view of old-style objectivity that was out of date.

Some thought that the press was wrong not to fight back, wrong to stay with past practice and scrupulously avoid any suggestion of subjectivity. How could journalists keep doing things the tried-and-true way when the president himself was so deeply abnormal, so disrespectful of the basics of how a democracy is supposed to function—including the role of the press?

Was Marty Baron out of sync with the times? He was dubbed "stubbornly retro" by the conservative *National Journal,* and a headline in *The Guardian* picked up on a description of him by *Times* media columnist Ben Smith as the "ultimate old-school editor." He certainly wasn't old-school in dealing with the realities of publishing in the digital era. Baron was skilled in moving the paper forward. By the time he retired, the Post had three million digital subscribers, was solidly profitable, largely due to that growth, and was hiring steadily, as well as opening bureaus all over the world. If this was old-school behavior, it was the kind that many other news executives would like to emulate, just as they would love to claim even a fraction of the ten Pulitzer Prizes the *Post* won during Baron's tenure. Was it, though, an accurate judgment on his journalism ideas? A judgment on "we're not at war . . . we're at work"? To put it bluntly: Is traditional objectivity in need of an update?

In the American press, objectivity has its roots in an effort to counter the irresponsible "yellow journalism" prevalent at the turn of the twentieth century. Beginning around 1920, the renowned writer and reporter Walter Lippmann promoted the idea that reporting should be based on verification and the examination of evidence. This more scientific approach would produce credible journalism very different from the sensationalized crime reporting of the earlier era with its "scare" headlines meant to inflame the public. It was a vast improvement.

Baron, in a 2019 speech, made it clear that while he believes in "objective" journalism and has no problem with using that adjective, it's not about false equivalency. It's about approaching every subject with an open mind, rigorously reporting without bias, and then telling the truth, as gleaned, in a straightforward manner. Just as we expect a judge or a police officer to put their own feelings aside when doing their jobs, so, too, should a journalist. That's objectivity, in his view.

This is not "on-the-one-hand, on-the-other-hand journalism as it is often wrongly defined," Baron said. It involves thorough, meticulous, fair-minded research and the clear relating to the public of what was discovered.

The "war/work" expression, though, had spurred debate. It became such an iconic sentence that New York University professor Jay Rosen, one of the nation's preeminent press critics, wrote a long thread about it on Twitter and mentioned it in a lengthy piece in *The New York Review of Books*. He viewed it as "genius"—but genius with some troubling limits built into it. First, he gave the phrase due credit. "Hard to overstate how seductive 'just do your job' is," Rosen wrote. "It combines the myth of taciturn manliness (Gary Cooper) with the appeal of the humble public servant (I'm no hero, ma'am, just doin' my job)."

Rosen then introduced his concerns: "To say 'we're not at war; we're at work' does not speak to the enormity of the problem. Somehow the press has to figure out how to fight back." You don't fight back effectively, he suggested, by staying with past practice even when it is time-honored. Somehow, he wrote, journalists actually *do* have to go to war against a political style embodied by Trump "in which power gets to write its own story."

Is there such a thing as objectivity and is it worth striving for? The inside-journalism fight about objectivity—which deals with questions like these—has been raging for decades. I wrote about one aspect of it at the *Times* when I considered the notion of "false balance" or "false equivalency" and rejected the ingrained journalistic practice of giving equal weight to both sides of an argument.

This debate intensified in the Trump era. In the aftermath of the 2020 election, followed by Trump's second impeachment for inciting the deadly riot at the Capitol on January 6, 2021, it ramped up even more.

To some observers, and some journalists, it seemed like traditional news coverage wasn't getting the job done in an era when there was so much bad-faith behavior. Wasn't it time to call out political misbehavior more forcefully? Wasn't it time to call a lie a lie? To use "racist" instead of "racially tinged"? Didn't we owe it to the public to emphasize *true* fairness over performative neutrality?

Wherever I traveled in recent years, whether on assignment or not, I always made a point to talk to people about where they got their news and what they liked and didn't like about the news media. I'd often hear that they wanted less opinion—less spin, as they saw it. They would say something like: "Just give me the facts and let me make up my own mind." I heard over and over that journalists should keep their own point of view out of their work, and that people were disgusted by what they called the "bickering" they saw on cable news.

They seemed to be seeking what Rosen called "the view from nowhere." Rosen opposed this; if objectivity is defined as having no point of view, then objectivity is impossible and not even worth striving for. Instead, he approvingly echoed a line from the author David Weinberger: "Transparency is the new objectivity." Declare your biases up front, and let the reader or viewer understand where you are coming from.

Rosen went further still. The old ways were *hurting* the cause of truth seeking, which is what journalism is supposed to be about. Everybody has beliefs and prejudices, and everybody has a point of view, Rosen said, so why not be honest about it? And others made the point that the media often presented "objective" reality from an outdated point of view: one based on society's white, male hierarchy.

On his blog in 2021, Rosen made a detailed case for journalists to be transparent with their audiences or readership about what they believe. For context, he harkened back to the longtime CBS News anchorman Walter Cronkite, whose famous sign-off was "And that's the way it is." This omniscient neutrality is one way to make a bid for trust. But a different way, perhaps better suited to this moment, is to say, in essence, "You can trust my reporting because I put myself into it, and I'm telling you who I am." Rosen gave examples of how this might work. The well-respected investigative journalism outlet ProPublica tells readers that it practices a particular kind of journalism, the point of which is "to expose abuses of power and betrayals of the public trust by government, business, and other institutions." Rosen calls this a disclosure of intent, one that is nonpartisan, neither red nor blue. He wrote:

If the powerful cannot be held accountable, democracy becomes a joke. Abuses of the public trust are a special category of wrongs to be righted. In journalism the point of investigating is not just to document wrongdoing but to get results. That—in my paraphrase—is where *ProPublica* is coming from: "Using the moral force of investigative journalism to spur reform through the sustained spotlighting of wrongdoing," as they put it.

Another example of this transparency, from the right-leaning website The Dispatch, does have a political stance and is clear about it: "We don't apologize for our conservatism. Some of the best journalism is done when the author is honest with readers about where he or she is coming from, and some of the very worst journalism hides behind a pretense of objectivity and the stolen authority that pretense provides."

Can these points of view be reconciled? I don't think Marty Baron and Jay Rosen are as far apart as one might think. While not in perfect sync, they don't really represent two ends of a continuum, even though Baron says he's in favor of old-fashioned objectivity and Rosen rejects that. But both believe in truth, and in good journalism as a bulwark of democracy. It's a difference in approach and in language.

I agree with the notion that more transparency would actually give journalists more credibility than pretending to be completely without viewpoint or, worse, presenting both sides of a given political controversy as equal. Too often, the allegiance to objectivity ends up with an unintended consequence, a kind of defensive neutrality sometimes described as "both-sides" journalism, in which unequal claims are treated as if they were equally valid. That's no good. To put it in simple terms: If one side claims it's raining outside, and the other side claims the sun is shining, it's not journalists' job to quote both equally; it's their job to walk outside, look at the sky, and report the truth.

Two think-tank scholars, Norman Ornstein and Thomas Mann, expressed the problem with "both-sides-equal" journalism beautifully in a 2012 opinion piece for *The Washington Post*. The italics are mine: "We understand the values of mainstream journalists, including the effort to report both sides of a story. *But a balanced treatment of an unbalanced phenomenon distorts reality.* If the political dynamics of Washington are unlikely to change any time soon, at least we should change the way that reality is portrayed to the public."

That makes sense. But for those who want to pass off a lie as truth—like that the 2020 election was stolen from Donald Trump through a rigged voting system—any reform of the old way is something to be fought off. Why? Because they want equal time to spout the lie. And in recent years they successfully made the case that they should get it. They often did, on the Sunday TV talk shows, on cable news panels of pundits, and in the columns of America's most prestigious newspapers, where "conservative" writers—sometimes misrepresenting reality—were hired to show how very nonpartisan the papers were.

Some journalists, though, were able to cut through all of that nonsense. One was Maria Ressa, the brilliant and admirable journalist who was persecuted relentlessly for her reporting on the autocratic Duterte administration in her country, the Philippines, and who won the Nobel Peace Prize in 2021. After the award was announced, her views on the subject were revisited and celebrated. "In a battle for facts, in a battle for truth, journalism is activism," she had told National Public Radio the previous year.

As she said in her Nobel Prize acceptance speech, talking about the social media platforms, particularly Facebook:

These American companies controlling our global information ecosystem are biased against facts, biased against journalists. They are—by design—dividing us and radicalizing us.

Without facts, you can't have truth. Without truth, you can't have trust. Without trust, we have no shared reality, no democracy, and it becomes impossible to deal with our world's existential problems: climate, coronavirus, the battle for truth.

I explored these subjects—truth, trust, and objectivity—over and over again at the *Post*, and in the process I figured out my own stance. Although I had come of age at a time when "the view from nowhere" was practiced religiously, my position became more and more like Ressa's.

Journalism, practiced in a democratic crisis, *is* a form of activism. How else to deal with the way the 2020 election and the January 6 insurrection at the Capitol were being lied about by Trump and by the Republicans, with whom he still held so much influence? Washington journalists were often guilty of taking things down the middle in exactly the way Ornstein and Mann had warned. In one column, I put the problem this way: "Mainstream journalists want their work to be perceived as fair-minded and non-partisan. They want to defend themselves against charges of bias. So they equalize the unequal. This practice seems so ingrained as to be unresolvable."

There were journalists, including on TV, who were able to take a constructive approach. On CNN, Jake Tapper made a decision not to have any members of the so-called insurrection caucus on his Sunday show, *State of the Union*. Why, he reasoned, should they be given the opportunity to spread their lies in the name of fairness? Others who didn't have Tapper's decision-making leeway found themselves frustrated by the old ways.

I interviewed Andrew Taylor, a well-respected and long-time reporter for the Associated Press, which prides itself on its impartiality and usually delivers the news in a direct "just the facts" way, with no opinion creeping in. In the minds of many news professionals and news consumers, the AP is the quintessential objective news organization: It plays everything straight. Taylor did it that way for a long time and developed a reputation as one of the most knowledgeable reporters covering Congress. But he was growing disillusioned with the way, in his words, politics had started going off the rails, particularly with the ascendancy of the Tea Party movement—the conservative Republicans who made it their business to oppose everything President Obama tried to get done. Then came January 6.

Taylor was at his desk in the Daily Press Gallery within the Capitol building on that day, and when the Senate abruptly stopped its session as rioters entered the building, he was one of those who huddled inside the chamber while the violence and chaos raged. He was physically unhurt but profoundly affected on a mental and emotional level, telling me he found himself angry and agitated in the weeks that followed. In the spring of 2021, he quit the AP. Part of the reason, he told me, was that he had become concerned about the kind of reporting he and his colleagues had been doing for many years; he had come to believe that it was no longer capable of really transmitting the full truth given how much dishonesty and political posturing he observed among members of Congress. He was particularly critical of House minority leader Kevin McCarthy, the California Republican and Trump loyalist, referring to him as among the worst of those lawmakers whose "approach to their jobs is too often bad-faith bullshit."

After decades in the business (Taylor began his career clipping news articles for reporters at *Congressional Quarterly* in the 1980s), he was done with daily news reporting. Part of the reason was how deeply he was affected by the trauma of January 6. Part of it was disillusionment.

"The rules of objective journalism require you to present facts to tell a true story, but the objective-journalism version of events can often obscure the reality of what's really going on," he told me. He was blunt about the unfortunate results: "It sanitizes things." Maybe objective-style journalism used to be an adequate way to cover Washington politics and government, he said—but no longer. Taylor's sentiments, which resonated deeply with many who read my column about him, probably couldn't have been uttered while he was still working for a mainstream news organization. To question the notion of objectivity is to open yourself up to charges of bias, of slanting the news to reflect your own politics. And so mainstream news organizations practice it—or they say they do. They don't stop to question whether they are, in Taylor's words, obscuring reality by presenting everything in a neutral way that normalizes the abnormal.

After I wrote about Taylor, I heard from Marty Baron, who had recently retired. He told me that what Taylor was describing wasn't objectivity at all. I followed up with him in person and by email to understand his point of view more fully. He wrote:

> Journalists use the word "objectivity" in all sorts of contexts without objection. In fact, we embrace it. We want objective judges. We want objective juries. We want police officers to be objective in how they make arrests and detectives to be objective in how they evaluate evidence. We want doctors to be objective in their diagnoses. We want scientists to be objective in their research; for example, in developing new drugs and therapies.
>
> Somehow, the concept of "objectivity" is fine and appropriate—even mandatory—when we assess the performance of other professionals. Suddenly, the term is anathema among many journalists, especially a younger generation, when applied to ourselves. We must think very little of ourselves as a profession if we feel incapable of achieving the very standards we expect of others who

hear testimony, examine documents and conduct independent research.

Objectivity doesn't mean both-sidesism. It doesn't mean balance. It doesn't mean neutrality or false equivalence. It does mean open-mindedness. It does mean a willingness to listen and learn. It does mean being thorough in our research. It means not thinking we start with the answers but rather that we go seeking them. It represents an acknowledgment on our part that what we know, or think we know, pales in comparison to what we don't know (and even may not have thought to ask). We should recognize that we as journalists are often seeing the world through a keyhole. Objectivity represents an acknowledgment that much can be out of sight, that we need to work hard to see what might be missing from view and that what's out of sight could alter our understanding.

When we've done our work with requisite rigor and thoroughness (also known as solid, objective reporting) we should tell people what we've learned and what remains unknown—directly, straightforwardly, unflinchingly— just as people in lots of other professions do when they're doing their jobs correctly. That's what "objectivity" was intended to mean when the term was developed for journalism more than a century ago. That's what it really means today.

In keeping with that, I was impressed by some news organizations that decided to step outside the mainstream as they covered the aftermath of the 2020 election, particularly the relentless efforts by Trump and his allies to claim that he was robbed of a second term. *The Philadelphia Inquirer,* long one of the most respected regional newspapers in the country, made a choice that I found both sensible and courageous. The paper decided not to use the word "audit" when referring to a bad-faith effort by Pennsylvania Republicans to investigate the 2020 election in their state. Editors made that choice because, as they told their readers, there was no indication that the Republicans' effort "would follow the best practices or the common understanding of an audit among nonpartisan experts." What it *did* follow was months of demands from Donald Trump for an investigation that would give weight to his false claim that the election was rigged. But there was nothing to back that up. Biden won the state by more than eighty thousand votes. County and state audits had already affirmed that outcome, and no one had turned up any meaningful fraud. What the *Inquirer* was doing was, in fact, not slanting the news by refusing to use the Republicans' language, but remaining true to actual reality. "We think it is critical to speak plain truths about efforts to make it harder to vote and about efforts to sow doubts about the electoral process," the paper's senior politics editor, Dan Hirschhorn, told me. "There is clear, objective truth here."

Another Pennsylvania news organization, WITF—the all-news public radio station in Harrisburg—made a similar decision. They didn't want to let the lies about the election, or the attempts to overturn it, simply get shoved down the memory hole. They decided they would remind their listeners, and the readers of their website, about how their elected officials had behaved. So in late January 2021, just weeks after the Capitol insurrection, the station posted an explanatory article stating that they would be regularly reminding their audience that some state legislators had signed a letter urging Congress to vote against certifying the state's election results, and that some members of Congress had voted against certifying the state's election results for President Biden, even though there was no evidence to support the claims of election fraud. In essence, the station was merely reminding its audience that these politicians had knowingly spread misinformation—in other words, they had lied—in an effort to give Trump a second term. The language was forthright: "This was an unprecedented assault on the fabric of American democracy."

"We struggled, because this is not the normal thing," Scott Blanchard, one of the editors who helped make the decision, told me when I interviewed him for my column. "We had to ask ourselves, 'Does this mean we are not independent journalists?'" In other words, the objectivity question had reared its head. Wouldn't they be seen as biased? Was this really the neutral coverage that is so prized in mainstream journalism? After a lot of discussion, the editors and their reporters came to believe that accountability was more important than the supposedly neutral practices to which so many news organizations are wed.

But it was a little scary. "We're out on a ledge here," another WITF editor, Tim Lambert, recalled thinking. They hoped that other news organizations would follow their lead, but what happened was quite the contrary: "It's been radio silence." How long would WITF keep this up? At least through the 2022 midterm elections and possibly through 2024. "Elected officials are going to run on this," Blanchard said as he explained the reasoning. "This is an example of their judgment."

I wrote columns about all of these decisions—Andrew Taylor's to quit the AP, the *Inquirer*'s not to use the word "audit," and WITF's to keep up the reminders—because they were rare. Most journalists and most news organizations didn't stray beyond the traditional ways. In addition, there was so much pressure to appear objective that they didn't want to join the others out on that ledge. But in my view, that fealty to the status quo was part of the reason that by the fall of 2021 millions of Americans had bought the lie about the supposedly stolen election.

The Reuters Institute, a think tank and research center based in the United Kingdom and affiliated with Oxford University, decided to take a sweeping look at this question of objectivity. Their researchers interviewed news consumers in Great Britain, Germany, Brazil, and the United States about their news preferences, specifically on the issue of impartiality. Their findings, released in the fall of 2021, were clear. Impartiality was still a very high value, but most people believed they weren't getting it: "Defenders of impartiality point to a continuing need for unbiased news that fairly represents different viewpoints in a world where extreme opinions, bias and misinformation is more available than ever." This is no surprise, of course. But maybe the key word here is "fairly."

Is it representing news *fairly* to give climate change deniers and vaccine skeptics equal time with those who base their views and actions on science and reason? Do we really want to split things down the middle and call that public service? The report does call for one major change: News, analysis, and opinion should be labeled more clearly so that consumers can readily tell if what they are reading or watching is meant to be coming from a specific point of view or if it's intended to be completely impartial. That's especially important in digital contexts, where all of these forms of journalism come at us in a never-ending flow of content, usually arriving via social media. The way news and opinion come at the audience now is a far cry from the old days of print newspapers, when the front page was for straight news, staff-written opinion pieces appeared on the editorial page, and other points of view were on the opposite (or "op-ed") page. Smartphones and laptops make no such distinction, nor does Facebook's news feed or Twitter's timeline. It's just a firehose spouting "content." A summary of the study did give a nod or two to some of the related issues roiling newsrooms: "While showing greater empathy is increasingly expected by a younger generation and can be compatible with impartiality, this should not tip over into taking sides in news reporting."

When I was running the *Buffalo News* newsroom, I discouraged staff from displaying their political beliefs. Although I never wanted to strictly forbid staffers from, for example, taking part in a march for or against abortion rights—a hot subject during my tenure—I sometimes asked them not to do so. I don't remember any instance of anyone ultimately flouting my request, but certainly I do remember some emotionally charged conversations. Could I have ordered them not to march or have a political sign on their lawn? Possibly, but I was trying to walk a line in which I respected their civil liberties and still protected the paper's reputation for impartiality. If Twitter had been more dominant then, that would have made it much more challenging.

Neil Barsky, the former *Wall Street Journal* reporter who in 2014 founded The Marshall Project, a nonprofit news organization dedicated to criminal justice reform, had worthwhile ideas on this subject. When he stepped down as Marshall Project chairman in 2021, he wrote a moving memo to the staff. "The tension between advocacy and journalism never goes away, and from time to time, I have heard people say we are too partisan or not partisan enough. Here, I am unwavering: Despite my strong personal views about the rancid criminal justice system, I am certain that our work will have the greatest impact only if it is independent and nonpartisan," Barsky wrote. But he drew a distinction between being nonpartisan—that is, not affiliated with any political party—and the notion of objectivity, which seemed to him to demand having no point of view at all.

"I don't believe 'objectivity' is achievable or desirable, and I don't think reporters need to check their humanity at the door while doing their jobs," he wrote. "But I do believe in fairness. I believe in letting the facts we uncover determine our conclusion rather than the other way around." (This is Baron's view, too, though Barsky rejects the word "objectivity.") Barsky urged the staff never to lose their sense of outrage over a criminal justice system that is terribly unfair.

"Despite some favorable developments over the past several years," he wrote, "the American criminal justice system remains a national disgrace. In my opinion, our courts, jails, police forces and prisons (also housing, education, transportation systems and more) greatly favor rich over poor, White over Black or brown. In other countries, this situation might be called a caste system or apartheid. It is easy to become numb to brutality, dehumanization and racism." In the six years after its founding, Barsky's nonprofit newsroom took home two Pulitzer Prizes, quite an accomplishment for a journalistic start-up. Like ProPublica, it was clearly coming from a point of view. Its journalism flowed from the belief that the criminal justice system is deeply flawed and needs investigative journalism to shine a light in order to bring about reform.

Whenever I dared to suggest, in my columns or in media appearances, that a new way of thinking about objectivity might be necessary, I would be disingenuously attacked from the right. ("Margaret Sullivan wants even more leftist bias from leftist media" was the gist.) I knew that I was independent and nonpartisan. I hadn't belonged to a political party in several decades, which meant I couldn't vote in primary elections. When I heard friends or relatives talking about what "we" need to do—meaning people with progressive views—I would often correct them. I'm not on the team. I'm not part of that "we." Still, I was often branded by conservatives as a raging liberal or a tool of the Democratic

National Committee, working off DNC talking points. That bothered me, but I knew I couldn't let it change my writing or my convictions.

I learned to shrug it off. I knew that I was right when, in a 2021 column for the *Post,* I wrote that Big Journalism (broadcast TV networks, the dominant national newspapers, the major cable networks) needed to have an open-minded, non-defensive recognition of what had gone wrong in politics and news coverage. I wasn't terribly hopeful because, as I wrote, mainstream journalists want their work to be perceived as fair-minded and nonpartisan. They want to defend themselves against charges of bias. So they equalize the unequal in a practice that seems so ingrained as to be unresolvable. But I urged them to get over it. Democracy itself depended on it.

Reporters for magazines and other publications with a clear political perspective were already doing this. Ari Berman, the excellent voting-rights reporter for *Mother Jones,* even touted this philosophy in a fund-raising letter to subscribers and would-be subscribers: "Being funded by readers like you means that I can give a damn, too—and not just dispassionately chronicle the brazen attacks on the foundation of our democracy as normal run-of-the-mill news." He emphasized that the spate of legislation that would suppress voting or even help a second effort to overturn a legitimate election should never be depicted as "partisan bickering." Berman was talking about extreme gerrymandering to redraw election districts for political purposes, about voter suppression efforts, and about replacing honorable secretaries of state with partisan actors willing to abdicate their responsibilities for political purposes.

But the mainstream press? Big Journalism? Many of its practitioners seemed far more reluctant to look this pressing issue in the face. In the fall of 2021 I asked representatives of the three major broadcast networks why they had essentially ignored the so-called Eastman Memo, the shocking six-point legal blueprint that a Trump lawyer wrote in order to coach Vice President Mike Pence on how to overturn the 2020 presidential election. Some of them told me they didn't think it was much of a story. After all, as one put it, what Eastman was proposing in his memo never came to pass. So, apparently, there was nothing to worry about. Meanwhile, the networks devoted nearly endless airtime, that very week, to the compelling but far less important story of Gabby Petito, the twenty-two-year-old woman whose remains had been found in Wyoming after she had gone missing. There was something really wrong with the media's priorities. I thought the Eastman Memo should have been a flashing warning sign, proof that Donald Trump's allies were planning the end of fair elections in America. Maybe the major media organizations were ignoring it, in part, because they didn't want to be seen as partisan. Was this kind of news judgment the result of the media's endless homage to objectivity?

Perhaps it's better to reframe this discussion by emphasizing words like "fairness," "impartiality," and "independence." The Reuters study, which surveyed not just the United States but also Germany, the United Kingdom, and Brazil, found that respondents used the words "objectivity" and "impartiality" almost interchangeably, and they put a high value on both. One young participant in the United Kingdom put it this way: "The way I see impartiality is like being fair, that is how I would define impartiality. Even when a judge is listening to a case he is not swayed, he has just come there open-minded and then he is listening to both sides and then he makes a decision."

Certainly, the ideals of independent, impartial reporting are worth holding to, whether it's called objectivity or simply open-mindedness and fairness. I would, however, point out that what people *say* they want, in an interview or survey, is not always what they seek out.

In real life, they actually click on content that makes them feel a strong emotion—like outrage or anger—or that feeds a preexisting belief. This is much of the basis of hyperpartisan media on both the left and the right. Outrage sells. Tell me what I want to hear, whether it's strictly true or not. This is why Fox News's Tucker Carlson is so popular, and it's why some of the most popular Facebook pages are those from people like Ben Shapiro and Dan Bongino, right-wing commentators who stir strong emotions in order to keep their audience hooked. The overkill coverage of the infamous Steele Dossier's unverified claims about Trump is more evidence of the demand for outrage-inducing coverage, even when unconstrained by the facts. Many of Trump's enemies and critics desperately wanted to portray him as a Russian agent. They latched on to anything that suggested such a thing, hoping revelations along those lines would bring him down.

News consumers may *claim* they want neutral reporting and information: "Be objective. Just give me the facts."

But their behavior isn't always consistent with that. In their choices of what to watch, read, and listen to, Americans often live comfortably ensconced in echo chambers resounding with emotionally charged opinions just like their own. Navigating that is a major challenge—mostly an unmet one, so far—for the reality-based press in a democracy that's teetering on the brink.

Related to all of this is a question that has increasingly roiled newsrooms. Should journalists be allowed to cover things they have strong personal feelings about (for example, transgender rights) or personal experience with (such as having been a victim of racism or sexual assault)?

That issue came up at *The Washington Post* in a way that rocked the staff and created discussion far beyond our paper. In the summer of 2021, a *Post* reporter, Felicia Sonmez, sued her employer and five senior editors, as well as Baron, who had retired at the beginning of the year. Her suit claimed that these editors had discriminated against her by preventing her from covering stories about sexual assault because she was a victim of such assault herself. Sonmez, a national politics reporter, wanted $2 million in damages to her career, to her mental and emotional health, and to her rights to equal employment. Her detailed claims, including many specific quotations from the editors, were stunning. According to the suit, Cameron Barr, the *Post*'s managing editor, had told her she had "'taken a side on the issue'" by going public about her own experience. For days after the suit was filed, many of us at the *Post* could talk about little else, though most conversations were moved off Slack (the messaging system used within the *Post*) and onto encrypted messaging services like Signal.

I felt torn. I had a great deal of loyalty to Baron and some of the other editors, whose journalism I admired and who had treated me supportively, including when my work was under fire. As a former top editor myself, who had dealt with thorny staff complaints, I could imagine how awful it would be to be sued by an unhappy employee and to have my every intemperate remark or ill-considered email made public. And I knew that in personnel matters, there's often a lot that managers can't say.

If I had ever met Sonmez, it was only in passing. The *Post*'s newsroom is a big place, with more than one thousand staffers, and she and I worked on different floors and in different departments. We'd had a little bit of contact over the years by email or in direct messages on Twitter. Because I've always tried to be helpful to younger journalists, especially women, and because, like Felicia, I had been the object of frightening online threats and abuse, I felt supportive of her. I had written columns about how women journalists are targeted online and about the psychological toll that takes. I understood that at a personal level. So although I didn't know her well, I found myself sympathizing, at least in some ways.

It certainly seemed an extreme measure for the *Post* to have suspended her in early 2020 after she tweeted a link to an article shortly after NBA superstar Kobe Bryant died in a helicopter crash with his daughter and seven others. The tweeted article, without any commentary from Sonmez, detailed the sexual assault allegations against Bryant from years before. At that moment, Bryant was being not just mourned but almost canonized in the immediate post-crash coverage, and Sonmez was clearly making a point that there was another aspect to remember. She brought an extra awareness to this, she has said, because she experienced sexual assault herself. But Bryant's multitudes of fans were disgusted by her tweet, especially given the timing immediately after his shocking death.

When she was swamped online with rape and death threats because of that, a *Post* editor suggested Sonmez stay with a friend or get a hotel room but, according to the suit, didn't provide or offer security. Soon after, she was put on paid leave—suspended, in other words—apparently on the grounds that she had violated the *Post*'s social media policy. Many newsroom staffers were outraged. They got together to support her strongly and in writing. The journalists' union, the Guild, circulated a petition that garnered hundreds of signatures. The *Post* soon ended the suspension and Sonmez returned to work.

The lawsuit also detailed how, at various times over several years, she was barred from covering some stories related to sexual assault, including Christine Blasey Ford's sexual misconduct allegations against Supreme Court nominee Brett Kavanaugh. Overall, Sonmez described a hostile work environment that hurt her and hindered her career. Reading the suit—particularly the disparaging or insensitive comments she said that high-ranking editors had made to her—was a startling experience. Equally shocking was the idea that a reporter would be angry and miserable enough to sue the news organization where she still worked. It hit many other journalists, especially women, the same way.

Months later, the *Post* filed a motion to dismiss the case. It argued that the editorial decisions to keep her away from certain coverage areas were the result of Sonmez's "public advocacy." The editors' decisions weren't about gender discrimination or Sonmez's background but rather were made to prevent any perception of bias. The *Post*'s motion called the case "nothing more than the continuation of a campaign [by Sonmez] against the journalistic and editorial policies" of the *Post*. In March 2022, D.C. Superior Court judge Anthony Epstein dismissed the suit, saying that Sonmez had not demonstrated that the *Post* showed "discriminatory motive" in making her reporting assignments, and that the paper was merely trying to maintain a public image of unbiased news coverage. Sonmez, through her lawyer, responded that she strongly disagreed with the judge's reasoning and that she would appeal his ruling. The whole episode was a strong indication that the relationship between newsroom leadership and rank-and-file staff had changed radically and permanently.

For many reasons, top-down management was less accepted. Some of this was generational; younger journalists were used to sharing their opinions and to absorbing those of others, instantly available on social media. Then, too, there was a widespread and growing feeling that—given the political, racial, environmental, and economic upheaval in the nation and world—the stakes were so high that it was wrong *not* to speak out.

In many newsrooms, issues of racial diversity and equity were at the heart of staff discontent. At *The Philadelphia Inquirer*, top editor Stan Wischnowski resigned after an uproar over an article on vandalism that carried the headline "Buildings Matter, Too"—an insensitive play on "Black Lives Matter" that seemed, however inadvertently, to mock the movement for racial justice. The internal reaction to that headline was immediate. Some *Inquirer* staffers called off work "sick and tired," explaining in a written protest that they were "tired of shouldering the burden of dragging this 200-year-old institution kicking and screaming into a more equitable age. . . . we're tired of being told of the progress the company has made, and being served platitudes about 'diversity and inclusion' when we raise our concerns."

The top opinion editor at *The New York Times,* James Bennet, resigned after his section published an editorial by Senator Tom Cotton of Arkansas, "Send In the Troops," which suggested using the U.S. military to quell violent protests in American streets after the death of George Floyd in Minneapolis. Many Black journalists at the *Times* were among those who found the piece not only inflammatory but threatening to their safety. Previously, Bennet had been a leading candidate to succeed Dean Baquet as executive editor.

Both the Bennet and Wischnowski resignations struck me as extreme outcomes, although when Bennet admitted that he hadn't even read the Tom Cotton piece before it was published, I did doubt his management skills. He should have made clear to his lieutenants long before this incident that anything so sensitive needed to be brought to him for his explicit sign-off. As always with such departures, there was more to the story than merely the precipitating event. Bennet had made a major editing mistake in an editorial in 2017, bringing about a most unwelcome defamation suit by former Alaska governor and vice presidential candidate Sarah Palin; and the unhappiness on the *Inquirer*'s staff had been mounting for years.

The controversy I mentioned earlier over the prominent science writer Donald McNeil caused lingering rancor at the *Times*, too. The anger from many of his colleagues about his uttering the "*n*-word" during a discussion about language with high school students was worsened by the way top editors didn't take complaints about what had happened seriously at first. McNeil (by his own description a prickly personality) could have made things better by fully apologizing and owning his error, but he initially resisted doing so. The outcome seemed to me like overkill; surely, the discipline could have been handled with a less draconian result—although I certainly had no sympathy for any white person uttering the *n*-word, especially as a representative of the paper while on a trip with teenagers, as McNeil was.

On balance I thought the newsroom reforms and self-examination were necessary—even overdue. The *Los Angeles Times*, where particularly strong protests over diversity, equity, and inclusion came from staff, published a thorough exploration of the paper's deeply flawed history of covering communities of color. "Our reckoning with racism" included something rare in journalism—an apology to readers.

Perhaps surprisingly, given my age and long experience in newsroom management, I found myself in sympathy with those demanding radical change. Often, I was on the side of what was disparagingly and falsely called the "woke mob"— the younger, more diverse staffers who were supposedly running roughshod through Big Journalism's newsrooms. I had learned enough after my mistake covering the City Grill shootings in Buffalo to understand how poorly traditional journalism had served some segments of our community, and how insular and insensitive we could be. Traditional journalism, however revered in some circles, hadn't always served its readers very well.

For many years I had believed deeply in staff diversity and in fair pay and equal access to career promotion, and I had acted on that. I was proud to have appointed a Black woman, Lisa Wilson, as the top sports editor at *The Buffalo News*—a rarity in the nation—and to have hired Dawn Bracely as the first Black woman to join our editorial board. I had named Rod Watson the first Black editor in newsroom management.

At the *Times,* I respected the work of Nikole Hannah-Jones, liked her very much personally, and was disgusted to see the racist rancor coming at her after the publication of "The 1619 Project," the Sunday magazine's reframing of America's history to put more emphasis on the consequences of slavery and on the contributions to society of Black Americans. Her introductory essay won the 2020 Pulitzer Prize for commentary, and it kicked off an incredible furor among those who refused to make room for what it had to say. Despite the pushback (a tiny portion of which was grounded in objections by a few historians to some of the project's assertions), it accomplished its goals: Whether they accept it or not, many more people—in the United States and around the world—are aware of this neglected and ignored history than before Hannah-Jones began to write about it.

If "woke" meant being fully conscious of all of this, I

was for it. If "mob," a misnomer, meant that staff finally had enough strength in numbers to force long-delayed change at hidebound institutions, I could get behind that, too. What it all amounts to is this: Every norm of journalism is being challenged, and that is playing out in newsrooms every day. The industry itself is in turmoil, and the changes brought about by the pandemic—working remotely, for example—are adding to that. All these changes will shape the next decade and beyond of journalism, of its role in society, and its relationship to the public it serves.

13

How to Clean Up the Mess We're In

I n early 2021 I taught a media ethics course at Duke University, provocatively titled "The News as a Moral Battleground." The class could just as easily have been called "Ripped from the Headlines." The twenty or so undergraduates, many of them public policy majors rather than journalism students, had plenty of compelling current events to consider. At this fraught moment in American history, not just the news was a moral battleground; the whole country had become one. Deeply woven into the stark division among citizens was the public health reality that the coronavirus pandemic hadn't abated. Hundreds of thousands already had died in the United States, but the vaccines hadn't yet arrived for the general public. The nation was at war about mask mandates, school policies, unemployment rates, and business lockdowns. The contentious presidential election had just concluded, followed by Donald Trump's appalling antidemocratic charges that he couldn't possibly have lost, so therefore the election must have been fraudulent and rigged.

The January 6 insurrection and riot at the Capitol, surely one of the hinge events in all of U.S. history, was fresh in our minds as we started the semester. Then, in the first few weeks of the class, Trump's second impeachment, on charges of inciting that mayhem, got under way. In the midst of all this, Biden's inauguration took place, with huge swaths of the nation convinced he wasn't the real president, and the right-wing news media playing along. In January, *New York* magazine graphically expressed the unending havoc by featuring three oversized words on the cover: "Insurrection. Impeachment. Inauguration." A phrase in tiny red letters nodded to the bizarre timing: "3 Wednesdays in America."

Even though I had run a newsroom after 9/11, and during a long period when a local battle was raging over abortion rights, I couldn't remember a time as tumultuous as this one. It was made more so by the knowledge that so many Americans not only believed the blatant lies about the election, but were beginning to believe the equally blatant lies about the riot itself—that it was caused by left-wing fanatics or that it really wasn't that major an event.

Trust in the legitimate press was at nearly its lowest point ever. In 2021, Gallup measured public trust in the media at 36 percent overall; it was much higher among Democrats and somewhat higher among independent voters, but only 11 percent of Republicans trusted the mainstream press.

This was the background of my Duke class. Because many students weren't on campus due to the pandemic, it needed to be taught entirely on Zoom. We met only once a week, on Monday afternoons, so each class was scheduled to be three hours long. A pure lecture format would have been sleep-inducing and dreary. I knew we desperately needed discussion, stimulation, and variety.

With that in mind, I almost always brought in a guest speaker, and was lucky enough to be able to lure prominent journalists of various generations whom I'd gotten to know over the years. Among the guests—and perhaps most memorable for me—was a less familiar name, unless you happened to be a close follower of Pulitzer Prize winners and investigative reporting. This was Alan Miller who, as a reporter at the *Los Angeles Times,* mostly in the 1990s, had done important investigative reporting, including revelations about illegal political contributions to the Democratic National Committee to support Bill Clinton's reelection. Later, with his reporting partner Kevin Sack, he investigated the dangers of a variety of Marine Corps jet that had been linked to the deaths of forty-five pilots. (Chillingly, that aircraft was so dangerous that it bore a nickname: "The Widow Maker.") Miller and Sack won the Investigative Reporters and Editors Medal and the 2003 Pulitzer Prize for National Reporting. By the time Alan Miller came to my class, he hadn't been a newspaper reporter for quite a while, despite his remarkable skills. His career took a radical turn in the mid-2000s after a visit to the school where his daughter was in the sixth grade. He spoke to the students about the crucial role of good journalism and the importance of learning to become well-informed citizens, and afterward received 175 thank-you notes. The enthusiastic response was part of what propelled him to leave the newsroom where he had worked for two decades and do something radically different. He founded the News Literacy Project, a nonprofit organization whose mission was to help students tell lies from truth, fiction from fact, all within a news environment that was rapidly deteriorating. Local newspapers were dying; hyperpartisan media was substituting outrage for truth; mainstream media was hungry for audience share to boost profits.

My media ethics students were always extraordinarily polite and respectful, but one student asked Miller a challenging question that might have seemed a little rude. Is what you're doing really *effective*? she wanted to know. Can your organization really make a difference, given all the misinformation and mistrust, amid all the lies, and all the politicized nonsense that tries to present itself as news? Miller clearly had thought a great deal about this, and he answered directly. What he and his team were doing, he had once acknowledged to interviewer Ted Koppel, "was like trying to empty the ocean with a teaspoon." Even so, Miller felt that there was no other choice but to try; the work is vital if American democracy is going to survive. The class and I found it hard to disagree.

I was moved by his appearance in my class. His sentiments corresponded closely with my own observations, but, as a columnist for *The Washington Post,* I was still seeing the ugly damage to democracy from the inside. Although my job was to observe and persuade, I knew that I was no longer able to change readers' viewpoints; with very few exceptions, their minds were made up.

I couldn't help but feel we were in real trouble, and I have serious doubts about whether America's news media will be up to the task and whether the level of most Americans' news literacy—the ability to tell lies from truth in the media—is high enough to support our system of government by the people. How do you battle against the social media algorithms that incentivize lying and outrage for the sake of profit? How do you introduce factuality and reason, not to mention civility, into disagreements that are getting more tribal all the time? In short, what can we do about it?

While I am worried and discouraged, I believe we can improve the situation by pressing ahead on four fronts, which to some extent are interrelated. First, the reality-based press has to reorient itself, framing its core purpose as serving democracy, not chasing clicks or fomenting outrage, not building egos or winning prizes, not worshipping corporate profits. Top editors need to take this goal seriously and communicate it to their staffs at every turn. I'll return to this.

Second, those who care about truth must do everything in their power to minimize the harm caused by those media outlets and platforms that traffic in lies and conspiracy theories. Accountability is paramount. Responsible lawsuits, like those of Dominion Voting Systems against right-wing news organizations who allowed or encouraged their staffs to broadcast lies about election fraud, will be a necessary part of this. Advertising boycotts can help. So will efforts to reduce the revenue of news organizations that spread misinformation—Fox News, in particular—by limiting the amount of money they make from lucrative cable transmission fees. (There's a movement called "UnFox My Cable Box," which urges consumers to demand that their cable providers change the way they, in essence, subsidize Fox News.) Part of these efforts involves meaningful regulation to counter the excesses of the social media platforms—particularly Facebook, which is such a behemoth. One way to do this, as many reformers have suggested, is to cautiously amend Section 230 of the Communications Decency Act of 1996, which protects social media platforms and other tech companies from legal liability when they post things that are harmful or dangerous. Reforming it could have potentially serious repercussions for free speech; it's a tricky balance.

A high-profile commission at the Aspen Institute took six months to study the problem of what they called "information disorder." In late 2021 they came out with a report that included fifteen recommendations. These included urging elected officials to take this problem seriously and dedicate resources to it, protecting local news sources, and increasing newsroom diversity in order to build public trust. It called for more transparency from large technology companies and for changing laws that shield digital platforms, like Facebook, from being held legally responsible for the content they magnify and amplify via their algorithms. As noted, all of this has to be carefully balanced with preserving free speech, but First Amendment concerns shouldn't be used as an all-powerful shield against regulation. The commission's study and its proposed solutions are worthwhile reading for anyone who is concerned about these problems, as we all should be; however, whether their recommendations have much chance of being widely adopted is another matter altogether. Reform, regulation, and leadership at the highest level are necessary, though hardly sufficient on their own, to deal with the scope of the disinformation and mistrust problem.

Third, in my view, we need a widespread effort to educate the public—not just schoolchildren but adults, too—about news literacy and about the deadly harm of not knowing the difference between truth and lies. The News Literacy Project, which has expanded to include adults, is a model; there are others springing up, and such efforts need to spread far and wide. It's important, too, for news consumers, also known as American citizens, to take responsibility for their own news literacy. I'm not terribly hopeful about this happening on its own, given the trends. I'm worried, too, about what it would mean to legislate it. Trying to get news literacy taught in public schools, given the turmoil over curriculum in recent years, could have unexpected negative consequences. I still think it's worth pursuing. I might even put Alan Miller in charge of it if I had the power.

And fourth—possibly the most important—we need to strengthen and shore up legitimate *local* news organizations, including, but not limited to, local newspapers. Study after study has shown that local news is relatively well trusted among a populace that increasingly disdains the national mainstream media. When local news fades, bad things happen in communities: polarization increases, civic engagement goes down, municipal costs go up. People retreat even further into political tribalism, not even able to talk to their neighbors about important concerns. How do we do this strengthening? This, too, has to happen on several fronts. Regular citizens should subscribe to or donate to news organizations in their communities; philanthropists and other powerful people should recognize how much is lost when these organizations fade away and do everything in their spheres of influence to help. That includes opening their own wallets and putting pressure on elected officials to pass legislation to provide relief.

I've been amazed and heartened by the good journalism I see done at the local level, even on staffs that have been so severely cut. I see that crucially important work at my former paper, *The Buffalo News*. I see it at papers like the *Times Union* in Albany, which did some of the most important investigations of sexual misconduct charges against former governor Andrew Cuomo. The challenges are unending, though. More than two thousand American newspapers went out of business between 2004 and 2020, and the trend hasn't stopped. Digital start-ups, including nonprofit newsrooms, increasingly— and admirably—are picking up some of the slack, but it's not nearly enough.

Again, this is personal. In late 2021, I was sickened when the dreaded news came that the chain that owned *The Buffalo News,* Lee Enterprises, had received an aggressive offer for its papers from the worst of the private-equity-based chains, Alden Global Capital. It was distressing enough that Warren Buffett, after decades of ownership, had recently sold the paper to Lee, itself a large chain, but I at least had some hope that, under Lee, the quality and staffing level would endure. There had even been some positive signs about the paper's profitability and digital-subscriber growth. I followed the *News*'s journalism closely, often admiringly, maintained ties to reporters and editors there, and, of course, was a subscriber. I took a seven-day print subscription in the summer months when I lived at a cottage on Lake Erie within the paper's circulation area. Everyone knew, though, that ownership by Alden would be tantamount to a death blow. That company is infamous for cutting newsroom staffs to the bone, chasing the highest possible profits, without regard for sustaining journalistic quality. It had happened in Denver, San Jose, and so many other places where robust newsrooms became ghosts of their former selves. Under Alden ownership, *The Buffalo*

News probably would survive in some form, but much of its quality journalism would not. For many of my friends and former colleagues this was personally frightening. It also was a symptom of a larger disaster, a deeply troubling trend visible everywhere in America, from which the dire effects on society were obvious.

The efforts to shore up existing local news outlets and to develop new ones deserve every bit of support that can be mustered. These include congressional action on tax credits to benefit local news organizations, philanthropy dedicated to digital start-ups, and ways to make it easier for legacy news organizations to turn themselves into nonprofit entities. There is, however, a strong sense of swimming against an inexorable tide, and almost a feeling of despair. Timothy Snyder, the celebrated Yale historian who wrote *On Tyranny,* has gone so far as to describe the decline of local news in the United States as the "essential problem of our republic."

Will these efforts get the job of saving democracy and curing misinformation done, if they all are somehow made to happen? Taken separately, no. If they are done simultaneously and with serious intentionality, though, America's democracy can survive. But it will take a mindset change, and for those in mainstream journalism it requires getting out of the inside-the-Beltway mentality.

Let's return to how the mainstream media can and must do better. First, they have to fully wake up to the challenge and to their role in it. If this is happening, it's happening slowly.

Too many journalists seem almost naive about the threats to democracy that they are enabling. Reviewing *Betrayal*, by ABC News chief Washington correspondent Jonathan Karl, about Trump's misdeeds before and after January 6, Jennifer Szalai of *The New York Times* mercilessly nailed what she found most notable about the book: the author's wide-eyed attitude about the president he had spent years covering. The book was packed with mini-scoops about Trump and his associates (for example, the way Trump loyalists purged anyone from the White House who would dare to disagree with the president), but that wasn't what struck the *Times* reviewer as the newsiest aspect. As Szalai put it, Karl's "expressions of surprise are so frequent and over-the-top that they are perhaps the most surprising parts of this book." She called the book "less insightful about the Trump White House and more revealing of Karl's own gradual, extremely belated awareness that something in the White House might in fact be awry." It made me wonder, too. Had Karl, one of the most prominent and experienced TV journalists in the nation, not noticed anything over the four preceding years? Perhaps chastened by this criticism, Karl later stated in a number of interviews that covering another Trump candidacy, replete with the former president's efforts to tear down democratic norms, would be a difficult challenge for political journalists, one they need to grapple with well before the campaign.

It's so rare for major news organizations to tell things through a clear, pro-democracy lens that when it happens, it's a cause for celebration. Consider this first sentence from a *New York Times* article: "Republicans in Wisconsin are

engaged in an all-out assault on the state's election system."
Eric Umansky, a high-ranking editor at ProPublica, com-
mended it on Twitter: "Now *this* is how to write about our
democracy." Why, though, is such straightforward clarity so
unusual?

What I've found, in every newsroom where I've ever
worked, is that reporters and editors are motivated by many
things. There's competition—trying to get the scoop, to break
the news first. This is a strong, impossible-to-extinguish
drive that can't be separated from the kind of ambition that
brings journalists to the highest levels of their business and,
to some extent, it's a positive force. There's finding the biggest
audience (or the most clicks); for some news organizations,
that is less about clicks than about converting one-time readers to subscribers. But it often amounts to the same thing:
getting the audience's eyeballs on your story and keeping
them on your site. There's the desire to sound smart, savvy,
and maybe a little jaded. There's the desire to win journalism
prizes by writing stories—sometimes very long stories—that
have gravitas and impact. There's the desire to look "balanced" and to avoid any accusations of bias, especially from
often extremely aggressive right-wing critics.

I wrote about this frequently in my *Post* media column,
calling for a new kind of framing. I identified what gets in the
way. "Mainstream journalists want their work to be perceived
as fair-minded and nonpartisan. They want to defend themselves against charges of bias," I wrote in one column. "So
they equalize the unequal. This practice seems so ingrained
as to be unresolvable."

Awareness of this has changed, but newsroom practices haven't followed suit to any great extent. How could this change be brought about? It would need leadership—patriotic leadership from the top of every major news organization, not the kind that involves mindless flag-waving but the kind that constantly communicates to staff and to the public what we're here for. I made some recommendations in my column:

- Toss out the insidious "inside-politics" framework and replace it with a "pro-democracy" framework. One way to do this is to establish new beats and teams of journalists to cover attacks on voting rights and other basic elements of a working democracy, and to treat this coverage as of utmost importance in how it is emphasized and displayed.
- Stop calling the reporters who cover what happens in Washington "political reporters." Start calling them "government reporters."
- Stop asking who the winners and losers are in the latest political skirmish. Start asking who is serving the democracy and who is undermining it.
- Stop being "savvy"—filled with smug insider knowledge—and start being patriotic. Again, I'm not talking about wearing American-flag lapel pins but about giving proper attention to the role of the press in a democracy, and letting the coverage reflect that.

I agree with Andrew Donohue, managing editor of the Center for Investigative Reporting's news site, Reveal, who in a piece for Harvard's Nieman Lab called for news organizations to put reporters on a new-style "democracy beat" to focus on voter suppression and redistricting: "These reporters won't see their work in terms of politics or parties, but instead through the lens of honesty, fairness, and transparency." But I called for something much more sweeping. The democracy beat shouldn't be some kind of narrow innovation but a widespread rethinking across the mainstream media.

Here's where I run into trouble about any likelihood of it happening. Big Journalism is notoriously bad at looking, in an open-minded way and without defensiveness, at what has gone wrong. If top editors were good at such things, we would have heard a lot more about the extreme overcoverage of Hillary Clinton's email practices and a lot more about how this can never happen again. We would have heard a lot more soul-searching, too, about how embarrassingly eager some of the Trump-as-Russian-agent speculators were—bearing in mind, however, that Russia certainly did intend to interfere in the 2016 election and did so. But improving this situation is not just about looking back; it's about anticipating what's to come next, and soon. What happens in 2024 if Trump runs again, with no intention of conceding loss even if the voters decide otherwise? Or if he doesn't, but a Trump-inspired candidate does the same?

Editors of leading news organizations, Sunday talk-show moderators, and other news executives should pull together their top people to think hard about this—every bit as hard as they think about digital innovation or increasing page views. They should be transparent and honest with their readers, viewers, and listeners about all of this. Some smaller news organizations have shown the way, quite admirably and bravely. I mentioned earlier that the Harrisburg, Pennsylvania, public radio station WITF clearly and consistently explained to their audience why they kept mentioning the actions of those public officials who tried to overturn the 2020 election results. Another model was *Cleveland Plain Dealer* editor Chris Quinn's letter to readers about how the paper and its sister website, Cleveland.com, refused to cover every reckless, attention-getting lie of Ohio Republican Josh Mandel during his run for U.S. Senate. Were these news organizations criticized for what they did? You can count on it. But that doesn't make it any less important or less correct.

There are good people thinking searchingly about these issues. Writing in The Bulwark in November 2021, Jonathan V. Last posed a question that should have sent chills down the spines of everyone who cares about this country, everyone with a patriotic bone in their body. "As we move toward 2024, the big concern should be how the media would cover an openly anti-democratic presidential candidate," he wrote. "Would they treat said candidate as a danger to America? Or would they attempt to remain neutral and pretend that he was just another generic politician doing normal political things?" If past is prologue, I'm afraid we already know the answer. That answer, though, is simply not adequate to the moment.

In late 2021 I got an unexpected email from the founder of a nonprofit organization dedicated to preserving democracy in the United States. He told me that his nonpartisan team was hoping to set up an event to explore how the media is, or isn't, adapting to the troubling dynamics within our democracy, and asked if he could send me a one-page draft of their proposal. I said I was happy to take a look at it, though I'm always wary of being on the "doing" side of things, accustomed as I am to staying strictly on the sidelines as an observer and commentator. When I received the proposal, I was surprised to see my name in the first sentence of the document. "This summer," it began, "Margaret Sullivan called for a widespread rethinking of how the media should cover issues related to our democracy, given the current political context facing the U.S." Well, he had my attention with that; the rest of the proposal would have captured it anyway. In partnership with a media platform or publisher, the organization wanted to host and support the production of an event, possibly at the National Press Club, with current and former journalists. The idea would be to foster conversation—among the practitioners of Washington journalism—about the media's current role, its responsibility, and the tools required to adequately cover today's political fights over elections, accountability for insurrection, and disinformation. This panel would look at "how media institutions can respond to changes in the industry and information landscape, and adequately cover today's democracy challenges in ways that are consistent with journalistic norms and practices." It would look at what's different about this moment in American history; what approaches various outlets are taking to covering issues, including January 6; disinformation, voting and election issues, and abuses of power. Ideally, there would be follow-up projects such as—and this is radical—an updated set of journalistic principles for threats to democracy in this era, or a sharing and highlighting of best practices.

I thought it sounded wonderful, but I told the founder that aspects of getting it done worried me. The very news organizations that most need to be involved would be resistant to participating. Why? Because it might make them look as if they were—horrors!—abandoning neutrality. The problem is a tautology, a Möbius strip looping around and around and ending up in the same place. To effect real change, you first must be willing to recognize the problem. Within the professional world I know so well, I doubt that there's a critical mass of powerful journalism leaders who want to do this. I was heartened—thrilled, in fact—when *The Washington Post* announced in early 2022 that it was starting a "democracy desk" that would put a good-sized group of reporters and editors on the story of American democracy in peril, with attention to voting suppression and the groundwork that's being laid to overturn elections in the future. Some of the reporters would be placed in the states that were most contested after the 2020 presidential election: Georgia, Arizona, Wisconsin, Michigan, and Pennsylvania. It's the kind of work that every serious news organization should be doing.

I gave my "Moral Battleground" class at Duke a daunting end-of-semester assignment. I asked them to imagine that they had been appointed Biden's anti-misinformation czar, the person responsible for solving these vexing problems of what has been called "truth decay." What would you do? Where would you start?

I didn't expect these students, bright and capable as they

were, to know all the answers, but I thought it would be worth having them think hard about the questions. They did, and overall, I was pleased with the way they grappled with the tricky intersection of public policy, social media reform, and free speech. Later that year, when the Aspen Institute released its report, I saw more developed and sophisticated versions of the same recommendations that my students had come up with, such as reforms that would hold social media platforms responsible for pushing lies, a big effort for media literacy, serious support for local news, and for government at the highest levels to treat these issues with the seriousness they deserve.

That the undergraduates in my class—many of them headed for public policy and journalism careers—were thinking so clearly and productively gave me tremendous hope. I also appreciated this surprising and provocative line in the Aspen Institute report about the seeming intractability of the problem: "The biggest lie of all, which this crisis thrives on, and which the beneficiaries of mis- and disinformation feed on, is that the crisis itself is uncontainable." That's right; it's not a lost cause, but citizens and leaders alike have to care enough to address it seriously and on many fronts simultaneously.

Amid all of this, I am somewhat encouraged by several developments. One is something mentioned briefly earlier: the growth of nonprofit digital-first newsrooms. One of the original and most successful ones, *The Texas Tribune*, is more than a decade old and does very important watchdog-journalism work for the entire state. Based in Austin, it is led now by Sewell Chan, whose background is in some of the largest newspapers in the country: *The New York Times* and the *Los*

Angeles Times. If every city and region in America could have its version of *The Texas Tribune,* I would sleep easier. But the problem is one of scale; how do you build a nationwide system to replace or augment newspapers? No one has solved that question yet, though many are working on it. The American Journalism Project, which directs philanthropy toward such newsrooms, has the right idea, as does the Institute for Non-profit News and others that are focused on keeping local news alive in this new era.

I'm also encouraged to see some traditional local news organizations adjusting successfully to the new business realities. *The Salt Lake Tribune*'s ownership turned the newspaper into a nonprofit. The *Tampa Bay Times* and *The Philadelphia Inquirer* have somewhat similar structures, in that they are owned by nonprofit organizations. Some large, for-profit local newspapers—including *The Boston Globe,* the *Los Angeles Times,* and the *Star Tribune* in Minneapolis—have managed to maintain robust newsrooms and do outstanding work. It's notable that they share a particular, important characteristic: They have local, civic-minded ownership. Through that, they have escaped the grim fate of so many papers damaged by large chains.

The Washington Post, The New York Times, and *The Wall Street Journal* are a hugely important and influential part of this ecosystem. To varying degrees, each has figured out a new business model for the digital era, but they have something the smaller papers don't have—the ability to market their products to the entire nation and even, to some extent, to the world. I'm also heartened by the growth of investigative reporting at local television stations, and the positive role of public radio and television. These need to be encouraged and supported, too.

Underlying all of this is an article of faith for me. I believe that most legitimate journalists and millions of citizens know some truths at a core level: that we serve the public interest and that good journalism is foundational to democracy. That belief, I'm convinced, needs to come out from hiding. It should be boldly and consistently articulated and deeply supported. Above all, the reality-based press should rededicate itself to being pro-democracy. Then, I think, America gets a fighting chance.

14

About Those Lessons

In the fall of 2021, I found myself sitting on a Central Park bench with a young CBS News journalist, Jason Silverstein. We had been talking for nearly two hours, and I wondered if it might be time to call it a day. "Well," I asked him, "shall we wrap this up?" His answer startled me: "I'll take as much time listening to Margaret Sullivan as I can get." I really didn't think I was dropping any great pearls of wisdom, though we had been discussing a challenging new project of his and I had tried to provide some guidance. It wasn't terribly profound, mostly amounting to "Well, just get started, and you can always fix it later in the process." Jason and I went way back. He had been a correspondent for our *Buffalo News* teen publication, called *NeXt*, as a high school student in a Western New York suburb, and then was a standout summer intern at the paper during his college years. He had gone on to Columbia Journalism School and then to the New York *Daily News* and *Newsweek* before CBS News. (By 2022, some months after our talk, he had moved to *The New York Times*.) I was proud to know him, and touched that he made a point of keeping up with me; we'd had a number of these park walks in recent years.

That same week, I encountered another former *News* intern, Marcus Yam, a remarkably talented *Los Angeles Times* photojournalist who had just returned from Afghanistan. The access that this quiet young man gets to the ordinary people enmeshed in historic events, all over the world, is as remarkable as his photographs, each one like a beautifully composed Renaissance painting, glowing with humanity. Marcus has been part of two Pulitzer Prize–winning teams; by March 2022, he was in Ukraine, covering the Russian invasion. Just weeks later, he won a Pulitzer Prize for his photojournalism in Afghanistan. We were delighted to see each other at a Manhattan awards dinner, and I smiled to myself when—as a friend prepared to take a photo of us together—Marcus suggested a relocation. "Let's move over here," he said in his low-key way, and, of course, the lighting turned out to be perfect.

When people have asked me over the years whether journalism is still a good field for young people, I hesitate. Certainly, it's a tough one to break into, and an uncertain one in which to navigate a career. The *Buffalo News* teen publication where Jason started—*NeXt*—is no more, another victim of endless budget cuts, despite nurturing budding journalists like my Style section colleague Dan Zak, one of *The Washington Post*'s best writers. The internship program at *The Buffalo News*, where I began, as did Marcus Yam, Jason Silverstein, and Dan Zak, was discontinued several years ago (although, I was glad to see, it was brought back in 2022). No, I'm tempted to say, it's not a particularly good field. Then I think about Sophie, Alison, and Peter, three young journalists whose careers I've watched with particular interest over the years because I had a personal connection to each.

Sophie Kleeman, who was my daughter's college roommate, is an investigations editor at Business Insider; her career has been almost entirely with digital publications. Alison Ingersoll, my son's former girlfriend, is a data journalism specialist at WRAL, the NBC-affiliated TV station in Raleigh, North Carolina; she has worked not only in television but also for a local investigative nonprofit and, during an internship, at Bloomberg News in London. Peter Sullivan, my nephew, had internships with *Foreign Policy* magazine and at the *Pittsburgh Post-Gazette* and now covers health care in Congress for *The Hill*. Their paths have been various and mostly not based in print. All are roughly thirty years old, doing important work, and paying the rent.

"The most satisfying thing you'll ever do in this business is bring along young journalists," was what Douglas Turner told me. He had been the top editor of the *Courier-Express*, the Buffalo newspaper that went out of business in 1982, and later was the Washington bureau chief of *The Buffalo News*. Few of these young journalists are as straightforward as Jason Silverstein in seeking guidance, but I do get asked for advice from time to time. There are five things I've figured out over the years, often through my own errors.

First, I tell them to be patient with themselves, especially with career setbacks and mistakes. Like fiction writers who could paper the walls with their rejection letters, journalists find out quickly that this is a tough, competitive, often unforgiving field. There will be jobs you want that you won't get; that's happened to all but the very fortunate few. (I'm not even sure it makes them fortunate; that humbling can be good for the soul.) There very likely will be humiliating errors that you will be lucky to survive.

Longtime journalists, if they're honest, can tell you all about their disasters, failures, and disappointments. I wrote a front-page story at the *Buffalo News* in my first year on the job that was essentially wrong because it was based on calculations about real estate square footage; I did the math correctly but with the wrong assumptions about what it meant. I've never forgotten that screw-up or the embarrassment of correcting it after a miserable conversation in my editor's office. Persistence goes along with being patient with yourself. Try to hang in there, since memories are short and, if you're lucky, you'll probably get another chance to right yourself and your reputation.

Second, I would tell them this: Do your own work, and when you borrow or find inspiration elsewhere, be generous in crediting others. In our digital age, it's never been easier to plagiarize, even without intending to, and it's never been easier to discover plagiarism. All it takes in one case is sloppy copy-and-pasting; all it takes in the other is a Google search. I would add that there's a solution: It's never been easier to give credit. Link out, give a phrase of attribution, and then do it again and again. It's amazing that journalists don't do more of this; it's always appreciated and, in almost all circumstances, it takes nothing away from your own work.

Third, I'd suggest some self-discipline in the use of social media. It's so easy to get involved in the digital equivalent of road rage. Put the phone down, walk away from the keyboard.

An errant tweet can wreck your career. Delete all you want, but if someone captured a screenshot, your momentary bad judgment will live forever. Despite what you may think, exactly no one is eagerly awaiting your words of wisdom on any platform. I'd like to see journalists doing less to build their reputations ("brands," in the somewhat dated parlance) on social media or in television appearances and more of the actual work of rigorous reporting. I say this knowing that, for many journalists, especially ones not attached to prestigious legacy news organizations, such reputation building is a career necessity. And done right, it can be a positive thing.

But for some, at least, a more muted approach—grounded in dogged reporting above all—is preferable. An example of this in action is my *Washington Post* colleague Stephanie McCrummen, whom I have worked alongside in the *Post*'s New York City office. She keeps a low profile and rarely does anything self-promotional, but her byline on a story is a clear signal that the reporting will be deep, original, and worthwhile. It was no surprise to me that she won both a Pulitzer Prize and a George Polk Award in 2018 after her investigative reporting, with colleagues Beth Reinhard and Alice Crites. Their work changed the course of a Senate race in Alabama by revealing that the Republican candidate, Roy Moore, had behaved inappropriately with teenage girls and then had tried to undermine the reporting that exposed that behavior. McCrummen kept her cool when the undercover group Project Veritas, which bills itself as a media watchdog, tried to trip her up by offering a fake story; the video of that encounter is a model for good journalistic behavior in tough circumstances. McCrummen's list of well-deserved awards is exceedingly long, but her name isn't widely known. In short, show some restraint and concentrate on the work first.

Fourth, and maybe most important, hold on tight to the qualities that make a good journalist. Stay idealistic. Stay curious. Stay mission driven, and know how much it matters or can matter. Remember what happened when Darnella Frazier, only seventeen years old, decided to video-record the murder of George Floyd in Minneapolis as a police officer knelt on his neck; although she's not a journalist per se, she certainly performed a journalistic service. It was heartening to see the Pulitzer Prize board recognize her world-changing action with a special award.

My *Washington Post* colleague Meryl Kornfield wrote about the strange turn of events—again, involving a crucial video—that led to the convictions of the killers of Ahmaud Arbery, the twenty-five-year-old Black man in Georgia who was out jogging when he was gunned down by three white men. Much of the case came down to the persistence and curiosity of a reporter, Larry Hobbs, with *The Brunswick News*, a daily newspaper with only four reporters.

Reading Kornfield's story, I loved one quote from Hobbs. After obtaining the (extraordinarily biased and incomplete) police report, Hobbs knew he had to pursue the story. "Red flags start going up," he said. "All the things started falling into place that this wasn't right." Later, a cellphone video, uploaded to a local radio station's website, bore out his suspicions, as it showed men chasing Arbery, cornering him, and shooting him.

Hobbs's dogged reporting was not the only factor that led to the convictions, but it surely helped. Prosecutors and police were failing to do their jobs, but a reporter did his. With considerable modesty, Hobbs put it in perspective in the *Post* story: "The main thing I did was just not let go of it. I didn't do any great writing. I didn't do any investigative reporting. I'm a small-town newspaper. We don't really have time to invest. I come in every day and there's an empty newspaper I have to do my part to fill up."

In other words, he just did the work, guided by his instincts and persistence. Honor that reporter's instinct, which will hardly ever steer you wrong and which might serve the public interest in unimaginable ways.

I'll add one more: Try to work with people you admire, who respect you, and whom you can trust, especially those in leadership positions. If you value your co-workers, nurture the relationships as best you can. That includes managing the boss, a skill worth developing. When I was the top editor in Buffalo, I had my disagreements with my direct supervisor, publisher Stan Lipsey; I sometimes found him too involved in the newsroom—in wanting to direct stories—when I thought he should leave that strictly to me and my team. We worked out the differences, though, and generally communicated well. There were probably times when he wanted to fire me—in fact, he was fond of pointedly reminding me who really had the upper hand in the publisher-editor dynamic. When we disagreed, I held my ground and was much more secure in doing so because the relationship was strong. It didn't hurt a bit that we had a regular doubles tennis game on Wednesday evenings after work. (It's one thing to fire the editor, but much worse when you lose her killer first serve, too.) The important thing, and one reason we lasted together for nearly thirteen years in our respective roles, is that there was mutual respect. If that's not the case, and there's nothing you can do about it, I would advise getting out. That's hard—sometimes almost impossible—in an industry where jobs can be hard to come by. I'm sympathetic to those who, for financial or other reasons, can't make a move. But I also know that staying can be corrosive to your work and even to your soul.

15

Sweeney (and Other Legends), Reconsidered

A flashback: My earliest mentor at *The Buffalo News*, Foster Spencer, was one of those newsroom characters whose mere presence made it fun to come to work. The paper's longtime managing editor, Foster often said that he was content in his number two editorial position and had no desire to join the "executive team" by ascending to the top job of chief editor. He would rather put out the paper every day than go to meetings with bean counters. Although he wasn't strictly handsome, Foster's humor and intelligence nonetheless gave him charisma. I can picture him ambling out of the newsroom at day's end in his loden-green trench coat and tweed flat cap with the paper's final edition tucked under his arm. In that pre-Twitter, pre-smartphone era, his workday was well and truly over, and here was the proof, in print.

Foster had all kinds of entertaining expressions and ideas, like the name he gave to boring-but-important stories, such as a nearly interminable series titled "Zoning and You" that the paper had once published. He called them "FWS," which stood for "Fraught with Significance." In Foster's parlance, an exclamation point was "an astonisher," and a headline that stretched across all eight columns of the paper's front page was a "screamer." (Thus, when I broke a big story as a rookie reporter, Foster gave me due credit; after giving his directions to the editor laying out the front page, he called across the newsroom in his Massachusetts accent, "Sully, you got your first *scream-ah*.")

And then there was Sweeney, an imaginary character whom Foster was fond of invoking. Sweeney was the average reader, presumably a working-class guy sitting on his front porch in Irish Catholic South Buffalo, cracking open a Labatt Blue and picking up *The Buffalo Evening News* to see what it had to say. Foster kept him in mind when he made news decisions: *What would Sweeney think?*

Foster hired me as a summer intern, and then, apparently pleased with my work and hustle, offered me a full-time reporting job in September, breaking with the tradition that most *Buffalo Evening News* hires would have three to five years' experience at a smaller outlet. I was fired up and wanted to prove my worth. Not long after I was hired full-time, all of twenty-three years old, I approached him as he stood chatting with more senior reporters and told him with some excitement that I had just scored an interview with Joyce Carol Oates, the Western New York native and author who had already won the National Book Award for her novel *them*, which I had read in Joanne Langan's English class at Nardin Academy. Foster seemed to have only the vaguest idea of who she was, but he was supportive. "That'll be a good one, Marge," he said, using a nickname I would tolerate only from him. He had a characteristic way of speaking from the side of his mouth that made every utterance seem wised-up and wry.

I interviewed Oates after a talk she gave at a college campus, and then drove out to talk to her parents in nearby Niagara County, where she had grown up. The profile appeared as the cover story of our Sunday magazine. I remember my mother, who looked for my work as soon as the paper arrived at their Lackawanna door, telling me that *this* one was good enough to stand the test of time. She may have been right; I got a chance to recall it more than thirty-five years later when Oates and I met again in 2019. As I walked through the door of the writer Molly Jong-Fast's Upper East Side apartment for a book party, my first vision was of Joyce Carol Oates and Erica Jong, Molly's mother and the author of the culture-changing novel *Fear of Flying*. Seeing two of the most famous authors of their generation, getting on in years and chatting over cocktails, I felt I had arrived in literary heaven. On that Manhattan evening, Oates told me that she remembered my *Buffalo News* profile, and I reminded her that she had written me a kind note, saying how pleased she was to see her parents quoted in it.

Foster was only sixty-four, and still held the managing editor's title, when he died in Roswell Park Comprehensive Cancer Center. Still in my thirties then, I didn't realize how young he was, but I certainly do now, since it is my age as I write. I directly succeeded Foster as managing editor in 1998 and inherited his office, which I used for another fourteen years until leaving for *The New York Times*. I stayed there rather than moving into the chief editor's slightly superior quarters when I got the top newsroom job two years later. I liked being at Foster's old desk, scorched in places by cigarettes that were set down, I assumed, while he worked the crossword puzzle between deadlines.

A longtime colleague of Foster's, Edward Cuddihy, who eventually would hold the managing editor title himself, recalled the mythical Sweeney when he provided a comment for Foster's obituary. As Cuddihy assembled a journalism contest entry, Foster told him he didn't think much about awards: "If I can inform Sweeney and a half million of his neighbors, I've won the only prize I want."

Much as I adored Foster and was grateful to him, we didn't always see eye to eye in his last years. He looked askance at my proposed innovations, including the redesigned front page that helped propel my career even though it was never implemented, and wasn't shy about saying so. He probably would have been lukewarm about some of my other eventual efforts: my drive to diversify a newsroom staff that was far too white for our readership, not because he didn't fully support the goal but because it required modifying the paper's traditional hiring practices; my desire to give women's and girls' sports more attention despite their much smaller fan base; my directive to represent people of color and women on our front page as often as possible, even if that meant expanding time-honored definitions of newsworthiness. Those things may not have mattered much to Sweeney, but I thought they would matter to a readership that wasn't always well served by the old ways. I knew they mattered to me.

Not just Sweeney needs reconsideration in our greatly

changed era, I've found. Even the wonders of "Woodstein," the famed Watergate reporting duo of Woodward and Bernstein, demand a fresh look. Never meet your heroes, goes the saying attributed to Marcel Proust. I wouldn't take it quite that far. I'd just be prepared for some nuance to replace the idol worship. As I wrote in the first chapter here, I was a teen when the young reporters doggedly revealed the scandal; they cultivated that secret source, Deep Throat, and, partly through him, slowly uncovered the corruption of the Nixon administration. They were *badass,* the essence of swashbuckling cool, especially when confused in my teenage mind with Robert Redford and Dustin Hoffman, shirt sleeves rolled up and wide ties askew as they made coded phone calls to their sources or tangled with their demanding editor. I wanted to be them, or at least immerse myself in that newsroom culture. Righteousness could be achieved, according to the self-important journalism adage, by "afflicting the comfortable and comforting the afflicted." That sounded good. So I did what Thoreau advised, advancing not just confidently in the direction of my dreams but at something of a breakneck pace. In the summer of 1974, Richard Nixon resigned the presidency in disgrace, and in the fall I became the editor of my high school's student newspaper.

Later, as celebrity-journalists, Woodward and Bernstein were the star speakers or award recipients at conferences I attended, and on one occasion, probably in the 1990s, I introduced myself. They were well accustomed to such admiration. In more recent years, I ran into Carl Bernstein in a CNN greenroom as we were both waiting to appear on the media show *Reliable Sources.* By then, I was a columnist at his old paper, the *Post*. I made sure to get his phone number and interviewed him soon after, asking him to compare Nixon to Donald Trump. Bernstein talked brilliantly, if incessantly. (In his memoir, *All About the Story*, former *Washington Post* executive editor Leonard Downie observes of Bernstein that it was "almost impossible to break off a conversation with him, even over the phone.") I remember, too, running into Bernstein during the intermission of a Carnegie Hall concert. As my date stood by, suitably impressed, Bernstein greeted me with a kiss and told me I was "killing it" in my *Post* columns. My seventeen-year-old self, editor of the Nardin *Kaleidoscope*, would have found this scene gratifying if she could have begun to imagine it.

Woodward, though, drew more ambivalence. Certainly, he had had a remarkable career; his reporting work was still occasionally appearing on *The Washington Post*'s front page, five decades after his and Bernstein's initial Watergate reporting. He was a top-selling author many times over, with thick tomes investigating presidential administrations, the Hollywood drug culture, and the Supreme Court. But like too many other journalist-authors, Woodward sometimes saved some of the revelations from his research for those books instead of writing them as news stories in real time. (Downie acknowledged this tension in his memoir, writing that while some readers complained about Woodward's practice, "I never felt that our readers were cheated.")

In another strange turn, as surreal as my encounter with Bernstein though in a very different way, I would take up a Woodward controversy in the same newspaper where the former Watergate reporter still held the honorary title of associate editor. My column revolved around Woodward's second book about Donald Trump, published in September 2020. His first one, *Fear*, had been a major bestseller. This one, *Rage*, promised to be one, too—especially because it contained some startling news: That Trump *knew* early in 2020 that the coronavirus pandemic would be deadly, far worse than the flu. But as president, he blatantly lied about the severity of the virus's threat, assuring Americans that it was nothing to worry about, that it would disappear.

I decided to write about why Woodward hadn't reported this news months before his book came out. Why hadn't he talked it over with *Post* editors and arranged to break off some of his book's revelations for an immediate news story? I had Woodward's phone number and was able to reach him quickly. He sounded defensive and wanted to avoid speaking to me on the record. Instead, he suggested we talk "on background"—meaning that I couldn't attribute whatever he said to him directly. I wasn't interested in that since I was seeking his rationale for holding back the news. I insisted that I wanted his response on the record. We tussled about the terms of our conversation for a while, as he explained that he had promised CBS's *60 Minutes* the first interview after his book's publication. I held my ground, making it clear that if he didn't want to speak on the record, I would just note in the column that he had declined comment. That would not be a good look for a legendary reporter, especially one dealing with his own newspaper.

At one point, Woodward nonetheless started talking with these words: "On background . . ." I stopped him. "Please don't try to manipulate me into doing a background interview" was the sentence I heard myself saying to one of the world's most famous journalists and my teenage inspiration. He made it clear that he didn't appreciate my reaction and thought it was out of line, but in the end he did speak to me on the record.

My column carried this rather soft headline: "Should Bob Woodward Have Reported Trump's Virus Revelations Sooner? Here's How He Defends His Decision." My takeaway, though, was more pointed. I duly considered his arguments that his reporting was more meaningful in book form, that earlier publication would not have helped to save any of the two hundred thousand lives that had then been lost, and that voters could still consider Trump's duplicity well before election day, which Woodward called the "demarcation." But I concluded:

> I don't know if putting the book's newsiest revelations out there in something closer to real time would have made a difference. They might very well have been denied and soon forgotten in the constant rush of new scandals and lies. Still, the chance—even if it's a slim chance—that those revelations could have saved lives is a powerful argument against waiting this long.

One reader, a former U.S. ambassador during the Clinton years, wrote to me, angry about Woodward's rationale and objecting to the notion that the "demarcation" was the election. "No, it was as soon as Trump made his revelations to Woodward," the reader fumed. "Which almost surely, if they had appeared in print at the time, would have caused an uproar that would have led to demands across the country for changes in Trump administration behavior that would al-most surely have saved thousands of American lives." Plenty of other readers accepted Woodward's reasoning and found my column pointlessly critical. But I felt good about getting him to state his case and about my conclusion.

As for my hero worship? I still admire the Watergate re-porting, still am happy to have spent a life inspired by it and to have come to work at the same newspaper where this enduring and consequential journalism history was made. But I thought Woodward made the wrong decision and, what's more, I was disturbed to see the way he responded to journalists who ques-tioned him at the annual Investigative Reporters and Editors (IRE) conference shortly after *Rage* was published. One of these was Shira Stein, a reporter for Bloomberg Law covering the pandemic; another was Karen Ho of Quartz. Both pressed Woodward, with more specificity than I did, about why he hadn't reported the Trump revelations earlier. He sounded dismissive, suggested they owed him an apology, and kept promoting his book. His behavior toward Jonathan Swan of Axios, who asked similar questions a few days later, was much more respectful. Maybe if Woodward had revealed the truth earlier and the nation had taken the virus more seri-ously early on, the IRE members would be meeting in person, not virtually. Maybe President Trump himself—who had for many months flouted social distancing recommendations and mocked mask-wearers—wouldn't have been hospital-ized with Covid only a few days after Woodward's remarks to Stein and Ho.

That's the odd thing about reporting. You never know what will happen when you put the truth out there in real

time. You might help banish a corrupt president, as Woodward and Bernstein did. Or you might shame another president into telling the truth about the worst public health crisis
in American history. If that were to happen, you might help
save thousands of lives. You don't know. And it's not your job
to make that calculation. It's your job to dig it out and to tell
it straight. And to publish without undue delay (as *The New
York Times* infamously failed to do with the warrantless-
wiretapping story in 2004).

The next year, Woodward came out with yet another
Trump-related book, *Peril*, co-authored with *Post* reporter
Robert Costa. Again, an excerpt appeared on the front page
of *The Washington Post*, and again, I wrote a column about
it. Woodward and Costa had unearthed the abhorrent memo
written by a Trump lawyer, John Eastman, that gave Vice
President Pence a detailed, six-point plan to declare the
2020 election invalid and falsely hand the presidency over
to Trump. It amounted to a blueprint for the insurrection.
I gave Woodward and Costa credit, and this time my point
wasn't to quarrel with the timing but to complain that the
Eastman Memo hadn't been treated as big news by most of
the mainstream media. Shockingly, there was zero on-air
news coverage on the three major broadcast networks of this
revelation immediately after it was made public, according to
a Media Matters for America study, and precious little in the
following days. As our democratic norms foundered, much
of the mainstream press was asleep at the switch, and seemed
perfectly content to stay that way.

I heard from Woodward about my Eastman Memo piece.
He had apparently let our earlier disagreement go, if he re-

membered it at all. "That was a terrific column," he wrote. "Thoughtful and aggressive." He gave me credit for prompting some follow-up coverage in *The New York Times*. (That credit was almost certainly undeserved; with a few rare exceptions, it wasn't like the *Times* to act on my advice.) I was glad that we remained on good terms. Proust notwithstanding, maybe it's not so bad, after all, to get to know your idols.

I have found, though, that the journalists I admire most aren't necessarily those with the biggest names or the best-selling books. The ones I have the greatest respect for are those—no matter how prominent or obscure—who are the most unflinching in seeking out the truth and presenting it straightforwardly. In the words of the classic *New York Times* axiom, they do their work "without fear or favor." Some of these are at major publications like the *Times* and the *Post;* others are in much smaller newsrooms or are fully independent. Some win Pulitzer Prizes; some don't get much recognition. As I mentioned in an earlier chapter, I admire Nikole Hannah-Jones of *The New York Times* for her bravery and vision in writing about the influence on American history of enslaved people's arrival in the English colonies in 1619, and her colleagues Jodi Kantor and Megan Twohey, who dug into film mogul Harvey Weinstein's sexual misconduct, revelations that led, in time, to his imprisonment. I admire the top editor of Albany's *Times Union*, Casey Seiler, who (while leading his paper's aggressive coverage of New York governor Andrew Cuomo's demise) insisted on keeping proper journalistic distance from sources, even if it hindered access. I give CNN's Jake Tapper credit for refusing to thoughtlessly magnify the voices of liars, as so many TV anchors do. I appreciate Will Bunch at *The Philadelphia Inquirer* for his incisive, pro-democracy commentary and Julie K. Brown at the *Miami Herald* for her persistent reporting about the disgraced financier Jeffrey Epstein, credibly accused of sex trafficking. There are far too many to list here, including many colleagues of mine, past and present, whose work inspires and awes me.

These days, however, I wonder if it's enough. A global study by a respected Stockholm-based think tank now describes the United States, for the first time, as a backsliding democracy. "The declines in civil liberties and checks on government indicate that there are serious problems with the fundamentals of democracy," concluded the International Institute for Democracy and Electoral Assistance. The "visible deterioration" of democracy in the United States includes the increasing tendency to contest credible election results, efforts to suppress participation in elections, and the country's "runaway polarization." This is not only true but obvious; it is staring us in the face.

American journalists should be putting the country on high alert, with sirens blaring and red lights flashing. The legitimate press should be trying to figure out how best to rise to this historic challenge. But too many journalists—worried about their reputations for neutrality, under pressure from corporate bosses, and mired in their comfortable traditions—are still doing their jobs the same old way. It's not good enough.

What if we did fully rise to meet the moment? Can an abundance of high-quality, mission-driven journalism overcome misinformation and break through to those indoctrinated in an alternative reality? Can the legitimate media—the reality-based press—ever recover lost public trust and credibility? I have serious doubts, but they don't make me completely disillusioned. I know that great journalism is powerful, that it can change the world. I'm worried, yes, but I remain moderately hopeful. For all kinds of reasons, I still believe in my craft.

And I still love practicing it, especially when I hear from readers like a woman in Texas who wrote to me after reading my *Post* column urging journalists and news organizations to refocus their coverage on the current threats to democracy. In Texas, she lamented, "democracy, voting rights and women's rights are pretty much DOA at this time." She offered some words of appreciation: "I want to take this opportunity to say thank you for your article on the importance of journalists speaking honestly and forthrightly on the attack on democracy in our country. While I'm not sure how much will change, I just feel a helluva lot better to see this articulated so honestly and directly in a major newspaper." Her brief note reminded me of why I've stayed in journalism for more than four decades. Some people get into journalism to expose corruption; others because they love to write; but for me, it's this relationship with the reader that means the most.

I'll conclude with a small story, a reconsideration of yet another legend. By the summer of 2021, I was getting burned out writing the media column. I had been doing it—at an average pace of two columns a week—for more than five years. I joked with my colleagues that there were really only five possible media columns, and I would write aspects of them over and over. There was the "Evils of Facebook" column; the one about the tragedy of local newspapers' decline at the hands of hedge-fund owners; the Fox News damage-to-society column; the "don't magnify political lies" column; and the one about the mainstream media's intransigent flaws. On the surface, my career was going well. I wrote a well-received book in 2020 and won a national award for my *Post* columns in 2021. Duke University's public policy school listed me as a faculty member. All of this was gratifying, but it didn't penetrate a deeper ennui.

Looking for variety, I started writing different kinds of pieces. One took up the reinvention of *Rolling Stone* magazine; another featured a new podcast that told the stories of inspiring people who were at least seventy years old. These were really feature stories, though, not opinion columns with a strong point to make. Readable, perhaps, but less important.

There was no denying that the Trump years had taken their toll on me, especially because of the distressing direction of the country, including the media's role in that, and because of all the nastiness and abuse that for years had been flooding my inbox, voicemail, and real-life encounters. The pandemic lockdown had isolated me from my newsroom colleagues. Even before that, I had isolated myself, to some extent, by moving back from Washington to New York City. I didn't regret that decision since New York suited me and endlessly fed my soul, but it did mean that I was only occasionally in the *Post*'s D.C. newsroom, working instead from the small New York City office. Once the pandemic hit, I worked solely from my Upper West Side apartment. Despite the burnout, I kept driving myself to write frequently, to keep going. It's what I had always done; but it was getting wearisome. I didn't want to admit it, but I was hitting the wall.

When I heard, via the newsroom's internal messaging system, from one of my favorite people, deputy features editor David Malitz, my curiosity was aroused. He surprised me by writing that he wanted to speak by phone—a rarity for him—about a story assignment. When we talked, Malitz said he wanted to send me to interview Joni Mitchell, the legendary musician who would soon be receiving a Kennedy Center lifetime achievement honor. I would fly out to California or British Columbia, depending on which of her homes she was living in, and spend a solid chunk of time with her. Then I would write a lengthy profile for the Sunday arts section. That sounded like a delightful change of pace, and a perfect fit. I had loved Joni Mitchell's music, as well as that of other singer-songwriters, for many years. Although I hadn't been on a plane in eighteen months because of the pandemic, I was vaccinated and more than ready.

There was just one problem. Joni Mitchell disliked interviews and mistrusted journalists. She felt burned by reporters who had sensationalized her comments or criticized her work without understanding it. At nearly seventy-eight, she wasn't in the best of health; she had suffered a brain aneurysm a few years earlier followed by a difficult recovery. So, after multiple conversations with her manager and her assistant, I was reluctantly ready to settle for something less than a lengthy in-person interview. A phone call. Or maybe a Zoom interview. Her staff took these ideas to her and the answer came back: a flat no. Nothing personal, but Joni Mitchell would not be talking to me. They offered me the option of emailing some questions to her assistant. If Mitchell chose to answer any of them, she would speak the answers aloud to the assistant, who would record, transcribe, and email them to me. Doing a written interview by proxy seemed an unproductive idea for this kind of personality-based story. Now it was time to think creatively, since the *Post* needed some sort of Joni Mitchell story to recognize her Kennedy Center honor. My colleagues were spending time with the other honorees, including Lorne Michaels of *Saturday Night Live* fame, legendary entertainer Bette Midler, and Motown founder Berry Gordy. I was the only one who had struck out, and the deadline was looming.

So I came up with an idea for a personal essay that wouldn't require Mitchell's cooperation. Her classic album *Blue* had turned fifty in 2021 and received endless recognition as one of the greatest of all time. My essay, though, would make the case that, excellent as it was, *Blue* wasn't her best. That had come three years later, I would argue, with *Court and Spark* in 1974. I listened anew to these albums and others, sometimes with musician friends helping me to hear them more perceptively. I remembered how much the album affected me as a young teen experiencing my first romantic turmoil, and I learned that Madonna had called *Court and Spark* her coming-of-age album. I got the chance to recall the harder-edged rock music that one of my older brothers, Phil, had introduced me to, like the Allman Brothers, the Rolling Stones, and The Who. Then I brainstormed with a colleague, movie critic Ann Hornaday, who offered an observation which I ended up quoting. *Blue* was like a glass of pure, cool water, Hornaday said, but *Court and Spark,* with its jazz-infused layers and glossy California production, was like a perfectly mixed tequila sunrise. A *Post* reader made me happy when he emailed to say that reading my piece gave him "that 'Roberta Flack' sensation—you were singing my life with your words. It is as if we were sitting on a sofa in 1974 listening together as it unfolded."

The whole episode was simply fun. Although it was a far cry from the Watergate investigation, it reminded me of how fortunate I've been to do all kinds of journalism over the years, from reviewing books and music to investigating government officials to supervising a big newsroom staff. With the Joni Mitchell essay, I once again was getting paid to report and observe, to think and communicate. Once again, I experienced the peculiar thrills of creativity under deadline. Like life itself, this assignment didn't go according to plan. Disappointments and unforeseen challenges forced me to go off-script. I had to scramble, improvise, and find another way. And it worked out pretty well. Against the odds, it gave me an unaccountable joy.

Acknowledgments

Writing a book is a solitary ordeal in many ways but, paradoxically, it's also a team effort. I'm deeply grateful to all of those at St. Martin's Press who helped along the way, especially my editor, Anna deVries, for her combination of sensitivity, knowledge, and mad skills. My wonderful agent, Pilar Queen, a force of nature, was always there to help. The cover design by Jonathan Bush not only perfectly captured my message but gave me great delight. The excellent Sujay Kumar, who fact-checked this manuscript, saved me from myself in several cases; whatever mistakes may remain are mine entirely. I benefited from the combined talents of my Macmillan team: Dori Weintraub in publicity and Danielle Prielipp in marketing, as well as Laura Clark in the publishers office. My former Duke student Maya Miller helped with research. I'm grateful to my early readers, including Joyce Pinchbeck Johnson (who not only wrote a classic memoir in the 1990s but was conveniently located in my Upper West Side apartment building), Brooke Kroeger, Brian Connolly, Neil Barsky, Linda Hirshman, Sophie Kleeman, and Betsey Higgins. For his invaluable technical help, I am indebted to Michael

Marissen. Thanks, too, to my supportive editors at *The Washington Post*, who understood when my column-writing fell off a bit, especially David Malitz, Liz Seymour, and Amy Argetsinger. I'm grateful to my brothers, David and Philip, who have provided guidance and wisdom from our Lackawanna days to the present, to their wonderful wives, Catherine and Maureen, and to their children—who are *almost* as dear to me as my own Grace and Alex. Finally, I am grateful to all the journalists whose work has inspired me over the decades: those I admired as an impressionable teenager; those I worked alongside in my forever newsroom, *The Buffalo News;* those I have known at *The New York Times*, *The Washington Post*, and elsewhere. Thank you for doing the work that is so necessary in helping our precious and fragile democracy to endure.

Michael Benabib

MARGARET SULLIVAN is an award-winning media critic and a groundbreaking journalist. She was the first woman appointed as public editor of *The New York Times* and went on to *The Washington Post* as media columnist. She started her career as a summer intern at her hometown *Buffalo News* and rose to be that paper's first woman editor in chief. She writes a weekly column for *Guardian* U.S. and teaches at Duke University. She tweets @sulliview.